The Phenomenological Mind

The Phenomenological Mind is the first book to properly introduce fundamental questions about the mind from the perspective of phenomenology. Key questions and topics covered include:

*   what is phenomenology?
*   naturalizing phenomenology and the cognitive sciences
*   phenomenology and consciousness
*   consciousness and self-consciousness
*   time and consciousness
*   intentionality
*   the embodied mind
*   action
*   knowledge of other minds
*   situated and extended minds
*   phenomenology and personal identity.

This second edition includes a new preface, and revised and improved chapters.

Also included are helpful features such as chapter summaries, guides to further reading, and a glossary, making *The Phenomenological Mind* an ideal introduction to key concepts in phenomenology, cognitive science and philosophy of mind.

Shaun Gallagher holds the Lillian and Morrie Moss Chair of Excellence in Philosophy at the University of Memphis. His secondary appointments include Research Professor of Philosophy and Cognitive Science at the University of Hertfordshire, and Honorary Professor of Philosophy at the University of Copenhagen. He is the author of *How the Body Shapes the Mind* (2005), and editor of *The Oxford Handbook of the Self* (2011).

Dan Zahavi is Professor of Philosophy and Director of the Center for Subjectivity Research at the University of Copenhagen. He is the author of *Self-Awareness and Alterity* (1999), *Husserl's Phenomenology* (2003), and *Subjectivity and Selfhood* (2005).

They jointly edit the journal *Phenomenology and the Cognitive Sciences*.

The Phenomenological Mind

Shaun Gallagher and Dan Zahavi

Second edition

Routledge
Taylor & Francis Group

LONDON AND NEW YORK

First published 2008 by Routledge
This edition published 2012 by Routledge
2 Park Square, Milton Park, Abingdon, Oxon, OX14 4RN

Simultaneously published in the USA and Canada by Routledge
711 Third Avenue, New York, NY 10017

Routledge is an imprint of the Taylor & Francis Group, an informa business

British Library Cataloguing in Publication Data
A catalogue record for this book is available from the British Library

Library of Congress Cataloging in Publication Data
Gallagher, Shaun, 1948–
The phenomenological mind / by Shaun Gallagher and Dan Zahavi. – 2nd ed.
p. cm.
Includes bibliographical references (p.) and index.
1. Phenomenology. 2. Philosophy of mind. 3. Cognitive science. 4. Consciousness. 5. Perception. I. Zahavi, Dan. II. Title.
B829.5.G27 2012
128'.2–dc23
2011050413

ISBN: 978-0-415-61036-0 (hbk)
ISBN: 978-0-415-61037-7 (pbk)
ISBN: 978-0-203-12675-2 (ebk)

Printed and bound in Great Britain by
TJ International Ltd, Padstow, Cornwall

Contents

Figures

Acknowledgements

A few comments about how we wrote this book. It is a co-authored work, and although we started out by dividing the chapters between us so that we each were first author on half of them, they were subsequently passed forth and back and rewritten so many times jointly that they now all stand as fully co-authored chapters.

In the process of writing the book, we have received very helpful comments from a number of people. We would like to thank Nils Gunder Hansen, Daniel Hutto, Søren Overgaard, Matthew Ratcliffe, Andreas Roepstorff, and especially Thor Grünbaum and Evan Thompson for their extensive comments on earlier drafts. We also want to thank Mads Gram Henriksen for helping with the compilation of the list of references.

A significant part of Shaun Gallagher's work on this book was supported by a Visiting Professorship at the University of Copenhagen, sponsored by the University's Research Priority Area: Body and Mind, and the Danish National Foundation's Center for Subjectivity Research.

Preface to the second edition

In preparing the revised second edition, we have greatly profited not only from ongoing discussions with our readers and colleagues, but also and in particular from the various reviews of and critical commentaries on the first edition. We have made various improvements, revisions and clarifications, and expanded each chapter with new material.

One change in particular calls for explanation. The first edition of our book was entitled *The Phenomenological Mind: An Introduction to Philosophy of Mind and Cognitive Science*. In this new revised edition, we have dropped the subtitle. The reason for this is simple. The subtitle unfortunately (but perhaps not so surprisingly) has been taken by many readers to suggest that our book is something it isn't, namely a comprehensive introduction to philosophy of mind and cognitive science. Arriving with this kind of expectation, some readers have subsequently expressed frustration over the fact that we failed to treat and discuss this or that central topic in philosophy of mind and cognitive science. This is also a frustration and criticism that some of our reviewers have given voice to. By dropping the subtitle, we hope to avoid this misinterpretation. The aim of our book, as made clear in the first chapter, was never to provide a general introduction to phenomenology, philosophy of mind, and cognitive science – a task that in any case would have been impossible to achieve in a single short volume. Our aim was to write an accessible and up-to-date introduction to phenomenology, but one that departed from other such introductions by its rather unique angle. On the one hand, we wanted to show people trained in phenomenology, how phenomenological philosophy could address issues also debated in contemporary philosophy of mind and cognitive science, and how the phenomenological analyses could profit from and be improved upon by such an engagement with empirical science and analytic philosophy. At the same time, however, and even more pronounced, we wanted to show readers not already familiar with phenomenology what kind of contribution phenomenological philosophy could make to the contemporary philosophical and scientific discussions of cognition and consciousness, be it by describing facets of experience that are somewhat overlooked in current debates, or by offering alternative conceptual frameworks for the interpretation of scientific data. These ambitions imposed some obvious limitations to our endeavour. On the one hand, we didn't extensively discuss topics in phenomenology that had little bearing on issues in analytic philosophy of mind or cognitive science. At the same time, we didn't touch and dwell on those areas of philosophy of mind and cognitive science where phenomenology has little or nothing to contribute. Some might consider the latter omission particularly problematic since one thereby misses out on the opportunity to show how phenomenology could be directly complemented by analyses of areas with which it has failed to grapple. But given our aims and the planned size of our book, this was a limitation that was practically unavoidable. Phenomenological interventions in and exchanges with cognitive science and philosophy of mind are ongoing. Our book was and is intended not as an exhaustive account, but as an introduction, and we think it has succeeded in that regard.

The approach we advocate in our book is an open-ended pluralistic methodology rather than a narrowly orthodox and rigorous phenomenological methodology. Strictly speaking, inference to best explanation and indirect arguments that proceed by way of eliminating competing positions is not phenomenological in nature. But we have adopted the view that the more arguments we could garner in support of our outlook the better. We are convinced that analytic philosophy of mind in many ways can, not only challenge, but also support, and enrich the phenomenological discussions. We wanted to convince our scientific colleagues that the problems addressed by the cognitive sciences – how the brain works, what counts as cognition, all the extremely difficult 'easy' problems, as well as the 'hard' problem of consciousness – are so complex that an adequate account of any one of them requires multidimensional studies from perspectives offered by many different disciplines, including neuroscience, artificial intelligence, psychology, philosophy of mind, and phenomenology. A complete neuroscience (even if that were possible) would not be a complete explanation of cognition; an exhaustive psychology would not exhaust what we can know about human nature; a perfect linguistics would not be a perfect account of everything we need to say about language. Cognitive science is not (or should not be) interdisciplinary for purposes of eliminating all but one discipline. Rather, the best account of cognitive science is that it consists of the cognitive *sciences*, and that these sciences have to stand together in order to develop the fullest account possible. It's not reduction, but multiplication – taking multiple perspectives on the problem – that characterizes the idea of the cognitive sciences that we defend in *The Phenomenological Mind*.

Let us end by expressing our gratitude to Rasmus Thybo Jensen, who in translating *The Phenomenological Mind* into Danish, called our attention to some points that needed clarification, a number of typos and some missing bibliographical information. We also want to thank Gottfried Vosgerau and Simona Chiodo, who guest-edited two comprehensive collections of commentaries on our book, and Roberta De Monticelli for organizing a Winter School on *The Phenomenological Mind* in Milan in 2010. Our thanks obviously also go to all the contributors to those special issues, and School participants, for their inspiring and challenging comments. Finally, we would like to thank Tony Bruce and Adam Johnson from Routledge for encouraging us to work on a second edition and for all their practical help, and James Thomas for his excellent copy-editing on the second edition.

1 Introduction

Philosophy of mind, cognitive science, and phenomenology

This is a book about the mind. What the mind is, and how it works, are currently the topics of many complex debates that span a number of disciplines: psychology, neuroscience, artificial intelligence, philosophy of mind – disciplines that belong to what is generally referred to as the cognitive sciences. The interdisciplinary nature of these debates is no coincidence. Rather, it is necessitated by the fact that no single discipline can do full justice to the complexity of the issues at hand. In this book, we want to explore a variety of issues that have traditionally been studied by philosophers of mind. However, we do not intend to take a *pure* philosophical approach – that is, we do not take a philosophical approach that would ignore the other sciences. We will frequently appeal to the details of scientific evidence from studies in cognitive neuroscience and brain imaging, developmental and cognitive psychology, and psychopathology. This is, however, a book on the *philosophy* of mind, and no matter how interdisciplinary it gets, it remains an attempt to address philosophical problems.

Everything we said so far, however, could be the basis for a standard philosophy of mind or philosophy of cognitive science textbook, of which there are already a sufficient number. We propose to do things differently, and for reasons that will become clear as we proceed, we think this difference is important and productive, and one that signals a change in the way things are developing in the cognitive sciences. Specifically, we will take a phenomenological perspective on the issues that are to be discussed, where phenomenology refers to a tradition of philosophy that originated in Europe and includes the work of Husserl,

Heidegger, Merleau-Ponty, Sartre, and other more recent thinkers. We will not try to do justice to all aspects of phenomenology. Rather, our treatment involves a selection of topics that we think are of particular importance for contemporary discussions in philosophy of mind and cognitive science. Also, our focus will not be historical or based on textual exegesis of figures in the phenomenological tradition, although we will certainly cite their work where relevant. To understand the motive for this selection of perspective, let us look briefly at the way philosophy and psychology have developed in the past century or so.

AN OVERSIMPLIFIED ACCOUNT OF THE LAST 100 YEARS

If we took a snapshot of the philosophical and psychological discussions of the mind around the end of the nineteenth century, we would find complex discussions about the nature of consciousness (for example, in the writings of the American philosopher/psychologist William James, and the European philosopher Edmund Husserl), the intentional structure of mental states (e.g. in the work of the Austrian philosopher and psychologist Franz Brentano, Bertrand Russell, and again, Husserl), as well as discussions about the methodology needed for a proper study of the mind (e.g. Wilhelm Wundt, Gustav Theodor Fechner, and again, James and Husserl). One would also notice that all of these people were influencing each other, sometimes directly (corresponding by letters in a pre-electronic age) or indirectly (by reading each other's work). So, for example, James was inspired by theorists and experimentalists in Europe, and in his 1890 *Principles of Psychology* (1950) he cited the work of Brentano and many of his students, including the psychologist Carl Stumpf. Although James did not cite Husserl, a student of both Brentano and Stumpf, the latter had recommended that Husserl read James's *Principles*. Husserl did so, and he clearly learned from James. Husserl also corresponded with the logician Frege. Both criticized the then prevalent doctrine of psychologism, that is, the idea that the laws of logic are reducible to laws of psychology.[1] Both of them had a strong interest in the philosophy of mathematics and logic, which was also of interest to Russell, who had a copy of Husserl's *Logical Investigations* in his prison cell (where he served time for civil disobedience).

As we move further into the twentieth century, these thinkers and their particular philosophical approaches start to move apart. James became less involved in psychology and occupied himself with the development of the philosophy of American pragmatism. The kind of logical analysis found in the work of Frege and Russell became the basis for what has become known as analytic philosophy. And Husserl developed an approach to consciousness and experience which he called phenomenology. By mid-century, and indeed throughout most of the latter part of the twentieth century, we find that with respect to discussions of the mind (as well as other topics) very little communication is going on between analytic philosophy of mind and phenomenology. In fact, on both sides, the habitual attitude towards the other tradition has ranged from complete disregard to outright hostility. Indeed, up until the 1990s, it was unusual to find philosophers from these different traditions even talking to each other. There has been plenty of arrogance on both sides of the aisle. Thus, for example, Jean-Luc Marion (1998) suggested that during the twentieth century phenomenology had essentially assumed the very role of philosophy, apparently ignoring any contribution by analytic philosophy. On the other side, Thomas Metzinger allegedly proclaimed phenomenology to be 'a discredited research programme ... intellectually bankrupt for at least 50 years'.[2] Even when phenomenologists do talk with analytic philosophers we find reactions such as John Searle's claim, in response to a critique by Dreyfus, that phenomenology suffers from serious limitations, or as he puts it, using the less reserved economic metaphor, 'I almost want to say ... bankruptcy – and [it] does not have much to contribute to the topics of the logical structure of intentionality or the logical structure of social and institutional reality' (Searle 1999a, pp. 1, 10).[3]

To explain how these different philosophers came to think of themselves as so opposed to each other, or perhaps even worse, indifferent towards each other, would involve telling a larger story than is necessary for our purposes. We endorse David Woodruff Smith's observation: 'It ought to be obvious that phenomenology has a lot to say in the area called philosophy of mind. Yet the traditions of phenomenology and analytic philosophy of mind have not been closely joined, despite overlapping areas of interest' (Smith 2003). In this book, however, you will be able to discern some of the important differences between the approaches of the analytic philosophy of mind and phenomenology, as well as some of their overlapping concerns.

Another part of the relevant history involves what happens in psychology. Here is the standard version, which is a somewhat distorted history of what actually happened, although it is the one given in almost every textbook account. At the end of the nineteenth and beginning of the twentieth century there was a great interest in explaining conscious experience and the cognitive processes involved in attention and memory. The early experimental psychologists relied on introspection as a method that aimed to produce measurable data about the mind. Around 1913, however, the emphasis shifted to the notion of behaviour as the proper object of psychological study. Behaviourism, as an approach to the study of animal and human psychology, was defended and articulated in the work of the American psychologist John Watson (1913), and came to dominate the study of psychology, especially in America, until the 1970s, peaking around 1950. The shift to behaviour and its emphasis on the measurement of observable action was at the same time a shift away from the interior life of the mind and the method of introspection. Behaviourism, however, was ultimately replaced by cognitive approaches that returned to the earlier interest in the interior processes of mental life, this time armed with computational models developed in computer science, and more recently, all of the scientific advancements in brain research. Finally, in the late 1980s and throughout the 1990s, researchers again focused on attempts to understand and explain consciousness.

This story is distorted and oversimplified even in its broad strokes. One could easily point to historical evidence that suggests, in complete contrast to the standard story, that behaviourist approaches and attempts to obtain objective measures were common in the earliest psychology laboratories of the nineteenth century, and introspection was frequently considered problematic, even by the so-called introspectionists, although it continued to play some part in psychological experimentation throughout the twentieth century. Furthermore, computational concepts of the mind can arguably be traced back to the eighteenth century;

and consciousness has been of continuing interest since the time of René Descartes, in the first half of the seventeenth century, and perhaps since the time of the ancient Greeks. One might also claim that the standard story is simply partisan, reflecting the interests of the people who pieced it together. As Alan Costall (2004, 2006) has argued, the understanding of the early history of psychology as introspectionist was an invention of John Watson, who wanted to put behaviourist psychology on everyone's agenda. Yet, the psychologist that Watson most associated with introspection, Wilhelm Wundt, expressed his own distrust of introspection: 'Introspective method relies either on arbitrary observations that go astray or on a withdrawal to a lonely sitting room where it becomes lost in self-absorption. The unreliability of this method is universally recognized' (Wundt 1900, p. 180; translated in Blumental 2001, p. 125). Furthermore, although cognitivists claimed to offer a revolution in psychology, as Costall (2004, p. 1) points out, 'Cognitivism is very much a continuation of the kind of mechanistic behaviorism it claims to have undermined.'

The story, then, is more complex than standard accounts indicate. The 'cognitive revolution', the emergence of cognitive science after 1950, and mid-century analytic philosophy of mind were all influenced by behaviourist thought. Gilbert Ryle, for example, wrote in his book *The Concept of Mind*, that what we call the mind simply is 'overt intelligent performances' (1949, p. 58), and he admits to the importance of behaviourism for this kind of insight (1949, p. 328).[4] In contrast, it is often thought that phenomenology was primarily an introspectionist enterprise. As we will show in the following, this is also a misconception (see Chapter 2). In terms of comprehending the relation between phenomenology and philosophy of mind, however, it is certainly the case that analytic philosophers of mind thought of phenomenology as being introspectionist, and from their point of view introspection, as a method for understanding the mind, was dead.

If we set the question of introspection aside for now, another way to characterize the difference between contemporary mainstream analytic philosophy of mind and phenomenology is by noting that whereas the majority of analytic philosophers today endorse some form of naturalism, phenomenologists have tended to adopt a non- or even anti-naturalistic approach. However, matters are somewhat complicated by the fact that naturalism is by no means an unequivocal term. We will discuss this point in more detail in Chapter 2. For now it will be sufficient to point out that science tends to adopt a naturalistic view, so that when finally the cognitive revolution occurred, that is, when psychology started to come under the influence of computational theories of mind in the 1950s and 1960s, and when the interdisciplinary study of the mind known as cognitive science started to emerge, the philosophical approach that seemed more attuned to science was analytic philosophy of mind. Moreover, there was quite a lot of work for philosophers of mind to do when the dominant model was a computational one. Logic and logical analysis play an essential role in the computational model. More importantly, however, philosophy of mind contributed important theoretical foundations and conceptual analyses to the emerging sciences of the mind. The philosophical definition of functionalism, for example, plays an important role in explicating the computational model so that it can apply both to natural and artificial intelligence.

In this organization of cognitive disciplines, the specific philosophical approach of phenomenology was pushed to the side and generally thought to be irrelevant. For a long time the one lone voice that insisted on its relevance to issues pertaining to the field of artificial intelligence and the cognitive sciences was Hubert Dreyfus (1967, 1972, 1992). But this situation has recently changed, and it is this change that motivates this book. Computationalism is not as dominant as it had been in the first 30 years of cognitive science. Three developments have pushed it off its throne. The first is a revived interest in phenomenal consciousness. Starting in the late 1980s (see, for example, Marcel and Bisiach 1988), psychologists and philosophers started to talk about consciousness in the context of the cognitive sciences. During the 1990s a broad debate about the 'hard problem' of consciousness began, led by David Chalmers (1995), in the wake of important writings by, among others, Thomas Nagel (1974), Searle (1992), Daniel Dennett (1991), Owen Flanagan (1992), and Galen Strawson (1994). When methodological questions arose about how to study the experiential dimension scientifically, and therefore, without resorting to old-style introspectionism, a new discussion of phenomenology was started. In other words, in some circles, *phenomenology* as a philosophical approach was thought to be of possible importance when consciousness was raised as a scientific question.

The second thing that happened to motivate a reconsideration of phenomenology as a philosophical-scientific approach was the advent of embodied approaches to cognition. In the cognitive sciences, the notion of embodied cognition took on strength in the 1990s, and it continues today. Scientists and philosophers such as Francisco Varela, Evan Thompson, and Eleanor Rosch (1991), Antonio Damasio (1994), and Andy Clark (1997) objected to the strong Cartesian mind–body dualism that, despite the best efforts of philosophers like Ryle, Dennett, and others, continued to plague the cognitive sciences. Functionalism led us to believe that cognition could be instantiated in a disembodied computer program, or 'brain in-a-vat', and that embodiment added nothing to the mind. Varela et al., as well as Clark and others, pointed back to the insights of the French phenomenologist Maurice Merleau-Ponty (1962) as a way to develop their objections to disembodied cognition. Indeed, we will see that Merleau-Ponty offers one of the best examples of how phenomenology can play an important role in the cognitive sciences.

A third development that has made phenomenological approaches to cognition relevant to experimental science has been the amazing progress of neuroscience. In the past 20 years we have been able to learn a tremendous amount about how the brain works. Technologies such as brain imaging (fMRI, PET) have generated new experimental paradigms. The science of brain imaging is complex, and is certainly not just a matter of taking a snapshot of what is going on inside the head. But the generation of images of neural processing using non-invasive technology has made possible a variety of experiments that depend on reports about the experience of the experimental subjects. Both in order to design the experiments properly and in order to interpret their results, experimenters often want to know what the subject's experience is like. Again, the issue of methodology calls for some consideration of dependable ways of describing conscious experience, and phenomenology offers just such a method.

It seems clear, then, that the time is ripe for a careful account of how phenomenological philosophy and method can contribute to the cognitive sciences. This book is an attempt to do that. What marks out the territory covered in this book, in contrast to other textbooks on philosophy of mind, then, is that it develops a *phenomenological* approach to the philosophy of mind. The idea, however, is not to displace or dismiss analytic philosophy of mind. Indeed, part of what we want to explore is how phenomenology can enter back into a communication with analytic approaches in a way that goes beyond generalities. To us the most exciting development of the past few years has been the growing interest of both analytic philosophers of mind and phenomenologists in experimental science. If, for a variety of historical and conceptual reasons, analytic philosophy and phenomenology have for a time been ignoring each other, the thriving field of consciousness research is certainly an area where communication has been re-sparked.

WHAT IS PHENOMENOLOGY?

Phenomenology, understood as the philosophical approach originated by Edmund Husserl in the early years of the twentieth century, has a complex history. In part it is the basis for what has become known as continental philosophy, where 'continental' means the European continent, despite the fact that much continental philosophy since 1960 has been done in America. Within this designation one finds a number of philosophical approaches, some building on the insights of phenomenology, such as existentialism and hermeneutics (theory of interpretation), and others reacting critically against phenomenology, including certain post-structuralist or postmodernist ideas. There is, however, a line of major philosophical thinkers, including Heidegger, Sartre, and Merleau-Ponty, who extend phenomenological philosophy from its origins in Husserl. Following this lineage means that we understand phenomenology to include a somewhat diverse set of approaches. To provide a basic idea of phenomenology, however, we will here focus on what these approaches have in common. In later chapters we will have the opportunity to explore insights provided by some of the individual phenomenologists.

Most introductory textbooks in philosophy of mind or in cognitive science start by or frame the entire discussion by describing various metaphysical positions: dualism, materialism, identity theory, functionalism, eliminativism … and so on (see, for example, Braddon-Mitchell and Jackson 2006; Chalmers 2002; Heil 2004; Kim 2005). Before we even know for sure what we are talking about, it seems that we have to commit ourselves metaphysically and declare our allegiance to one or the other of these positions. Phenomenology pushes these kinds of questions aside, brackets them, sets them out of play, and asks us instead to pay attention to the phenomenon under study. One of the underlying ideas of phenomenology is that the preoccupation with these metaphysical issues tends to degenerate into highly technical and abstract discussions that lose touch with the real subject matter: *experience*. It is no coincidence that Edmund Husserl's maxim for phenomenology was, 'Back to the things themselves!' (Husserl 1950/1964, p. 6). By this he meant that phenomenology should base its considerations on the way things are experienced rather than various extraneous concerns which might simply obscure and distort what is to be understood. One important concern of the philosophy of mind and cognitive science should be to provide a phenomenologically sensitive account of the various structures of experience.

But what is the thing under study? Don't we have to know whether we are studying the mind, or the brain, or whether it is something material or immaterial? Is consciousness generated by specific brain processes, or not? How can the phenomenologist set such questions aside and hope to make any progress? Or, someone might object, 'How can the phenomenologist deny that the brain causes consciousness?' The proper response to this is that phenomenologists do not *deny* it; nor do they *affirm* it. They suspend these kinds of questions and all judgements about them. They start with experience.

Take perception as an example. When I look out of the window and see my car parked in the street, I am having a visual perception. An experimental psychologist would want to provide a causal explanation of how visual perception works, perhaps in terms of retinal processes, neuronal activation in the visual cortex and association areas in the brain that allow me to recognize the car as my own. She might devise a functionalist account that explains what sorts of mechanisms do the work, or what sort of information (colour, shape, distance, etc.) needs to be processed in order for me to have the visual perception of my car. These are important explanations for science to develop. The phenomenologist, however, has a different task. She would start with the experience itself and by means of a careful description of that experience she would attempt to say what perceptual experience is like, what the difference is between perception and, for example, an instance of imagination or recollection, and how that perception is structured so that it delivers a meaningful experience of the world. Without denying that brain processes contribute causally to perception, such processes are simply not part of the perceiver's experience.

There is of course a relationship between what the phenomenologist is doing and what the psychologist is doing. Clearly they are trying to give an account of the same experience. But they are taking different approaches, asking different questions, and looking for different kinds of answers. To the extent that phenomenology stays with experience, it is said to take a first-person approach. That is, the phenomenologist is concerned to understand the perception in terms of the meaning it has for the subject. My perceptual experience of seeing my car in the street, for example, includes nothing about processes that are happening in my brain. The typical cognitive scientist, on the other hand, takes a third-person approach, that is, an approach from the perspective of the scientist as external observer rather than from the perspective of the experiencing subject. She attempts to explain perception in terms of something other than the experience, for example certain objective (and usually subpersonal) processes like brain states or functional mechanisms.

One might think that there is nothing much to say about experience itself. One simply experiences as one experiences. The phenomenologist finds quite a lot to say, however. For example, the phenomenologist notes that my visual perception of the car has a certain structure that characterizes all conscious acts, namely an intentional structure. Intentionality is a ubiquitous character of consciousness, and as the phenomenologists put it, it means that all consciousness (all perceptions, memories, imaginings, judgements, etc.) is *about* or *of something*. In that sense, experience is never an isolated or elemental process. It always involves reference to the *world*, taking that term in a very wide sense to include not just the physical environment, but the social and cultural world, which may include things that do not exist in a physical way (for example, Hamlet, the Prince of Denmark). The phenomenological analysis of intentionality leads to a number of insights. For example, the intentionality of perception is richly detailed in the following sense. When I see a particular object in the street, I see it as my car. Perception is not a simple reception of information; rather, it involves an interpretation, which frequently changes according to context. To see my car as my car already suggests that perception is informed by previous experience, and at least in this sense Locke and the empiricists were correct to suggest that perception is educated by experience. One should think of this as perception enriched by experience and by habitual, as well as customary, ways of experiencing things rather than as a case of perception plus thought. It's not that I perceive x and then add something quite different and novel, namely the thought that this is my car. One way to put this is to say that perception is 'smart'. To say that perception involves interpretation doesn't mean that first we perceive some nebulous entity and then we add an interpretation – something over and above perception that bestows meaning on it. Rather, perception *is* interpretational. I see the car already as my car.

Perception is smart; it's already meaningful. In part this means that it is already enriched by the circumstances and possibilities of my embodied existence and surrounding environment. The phenomenologist would say that perceptual experience is embedded in contexts that are pragmatic, social, and cultural and that much of the semantic work (the formation of perceptual meaning) is facilitated by the objects, arrangements, and events that I encounter. In a particular instance I may see the object as a practical vehicle that I can use to get me to where I'm going. In another instance I may see the exact same object as something I have to clean, or as something I have to sell, or as something that is not working properly. The way that I see my car will depend on a certain contextual background, which can also be explored phenomenologically. To encounter my car as something to drive is to encounter it as something I can climb into, as something located in a place that affords the kind of motion the car is built for. My perceptual experience will consequently be informed by the bodily abilities and skills I possess. It has been customary to say that perception has representational or conceptual content. But perhaps this way of talking fails to fully capture the situated nature of perceptual experience. Rather than saying that I represent the car as driveable, it might be better to say that – given the design of the car, the shape of my body and its action possibilities, and the state of the environment – the car is driveable and I perceive it as such.

The intentional structure of perception also involves spatial aspects that can be explored phenomenologically. My embodied position places precise limitations on what I can see and what I can't. From where I am standing I can see the driver's side of the car. The car appears in that profile, and in such a way that what I do see of the car occludes other aspects or profiles of the car. Standing where I am I cannot literally see the passenger side of the car, for example – it is not in my visual field. Nonetheless, I see the car *as having* another side to it, and I would be extremely surprised if I walked around the car and found that the passenger side was missing. The surprise that I would feel indicates that I have a certain tacit anticipation of what my possible action in the immediate future will bring. I am surprised because my anticipation is disappointed. This temporal structure of our experience has been described in great detail by phenomenologists, and it is a feature that we will return to repeatedly in the following chapters.

In any perception of a physical object, my perception is always incomplete in regard to the object – I never see a complete object all at once. Let's call this 'perspectival incompleteness'. There is always something more to see that is implicitly there, even in the perception of the simplest object. If I move around a tree in order to obtain a more exhaustive perception of it, then the various profiles of the tree, its front, sides, and back, do not present themselves as disjointed fragments, but are perceived as synthetically integrated moments. This synthetic process is once again temporal in nature.

Phenomenologically, I can also discover certain *gestalt* features of perception. Visual perception comes with a characteristic structure such that, normally, something is always in focus while the rest is not. Some object is at the centre of my focus, while others are in the background, or on the horizon, or at the periphery. I can shift my focus and make something else come into the foreground, but only at the cost of shifting the first object attended to out of focus and into the horizon.

Notice that in these kinds of accounts the phenomenologist is concerned with particular experiential structures of perception, and precisely as they relate to the world in which the perceiver is situated. That is, even as she attends to experience, the phenomenologist does not get locked up in an experience that is purely subjective, or detached from the world. The phenomenologist studies perception, not as a purely subjective phenomenon, but as it is lived through by a perceiver who is *in the world*, and who is also an embodied agent with motivations and purposes.

In addition to this kind of intentional analysis of how we experience the world, or how the world appears to us, the phenomenologist can also ask about the phenomenal state of the perceiver. This is sometimes referred to in the philosophy of mind literature as the qualitative or phenomenal features of experience – or, in a fortuitous phrase made famous by Nagel (1974), the 'what it is like' to experience something. The phenomenal features of experience are not divorced from the intentional features. What it is like to stand around and admire my new car is obviously quite different from what it is like to stand around and see my new car get smashed by another car.

In a short reflection we have identified some ubiquitous aspects or structures of perception: its intentionality, its gestalt character, its perspectival incompleteness, its phenomenal and temporal character. There is much more to say about temporality (see Chapter 4), perception (Chapter 5), intentionality (Chapter 6), and phenomenality (Chapter 3). Notice, however, that what we have been outlining here amounts to a description of experience, or more precisely a description of the structures of experience, and that as phenomenologists we have not once mentioned the brains behind this experience. That is, we have not tried to give an account in terms of neuronal mechanisms that might cause us to perceive the car in the way that we perceive it. So in this way a phenomenological account of perception is something quite different from a psychophysical or neuroscientific account. Phenomenology is concerned with attaining an *understanding* and proper *description* of the experiential structure of our mental/embodied life; it does not attempt to develop a naturalistic *explanation* of consciousness, nor does it seek to uncover its biological genesis, neurological basis, psychological motivation, or the like.

This kind of phenomenological account is consistent with Husserl's original conception of phenomenology. In his view, phenomenology is not interested in an analysis of the psycho-physical constitution of the human being, nor in an empirical investigation of consciousness, but in an understanding of what intrinsically and in principle characterizes perceptions, judgements, feelings, etc.

Nonetheless, and this is an important point for our purposes, we can also see that this phenomenological account is not irrelevant for a *science* of perception. There is currently a growing realization that we will not get very far in giving a scientific account of the relationship between consciousness and the brain unless we have a clear conception of what it is that we are trying to relate. To put it another way, any assessment of the possibility of reducing consciousness to neuronal structures and any appraisal of whether a *naturalization* of consciousness is possible will require a detailed analysis and description of the experiential aspects of consciousness. As Nagel once pointed out, a necessary requirement for any coherent reductionism is that the entity to be reduced is properly understood (1974, p. 437). Without necessarily endorsing a reductionist strategy, it is clear that if, in a methodical way, we pursue a detailed phenomenological analysis, exploring the precise intentional, spatial, temporal, and phenomenal aspects of experience, then we will end up with a description of just what it is that the psychologists and the neuroscientists are trying to explain when they appeal to neural, information processing, or dynamical models. Indeed, the phenomenologist would claim that this kind of methodically controlled analysis provides a more adequate model of perception for the scientist to work with than if the scientist simply starts with a common-sense approach.

Compare two situations. In the first situation we, as scientists who are interested in explaining perception, have no phenomenological description of perceptual experience. How would we begin to develop our explanation? We would have to start somewhere. Perhaps we would start with a pre-established theory of perception, and begin by testing the various predictions this theory makes. Quite frequently this is the way that science is done. We may ask where this pre-established theory comes from, and find that in part it may be based on certain observations or assumptions about perception. We may question these observations or assumptions, and based on how we think perception actually works, formulate counter-arguments or alternative hypotheses to be tested out. This seems somewhat hit or miss, although science often makes progress in this way. In the second situation, we have a well-developed phenomenological description of perceptual experience as intentional, spatial, temporal, and phenomenal. We suggest that starting with this description, we already have a good idea of what we need to explain. If we know that perception is always perspectivally incomplete, and yet that we perceive objects as if they have volume, and other sides that we cannot see in the perceptual moment, then we know what we have to explain, and we may have good clues about how to design experiments to get to just this feature of perception. If the phenomenological description is systematic and detailed, then to start with this rich description seems a lot less hit or miss. So phenomenology and science may be aiming for different kinds of accounts, but it seems clear that phenomenology can be relevant and useful for scientific work.

Currently, the term 'phenomenology' is increasingly used by philosophers of mind and cognitive scientists to designate a first-person description of the 'what it is like' of experience. In the next chapter we will show why this non-methodical use of the term, as an equivalent to introspection, is misleading, and that quite a lot depends on the methodological nature of phenomenology.

As we indicated, many philosophy of mind textbooks start off by reviewing various theories about the mind – dualism, identity theory, functionalism, etc. It is also the case that psychology and cognitive science may already be informed by specific theories of the mind. Phenomenology, however, does not start with a theory, or with a consideration of theories. It seeks to be critical and non-dogmatic, shunning metaphysical and theoretical prejudices, as much as possible. It seeks to be guided by what is actually experienced rather than by what we expect to find, given our theoretical commitments. It asks us not to let preconceived theories form our experience, but to let our experience inform and guide our theories. But, just as phenomenology is not opposed to science (although its task is somewhat different from empirical science), neither is phenomenology opposed to theory. It would be an oversimplification if we considered phenomenology as simply a set of methods for the pure description of experience. Using such methods, however, phenomenologists are led to insights about experience, and they are also interested in developing these insights into theories of perception, intentionality, phenomenality, etc. The overarching claim of this book is that these phenomenological-based theoretical accounts and descriptions can complement and inform ongoing work in the cognitive sciences. In fact, we think they can do so in a far more productive manner than the standard metaphysical discussions of, say, the mind–body problem that we find in mainstream philosophy of mind.

OUTLINE OF THIS BOOK

In contrast to many textbooks on philosophy of mind and cognitive science, then, we will not begin by wrestling with the various metaphysical positions. Without doubt we will meet up with these different positions in the following chapters, but the framework for this book will be set by starting closer to experience and scientific practice.

In Chapter 2 we will take up certain methodological questions which are directly relevant to the practice of experimental science. We want to ask about what actually happens in the lab, in the experiment, and how scientists go about studying the mind. If part of what psychologists and neuroscientists want to study is experience, what kind of access do they have to it? We also want to provide a clear explication of phenomenological methods. This is something that we have often been asked to do by scientists who are interested in using phenomenological approaches, but who are puzzled about how phenomenological methods are supposed to work.

In Chapter 3 we discuss diverse concepts of consciousness. In contemporary analytic philosophy of mind there is an important debate going on about higher-order theories of consciousness, and we want to review that debate and suggest an alternative way to approach the problem of consciousness. This debate involves fascinating questions about issues that range from the common experience of driving a car, to certain experimental results about non-conscious perception, to some exotic cases of pathology, such as blindsight.

In Chapter 4 we explore one of the most important, but also one of the most neglected aspects of consciousness and cognition, as well as action – the temporality of experience. William James had described consciousness metaphorically as having the structure of a stream. He also argued that the present moment of experience is always structured in a threefold temporal way, to include an element of the past and an element of the future. He called this, following Robert Kelly (aka E. R. Clay), the 'specious present'. For phenomenologists, this issue goes to the very foundational structure of experience.

In Chapter 5 we dig deeper into perception. Contemporary explanations of perception include a number of non-traditional, non-Cartesian approaches that emphasize the embodied and enactive aspects of perception, or the fact that perception, and more generally cognition, are situated, both physically and socially, in significant ways. We'll try to sort these approaches out in order to see on what issues they agree or disagree. This will lead us to consider the debate between non-representationalist views and representationalist views of the mind.

Chapter 6 takes us to one of the most important concepts in our understanding of how the mind is in the world – intentionality. This is the idea that experience, whether it is perception, memory, imagination, judgement, belief, etc., is always directed to some object. Intentionality is reflected in the very structure of consciousness, and involves notions of mental acts and mental content. It is also a concept that is of direct relevance for the contemporary debate between externalism and internalism.

Chapter 7 takes up the question of embodiment. Here, we examine the classic phenomenological distinctions between the lived body (*Leib*) and the objective body (*Körper*). But we also want to show how biology and the very shape of the body contribute to cognitive experience. We explore how embodied space frames our experiences and we discuss cases of phantom limbs, unilateral neglect, and deafferentation. We also pursue some implications for the design of robotic bodies.

Chapter 8 shows how an adequate scientific account of human action depends on certain phenomenological distinctions between the sense of agency and the sense of ownership for bodily movement. We suggest, however, that human action cannot be reduced to bodily movement, and that certain scientific experiments can be misleading when their focus is narrowed to just such bodily movements. Here too a number of pathological cases, including schizophrenic delusions of control, will help us to understand non-pathological action.

Chapter 9 concerns the question of how we come to understand other minds. We explore some current 'theory of mind' accounts ('theory theory' and 'simulation theory'), and introduce a phenomenologically based alternative that is consistent with recent research in developmental psychology and neuroscience.

In Chapter 10 we come to a question that has been gaining interest across the cognitive sciences – the question of the self. Although this question has long been explored by philosophers, neuroscientists and psychologists have recently revisited the issue. What we find is that there are almost as many different concepts of the self as there are theorists examining them. To make some headway on this issue, we focus on the basic pre-reflective sense of unity through temporal change that is implicit in normal experience. We examine how this pre-reflective sense of self can break down in cases of schizophrenia, and what role it plays in the development of a more reflective sense of self, expressed in language, narrative, and cultural contexts.

NOTES

1 Psychologism is not entirely defeated, and it has recently been revived in the form of what might be called *neurologism*. The well-known neuroscientist Semir Zeki wrote in a recent article: 'My approach is dictated by a truth that I believe to be axiomatic – that all human activity is dictated by the organization and laws of the brain; that, therefore, there can be no real theory of art and aesthetics unless neurobiologically based' (Zeki 2002, p. 54). The limitations and problematic nature of this proposal become obvious the moment one simply replaces the claims about art and aesthetics with claims about other human activities such as astrophysics or archaeology.

2 See the editorial in *Journal of Consciousness Studies* 4/5–6 (Editors 1997, p. 385).

3 For a more sober and forward-looking discussion of the relation between analytic philosophy and phenomenology, see D. Moran (2001).

4 Was Ryle really a behaviourist? No. See Dennett (2000).

2 Methodologies

Let's admit it right from the beginning. Discussions of methodology are quite good as sleeping aides. They tend to put us right to sleep. Most of us want to get on with it and get to the issues, the 'things themselves', the experiments, and so on. But in this chapter we are not going to give you a boring outline of the details of a method, or provide a set of rules. Rather, we are going to jump into the middle of a debate that is raging within the cognitive sciences. People are being accused of being *introspectionists* or *heterophenomenologists* or *neurophenomenologists*, or, worse, just plain *phenomenologists*. It is even the case that there has been a recent outbreak of terminological hijacking. That is, some theorist will come up with an extraordinarily good term for something, and next thing you know, other theorists are using that term to refer to something quite different.[1] What we need to do in the following is to sort out the differences between these various approaches.

It may be helpful to begin by noting that in philosophical and scientific discussions of cognition and consciousness one often finds a distinction made between first-person and third-person perspectives. Indeed, traditional and contemporary definitions of the mind–body problem, the 'hard' problem, or the problem of the explanatory gap, have often been framed by this distinction. Scientific objectivity, it is said, requires a detached, third-person approach to observable phenomena, and for this we need, and usually have, good observational access to things in the environment, some of which are brains. Brain science depends on taking a third-person, observational perspective. In contrast, even if we have a kind of direct access to our own experience from the first-person perspective, some philosophers and scientists would consider this to be too subjective to generate scientific data. Dennett (2001) has recently remarked: 'First-person science of consciousness is a discipline with no methods, no data, no results, no future, no promise. It will remain a fantasy.'

If this is so, then there seems to be a real problem. Seemingly there can be no *science of consciousness per se* if (1) consciousness is intrinsically first-person, if (2) science only accepts third-person data, and if (3) any attempt to explain something that is first person in third-person terms distorts or fails to capture what it tries to explain. Perhaps, then, it was simply a nineteenth- and early twentieth-century fantasy to think that one could base a scientific study of consciousness on careful introspection. Let's take a closer look at these claims.

FANTASIES IN THE SCIENCE OF CONSCIOUSNESS

> *Introspective observation is what we have to rely on first and foremost and always.* The word introspection need hardly be defined – it means, of course, looking into our own minds and reporting what we there discover.
>
> (James 1890/1950, I, p. 185)

Let's first ask what has been the fate of introspection as a method in the experimental science of the mind? The standard view is that it has been left behind in the same way that we have left the nineteenth century behind. As John Watson wrote in 1913:

> Psychology as the behaviorist views it is a purely objective experimental branch of natural science. Its theoretical goal is the prediction and control of behavior. Introspection forms no essential part of its methods, nor is the scientific value of its data dependent upon the readiness with which they lend themselves to interpretation in terms of consciousness.
>
> (Watson 1913, p. 158)

Even after the official demise of behaviourism, many have continued to deny that intro-spection is even possible, and philosophers like William Lyons (1986) have charted the complete dismissal of this method in psychology. But the situation is in fact less clear. In a recent paper, Price and Aydede (2005), a psychologist and a philosopher, respectively, claim that introspection continues to be used in experimental science because 'the subjects' verbal reports [or non-verbal behaviours like button-pushes] about their own cognitive states have routinely been taken as evidence for the cognitive models postulated' (2005, p. 245). Furthermore, according to Jack and Roepstorff (2002), two cognitive scientists: 'Introspective observation is not just a pervasive feature of our personal lives. Cognitive scientists use this source of evidence to inform virtually every stage of their work' (p. 333). Perhaps James was wrong, however; it may not be so clear what various people mean by introspection. On a very basic level one might argue that *all* reports given by subjects, even if directly about the world, are in some sense, indirectly, about their own cognitive (mental, emotional, experiential) states. If, in a psychophysical experiment one instructs a subject to push a button, or say 'now' when they see a light come on, then the subject is reporting about the light, but also about their visual experience. Even if one neutralizes the instruction in a way that carefully avoids mention of an experiential state ('Push the button when the light comes on'), the only access that the subject has to the fact of the light coming on is by way of her experience of the light coming on. In this sense the first-person perspective is inherent in all experiments that depend on subjects' reports. This seems to be what Price and Aydede mean. But does this mean that all such reports are introspective?

For example, the experimenter may ask the subject to say 'now' when she sees the light come on. How precisely does the subject know when she sees the light come on? Does she introspect her experience looking for the particular visual state of seeing-the-light-come-on? Or does she simply see the light come on and report that? One might ask, 'How could she possibly report that she sees the light come on if she doesn't introspectively observe that she sees the light come on?' There is a long tradition in philosophical phenomenology (specifically the tradition that follows Husserl) that explains how. We are aware of what we experience without using introspection precisely because we have an implicit, non-objectifying, pre-reflective awareness of our own experience as we live it through. At the same time that I see the light, I'm aware that I see the light. The awareness in question is not based on reflectively or introspectively turning our attention to our own experience. It is, rather, built into our experience as an essential part of it, and it is precisely this which defines our experience as conscious experience (for a more extended argument, see Chapter 3). On this view, I consciously experience the light coming on just when I see the light coming on. I don't have to verify through introspection that I have just seen the light come on, since my first-order phenomenal experience is already something of which I am aware in the very experiencing.

The idea of 'ascent routines' suggests in a similar fashion that reports on experience are not necessarily introspective (Evans 1982). For example, if a subject is asked 'Do you believe that p?', the subject does not start searching in her mind for the belief that p. Rather, she straightforwardly considers whether p is or is not the case about the world. So too, in regard to perceiving the world, the perceiver does not have to introspect for perceptual representations in her mind; she can say what she perceives simply by consciously perceiving the world. If you were asked whether it is raining outside, you would look out the window rather than inside your mind.

In this sense it does not seem correct to say, as Price and Aydede do, that from a first-person perspective 'conscious experiences seem accessible only through introspection' (2005, p. 246) or 'introspection seems to be the *only* available method of access to qualia' (ibid., p. 249). First-person reports of this kind are not introspective reports, if we think of introspection as a matter of reflective consciousness. They are nonetheless *first-person*, pre-reflective reports expressive of experience. But, one might ask, even if I can report *what* I am seeing without using introspection, can I also report *that* I am *seeing* without using introspection? Again, if I am asked 'Do you see the light?' I can certainly say yes, without initiating a second-order introspective cognition that takes my own experience as an object. If, in contrast, the question were 'Do you *taste* the light?' that would likely motivate a reflective attitude in me, likely with the goal of ascertaining whether I understand your use of the word 'taste'. But even this reflective attitude would not constitute an introspective cognition, since my attention would be on the word you used and its relation to what I've just experienced (to which I still have pre-reflective access), rather than directed to my consciousness of the word, or to the details of my consciousness of the world. If the linguistic articulation of my experience might be considered a type of reflection in this sort of case, it is not neces-sarily an introspective sort of reflection where I am focusing my attention on my experience. Rather, I'm focused on the light, on your question, on its meaning.

Even in the case where consciousness itself is the object of study, then, we need a distinction between straightforward reports about the world (e.g. Did the light come on or not?) and reflective reports about experience (e.g. What is it like to experience the light coming on?). In the first case we may be measuring reaction times or looking into the subject's brain to see what lights up in there when the light comes on out there. In the second case we are asking about the phenomenology – the first-person experience itself. Consequently, we seem to get a clean distinction between third-person, objective data (reaction times, brain images), and first-person data (What does it feel like? On what is the subject focused?). But let's be careful. Things are more complicated, as we will discover shortly.

To begin with, when the investigation is about consciousness, the third-person data are supposedly *about* the subject's first-person experience. After all, in such experiments, the scientist is not concerned about the light, but about the subject's experience. Even if it is an attempt to capture what is objectively happening inside the brain, an fMRI or PET scan lacks any pertinence for the study of consciousness unless it is correlated with the subject's first-person experience. Indeed, the only reason brain states or functional states assume the relevant importance they do is through their putative correlation with mental states identified on other, experiential grounds. Without experiential classification and subsequent corre-lation, we would simply have a description of neural activity, and it would not be informative in the way we want it to be. We would not know, at least in the first case, whether the brain activation had something to do with memory, or face recognition, or feelings of agency, or light perception, etc. So the interpretation of third-person data, when such data are about consciousness, requires us to know something about the first-person data. The terrain of the explanandum (the thing to be explained) has to be properly investigated before explanatory proposals can make any sense.

In the practice of experimental psychology more stock is put in non-introspective reports about the world than in introspective reports. How reliable are such non-introspective reports about the world? In general and for many cases, these kinds of reports do seem very reliable. If an experimenter applies or presents a sensory stimulus that is well above threshold, the subject's report that they experience the stimulus as, for example, clearly present seems above suspicion. Reliability may decrease, however, when the stimulus is closer to threshold, and it may depend on the mode of report, or other subjective factors that qualify the report. Marcel (1993), for example, has shown that requests for quick reports of close-to-threshold stimuli using diverse modes of report (verbal, eye blink, button push) elicit contradictory responses. At the appearance of a just-noticeable light stimulus, subjects will report with a button push that they did see the light and then contradict themselves with a verbal report. This kind of data, and more generally, uneven or inconsistent data, can motivate two different strategies. Most often, following established scientific procedure, data are averaged out across trials or subjects, and the inconsistencies are washed away.

Less often, scientists are motivated to take this first-person data seriously and to employ further methods to investigate it.

Let's consider one methodological statement of how this third-person treatment of first-person data gets started. This is the method that Dennett calls 'heterophenomenology' (1991, 2001, 2007).[2] Dennett has on many occasions made it clear that his goal is to explain every mental phenomenon within the framework of contemporary physical science. More specifically, the challenge he has set himself is to construct a convincing and adequate theory of consciousness on the basis of data that are available from the third-person scientific perspective (Dennett 1991, pp. 40, 71). However, if this enterprise is to succeed, we first need a clear and neutral method that will allow us to collect and organize the data that subsequently are to be explained. Dennett's name for this method is *heterophenomenology*. According to heterophenomenology we need to adopt a strict third-person methodology in the study of consciousness. This means that its only access to the phenomenological realm will be via the observation and interpretation of publicly observable data. Accordingly, the heterophenomenologist intends to access consciousness from the outside. His focus is on the mental life of *others* as it is publicly expressed or manifested. In other words, the heterophenomenologist will interview subjects and record their utterances and other behavioural manifestations. He will then submit the findings to an intentional interpretation, that is, he will adopt the intentional stance and interpret the emitted noises as speech acts that express the subject's beliefs, desires, and other mental states. If there are any ambiguities, he can always ask for further clarifications by the subject, and through this process, he will eventually be able to compose an entire catalogue consisting of the things the subject (apparently) wants to say about his own conscious experiences (Dennett 1991, pp. 76–77; 1982, p. 161).

For the heterophenomenologist, the subjects' reports about their conscious experiences are the primary data in consciousness research: 'the reports *are* the data, they are not reports *of* data' (Dennett 1993a, p. 51). It is consequently no coincidence that Dennett characterizes heterophenomenology as a black box psychology (Dennett 1982, p. 177). Strictly speaking, heterophenomenology doesn't study conscious phenomena, since it is neutral about whether they exist; rather, it studies reports that purport to be about conscious phenomena. Thus, Dennett urges us to adopt a neutral stance and to bracket the question concerning the validity of the subjects' expressed beliefs, and he argues that this manoeuvre amounts to a third-person version of the phenomenological method (Dennett 2003, p. 22).

Why is the neutrality required? Dennett provides different reasons. Occasionally, he compares the neutrality in question with the neutrality that is required in an anthropological investigation. Just as we shouldn't prejudge our anthropological fieldwork by declaring certain mythical gods real divinities (Dennett 1993a, p. 51), we shouldn't prejudge the phenomenological investigation by declaring conscious phenomena real. Dennett also refers to the existence of false positives and false negatives. Our access to our own mind is neither infallible nor incorrigible. We sometimes get things wrong about our own experience; some of the beliefs that we have about our own conscious states are provably false. And some of the psychological processes that happen in our minds take place without our knowledge.

Given these possibilities of error, Dennett thinks it is best to adopt a policy of moderation and simply abstain from commitment (2001).

People believe they have experiences, and these facts – the facts about what people believe and express – are phenomena any scientific study of the mind must account for (Dennett 1991, p. 98), but from the fact that people believe that they have experiences, it doesn't follow that they do in fact have experiences (Dennett 1991, p. 366). To put it differently, we shouldn't simply assume that every apparent feature or object of our conscious lives is really there, as a real element of experience. By adopting the heterophenomenological attitude of neutrality, we do not prejudge the issue about whether the apparent subject is a liar, a zombie, a computer, a dressed-up parrot, or a real conscious being (ibid., p. 81). Thus, heterophenomenology can remain neutral about whether the subject is conscious or a mere zombie (Dennett 1982, p. 160), or to be more precise, since heterophenomenology is a way of interpreting behaviour, and since (philosophical) zombies, per definition, behave like real conscious people, there is no relevant difference between zombies and real conscious people as far as heterophenomenology is concerned (Dennett 1991, p. 95).

But from this alleged stance of neutrality where we bracket the question of whether or not there is a difference between a zombie and a non-zombie, Dennett quickly moves a step further, and *denies* that there is any such difference. As he puts it, zombies are not just possible; they are real, since all of us are zombies. If we think we are more than zombies, this is simply due to the fact that we have been misled or bewitched by the defective set of metaphors that we use to think about the mind (Dennett 1993b, p. 143; 1991, p. 406). It is important not to misunderstand Dennett at this point. He is not arguing that nobody is conscious. Rather he is claiming that consciousness does not have the first-person phenomenal properties it is commonly thought to have, which is why there is in fact no such thing as actual phenomenology (Dennett 1991, p. 365). The attempt to investigate the first-personal dimension phenomenologically is consequently a fantasy.

Heterophenomenology itself, however, involves something of a fantasy. The fantasy here is the idea that in the study of consciousness or the mind, science can leave the first-person perspective behind, or neutralize it without remainder. In attempting to say something about consciousness (or specifically about the experience *X*), heterophenomenology fails to acknowledge that its interpretations of first-person reports must be based on either the scientist's own first-person experience (what he understands from his own experience to be the experience of *X*), or upon pre-established (and seemingly objective) categories that ultimately derive from folk psychology or from some obscure, anonymous, and non-rigorous form of phenomenology. Thus, as Jack and Roepstorff suggest, from 'the moment we conceive of an experimental paradigm, through piloting and refinement, to the interpretation of results, we are guided by considerations of our own experience and the experiences we attribute to others, understood by proxy to our own' (2002, p. 333). The scientist's own intentional stance, required for the interpretation of the subject's report, is not itself something that has come under scientific control; it is nonetheless infected, directly or indirectly, by the first-person perspective. This is why Merleau-Ponty, in *Phenomenology of Perception*, criticizes the one-sided focus of science on what is available from a third-person perspective for being both naive and dishonest, since the scientific practice constantly presupposes the scientist's first-personal and pre-scientific experience of the world (Merleau-Ponty 1962, p. ix). This is also why the usual opposition of first-person versus third-person accounts in the context of the study of consciousness is misleading. It makes us forget that so-called third-person objective accounts are accomplished and generated by a community of conscious subjects. There is no pure third-person perspective, just as there is no view from nowhere.

PHENOMENOLOGICAL METHOD

Is it possible to gain a more controlled approach to first-person experience? Can we approach consciousness scientifically? Phenomenologists have answered these questions in the affirmative. Phenomenology is important here, as Evan Thompson explains, because 'any attempt to gain a comprehensive understanding of the human mind must at some point confront consciousness and subjectivity – how thinking, perceiving, acting, and feeling are experienced in one's own case. Mental events do not occur in a vacuum; they are lived by someone. Phenomenology is anchored to the careful description, analysis, and interpretation of lived experience' (Thompson 2007, p. 16). To understand what phenomenology can deliver, and to exploit it for experimental science, we need to understand the methodology that defines the phenomenological stance or attitude. We then need to see how this stance can be incorporated into scientific practice.

Let's take a closer look at the phenomenological method. Like ordinary scientific method, it also aims to avoid biased and subjective accounts. Some people mistake phenomenology for a subjective account of experience; but a subjective account of experience should be distinguished from an account of subjective experience. In a similar way, some people confuse an objective account of experience with the idea that we can understand subjective experience by turning it into an object that can be examined using third-person methods. The problem is that these terms, 'subjective' and 'objective', are ambiguous; they can mean different things in different contexts. In science, objectivity, in the sense of avoiding prejudice or bias, is important. It is one of the reasons that controls are used in experiments, and there are various methodological steps one takes to maintain objectivity. Phenomenology is also concerned to maintain objectivity in this sense. It does so by way of a carefully delineated method.

Phenomenology and introspection

First, let's return to an issue that tends to confuse things. Is phenomenology the same as introspection? Husserl once raised the following question: Why introduce a new science entitled phenomenology when there is already a well-established explanatory science dealing with the psychic life of humans and animals, namely psychology? Could it not be argued that a mere description of experience – which is supposedly all that phenomenology can offer – does not constitute a viable scientific alternative to psychology, but merely a – perhaps indispensable – descriptive preliminary to a truly scientific study of the mind

(Husserl 1987, p. 102)? As Husserl remarked in these lectures from the early part of the twentieth century, this line of thought had been so convincing that the term 'phenomeno-logical' was being used in all kinds of philosophical and psychological writings to signify a direct description of consciousness based on introspection (ibid., p. 103). The parallel to contemporary discourse is quite striking. Currently, the term 'phenomenology' is increasingly used by cognitive scientists to designate a first-person description of what the 'what it is like' of experience is really like. And against that background, it might be difficult to under-stand why phenomenology should not simply be seen as a kind of psychology or even as a form of introspectionism.

In *Consciousness Explained*, for instance, Dennett criticizes phenomenology for employing an unreliable introspectionist methodology and argues that it has failed to find a single, settled method that everyone could agree upon (Dennett 1991, p. 44). A comparable view can be found in Metzinger, who recently concluded that 'phenomenology is impossible' (2003, p. 83). What kind of argument do these theorists provide? The basic argument seems to concern the epistemological difficulties connected with any first-person approach to data generation. If inconsistencies in two individual data sets should appear, there is no way to settle the conflict. More specifically, Metzinger takes data to be such things that are extracted from the physical world by technical measuring devices. This data extraction involves a well-defined intersubjective procedure, it takes place within a scientific community, it is open to criticism, and it constantly seeks independent means of verification. The problem with phenomenology, according to Metzinger, is that first-person access to the phenomenal content of one's own mental state does not fulfil these defining criteria for the concept of data. In fact, the very notion of first-personal data is a contradiction in terms (ibid., p. 591).

But is it really true that classical phenomenology is based on introspection? Consider Husserl's *Logical Investigations*, a recognized milestone in twentieth-century philosophy and indisputably a work in phenomenological philosophy. In fact, Husserl himself took it to be his 'breakthrough' to phenomenology. What kind of analyses does one find in this book? One finds Husserl's famous attack on and rejection of psychologism; a defence of the irreduc-ibility of logic and the ideality of meaning; an analysis of pictorial representations; a theory of the part–whole relation; a sophisticated account of intentionality; and an epistemological clarification of the relation between concepts and intuitions, to mention just a few of the many topics treated in the book. Does Husserl use an introspective method, and is this a work in introspective psychology? Anyone who reads *Logical Investigations* should answer 'no', since what we find there are clearly philosophical arguments and analyses. Rather than concluding that this work is not phenomenology, one should rather reconsider the hasty identification of phenomenology and introspective psychology.

Phenomenological disputes as well as disputes among phenomenologists are philo-sophical disputes, not disputes about introspection. Although it would be an exaggeration to claim that Husserl's analyses in *Logical Investigations* found universal approval among the subsequent generations of phenomenologists, we don't know of any instance at all where Husserl's position was rejected on the basis of an appeal to 'better' introspective evidence. On the contrary, Husserl's analyses gave rise to an intense discussion among phenomeno-logical philosophers, and many of the analyses were subsequently improved and refined by thinkers like Sartre, Heidegger, Lévinas, and Derrida (see Zahavi and Stjernfelt 2002). This clearly contrasts with Metzinger's claim that the phenomenological method cannot provide a method for generating any growth of knowledge since there is no way one can reach inter-subjective consensus on claims like 'this is the purest blue anyone can perceive' versus 'no it isn't, it has a slight green hue' (Metzinger 2003, p. 591). These kinds of claims are simply not the kind that are to be found in works by phenomenological philosophers and to suggest so is to reveal one's lack of familiarity with the tradition in question.

Although phenomenology is interested in the phenomena (how things are experienced; or as phenomenologists like to say, how they are 'given' or presented to the subject in experience) and in their conditions of possibility, phenomenologists would typically argue that it is a metaphysical fallacy to locate the phenomenal realm within the mind, and to suggest that the way to access and describe it is by turning the gaze inwards (*introspicio*). As Husserl already pointed out in *Logical Investigations*, the entire facile divide between inside and outside has its origin in a naive commonsensical metaphysics and is phenomenologi-cally suspect and inappropriate when it comes to understanding the nature of consciousness (Husserl 2001a, II, pp. 281–82, 304). But this divide is precisely something that the term 'introspection' buys into and accepts. To speak of introspection is to (tacitly) endorse the idea that consciousness is inside the head and the world outside. The same criticism can also be found in Heidegger, who denies that the relation between human existence (*Dasein*) and the world can be grasped with the help of the concepts 'inner' and 'outer' (Heidegger 1986/1996, p. 62), and in Merleau-Ponty, who suggests in this context that it is imposs-ible to draw a line between inner and outer (Merleau-Ponty 1962, p. 407). Indeed, all the major figures in the phenomenological tradition have openly and unequivocally denied that they are engaged in some kind of introspective psychology and that the method they employ is a method of introspection (see Gurwitsch 1966, pp. 89–106; Heidegger 1993, pp. 11–17; Husserl 1984, pp. 201–16; Merleau-Ponty 1962, pp. 57–58). Husserl, who categorically rejects the suggestion that the notion of phenomenological intuition is a form of inner experience or introspection (1987, p. 36), even argues that the very suggestion that phenomenology is attempting to restitute the method of introspection or inner observation (*innerer Beobachtung*) is preposterous and perverse (Husserl 1971/1980, p. 38). What is behind this categorical dismissal? There are many different reasons. To understand some of them, we must return to the issue of the phenomenological method.

Phenomenological reduction

Phenomenology is supposed to be concerned with phenomena and appearances and their conditions of possibility, but what precisely is a phenomenon? For many philosophers, the phenomenon is understood as the immediate 'givenness' of the object, how it appears to us, how it *apparently* is. The assumption has frequently been that the phenomenon is something merely subjective, a veil or smokescreen that conceals the objectively existing reality. According to such a view, if one wished to discover what the object was really like, one would have to surpass the merely phenomenal. If phenomenology employed this concept of the phenomenon it would be nothing but a science of the merely subjective, apparent, or superficial. But not surprisingly the phenomenologists endorse a rather different understanding of what a phenomenon amounts to. In their view, the reality of the object is not to be located behind its appearance, as if the appearance in some way or other hides the real object. Although the distinction between appearance and reality must be maintained (since some appearances are misleading), phenomenologists do not understand this as a distinction between two separate realms (falling in the province of, say, phenomenology and science, respectively), but as a distinction internal to the phenomenon – internal to the world we are living in. It is a distinction between how objects might appear to a superficial glance, or from a less than optimal perspective, and how they might appear in the best of circumstances, be it in practical use or in the light of extensive scientific investigations. Indeed, only insofar as the object appears in one way or the other can it have any meaning for us. Rather than regarding questions concerning structures and modes of appearance as something insignificant or merely subjective, phenomenologists consequently insist that such an investigation is of crucial philosophical importance.

Indeed from Husserl's early formulations of the phenomenological research programme it is clear that he considered the task of phenomenology to be that of providing a new epistemological foundation for science. He soon realized, however, that this task would call for an 'unnatural' change of interest. Rather than focusing exclusively on the objects of knowledge, we should describe and analyse the experiential dimension in detail in order to disclose the cognitive contribution of the knowing subject (Husserl 2001a, I, p. 170); a contribution that in his view had been virtually ignored by ordinary science.

Ordinary science is, naturally, so absorbed in its investigation of the natural (or social/cultural) world that it doesn't pause to reflect upon its own presuppositions and conditions of possibility. The ordinary sciences operate on the basis of a natural (and necessary) naivety. They operate on the basis of a tacit belief in the existence of a mind-, experience-, and theory-independent reality. Reality is assumed to be out there, waiting to be discovered and investigated. And the aim of science is to acquire a strict and objectively valid knowledge about this given realm.[3] This realistic assumption is so fundamental and deeply rooted that it is not only accepted by the positive sciences, it even permeates our daily pre-theoretical life, for which reason Husserl called it the *natural attitude*. But this attitude must be contrasted with the properly philosophical attitude, which critically questions the very foundation of experience and scientific thought (Husserl 1987, pp. 13–14). A strict naturalism denies the existence of a unique philosophical method, and claims that philosophers should consider their own work to be directly continuous with the natural sciences. In contrast to this, phenomenologists consider philosophy to be doing work that is different from natural scientific research. Philosophy is a discipline which doesn't simply contribute to or augment the scope of our positive knowledge, but instead investigates the basis of this knowledge and asks how it is possible. As Heidegger remarks, philosophers should be 'aroused by and immediately sensitive to the completely enigmatic character of what, for sound common sense, is without question and self explanatory' (1976, pp. 23–24). Indeed, according to one reading it is precisely this domain of ignored obviousness that phenomenology seeks to investigate.

But how is phenomenology supposed to accomplish this? How should it proceed? In a first step, we need to suspend or bracket our acceptance of the natural attitude in order to avoid commonsensical naivety (as well as various speculative hypotheses about the metaphysical status of reality). This bracketing doesn't amount to a form of scepticism. That the world exists is, as Husserl writes, beyond any doubt. But the great task is to truly understand this indubitability (which sustains life and positive science) and to clarify its legitimacy, and we cannot do so as long as we simply take its validity for granted (Husserl 1971/1980, pp. 152–53; 1970, p. 187). Husserl has a technical term for the suspension of our natural realistic inclination; he calls the procedure *epoché*.

The purpose of the epoché is not to doubt, neglect, abandon, or exclude reality from consideration; rather the aim is to suspend or neutralize a certain dogmatic *attitude* towards reality, thereby allowing us to focus more narrowly and directly on reality just as it is given – how it makes its appearance to us in experience. In short, the epoché entails a change of attitude towards reality, and not an exclusion of reality. The only thing that is excluded as a result of the epoché is a certain naivety, the naivety of simply taking the world for granted, thereby ignoring the contribution of consciousness.

Descriptions of phenomenological method often seem to imply that once one carries out the epoché, one then fully achieves a certain attitude and can simply go about the business of developing phenomenological descriptions. But one shouldn't think of the epoché as something that is accomplished for good in one first step, then to be followed by several other procedures. The epoché is an attitude that one has to keep accomplishing.

Importantly, the epoché does not involve an exclusive turn inward. On the contrary, it permits us to investigate the world we live in from a new reflective attitude, namely in its significance and manifestation for consciousness. Although this reflective investigation differs from a straightforward exploration of the world, it remains an investigation of reality; it is not an investigation of some other-worldly, mental realm. We should consequently not commit the mistake of interpreting the notion of experience in purely mentalistic terms, as if it were something that happened in a pure mental space.

For example, how do we go about describing the experiential difference between tasting wine and tasting water, between hearing a foghorn and seeing the full moon, or between affirming and denying that the Eiffel Tower is taller than the Empire State Building? Do we do so by severing our intentional link with the world and by turning some spectral gaze inwards? No, rather, we discover these differences, and we analyse them descriptively by paying attention to how worldly objects and states of affairs appear to us. The phenomenological descriptions take their point of departure in the world in which we live.[4] Indeed, for phenomenology, as Donn Welton (2000, p. 17) indicates, mental acts do 'not belong to a closed interior realm available only to introspection. Rather, they have their being by virtue of their relationship to that which transcends them'.

This is why Merleau-Ponty, in *Phenomenology of Perception*, can declare that phenomenology is distinguished in all its characteristics from introspective psychology and that the difference in question is a difference in principle. Whereas the introspective psychologist considers consciousness as a mere sector of being, and tries to investigate this sector as the physicist tries to investigate the physical world, the phenomenologist realizes that consciousness ultimately calls for a transcendental clarification that goes beyond common-sense postulates and brings us face to face with the problem concerning the constitution of the world (Merleau-Ponty 1962, p. 59).

The concept of the transcendental calls for further clarification, however. The simplest way to understand Merleau-Ponty's claim is by acknowledging that phenomenology – despite all kinds of other differences – is firmly situated within a certain Kantian or post-Kantian framework. One way to interpret Kant's revolutionary *Copernican turn* in epistemology (1956/1999, B xvi) is by seeing it as the realization that our cognitive apprehension of reality is more than a mere mirroring of a pre-existing world. Rather, a philosophical analysis of reality, a reflection on what conditions something must satisfy in order to count as 'real', should not ignore the contribution of consciousness. Thus, and this pinpoints a main difference from at least a good part of recent analytic philosophy's preoccupation with consciousness, the phenomenological interest in the first-person perspective is not primarily motivated by the relatively trivial insight that we need to include the first-person perspective if we wish to understand mental phenomena. Rather, the phenomenologists' focus on the first-person perspective is as much motivated by an attempt to understand the nature of objectivity, as by an interest in the subjectivity of consciousness. Indeed, rather than taking the objective world as the point of departure, phenomenology asks how something like objectivity is possible in the first place. What are the primitive modes of understanding that precede our belief in objectivity? How is objectivity constituted?

In phenomenological texts the term 'constitution' is a technical one. This concept should not be understood as involving any kind of creation or fabrication (Heidegger 1979, p. 97). Constitution must be understood as a process that allows for the manifestation or appearance of objects and their signification, that is, it is a process that permits what is constituted to appear, to manifest and present itself as what it is (Husserl 1973a, p. 47; 1973b, p. 434). And this process is something that in significant ways involves the contribution of consciousness. Without consciousness, no appearance; consciousness constitutes the way in which the world appears as meaningful. Incidentally, this also makes it clear that phenomenology, despite its emphasis on how things are *given* in experience, does not succumb to what philosophers call the 'myth of the given', the idea that experience is pure reception of the world, and that cognition is a purely receptive attitude.

Thus, the phenomenological interest in the first-person perspective is motivated by transcendental philosophical concerns. It makes use of a distinction between the subject conceived as an object *within the world* and the subject conceived as a subject *for the world*, i.e. considered as a necessary (though not sufficient) condition of possibility for cognition and meaning (see Carr 1999). Objects are constituted, that is, experienced and disclosed in the ways they are, thanks to the way consciousness is structured. As Husserl writes, '[T]he objects of which we are "conscious", are not simply *in* consciousness as in a box, so that they can merely be found in it and snatched at in it; ... they are first *constituted* as being, what they are for us, and as what they count as for us, in varying forms of objective intention' (2001a, I, p. 275). Phenomenologists consequently reject the suggestion that consciousness is merely one object among others in the world, on a par with – though possibly more complex than – volcanoes, waterfalls, ice crystals, gold nuggets, rhododendrons, or black holes, since they would consider it to be a necessary (though not sufficient) condition of possibility for any entity to appear as an object in the way it does and with the meaning it has.[5] Phenomenologists argue that a view from nowhere is unattainable, just as they would deny that it is possible to look at our experiences sideways to see whether they match with reality. This is so, not because such views are incredibly hard to reach, but because the very idea of such views is nonsensical.

It is at this point necessary to introduce yet another technical term, namely the notion of the *phenomenological reduction*. The epoché and the reduction can be seen as two closely linked elements of a philosophical reflection, the purpose of which is to liberate us from a natural(istic) dogmatism and to make us aware of our own constitutive (i.e. cognitive, meaning-disclosing) contribution to what we experience. Whereas the purpose of the epoché is to suspend or bracket a certain natural attitude towards the world thereby allowing us to focus on the modes or ways in which things appear to us, the aim of the phenomenological reduction is to analyse the correlational interdependence between specific structures of subjectivity and specific modes of appearance or givenness. When Husserl speaks of the reduction, he is consequently referring to a reflective move that departs from an unreflective and unexamined immersion in the world and 'leads back' (*re-ducere*) to the way in which the world manifests itself to us. Thus, everyday things available to our perception are not doubted or considered as illusions when they are 'phenomenologically reduced', but instead are envisaged and examined simply and precisely *as perceived* (and similarly for remembered things *as remembered*, imagined things *as imagined*, and so on). In other words, once we adopt the phenomenological attitude, we are no longer primarily interested in *what* things are – in their weight, size, chemical composition, etc. – but rather in *how* they appear, and thus as correlates of our experience.

When we perceive, judge, or evaluate objects, a thorough phenomenological examination will lead us to the experiential structures and modes of understanding to which these types of appearance are correlated. We are led to the acts of presentation – the perception, judgement, or valuation – and thereby to the experiencing subject (or subjects) in relation to whom the object as appearing must necessarily be understood. By adopting the phenomenological attitude, we pay attention to how public objects (trees, planets, paintings, symphonies, numbers, states of affairs, social relations, etc.) appear in our experience. But we do not simply focus on the objects precisely as they appear; we also focus on the subjective side of consciousness, thereby becoming aware of our subjective accomplishments and of the intentionality that is at play. If we want to understand how physical objects, mathematical models, chemical processes, social relations, or cultural artefacts can appear as they do, with the meaning they have, then we also need to examine the experiencing subject to whom they appear.

The phenomenological investigation of consciousness is not motivated by the wish to find a place for consciousness within an already well-established materialistic or naturalistic framework. In fact, the very attempt to do so, assuming that consciousness is merely yet another object in the world, would prevent one from discovering and clarifying some of the most interesting aspects of consciousness, including the true epistemic and ontological significance of the first-person perspective. The problem of consciousness should not be addressed on the background of an unquestioned objectivism. Too frequently the assumption has been that a better understanding of the physical world will allow us a better understanding of consciousness; rarely has it been thought that a better understanding of consciousness might allow for a better understanding of what it means for something to be real. That something like a conscious appropriation of the world is possible does not merely tell us something about consciousness, but also about the world. But, of course, this way of discussing consciousness, as the constitutive dimension, as the 'place' 'in' which the world can reveal and articulate itself, is quite different from any attempt to treat it naturalistically as merely yet another (psychical or physical) object in the world.

It should now be clear why phenomenology is not simply a collection of descriptions of phenomenal consciousness, which we might generate if we start to introspect on our experience. In some respects phenomenology does engage in a kind of reflective process. Phenomenology, however, is also about describing the world and how it appears in such experience. It includes an examination of the world from the first-person perspective. So although it requires a suspension of our natural, everyday attitude, it also takes that attitude, that *being-in-the-world*, as part of the subject matter to be investigated. In this sense, phenomenology is not just about consciousness, as if consciousness could be considered in isolation from everything else in our lives. It's about how we are immersed in our everyday situations and projects, how we experience the world, relate to others, and engage in the kinds of actions and practices that define our lives.

Phenomenology has as its goal, not a description of idiosyncratic experience – 'here and now, this is just what I experience' – rather, it attempts to capture the invariant structures of experience. In this sense, it is more like science than like psychotherapy. Psychotherapy is focused on the subject as a particular person and may appeal to introspection in its concern about the way and the why of the person's experience of the world, here and now. By contrast, phenomenology is not interested in understanding the world according to Gallagher, or the world according to Zahavi, or the world according to you; it's interested in understanding *how it is possible* for *anyone* to experience a world. In this sense, phenomenology is not interested in qualia in the sense of purely individual data that are incorrigible, ineffable, and incomparable. Phenomenology is not interested in psychological processes (in contrast to behavioural processes or physical processes). Phenomenology is interested in the very possibility and structure of phenomenality; it seeks to explore its essential structures and conditions of possibility. Phenomenology aims to disclose structures that are intersubjectively accessible, and its analyses are consequently open for corrections and control by any (phenomenologically attuned) subject.

One reason why any account of the phenomenological approach to the study of consciousness must mention the epoché and reduction, is because this reference situates the investigation in question, it provides its systematic context. The epoché and the reduction are elements in the reflective move that makes phenomenology a transcendental philosophical enterprise. Any attempt to downplay the significance of these methodological elements runs the risk of confusing phenomenological analyses with psychological or anthropological descriptions. We could put this transcendental view in a somewhat paradoxical way: phenomenologists are not interested in consciousness per se. They are interested in consciousness because they consider consciousness to be our only access to the world. They are interested in consciousness because it is world-disclosing. Phenomenology should therefore be understood as a philosophical analysis of the various types of world-disclosure (perceptual, imaginative, recollective, etc.), and in connection with this as a reflective investigation of those structures of experience and understanding that permit different types of beings to show themselves as what they are.

Another reason why it has been necessary to spend some time discussing these methodological concepts is that we can thereby ward off a number of widespread misunderstandings that again and again have blocked a proper appreciation of the import and impact of phenomenology, especially as it has been proposed by Husserl. Thus, according to one reading, Husserl makes use of a methodological procedure that separates mind from world (Dreyfus 1991, pp. 73–74). As a consequence, he not only loses sight of the world, but also remains incapable of providing a satisfactory account of such central issues as intersubjectivity and embodiment. In the light of the account just given of the aim and focus of Husserl's phenomenological method, we can see why such a reading is quite problematic. This will become even clearer in some of the later chapters.

Eidetic variation and intersubjective verification

But what does the phenomenological reduction accomplish, especially if we are interested in the cognitive sciences? Remember that phenomenology, in contrast to the objective or positive sciences, is not particularly interested in the causal or substantial nature of objects, i.e. in their weight, rarity, or chemical composition, but in the way in which they show themselves in experience. There are essential differences between the ways in which a physical thing, a utensil, a work of art, a melody, a state of affairs, a number, an animal, a social relation, etc., manifest themselves. Moreover, it is also possible for one and the same object to appear in a variety of different ways: from this or that perspective, in strong or faint illumination, as perceived, imagined, wished for, feared, anticipated, or recollected. Rather than regarding questions concerning the way things are given in experience as insignificant or merely subjective, such questions concern something very basic; something presupposed by all ordinary sciences. For a scientist to be in a position to ask about X, to examine how X works, and what causes it, she must first be conscious of X. Phenomenology investigates the character and structure of that consciousness. In later chapters, we discuss some phenomenological findings that are directly related to the study of consciousness and the cognitive sciences – that perception is always egocentric and embodied, that it is always from a perspective that delivers the perceived thing in an incomplete series of profiles, that it always has an intentional structure, that it is never momentary, etc. – as well as diverse aspects of memory, imagination, judgement, etc.

But how do phenomenologists manage to accomplish all of this? In addition to the epoché and phenomenological reduction, phenomenology adds two further instruments to its toolbox of methods. The first is called *eidetic variation*. Philosophers have always been on the lookout for what Plato called the *eidos* or essence of things. In developing his phenomenological method, Husserl proposed a way that would draw out the essential and invariant characteristics of the things that we experience. Quite simply, it involves using our imagination to strip away the unessential properties of things. If the object that I am examining happens to be a book, what features of it can I imaginatively vary without destroying the fact that it is a book. I can change the colour and design of the cover; I can imaginatively subtract from the number of pages, or add to them; I can change the size and weight of the book; I can vary the binding. In all of this, I can use my previous experience of books, and I can imagine further variations. The result is that the core set of properties that resist change – those properties that belong to the book per se and which, if changed, would make the object cease being a book – constitute the essence, the 'what makes a book a book'.

'But wait,' you say. 'That's nice, but the cognitive scientist doesn't want to study books – at least not in this sense.' Right. But we can also do the same kind of eidetic analysis of the act of cognition through which I experience the book. For example, if I am remembering the book, what can I change about the process of remembering and still have memory; what is it that I cannot change and that remains essential to the cognitive activity of remembering? The phenomenologist can do the same with perception, face recognition, decision-making, social perception, and so on. Certainly this would be interesting, and of use, to the cognitive scientist. It would in fact give her a good idea of the kinds of things – the cognitive acts – that she wants to study.

It is important not to mystify eidetic variation. The idea is not that we, by merely gazing passively at the object, can obtain infallible insights into its invariant structure. In fact, when it came to the realm of cognitive phenomena, Husserl was quite explicit about all of them being characterized by an essential vagueness, and he consequently argued that any attempt to classify and define them with the same kind of exactness and precision that one might find in, say, geometry would do violence to them. 'The *vagueness* of such concepts, the circumstances that their spheres of application are fluid, does not make them defective; for in the spheres of knowledge where they are used they are absolutely indispensable, or in those spheres they are the only legitimate concepts' (Husserl 1976/1982, p. 155/166). Thus, when Husserl mentions the eidetic variation as one of the phenomenologist's tools, this is not to be understood as any claim to the effect that phenomenologists can intuit the eternal and immutable essence of, say, memory or imagination. The phenomenological investigation of these highly complex topics involves demanding analyses that in many cases are defeasible – which means that the phenomenologist is not infallible. This fact makes another tool at the phenomenologist's disposal extremely important.

This other tool is simply the fact that phenomenologists do not have to do their phenomenological analyses alone. Descriptions allow for intersubjective corroboration. And again, the quest for invariant, essential structures of experience is not narrowly tied to the peculiarities of my own experience. We can and should compare our phenomenological descriptions with those of others. Of course this is not a straightforward process, any more than the heterophenomenological interpretation of reports is. But it is no messier than science, and in this process we are guided by the methodological steps we follow.

The method of phenomenology can get more specialized, depending on the kind of experience that is being studied. But these four steps are the basic ones:

(1) The *epoché* or suspension of the natural attitude.
(2) The *phenomenological reduction*, which attends to the correlation between the object of experience and the experience itself.
(3) The *eidetic variation*, which keys in on the essential or invariant aspects of this correlation.
(4) *Intersubjective corroboration*, which is concerned with replication and the degree to which the discovered structures are universal or at least shareable.

NATURALIZING PHENOMENOLOGY

One of the contentious issues about whether the phenomenological method can be used in the experimental natural sciences of the mind (the cognitive sciences) is centred on the fact that Husserl constantly emphasized the limitations of a naturalistic account of consciousness. His own phenomenological method was introduced precisely as a non-naturalistic alternative. He intended phenomenology to be a transcendental inquiry. In general, a *transcendental* study is one that is concerned with the necessary, a *priori* conditions of experience. We can think of this just in the terms that we have already discussed: the ability to do science presupposes consciousness (cognition, the mind). Consciousness is a *sine qua non*, an a *priori* condition for doing science. A natural scientific study of consciousness, then, presupposes the very thing that it studies. We have to be conscious (In a first-person subjective way) to study consciousness as an object. A transcendental study focuses on consciousness, not as an object, but as subjectivity. It can ask, 'What limitations does consciousness, in its subjective structure and in the way that it operates, place on the practice of science?' In fact, as we have noted, this was Husserl's motive for developing phenomenology – and in this regard, he was motivated by some of the same concerns as Descartes and Kant in attempting to provide an epistemological foundation for the proper practice of science.

But is it even possible to provide this kind of foundation? There are debates about this even within phenomenology, but this is not a question we need to be concerned with here. Rather the issue we want to address is simply whether phenomenology can be put to work in experimental science. In the following chapters, we will offer plenty of evidence that this is the case. We will demonstrate to what extent phenomenology addresses issues and provides analyses that are crucial for an understanding of the true complexity of consciousness and cognition and which are nevertheless frequently absent from current debates, and show how it can offer a conceptual framework for understanding the mind that might be of considerably more value than some of the models currently in vogue in cognitive science. Let us end this chapter, however, by briefly reviewing three recent and quite general proposals in regard to how phenomenology can work with science rather than in opposition to it.

Phenomenology is a philosophical enterprise; it is not an empirical discipline. This doesn't rule out, of course, that its analyses might have ramifications for and be of pertinence to an empirical study of consciousness and cognitive sciences, even if this was not the primary aim of Husserl and his followers. Husserl and phenomenology are not anti-scientific, even if they are anti-scientistic. In fact, since one of Husserl's primary concerns in developing phenomenology was his worry about doing science properly, one can understand phenomenology as designed to support science. And in terms of whether we can put the insights gained in transcendental phenomenology to use in science, Husserl himself puts it this way: 'every analysis or theory of transcendental phenomenology – including ... the theory of the transcendental constitution of an objective world – can be developed in the natural realm, by giving up the transcendental attitude' (1950/1999, p. 159). That is, just as we can move through methodological steps into the phenomenological stance, we can also take the insights developed in that stance and carry them back into science.

In regard to the issue of naturalizing phenomenology, it is important to realize that this catchphrase has taken on several different meanings; a development not unrelated to the fact that both terms involved are equivocal. On some readings, a commitment to naturalism simply amounts to taking one's departure in what is natural (rather than supernatural). But it is fair to say that the use of the term in current discourse mainly signals an orientation towards natural science, and further that many contemporary naturalists endorse a form of scientism according to which natural science is the measure of all things. In other words, on a dominant reading naturalism is committed to the idea that the only legitimate way to study the mind is by means of objective natural science.

As for the term 'phenomenology', it is also used in several different ways. As we noted in Chapter 1, one can distinguish between a non-technical and technical use of the term. According to the former, 'phenomenology' is merely another word for experience. To discuss whether phenomenology can be naturalized is consequently to discuss the metaphysical question of whether experiences can be naturalized. Is it possible, for instance, to identify experience with the biological (neurological) processes that occur in the organism (brain)? This is precisely the kind of question that will not be of any major concern for the approach outlined in this book. According to the more technical use of the term, 'phenomenology' refers to the philosophical tradition and methodology we have been discussing. To ask whether this kind of phenomenology can be naturalized might then mean a number of different things, as we shall see.

The last subchapter of Merleau-Ponty's *The Structure of Behavior* carries the heading 'Is There Not a Truth in Naturalism?' It contains a criticism of Kantian transcendental philosophy, and on the very final page of the book, Merleau-Ponty calls for a redefinition of transcendental philosophy that makes it pay heed to the real world (1963, p. 224). Thus, rather than making us choose between an external scientific explanation and internal phenomenological reflection, a choice which according to Merleau-Ponty would rip asunder the living relation between consciousness and nature, he asks us to reconsider the very opposition, and to search for a dimension that is beyond both objectivism and subjectivism. What is interesting and important, however, is that Merleau-Ponty doesn't conceive of the relation between phenomenology and positive science as a question of how to apply already established phenomenological insights on empirical issues. It isn't simply a question of how phenomenology might constrain positive science. On the contrary, Merleau-Ponty's idea is that phenomenology itself can be changed and modified through its dialogue with the empirical disciplines. In fact, it needs this confrontation if it is to develop in the right way. Importantly, Merleau-Ponty holds this view without thereby reducing phenomenology to merely yet another positive science, without thereby dismissing its truly philosophical nature.

As we try to make clear in this book, phenomenology is not only engaged in fundamental transcendental philosophical clarifications, it also studies concrete phenomena that are open to empirical investigation, and insofar as phenomenology concerns itself with such phenomena our claim would be that it should be informed by the best available scientific knowledge, and vice versa, so that a fuller account of experience will involve some integration of phenomenology and science.

To be more specific, the phenomenological motto: 'To the things themselves' (*Zu den Sachen selbst*) calls for us to let our experience guide our theories. We should pay attention to the way in which we experience reality. Cognitive scientists might not pay much attention to the formal structure of phenomenality, but as empirical researchers they do in fact pay quite a lot of attention to concrete empirical phenomena, and might consequently be less apt to underestimate the richness, complexity and variety of phenomena than the average philosopher. Even if one aim of phenomenology is to provide a transcendental philosophical clarification, there is more to phenomenology than this. Phenomenology also offers detailed analyses of various aspects of consciousness, including perception, imagination, embodiment, memory, self-experience, temporality, etc. In offering such analyses, phenomenology addresses issues that are crucial for an understanding of the true complexity of consciousness and develops a conceptual framework for understanding the mind that is a viable alternative to some of the models currently in vogue in cognitive science. But for the very same reason, it should also be clear that phenomenology deals with topics that it shares with other disciplines, and it would be wrong to insist that it should simply ignore empirical findings pertaining to these very topics. The phenomenological investigations can not only profit directly from insights obtained through empirical studies of psychopathological or neuropathological disorders, studies of infantile social interaction, perception, memory, and emotion, etc., they can also profit indirectly from the problem-oriented approach found in these empirical sciences. The very attempt to engage in dialogue with cognitive science forces phenomenology to become more problem oriented and may thereby counteract what still remains one of its greatest weaknesses: its preoccupation with exegesis. We are obviously not denying that there is still very much to learn from such authors as Husserl, Heidegger, Sartre, Merleau-Ponty, Lévinas, etc., but phenomenologists should not ignore opportunities to engage in critical dialogue, not only with empirical science, but also with other philosophical traditions. It is exactly by confronting, discussing, and criticizing alternative approaches that phenomenology can demonstrate its vitality and contemporary relevance.

'But wait a second,' someone might ask. 'Are you really proposing that a phenomenological account of perception or action should necessarily be informed and constrained by, say, investigations of the neuronal mechanisms and processes involved in action and perception?' The question is motivated by the thought that generally speaking a phenomenological account of perception and action is an attempt to do justice to the first-person perspective; it seeks to understand experience in terms of the meaning it has for the subject, and doesn't address the subpersonal mechanisms that might enable us to experience the way that we do. Two things can be said in response. First, we shouldn't overlook the fact that disciplines such as psychopathology, neuropathology, developmental psychology, cognitive psychology, anthropology, etc. can provide *personal-level descriptions* that might be of phenomenological relevance. The examples are legion, but if one were to mention a few, one could single out

(1) neuropsychological descriptions of various disorders of body-awareness, Consider, for example, Jonathan Cole's (1995) careful analysis of Ian Waterman, who at the age of 19, due to illness, lost all sense of touch and proprioception from the neck down; compare Cole's analysis of how dramatic and disabling this impairment is, with the classical phenomenological investigation of the lived body.
(2) psychopathological descriptions of schizophrenic disturbances of self-experience and intentionality. Psychiatrists and clinical psychologists, for example, sometimes provide careful analyses of the disturbed self- and world-experience we find in schizophrenic patients; compare such accounts to the phenomenological discussion of natural evidence and non-objectifying pre-reflective self-awareness.
(3) developmental descriptions of social interactions in early childhood. Compare, for example, the careful analyses provided by contemporary developmental psychologists of primitive but fundamental forms of social understanding found in infants and young children to the work on empathy, pairing and intercorporeity that we find in Scheler, Stein, Husserl and Merleau-Ponty.

Second, not only personal-level accounts, but subpersonal accounts may have relevance for phenomenological analysis. For example, assume that our initial phenomenological description presents us with what appears to be a simple and unified perceptual phenomenon. When studying the neural correlates of this phenomenon, however, we discover that not only areas associated with perception, but also those associated with episodic memory are activated. This discovery might motivate us to return to our initial phenomenological description in order to see whether the phenomenon in question is indeed as simple as we thought. Assuming that phenomenologists are not infallible and that their first attempts are not always perfect, it's possible that a more careful phenomenological analysis will reveal that the experience harbours a concealed complexity. It is important, however, to emphasize that the discovery of a significant complexity on the subpersonal level – to stick to this simple example – cannot by itself force us to refine or revise our phenomenological description. It can only serve as motivation for further inquiry. There is no straightforward isomorphism between the subpersonal and personal level, and ultimately the only way to justify a claim concerning a complexity on the phenomenological level is by cashing it out in experiential terms.

Accordingly, what we are proposing is in fact not merely that phenomenological analyses and distinctions might be useful for cognitive science. The point isn't merely that phenomenology might prove indispensable if we wish to obtain a precise description of the explanandum – a *sine qua non* for any successful cognitive neuroscience. Rather, the idea is that the influence goes both ways, i.e., it is also a question of letting phenomenology profit from – and be challenged by – empirical findings. This is why it is entirely appropriate to speak of *mutual enlightenment* (Gallagher 1997). To put it differently, phenomenology does not necessarily have the last word regarding the explanandum, since phenomenological descriptions are revisable under the influence of available explanations. There is, in short, a dialectical relation between the descriptions we offer and the (theoretical) concepts we use, and the latter can influence the former. In other words – and again, this is a familiar herme-neutical point – one might question the purity of the phenomenological descriptions. Do they not inevitably contain an element of conceptual reconstruction? If there is a conflict between a phenomenological description and a theoretical assumption, we shouldn't necessarily in each and every case reject the theory. We might also in some cases have to reconsider the description; indeed, new theories might offer and encourage us to attempt new descriptions. So the relation between description and theory is dialectical. It goes both ways. It is not merely a question of descriptions constraining available theories. How best to go about seeking this enlightenment and how far it should go remain contentious issues.

A formal affair

One approach suggests that the way to naturalize phenomenology is to translate the results of phenomenological analysis into a language that is clearly understood by science, namely, mathematics. We'll look at two versions of this approach. The first one has been proposed by the phenomenologist Eduard Marbach (1993). He suggests that by formalizing the language of phenomenological description, scientists and phenomenologists will be better able to communicate about mental phenomena. The second proposal has been made by an interdisciplinary group of researchers at the Centre de Recherche en Epistémologie Appliquée in Paris, including Jean Petitot (a mathematician), Jean-Michel Roy (a philosopher), Bernard Pachoud (a psychiatrist), and the late Francisco Varela (a neurobiologist). They write, 'It is our general contention ... that phenomenological descriptions of any kind can only be naturalized, in the sense of being integrated into the general framework of natural sciences, if they can be mathematized. We see mathematization as a key instrument for naturalization ... ' (Roy et al. 1999, p. 42).

The very first question that this kind of approach raises is whether it is possible for mathematics to capture the lived experience described by phenomenology. Yes, Marbach (1993) argues, if we agree that a linguistic description can express lived experience, we simply need to formalize that description. For him, this is a strategy to deal with the problem of meaning and scientific communication. In contrast to Dennett's idea of heterophenomenology, where we simply treat first-person reports as texts for interpretation, Marbach proposes to start with methodically controlled phenomenological descriptions and then to appeal to formalized and intersubjectively shareable meanings. Indeed, this is usually the way it is done in scientific contexts, where terminological problems are addressed through the use of formalized language systems such as one finds in mathematics. Marbach thus attempts to develop a formalized language, a phenomenological notation, to express phenomenological findings.

Marbach's phenomenological notation expresses, not the content, but the formal structure of experience. It reflects how various mental activities can be different from, yet also related to, one another. Marbach shows, for example, how episodic memory depends upon perception. The precise phenomenological description of memory requires the notion of 're-presentation' (*Vergegenwärtigung* – literally, to make something present again). In contrast to perception, which establishes intentional reference to something present and is therefore an activity of 'presentation', memory refers to something that is absent. To establish conscious reference to something, however, an activity that involves presentation is required. For something like memory or imagination, Marbach suggests, consciousness establishes reference to what is not present in such a way that it is 'as if' it were given to me in perception (1993, p. 61). The 'as if' indicates a modification of the perceptual element, which Marbach, following Husserl, calls a re-presentation. To explicate and clarify the structure of such a representational act, Marbach develops his notation. An act of actually perceiving some object, x, is signified as

(PER)x

The representation of x in an act of episodic memory involves (PER)x, not as an actual and occurrent act of perception, but as a re-enactment of a past perception which Marbach designates as

[PER]x

The fact that memory is a re-enactment rather than just an imaginary enactment means, according to Marbach, that there is an element of belief involved (signified by |–, the belief-stroke). That is, episodic memory involves a belief that at some point in the past I actually did perceive x, and this differentiates it from imagination. The fact that the perception of x is in the past rather than in the future, that is, the fact that it is an act of memory rather than expectation, can be indicated by the letter p. So Marbach formalizes an act of memory, that is, a re-presentation of x by means of 'a perceiving of x bestowed with the belief of it having actually occurred in the past', as follows:

(REP p |–[PER])x

Things get more complicated, of course, but one can see the virtue of developing a notation like this. The notation helps to clarify the complexity of consciousness and shows how that complexity might be explicated by means of phenomenological reflection. It also helps to suggest alternative structures that might be implicated, for example, in various memory systems. If, as Marbach, following Husserl, contends, memory involves, in some fashion, a re-enactment of perception, one would expect precisely the kind of neural activity associated with memory that Damasio describes as occurring in 'the same early sensory cortices where the firing patterns corresponding to perceptual representations once occurred' (1994, p. 101). As Marbach's notation makes clear, phenomenological analysis confirms and supports this neuroscientific model of memory; and reciprocally, the neurological evidence supports Marbach's description.[6] Furthermore, it seems quite possible that neuroscience could develop a formal notation that would express this model of memory, albeit a notation that would express something about the subpersonal, neuronal level. One could then hypothesize that at some suitable level of abstraction, the phenomenological and the neurological notations would turn out to be consistent. This brings us to the proposal made by Roy et al., which carries things a bit further.

Mathematics represents a formal and therefore neutral realm within which we can set out results that are either first-person (phenomenological) or third-person (natural scientific). While mathematics is a common tool in science, phenomenologists might object that even if we can formalize phenomenological descriptions in Marbach's notation, first-person data cannot be fully reduced to mathematical formula. Indeed, Husserl, himself a trained mathematician, argued that, technically, mathematical formula are incapable of capturing phenomenological results. Roy et al. argue that although this may have been true of the mathematics of Husserl's time, the development of dynamic systems theory has made Husserl's objection obsolete (1999, p. 43). To the extent that the mathematics of dynamical systems can be applied to the mind, it provides an explanatory framework that can integrate first-person and third-person data. To put it differently, the idea is that a sufficiently complex mathematics can facilitate the translation of data from phenomenological and naturalistic realms into a common language. See Figure 2.1. Something like this happened in the field of classical mechanics:

> Thanks to an appropriate mathematical interpretation (requiring in fact the highly sophisticated techniques of integral and differential calculus, of Poincaré's quali- tative dynamics, of complex dynamical systems theory, and of symplectic geometry) concepts can be transformed into algorithms capable of generating a diversity of constructed (computed) phenomena that can then be placed in relation (right up to complete coincidence) with the data of observation.
>
> (Roy et al. 1999, p. 47)

The claim is that we are ready to do the same kind of translation in the field of consciousness, with the primary idea being that this can be extended to phenomenological data.[7] Indeed, as Roy et al. suggest, the first step of the translation to mathematics involves eidetic variation, insofar as it involves a degree of abstraction from the natural psychophysical dimension of individual embodied lived experience.[8]

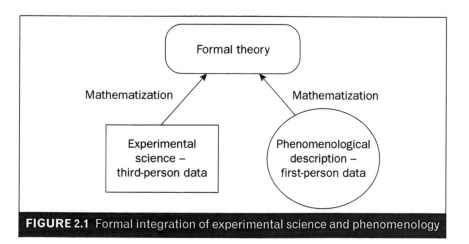

FIGURE 2.1 Formal integration of experimental science and phenomenology

Perhaps what is most important in the contemporary proposal outlined by Roy et al. is that the mathematical (computational) models of traditional cognitive science are insufficient for this project. Specifically, if mathematical formalization involves an abstraction from experience, it is important to understand precisely what full-bodied, dynamic experience is and to start with that. In other words, the starting point, on the phenomenological side, is with embodied, in-the-world experience, rather than with an intellectualized version of experience. Similarly, in terms of understanding the physical side of mental processes, we need the recently developed dynamical models of the brain. Once we have these starting points right, we quickly learn that the computational models of traditional cognitive science are inadequate. 'Embodiment, thus, implies that sensori-motor coupling modulates (but does not determine) an ongoing [neuro-logical] activity that it configures into meaningful world items in an unceasing flow. This makes it naturally framed in the tools derived from dynamical systems, which [this approach] shares with connectionism' (ibid., p. 61). Jean Petitot provides a good example of this approach in his analysis of spatial perception (Petitot et al. 1999), as does Varela in his dynamical analysis of time-consciousness (Gallagher and Varela 2003; Varela 1999). For our purposes, we will return to this kind of analysis in the chapter on time-consciousness. Right now, however, with the promise of avoiding the higher mathematics this entails, we will look at an example of how phenomenology, experimental brain science, and dynamical systems theory can be integrated in Varela's more specific proposal for a neurophenomenology.

Neurophenomenology

So far, proposals to formalize phenomenological description seem to lend themselves to the task of developing scientific models. Phenomenology itself, however, has always tried to stay closer to experience than to theory. So it is important to ask whether there is a way for phenomenology to contribute directly to scientific experimentation. Neurophenomenology, as espoused by Varela (1996), fills this order. Neurophenomenology attempts to integrate three elements: (1) phenomenological analysis of experience; (2) dynamical systems theory; and (3) empirical experimentation on biological systems (see Thompson 2007, ch. 10). Neurophenomenology follows Husserl in understanding phenomenology to be a method-ologically guided reflective examination of experience, and it maintains that, for purposes of studying consciousness and cognition, both empirical scientists and experimental subjects ought to receive some level of training in phenomenological method. Varela proposes that this training would include learning to practise the epoché and phenomenological reduction, that is, the setting aside or 'bracketing' of opinions or theories that a subject may have about experience or consciousness, and focusing on the way things are experienced. If an approach that involves training experimental subjects in this method might at first seem methodologically impractical, remember that experimental psychologists often spend good amounts of time training chimps and monkeys to do experimental tasks. Should it be much more difficult to train human subjects in phenomenological method? In any case, Lutz et al. (2002) have done it, and have shown its feasibility with some success. So let's take a look at their work, which is an exemplary instance of neurophenomenology in that it combines the three elements just mentioned: phenomenology, dynamical systems theory, and experimental brain science.[9]

In many empirical testing situations that target specified cognitive tasks, the brain activity associated with successive responses to repeated and identical stimulations (recorded, for example, by EEG) is highly variable. The source of this variability is presumed to reside mainly in fluctuations that may be due to a variety of cognitive parameters defined by the subject's attentive state, for example distractions, spontaneous thought processes, strategy decisions for carrying out the task, etc. In other words, experimental subjects sometimes get distracted from the experimental tasks, and sometimes by their own thoughts. For our purposes, let's call the cause of these distractions *subjective parameters*. Experimental control of subjective parameters is difficult. As a result, they are usually classified as unintelligible noise (Engel et al. 2001) and ignored or neutralized by a method of averaging results across a series of trials and across subjects. Lutz and his colleagues decided to approach the problem of subjective parameters in a different way. They followed a neurophenomenological approach that combined first-person data and the dynamical analysis of neural processes to study subjects exposed to a 3D perceptual illusion (see the box overleaf – Figure 2.2). They used the first-person data not simply as more data for analysis, but as contributing to an organizing analytic principle.

In preliminary trials, Lutz et al. presented subjects with visual stimuli and asked them to report on some detail that appeared in the stimuli. Subjects were phenomenologically trained to develop their own descriptions of the subjective parameters (distractions, etc.) that occurred as they did the task. The language used to describe these experiences was formalized and then used in the main experimental trials. In the main trials, reports of subjective parameters were correlated with reaction times for the response as well as with EEG measures of brain activity.

To be clear, phenomenological training in this experiment did not involve teaching subjects about the philosophical work of Husserl or the phenomenological tradition. Rather, as described by Lutz et al., following Varela (1996), it consisted in training subjects to employ the epoché, and to deliver consistent and clear reports of their experience. Specifically, Varela (1996) identified three steps in phenomenological method that correspond closely to the method as we described it above (p. 31):

(1) suspending beliefs or theories about experience (the *epoché*)
(2) gaining intimacy with the domain of investigation (*focused description*)
(3) offering descriptions and using intersubjective validations (*intersubjective corroboration*).

The epoché can be either self-induced by subjects familiar with it, or guided by the experimenter through open questions – questions not directed at opinions or theories, but at experience. Rather than employing predefined categories, and asking, 'Do you think this experience is like *X* or *Y* or *Z*?', the open question asks simply, 'How would you describe your experience?'[10] In the context of this experiment, questions posed immediately after the task help the subject to redirect her attention towards the implicit strategy or degree of attention she implemented during the task. Subjects can be re-exposed to the stimuli until they find 'their own stable experiential invariants' to describe the specific elements of their experiences. These invariants then become the defining elements that are used as analytic tools in the main trials.

A neurophenomenological experiment

In Lutz et al. (2002) the trials were grouped according to the subjects' descriptive reports concerning their experience of subjective parameters. For each group (or experiential cluster) separate dynamical analyses of electrical brain activity, recorded by EEG, were conducted. The results were different and significant in comparison with a procedure of averaging across trials.

The phenomenological part of the experiment involved the development of descriptions (refined verbal reports) of the subjective parameters through a series of preliminary or practice trials, using a well-known depth perception task – see Figure 2.2.

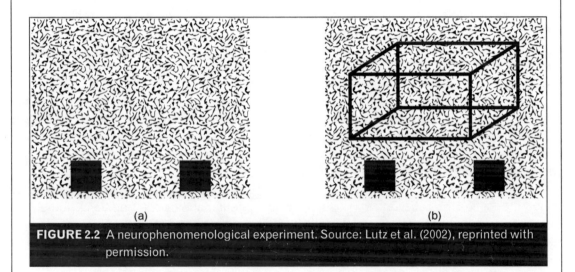

(a)   (b)

FIGURE 2.2 A neurophenomenological experiment. Source: Lutz et al. (2002), reprinted with permission.

In these trials subjects are shown random-dot static images on a digital monitor (as in Figure 2.2a). At an auditory signal the subjects were asked to adjust their focus in order to fuse the two squares at the bottom of the screen and to remain in this eye position for seven seconds. The experimenters then changed the pattern to a slightly different random-dot pattern with binocular disparities (an autostereogram). In this condition the subjects were able to see a 3D illusory geometric shape emerge in their visual field (represented in Figure 2.2b). They were asked to press a button as soon as the shape had completely emerged and they then gave a brief verbal report of their experience.

In the preliminary trials, subjects reflected on their experience, defined their own categories descriptive of the subjective parameters, and could report on the presence or absence or degree of distractions, inattentive moments, cognitive strategies, etc. Based on these trained reports, descriptive categories were defined *a posteriori* and used to divide the trials into phenomenologically based clusters. For example, with regard to the subject's experienced readiness for the stimulus, the results specified three readiness states:

- **Steady readiness (SR):** subjects reported that they were 'ready', 'present', 'here', or 'well-prepared' when the image appeared on the screen and that they responded 'immediately' and 'decidedly'.
- **Fragmented readiness (FR):** subjects reported that they had made a voluntary effort to be ready, but were prepared either less 'sharply' (due to a momentary 'tiredness') or less 'focally' (due to small 'distractions', 'inner speech', or 'discursive thoughts').
- **Unreadiness (SU):** subjects reported that they were unprepared and that they saw the 3D image only because their eyes were correctly positioned. They were surprised by it and reported that they were 'interrupted' by the image in the middle of an unrelated thought.

Subjects were then able to use these categories as a kind of reporting shorthand during the main trials when the experimenters recorded both the electrical brain activity and the subject's own report of each trial. The reports during the main trials revealed subtle changes in the subject's experience due to the presence and variation in the subjective parameters. The clustered first-person data were correlated with reaction times (Figure 2.3) and dynamic neural signatures (DNSs), i.e.

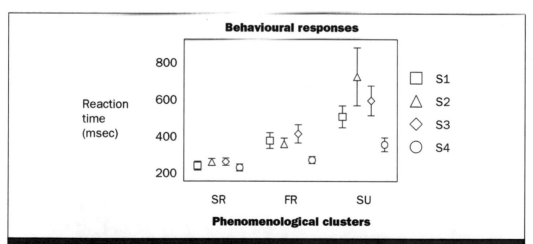

FIGURE 2.3 Correlation of behavioural responses and phenomenological clusters.
Note: for four subjects, reaction times were faster in SR, slower in FR, and slowest in SU.
Source: Lutz et al. (2002), reprinted with permission.

continued

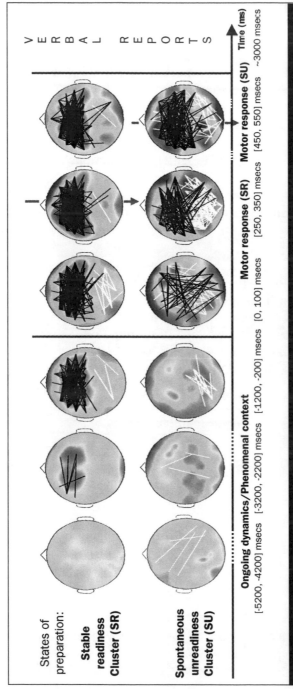

FIGURE 2.4 Dynamical neural signature for Subject 1 during SR (154 trials) and SU (38 trials).

Note: Colour-coding indicates scalp distribution of time-frequency gamma power around 35Hz normalized compared to distant baseline B0 average for trials and for time windows indicated by an arrow. Black and white lines correspond to significant increase and decrease in synchrony, respectively.

Source: Lutz et al. (2002), reprinted with permission.

dynamic descriptions of the transient patterns of local and more global synchronies occurring between oscillating neural populations (Figure 2.4). According to the dynamical systems approach to neuroscience, the neural activation that underlies our experience is not localized in a specific brain area, but involves the rapid and transient integration of functionally distinct and widely distributed brain areas. This kind of integration is effected by the dynamic links among the different areas. Thus, using the sophisticated mathematics and models of dynamical systems theory, the neurophenomenologist investigates the neural correlates of experience in terms of these emergent and changing patterns of integration, here captured in the concept of a DNS (see Thompson 2007; Varela et al. 2001).

The experimenters were able to show that distinct subjective parameters, described in the subjects' trained phenomenological reports, correlated to distinct DNSs just prior to presentation of the stimulus. For example, characteristic patterns of phase synchrony recorded in the frontal electrodes prior to the stimulus depended on the degree of experienced readiness as reported by subjects.

In this way, the experimental protocol used in Lutz et al. (2002) might be said to employ a form of phenomenological reduction. The subjects are asked to provide a description of their own experience using an open-question format, and thus without the imposition of prede-termined theoretical categories. They are trained to gain intimacy with their own experience in the domain of investigation. The descriptive categories are intersubjectively and scientifi-cally validated and used to interpret results that correlate with objective measurements of behaviour and brain activity. As indicated (see the box above), the experiments showed that distinct subjective parameters, described in the subjects' trained phenomenological reports, correlated to distinct dynamic neural signatures just prior to presentation of the stimulus and that these dynamic signatures then differentially conditioned the behavioural and neural response to the stimulus.[11]

This combination of behavioural, neural and phenomenological dimensions, and the establishment of their close correlations, represent a useful and productive way to integrate phenomenological method into empirical experimentation. Use of the first-person method clarifies in precise terms what is being measured in the third-person data, and the behav-ioural and neural results ground experience in embodied perceptual processes. Similar neurophenomenological procedures have been employed in the study of epilepsy and have contributed to cognitive therapies for certain types of this disorder (Le Van Quyen et al. 2001; Le Van Quyen and Petitmengin 2002).

Front-loading phenomenology

A third view of a phenomenologically enlightened experimental science is what has been called 'front-loaded phenomenology' (Gallagher 2003a). Rather than starting with the empirical results (as one would do in either heterophenomenology or the formal mathematical approach), or with the training of subjects (as one would do in neurophenomenology), this approach starts with the experimental design. The idea is to build experimental design on or around phenomenological insights, that is, to allow the insights developed in phenomenological analyses to inform the way experiments are set up. The phenomenological insights might be found in Husserlian transcendental investigations, or in the more empirically oriented phenomenological analyses found, for example, in Merleau-Ponty (1962), or developed in neurophenomenological experiments. To front-load phenomenology, however, does not mean to simply presuppose or accept the phenomenological results obtained by others. Rather it involves testing those results and more generally it incorporates a dialectical movement between previous insights gained in phenomenology and preliminary trials that will specify or extend these insights for purposes of the particular experiment or empirical investigation. An example may be helpful to see how this works.

First, however, let's note that according to this approach, one can incorporate the insights of phenomenology into experimental protocols without training subjects in the method. This is not meant as a rejection of the neurophenomenological approach. As indicated, phenomenological insights developed in neurophenomenological experimentation can be front-loaded into the design of subsequent experiments. Front-loaded phenomenology, however, can address certain limitations involved in neurophenomenological procedures that involve training. Specifically, not every psychological experiment can be designed to allow for the training of subjects. In some cases one wants the subject to be naive about what is being tested, for example. In other cases one might be testing subjects who are unable to follow phenomenological method, as when subjects might be suffering from pathologies. In such cases, it may still be possible to front-load the phenomenology into experimental design.

As an example we focus on some experiments that incorporate the phenomenological distinction between the sense of agency that I may have for my action, and the sense of ownership I feel for my own body and its movement. In the normal experience of intentional action, these two aspects are close to indistinguishable. But consider the phenomenology of involuntary action. If, for example, someone pushes me from behind, I sense that it is my body that is moving – it is *my* movement, not someone else's, so I experience ownership for the movement – but I do not experience agency for the initial movement since I have no sense that I intended or caused the movement. That is, in the case of involuntary movement, I directly experience the movement as happening to me (sense of ownership), but not as caused by me (no sense of agency). Both the sense of agency and the sense of ownership (what phenomenologists refer to as a sense of 'mineness') are first-order, pre-reflective phenomenal experiences.

Employing this distinction neuroscience can ask what neurological processes generate these first-order experiences. Furthermore, if this distinction is in fact implicit in first-order experience rather than being the product of second-order introspective attribution, then this suggests that neuroscientists should look for a more basic set of primary processes that are activated in motor control mechanisms rather than in areas that may be responsible for higher-order cognitive processes.

This phenomenologically based supposition is not only empirically testable; it has already informed the design of several recent experiments that attempt to distinguish the neural correlates of the sense of agency for one's own actions (self-agency) in contrast to the sense that the action belongs to someone else (other-agency) (e.g. Chaminade and Decety 2002; Farrer and Frith 2002; Farrer et al. 2003; Nahab et al. 2011). We discuss these experiments in some detail in Chapter 8. For now, however, we simply want to note that in the experiments subjects can remain perfectly naive about the phenomenological details of their own experience. They are not even required to give a report of their experience. Yet in these experiments the phenomenological description of the sense of agency both informs the experimental design (the experiments are set up to find the neural correlates of precisely this experiential component) and is part of the analytic framework for interpreting the results. Moreover, these experiments do not simply presuppose the phenomenological description. Rather the experiments test and attempt to corroborate that description.

CONCLUSION

How distinct is the phenomenological methodology? Do neurophenomenology and front-loaded phenomenology really differ from existing scientific methodologies employed by cognitive scientists when they try to identify the neural correlates of experience. After all, isn't the point in each case to correlate subject's reports with measurements of brain activity? But if the phenomenological paradigms don't possess unique features why should they then be attractive to experimentalists?

In our view, however, one reason phenomenology can make a contribution to the investigation of the involved cognitive mechanisms is that it offers conceptual tools and descriptive distinctions (say between reflective and pre-reflective consciousness, between *Leib* and *Körper*, or between primal impression, retention and protention – to mention some of the notions that we will examine in more detail in subsequent chapters) that allow for a better grasp of the topic under investigation. As long as these conceptual tools and descriptive distinctions differ productively from those employed by researchers working in types of cognitive science not informed by phenomenology, there is something to be gained by making the phenomenological move.

Some might think that phenomenology's truly distinctive contribution to cognitive science is that it can provide a meticulous description of the explanandum, one that can then serve as the basis for a subsequent explanatory account that employs inferences to best explanation regarding the underlying causal mechanisms. After all, phenomenology is not in the business of offering accounts of the actual neural underpinnings of cognition. Nor does it allow us a better grasp of the procedural level, i.e. of the physical dynamical processes involved in cognition. While it is certainly true that phenomenology can offer careful descriptions, we also think that phenomenology can do more than that. Not only does it address issues that are crucial for an understanding of the true complexity of consciousness and which are nevertheless frequently absent from the current debate, but it can also offer a theoretical and conceptual framework that allows it to challenge standard interpretations of the empirical data and to offer alternative interpretations that can be further tested out empirically.

We want to emphasize the interaction between phenomenology and, for example, the cognitive neurosciences; and we are claiming that the interaction can often add up to more than anything that phenomenology or cognitive neuroscience can do on its own. At the same time, our view is not that all parts of phenomenology are amenable to the agenda espoused by cognitive science, quite to the contrary in fact, since, in other writings, we have argued explicitly for the irreducible philosophical nature of some parts of phenomenology.

We conclude by emphasizing once more that the phenomenological analysis of the first-person perspective is much more than a mere compilation of descriptive findings. When speaking of a first-person perspective, or of a dimension of first-person experiencing, it would be a mistake to argue that this is something that exclusively concerns the type of access a given subject has to her own experiences. It would be a mistake to argue that access to objects in the common world is independent of a first-person perspective, precisely in that it involves a third-person perspective. This line of thought will not do; obviously, I can be directed at intersubjectively accessible objects, and although my access to these objects is of the very same kind available to other persons, this does not imply that there is no first-person perspective involved. Rather, intersubjectively accessible objects are intersubjectively accessible precisely insofar as they can be accessed from each first-person perspective. There is no *pure* third-person perspective, just as there is no view from nowhere. To believe in the existence of such a pure third-person perspective is to succumb to an *objectivist illusion*. This is, of course, not to say that there is no third-person perspective, but merely that such a perspective is exactly a perspective from somewhere. It is a view that we can adopt of the world. It is a perspective founded upon a first-person perspective, or to be more precise, it emerges out of the encounter between at least two first-person perspectives; that is, it involves intersubjectivity.[12]

Phenomenological analysis also goes beyond a narrow contribution to issues of relevance for philosophy of mind. In fact, the systematic import of the analysis can only be fully appreciated the moment the link to the overarching transcendental philosophical considerations is made visible. In this regard, it entails a showdown with metaphysical and scientific realism.

One way to define scientific realism is to say that it is guided by a certain conception of knowledge. Knowledge is taken to consist of a faithful mirroring of a mind-independent reality. It is taken to be knowledge of a reality which exists independently of that knowledge, and indeed independently of any thought and experience (Williams 2005, p. 48). If we want to know true reality, we should aim at describing the way the world is, not just independently of its being believed to be that way, but independently of all the ways in which it happens to present itself to us human beings. An *absolute conception*, on this view, would be a dehumanized conception, a conception from which all traces of ourselves had been removed. Nothing would remain that would indicate whose conception it is, how those who form or possess that conception experience the world, and when or where they find themselves in it. It would be as impersonal, impartial, and objective a picture of the world as we could possibly achieve (Stroud 2000, p. 30).

Scientific realism assumes that everyday experience combines subjective and objective features and that we can reach an objective picture of what the world is really like by stripping away the subjective. It consequently argues that there is a clear distinction to be drawn between the properties things have 'in themselves' and the properties which are 'projected by us'. Whereas the world of appearance, the world as it is for us in daily life, combines subjective and objective features, science captures the objective world, the world as it is in itself. But to think that science can provide us with an *absolute* description of reality, that is, a description from a view from nowhere, to think that science is the only road to metaphysical truth, or that science simply mirrors the way in which nature classifies itself, is according to the phenomenologists an objectivist and scientistic illusion (see Zahavi 2003e). We cannot hold all our current beliefs about the world up against the world and somehow measure the degree of correspondence between the two.

Phenomenology endorses a *this-worldly* conception of objectivity and reality and seeks to overcome the scepticism that argues that the way the world appears to us is compatible with the world really being completely different (Husserl 1950/1999, p. 117; Heidegger 1986/1996, p. 229). Phenomenology also rejects the view – currently endorsed by many naturalists – according to which natural science is the measure of all things, of what is that it is, and of what is not that it is not (see Sellars 1963, p. 173). For phenomenology, science is not simply a collection of systematically interrelated justified propositions. Science is performed by somebody; it is a specific theoretical stance towards the world. This stance did not fall down from the sky; it has its own presuppositions and origins. Scientific objectivity is something to strive for, but it rests on the observations and experiences of individuals; it is knowledge shared by a community of experiencing subjects and presupposes a triangulation of points of view or perspectives. In short, if we wish to understand knowledge, truth, objectivity, meaning, and reference we will have to investigate the forms and structures of intentionality that are employed by cognizing and acting subjects. Failing to do so, failing to effect the reflective move of transcendental phenomenology, would be to succumb to a naive objectivism. Thus, according to this view, rather than being a hindrance or obstacle, subjectivity turns out to be a far more important requisite for objectivity and the pursuit of scientific knowledge than, say, microscopes and scanners, which are of no use unless the scientist is an experiencing subject. At the same time, it is important to recognize that, although phenomenology involves a transcendental critique of scientism, it by no means entails a rejection of science. Rather, as we have seen from the discussion of naturalizing phenomenology, it offers unique resources that can enhance or complement the natural science of the mind.

NOTES

1 The term 'neurophenomenology', for example, was originally defined by Francisco Varela (1996) to signify an approach to the neuroscience of consciousness that incorporates the phenomenological methodology outlined in the Husserlian tradition. In recent years, however, the term has

been used in a much looser sense to signify any kind of appeal to first-person data in combination with data from neuroscience. See, for example, Metzinger (2003).

2 See the special issue of *Phenomenology and the Cognitive Sciences* (Noë 2007b) on heterophenomenology. Dennett (2007, p. 252), in his response to this issue, insists that heterophenomenology describes how empirical science already does what it does, but he rejects the characterization of heterophenomenology as 'averaging out' first-person data. But if averaging out is not the correct way to put it, then perhaps the 'elimination' of first-person data might be a more apt phrasing. After all, Dennett does claim that consciousness does not have the first-person phenomenal properties it is commonly thought to have (1991, p. 365). That something has subjective or experiential reality for the subject just means that the subject believes in it (Dennett 1993b, p. 139). There are the public reports we utter, there are the episodes of propositional thinking, and then there is, as far as introspection is concerned, darkness (Dennett 1979, p. 95). Indeed, for Dennett, our stream of consciousness consists of nothing but propositional episodes (ibid., pp. 94–95, 109).

3 Of course, developments in physics, particularly the rise of relativity theory and quantum physics, have called this fundamental assumption into question. It is, however, questionable whether the full theoretical implications of Einstein's and Bohr's ideas – the exact interpretation of which is still debated – have yet been absorbed by standard science and reflected in its understanding of reality. On a side note, it is worth mentioning that the outstanding mathematician Hermann Weyl who was one of Einstein's colleagues in Zürich, and who contributed decisively to the interpretation and further development of both the general theory of relativity and the field of quantum mechanics, not only drew quite extensively from Husserl's criticism of naturalism, but was also deeply influenced by Husserl's transcendental idealism (see Ryckman 2005).

4 For a recent, quite similar claim, see Noë (2004, p. 179).

5 A proper understanding of the phenomenological analyses of consciousness must recognize their transcendental philosophical character. Some still find this claim controversial when it concerns the work of Heidegger and Merleau-Ponty. For a defence of such a reading, which emphasizes the commonality between the three phenomenologists, see Zahavi (2006, 2008b).

6 Further support for the Husserlian view that memory involves the re-enactment of a previous perceptual experience is to be found in neurological differences involved in illusory versus veridical memory. See Schacter et al. (1996).

7 It's important to note how controversial this proposal is from a strict Husserlian viewpoint. As Husserl writes in the very beginning of *Ideen I*: 'One cannot define in philosophy as in mathematics; any imitation of mathematical procedure in this respect is not only unfruitful but wrong, and has most injurious consequences' (Husserl 1976/1982, p. 9). See Yoshimi 2007 for support of the position outlined by Roy et al. For some critical remarks see Zahavi 2004e.

8 Froese and Gallagher (2010) have recently suggested a high-tech enhancement of eidetic variation as a phenomenological tool, consistent with the proposal of using dynamic systems theory. They suggest that the use of computer simulation, specifically in the field of artificial life, could play a similar role as, or in fact supplement the use of eidetic variation.

9 The following summary is based on Gallagher (2003a), but see Thompson (2007) for a more developed account.

10 'To train the subjects, open questions were asked to try to redirect their attention towards their

own immediate mental processes before the recordings were taken ... For example: Experimenter: "What did you feel before and after the image appeared?" Subject S1: "I had a growing sense of expectation, but not for a specific object; however when the figure appeared, I had a feeling of confirmation, no surprise at all"; or subject S4: "it was as if the image appeared in the periphery of my attention, but then my attention was suddenly swallowed up by the shape"' (Lutz et al. 2002, p. 1587).

11 For further theoretical and methodological discussion of this experiment, see Lutz 2002, Lutz and Thompson 2003, and Thompson et al. 2005. In his recent book, Thompson makes it clear that the phenomenological methods employed in experimental neurophenomenology are not necessarily limited to those found in the Husserlian tradition of phenomenology. They can include 'any systematic project of investigating and describing experience. So understood, phenomenology includes Asian traditions, in particular the various Buddhist and Hindu philosophical analyses of the nature of the mind and consciousness, based on contemplative mental training' (Thompson 2007, p. 474).

12 For a more elaborate argument, see Zahavi (2001b).

FURTHER READING

Natalie Depraz, Francisco Varela, and Pierre Vermersch, On Becoming Aware. Amsterdam: John Benjamins, 2003.

Owen Flanagan, Consciousness Reconsidered. Cambridge, MA: MIT Press, 1992.

Aron Gurwitsch, Studies in Phenomenology and Psychology. Evanston: Northwestern University Press, 1966.

Anthony Jack and Andreas Roepstorff (eds.), Trusting the Subject I? Special double issue of Journal of Consciousness Studies 10/9–10, 2003.

Eduard Marbach, Mental Representation and Consciousness: Towards a Phenomenological Theory of Representation and Reference. Dordrecht: Kluwer Academic Publishers, 1993.

Dermot Moran, Introduction to Phenomenology. London: Routledge, 2000.

Alva Noë (ed.), Dennett and Heterophenomenology. Special double issue of Phenomenology and the Cognitive Sciences 6/1–2, 2007.

Jean Petitot, Francisco J. Varela, Bernard Pachoud, and Jean-Michel Roy (eds), Naturalizing Phenomenology: Issues in Contemporary Phenomenology and Cognitive Science. Stanford: Stanford University Press, 1999.

Robert Sokolowski, Introduction to Phenomenology. Cambridge: Cambridge University Press, 2000.

Evan Thompson, Mind in Life: Biology, Phenomenology, and the Sciences of Mind. Cambridge, MA: Harvard University Press, 2007.

Francisco Varela, Evan Thompson, and Eleanor Rosch, The Embodied Mind: Cognitive Science and Human Experience. Cambridge, MA: MIT Press, 1991.

Donn Welton (ed.), The New Husserl: A Critical Reader. Bloomington: Indiana University Press, 2003.

Dan Zahavi, Husserl's Phenomenology. Stanford: Stanford University Press, 2003.

3 Consciousness and self-consciousness

After putting in a long day's work, I climb into my sleek new hybrid, make my way onto the highway and head for home. It was an amazing waste of time, I think to myself, to go to all those meetings today. Nothing ever gets accomplished at them. And that jerk who suggested that Plan A was beyond budget sounded like he never had a course in economics. But that new person seemed to know what she was talking about. I wonder whether she would like to get a drink sometime.

... Ah, here I am. I pull into my driveway and I'm home. That didn't take long. Actually, now that I think of it, I hardly remember making the trip home. I remember pulling onto the highway, and the next thing I knew I was here. Let me think – which route did I actually take? Hmm. I can't recall anything about the actual driving I must have been doing. I must have been on automatic pilot. Does this mean that I was not conscious of my driving?

The situation we have just described is a version of what has become known in the literature as the 'long-distance truck driver' problem (Armstrong 1968). Can I have unconscious perceptions and perform unconscious actions? Can I perceive events in the world without being conscious of my perceptions? If so, what difference does it make, if any, when the perceptions are in fact conscious? And what perceptions and actions should we call conscious? If conscious perceptions are perceptions that in addition to being conscious of something in the world, are also themselves something one is conscious of, would they then entail a form of self-consciousness? We are here faced with the large philosophical issue concerning the relation between consciousness and self-consciousness. What is the right way to think about these concepts?

In this chapter, we discuss some central problems that have to be addressed by any account of consciousness. We'll focus on a phenomenological account and compare it with other accounts. Like any other tradition, the phenomenological tradition spans many differences, yet even if phenomenologists disagree on important questions concerning methods and focus, they are in nearly unanimous agreement when it concerns the relation between consciousness and self-consciousness. Literally all of the major figures in phenomenology defend the view that a minimal form of self-consciousness is a constant structural feature of conscious experience. Experience happens for the experiencing subject in an immediate way and as part of this immediacy, it is implicitly marked as *my* experience. For the phenomenologists, this immediate and first-personal character of experiential phenomena must be accounted for in terms of a 'pre-reflective' self-consciousness.

By calling the type of self-consciousness in question 'pre-reflective', we wish to emphasize that it does not involve an additional second-order mental state that in some way is directed in an explicit manner towards the experience in question. Rather, self-consciousness must be understood as an intrinsic feature of the primary experience. Moreover, it is not thematic or attentive or voluntarily brought about; rather it is tacit, and very importantly, thoroughly non-observational (that is, it is not a kind of introspective observation of myself) and non-objectifying (that is, it does not turn my experience into a perceived or observed object). I can, of course, reflect on and attend to my experience, I can make it the theme or object of my attention, but prior to reflecting on it, I wasn't 'mind- or self-blind'. The experience was already present to me, it was already something *for me*, and in that sense it counts as being pre-reflectively conscious.

CONSCIOUSNESS AND PRE-REFLECTIVE SELF-CONSCIOUSNESS

When I look out my window I see the car that I have just parked in the driveway. In this case, it makes sense to say that I am conscious of the car, or that I have a first-order consciousness of it. I can tell you what it looks like, and I can tell you that, yes, there it is, located in the driveway. But can I be conscious of the car, and can I be in a position to tell you *what* I am conscious of, unless I am also, somehow, familiar or acquainted with my very experience of the car? Since the latter would amount to a consciousness of myself being conscious, we would say that it is a form of self-consciousness. The question would then be, what precisely is the nature of this self-consciousness? And is it right to say that in *all* cases of being conscious of something, we are also conscious that we are conscious of something, or wouldn't this generate an infinite regress?

Husserl, for example, contends that the individual's stream of experience is characterized by a self-appearance or self-manifestation (1959, p. 189). He argues that self-consciousness, rather than being something that occurs only during exceptional circumstances, namely whenever we pay attention to our conscious life, is a feature characterizing the experiential dimension as such, no matter what worldly entities we might otherwise be conscious of and occupied with. As he puts it, 'To be a subject is to be in the mode of being aware of oneself' (Husserl 1973a, p. 151).

We find very similar ideas in other phenomenologists. Heidegger, for example, argues that the self is present whenever one is conscious of something. Every worldly experience involves a component of self-acquaintance and self-familiarity; every experiencing is characterized by the fact that 'I am always somehow acquainted with myself' (Heidegger 1993, p. 251), or as he puts it – this time adopting a more traditional terminology – 'Every consciousness is also self-consciousness' (Heidegger 2001, p. 135).

Phenomenologists refer to the idea that our consciousness is *of* or *about something* as the *intentionality* of consciousness (more on this in Chapter 6). Sartre, probably the best-known defender of a phenomenological theory of self-consciousness, also claimed that each intentional experience is characterized by self-consciousness. Sartre took pre-reflective self-consciousness to constitute a necessary condition for being conscious of something. To perceive a withering oak, a dance performance, or a red pillow consciously without being aware of perceiving it, i.e. without having a sense that I am experiencing it or being acquainted with the experience in question, is, according to Sartre, a manifest absurdity (1956, pp. l–lxii; 1967). An experience does not simply exist, it exists in such a way that it is implicitly self-given, or as Sartre puts it, it is 'for itself'. This self-givenness of experience is not simply a quality added to the experience, a mere varnish; it rather constitutes the very mode of being of the experience. This line of thought is elaborated in the important introduction to *Being and Nothingness*, where Sartre claims that an ontological analysis of consciousness – that is, an analysis of the very being of consciousness – shows that it always involves self-consciousness – the *mode of being* of intentional consciousness is to be *for-itself* (*pour-soi*), that is, self-conscious: 'This self-consciousness we ought to consider not as a new consciousness, but as *the only mode of existence which is possible for a consciousness of something*' (Sartre 1956, p. liv).

These claims should not be misunderstood. The phenomenologists are not advocating a strong thesis concerning total and infallible self-knowledge; rather, they are calling attention to the constitutive link between experiential phenomena and the first-person perspective. As we shall see in a moment, many analytic philosophers have more recently made similar claims.

Husserl, Heidegger, Sartre, and others all emphasize the importance of considering the first-person perspective when elucidating phenomenal consciousness. When speaking of a first-person perspective it is important to be clear about the distinction between having or embodying such a perspective and being able to articulate it linguistically (we'll call this a weak and strong first-person perspective, respectively). Whereas the latter presupposes mastery of the first-person pronoun, the former is simply a question of the first-personal, subjective manifestation of one's own experiential life. Although both capabilities deserve to be investigated, phenomenologists have mainly been accentuating the significance of the former, since they take it to provide an experiential grounding of the latter. To emphasize the importance of the first-person perspective should consequently not be seen as an endorsement of a perceptual model of self-knowledge, as if our acquaintance with our own experiences literally came about by taking up a position in relation to ourselves, or through an explicit perspective-taking. Rather, the point is simply that there is a distinctive way experiential episodes are present to the subject whose episodes they are. Experiential episodes have, to use Searle's terminology, a *first-person ontology* from the start, i.e. even before the subject acquires the conceptual and linguistic skills to classify them as his own.

Different forms of self-consciousness

Despite the consensus among the philosophers we have just named, the term 'self-consciousness' is notoriously ambiguous, and the philosophical, psychological, and neuroscientific literatures are filled with competing, conflicting, and complementary definitions. Let us take a quick look at some of the main candidates:

- In philosophy, many have sought to link self-consciousness to the ability to think 'I'-thoughts. A recent defence of such an approach can be found in Lynne Rudder Baker, who has argued that all sentient beings are subjects of experience, that they all have perspectival attitudes, and that they all experience the world from their own egocentric perspective. In doing so, they show that they are in possession of what Baker calls weak *first-person phenomena* (2000, pp. 60, 67). Merely having a subjective point of view, however, is not enough for having self-consciousness. In order to be in possession of self-consciousness, which for Baker is a *strong first-person phenomenon*, one must be able to think of oneself as oneself. It is not enough to have desires and beliefs, it is not enough to have a perspectival attitude, nor is it enough to be able to distinguish between self and non-self; one must also be able to conceptualize this distinction. Baker consequently argues that self-consciousness presupposes the possession of a first-person concept. One is only self-conscious from the moment one can conceive of oneself as oneself and has the linguistic ability to use the first-person pronoun to refer to oneself (Baker 2000, pp. 67–68; see also Block 1997, p. 389). Given this definition, self-consciousness is obviously taken to be something that emerges in the course of a developmental process, and that depends upon the eventual acquisition of concepts and language.
- Another popular and related philosophical move has been to argue that self-consciousness, in the proper sense of the term, requires consciousness of a self. In other words, for a creature to be self-conscious it is not sufficient that it be able to self-ascribe experiences on an individual basis without recognizing the identity of that to which the experiences are ascribed. Rather, the creature must be capable of thinking of the self-ascribed experiences as belonging to one and the same self. Thus, genuine self-consciousness requires that the creature is capable of being conscious of its own identity as the subject, bearer, or owner of different experiences (see Cassam 1997).
- If we shift terrain and move into social psychology, we will frequently encounter the claim, famously defended by George Herbert Mead, that self-consciousness is a matter of becoming an object to oneself in virtue of one's social relations to others, i.e. that self-consciousness is constituted by adopting the perspective of the other towards oneself (Mead 1962). According to this account, self-consciousness is per se a social phenomenon. It is not something you can acquire on your own. As Mead wrote: 'Consciousness, as frequently used, simply has reference to the field of experience, but self-consciousness refers to the ability to call out in ourselves a set of definite responses which belong to the others of the group. Consciousness and self-consciousness are not on the same level. A man alone has, fortunately or unfortunately, access to his own

toothache, but that is not what we mean by self-consciousness' (Mead 1962, p. 163; see also pp. 171–72).

- Within developmental psychology, the so-called mirror-recognition task has occasionally been heralded as the decisive test for self-consciousness. Chimps (and a few other animals) can recognize themselves in the mirror, and humans begin to do so around the age of 18 months. Hence, it has been argued that self-consciousness is only present from the moment the child is capable of recognizing itself in the mirror (see Lewis 2003).

- Some, however, have raised the stakes even further and have argued that self-consciousness presupposes possession of a theory of mind. Roughly, the idea is that self-consciousness requires the ability to be aware of experiences as experiences, which in turn requires possession of a concept of experience. However, this concept cannot stand alone. It gets its significance from being embedded in a network of theoretical concepts. In particular, to think of experiences as experiences requires one to have the conception of objects or states of affairs that are capable of being experienced but that can exist even if they are not experienced. This motivates some to argue that children do not gain self-consciousness until around the age of four years, and that one can test the presence of self-consciousness by using classical theory of mind tasks, such as the false belief task or the appearance–reality task (see Chapter 7). Such claims have been recently complicated by experiments that supposedly show that infants as young as 13–15 months are capable of passing false-belief tests (see, e.g. Baillargeon et al. 2010). How precisely to understand these experiments, however, is still under debate (but see Chapters 5 and 9 in this book).

- Finally, narrative theorists suggest that a fully fledged self-consciousness comes about only on the basis of being in command of our own life story. Self-consciousness is tied to our ability to develop self-narratives, to tell stories about ourselves, and to make sense out of our own life in a narrative way.

There are kernels of truth in all of these definitions in the sense that they all capture various important aspects of the phenomenon of self-consciousness, yet none of them have much to do with the idea of a minimal, pre-reflective self-consciousness. Rather, the phenomenological line of thought can be construed as follows: self-consciousness is not merely something that comes about the moment one scrutinizes one's experiences attentively (let alone something that only comes about the moment one recognizes one's own mirror image, refers to oneself using the first-person pronoun, or is in possession of a theory of mind, or an identifying knowledge of one's own life story). Rather, self-consciousness comes in many forms and degrees. It makes perfect sense to speak of self-consciousness whenever I consciously perceive an external object – a chair, a chestnut tree, or a rising sun – because to consciously perceive something is not simply to be conscious of the perceptual object, but also to be acquainted with the experience of the object. In its most primitive and fundamental form, self-consciousness is simply a question of the ongoing first-personal manifestation of experiential life.

PRE-REFLECTIVE SELF-CONSCIOUSNESS AND 'WHAT IT IS LIKE'

The notion of pre-reflective self-consciousness is related to the idea that experiences have a subjective 'feel' to them, a certain (phenomenal) quality of 'what it is like' or what it 'feels' like to have them. As it is usually expressed outside of phenomenological texts, to undergo a conscious experience necessarily means that there is something it is like for the subject to have that experience (Nagel 1974; Searle 1992). However, there is more to experience than the fact that what it is like to perceive a black triangle is subjectively distinct from what it is like to perceive a red circle (see Nagel 1974). Not only is what it is like to perceive *red* different from what it is like to perceive *black*, but what it is like to *perceive* red is different from what it is like to *remember* or *imagine* red. Furthermore, all of these phenomenal experiences involve a reference to a subject of experience. In perceiving or imagining an object consciously, one is aware of the object as appearing in a determinate manner to oneself. When I consciously imagine Santa Claus, desire a hot shower, anticipate my next holiday, or reflect on Aristotle's notion of an unmoved mover, all of these intended objects are given in correlation to a variety of subjectively distinct intentional experiences. One reason these experiences are said to be subjective is that they are characterized by a subjective mode of existence, in the sense that they necessarily feel like something *for somebody*. Our experiential life can consequently be said to entail a primitive form of self-referentiality or for-me-ness.

So although I live through various different experiences, there is also something experiential that in some sense remains the same, namely, their distinct first-personal presence. When I am aware of a current pain, perception, or thought, the experience in question is immediately, non-inferentially, and non-criterially *mine*. I do not first have a neutral or anonymous experience only to infer in a subsequent move that it is mine. In fact, if I am dizzy I can neither be in doubt nor be mistaken about who the subject of that experience is, and it is nonsensical to ask whether I am sure that I am the one who is dizzy, or to demand a specification of the criteria being used by me in determining whether or not the felt dizziness is really mine. In effect, all of my experiences are characterized implicitly by a quality of *mineness*, that is, as having the quality of being experiences *I* am undergoing or living through. This is not to say that I always attend to this quality, or that I am always thematically aware of my experiences as being mine. But we need an account that can explain how I can return to an experience and remember it as my experience even though it might not have been given thematically as mine when it was originally lived through. Had the experience in fact been completely anonymous, had it lacked first-personal mineness altogether when originally lived through, such a subsequent appropriation would be rather inexplicable.

Furthermore, it is also important to point to the special nature of this mineness. It is not meant to suggest that I own the experiences in a way that is even remotely similar to the way I possess external objects of various sorts (a car, my trousers, or a house in Sweden). Nor should it be seen primarily as a contrastive determination. When young children start to use the possessive pronoun, it frequently means 'not yours'. But as Husserl observes in one of his manuscripts, when it comes to the peculiar mineness (*Meinheit*) character-izing experiential life, this can and should be understood without any contrasting others (Husserl 1973b, p. 351), although it may form the basis of the self–other discrimination. To put it differently, the for-me-ness in question is not a quality like yellow, salty, or spongy. It doesn't refer to a specific content of experience, to a specific *what*, but to the unique mode of givenness or how of experience. It refers to the first-personal presence of experience; it refers to the fact that experiences I am living through present themselves differently (but not necessarily better) to me than to anybody else. It could consequently be claimed that anybody who denies the mineness or for-me-ness of experiences simply fails to recognize an essential constitutive aspect of experience. Indeed, to stress the intimate link between consciousness and self-consciousness as we have been doing is simply to take the subjec-tivity of experience seriously.

It is thus crucial not to misconceive of the ubiquitous pre-reflective self-consciousness as if it was something distinct from phenomenal consciousness as such, something that could and should be found in addition to the ordinary phenomenal consciousness of sweet oranges or hot coffee. Rather, the claim is that pre-reflective self-consciousness is a consti-tutive feature and integral part of phenomenal consciousness.To put the point differently, on our view, every experience is characterized by what has recently been called *perspectival ownership* (Albahari 2006). For a subject to own something in a perspectival sense is for the experience in question to present itself in a distinctive manner to the subject whose experience it is.

As already noted, one finds similar views in analytic philosophy as well. Consider the following quotes from Frankfurt and Goldman, respectively:

> What would it be like to be conscious of something without being aware of this consciousness? It would mean having an experience with no awareness whatever of its occurrence. This would be, precisely, a case of unconscious experience. It appears, then, that being conscious is identical with being self-conscious. Consciousness is self-consciousness. The claim that waking consciousness is self-consciousness does not mean that consciousness is invariably dual in the sense that every instance of it involves both a primary awareness and another instance of consciousness which is somehow distinct and separable from the first and which has the first as its object. That would threaten an intolerably infinite proliferation of instances of consciousness. Rather, the self-consciousness in question is a sort of *immanent reflexivity* by virtue of which every instance of being conscious grasps not only that of which it is an awareness but also the awareness of it. It is like a source of light which, in addition to illuminating whatever other things fall within its scope, renders itself visible as well.
>
> (Frankfurt 1988, p. 162)

> [Consider] the case of thinking about *x* or attending to *x*. In the process of thinking about *x* there is already an implicit awareness that one is thinking about *x*. There is no need for reflection here, for taking a step back from thinking about *x* in order to examine it. ... When we are thinking about *x*, the mind is focused on *x*, not on

our thinking of *x*. Nevertheless, the process of thinking about *x* carries with it a non-reflective self-awareness.

(Goldman 1970, p. 96)

Related views have been defended by Owen Flanagan, who not only argues that consciousness involves self-consciousness in the weak sense that there is something it is like for the subject to have the experience, but has also spoken of the low-level self-consciousness involved in experiencing my experiences as mine (1992, p. 194). Arguing along similar lines, Uriah Kriegel has more recently claimed that peripheral self-consciousness is an integral moment of phenomenal consciousness. As he writes, 'It is impossible to think or experience something consciously without thinking or experiencing it self-consciously, i.e. without being peripherally aware of thinking or experiencing it' (Kriegel 2004, p. 200). Thus, in his view, unless a mental state is self-conscious, there will be nothing it is like to undergo the state, and it therefore cannot be a phenomenally conscious state (Kriegel 2003, pp. 103–6).[1]

To avoid misunderstandings, it is however important to emphasize that the phenomenologists don't endorse the strong view that consciousness and self-consciousness are identical; rather, the claim is merely that (phenomenal) consciousness entails (a weak or thin) self-consciousness. Compare three different experiences: the smelling of crushed basil leaves, the seeing of the full moon, and the hearing of Bartok's *Music for Strings, Percussion & Celesta*. Although all three experiences are characterized by the same kind of pre-reflective self-consciousness, which tells me that I am the one experiencing these different things, they nevertheless differ in what it is like to have or undergo them. This should be sufficient to show that consciousness and self-consciousness cannot simply be identified.

First- and higher-order accounts of consciousness

The claim that there is a close link between consciousness and self-consciousness is less exceptional than might be expected. In fact, it could even be argued that such a claim is part of current orthodoxy since it is a claim defended by various higher-order theorists. Consider that in the current debate about consciousness it has become customary to distinguish between two uses of the term 'conscious', a transitive and an intransitive use. On the one hand, we can speak of somebody being conscious of something, be it apples, lemons, or roses. On the other, we can speak of somebody (or a mental state) being conscious *simpliciter* (rather than non-conscious). This latter use of the term 'conscious' is obviously connected to the notion of phenomenal consciousness, to the idea that there is something (rather than nothing) it is like to be in a certain mental state. Now, for the past two or three decades, a dominant way to account for intransitive consciousness in cognitive science and analytical philosophy of mind has been by means of some kind of higher-order theory (see Armstrong 1968; Carruthers 1996; Lycan 1987; Rosenthal 1986). According to these authors, the difference between conscious and non-conscious mental states rests upon the presence or absence of a relevant meta-mental state. As Carruthers puts it, the subjective feel of experience presupposes a capacity for higher-order awareness; 'such self-awareness is a conceptually necessary condition for an organism to be a subject of phenomenal feelings, or for there to be anything that its experiences are like' (1996, p. 152).

One way to illustrate the guiding idea of this approach is to compare consciousness to a spotlight. Some mental states are illuminated; others do their work in the dark. What makes a mental state conscious (illuminated) is the fact that it is taken as an object by a relevant higher-order state. It is the occurrence of the higher-order representation that makes us conscious of the first-order mental state. In short, a conscious state is a state we are conscious of, or as Rosenthal puts it, 'the mental state's being intransitively conscious simply consists in one's being transitively conscious of it' (1997, p. 739). Thus, intransitive consciousness is taken to be a non-intrinsic, relational property (ibid., pp. 736–37), that is, a property that a mental state has only in so far as it stands in the relevant relation to something else.

There have generally been two ways of interpreting this. Either we become aware of being in the first-order mental state by means of some higher-order perception (HOP) or monitoring (Armstrong 1968; Lycan 1997), or we become aware of it by means of some higher-order thought (HOT), that is, the state is conscious just in case we have a roughly contemporaneous thought to the effect that we are in that very state (Rosenthal 1993a, p. 199). Thus, the basic divide between the HOP and HOT models has precisely been on the issue of whether the conscious-making metamental states are perception-like or thought-like in nature.[2] In both cases, however, consciousness has been taken to be a question of the mind directing its intentional aim upon its own states and operations. Self-directedness has been taken to be constitutive of (intransitive) consciousness, or to put it differently, higher-order theories have typically explained (intransitive) consciousness in terms of self-consciousness.

But one might share the view that there is a close link between consciousness and self-consciousness and still disagree about the nature of the link. And although the phenomenological view might superficially resemble the view of the higher-order theories, we are ultimately confronted with two radically divergent accounts. In contrast to the higher-order theories, phenomenologists explicitly deny that the self-consciousness that is present the moment I consciously experience something is to be understood in terms of some kind of reflection, or introspection, or higher-order monitoring. It does not involve an additional mental state, but is rather to be understood as an intrinsic feature of the primary experience. That is, in contrast to the higher-order account of consciousness that claims that intransitive consciousness is an extrinsic property of those mental states that have it, a property bestowed upon them externally by some further states, phenomenologists typically argue that intransitive consciousness is an intrinsic property and constitutive feature of those mental states that have it. Moreover, not only do they reject the view that a mental state becomes conscious by being taken as an object by a higher-order state, they also reject the view – generally associated with Franz Brentano – according to which a mental state becomes conscious by taking itself as an object.

Franz Brentano (1839–1917) was an influential philosopher and psychologist of the nineteenth century. Husserl attended his seminars in Vienna – and so did Freud and several of the founders of gestalt psychology. The novelist Franz Kafka also visited Brentano's seminars. Brentano wrote books on psychology, but also on Aristotle's metaphysics. Whereas his work *Psychology from an Empirical Standpoint* was of decisive importance for Husserl, Brentano's *On the Several Senses of Being in Aristotle* greatly influenced Heidegger.

According to Brentano, as I listen to a melody I am aware that I am listening to the melody. He acknowledges that I do not have two different mental states: my consciousness of the melody is one and the same as my awareness of hearing it; they constitute one single psychical phenomenon. On this point, and in opposition to higher-order representation theories, Brentano and the phenomenologists are in general agreement. But according to Brentano, by means of this unified mental state, I have an awareness of *two objects*: the melody and my auditory experience:

> In the same mental phenomenon in which the sound is present to our minds we simul-taneously apprehend the mental phenomenon itself. What is more, we apprehend it in accordance with its dual nature insofar as it has the sound as content within it, and insofar as it has itself as content at the same time. We can say that the sound is the *primary object* of the act of hearing, and that the act of hearing itself is the *secondary object*.
>
> (Brentano 1973, pp. 127–28)

Husserl disagrees on just this point, as do Sartre and Heidegger: pre-reflectively, my experience is not itself an object for me. I do not occupy the position or perspective of an observer, spectator, or in(tro)spector who attends to this experience. That something is experienced, 'and is in this sense conscious, does not and cannot mean that this is the *object* of an act of consciousness, in the sense that a perception, a presentation or a judgement is directed upon it' (Husserl 2001a, I, p. 273). In pre-reflective or non-observa-tional self-consciousness, experience is given, not as an object, but precisely as subjective experience. On this view, my intentional experience is lived through (*erlebt*), but it does not appear to me in an objectified manner, it is neither seen nor heard nor thought about (Husserl 1984, p. 399; Sartre 1957, pp. 44–45).

We have emphasized that pre-reflective self-consciousness is not a matter of taking an intentional or objectifying stance, and consequently it is neither some kind of inner perception, nor more generally a type of conceptual knowledge. Some have objected that even if something like non-objectifying self-consciousness is possible, it will be far too weak and vague to allow for or to explain the distinctive character of our first-person *knowledge* (Caston 2006, 4; Thomasson 2006, 6). In our view, this is a rather puzzling objection. As

Chalmers has recently argued having an experience is automatically to stand in an intimate epistemic relation to the experience, a relation more primitive than knowledge that might be called 'acquaintance' (1996, p. 197). We would concur and so would the classical phenomenologists. In their view, pre-reflective self-consciousness doesn't amount to first-person knowledge. This is, for instance, why Sartre carefully distinguishes self-consciousness (*conscience de soi*) from self-knowledge (*connaissance de soi*). In order to obtain knowledge about one's experiences something more than pre-reflective self-consciousness is needed. This is precisely why we find in the central works of the phenomenologists extensive and sophisticated analyses of the contribution of *reflection*. Qua thematic self-experience, reflection does not simply reproduce the lived experiences unaltered, rather the experiences reflected upon are transformed In the process, to various degrees and manners depending upon the type of reflection at work. This transformation is precisely what makes reflection cognitively valuable. But from the fact that pre-reflective self-consciousness isn't sufficient for first-person knowledge, one can obviously not conclude that it is therefore also unnecessary if such knowledge is to obtain.

Although, as pre-reflectively self-aware of my experience, I am not unconscious of it, I tend to ignore it in favour of its object. In my everyday life, I am absorbed by and preoccupied with projects and objects in the world, and as such I do not attend to my experiential life. Therefore, it's clear that my pervasive pre-reflective self-consciousness Is not to be understood as complete self-comprehension. Thus, one should distinguish between the claim that consciousness as such involves an implicit self-consciousness and the claim that consciousness is characterized by total self-transparency. One can easily accept the first and reject the latter (Ricoeur 1966, p. 378).

If I am engaged in some conscious activity, such as the reading of a story, my attention is neither on myself nor on my activity of reading, but on the story. If my reading is interrupted by someone asking me what I am doing, I immediately reply that I am (and have for some time been) reading; the self-consciousness on the basis of which I answer the question is not something acquired at just that moment, but a consciousness of myself which has been implicit in my experience all along. To put it differently, it is because I am pre-reflectively conscious of my experiences that I am usually able to respond immediately, i.e. without inference or observation, if somebody asks me what I have been doing, or thinking, or seeing, or feeling immediately prior to the question.

Sartre emphasized quite explicitly that the self-consciousness in question is not a new consciousness (1956, p. liv). It is not something added to the experience, an additional mental state, but rather an intrinsic feature of the experience. Thus, when he spoke of self-consciousness as a permanent feature of consciousness, Sartre was not referring to what he called reflective self-consciousness. Reflection (or higher-order monitoring) is the process whereby consciousness directs its intentional aim at itself, thereby taking itself as its own object. According to Sartre, however, this type of self-consciousness is derived; it involves a subject–object split, and the attempt to account for self-consciousness in such terms is, for Sartre, bound to fail. It either generates an infinite regress or accepts a non-conscious starting point, and he considered both of these options to be unacceptable (ibid., p. lii).

On the view espoused by most phenomenologists, the weak self-consciousness entailed by phenomenal consciousness is not intentionally structured; it does not involve a subject–object relation. It is not just that self-consciousness differs from ordinary object-consciousness; rather it is not an object-consciousness at all. When one is pre-reflectively self-conscious one does not take oneself as an intentional object, one is not aware of oneself as an object that happens to be oneself, nor is one aware of oneself as one specific object rather than another. Rather, my first-person, pre-reflective self-experience is immediate and non-observational. It involves what has more recently been called either 'self-reference without identification' (Shoemaker 1968) or 'non-ascriptive reference to self' (Brook 1994).

What is the actual argument for these claims, however? When it comes to defending the existence of a tacit and non-thematic self-consciousness, the argument is occasionally an indirect argument by elimination and consists in a rejection of the two obvious alternatives. Phenomenologists first deny that we could consciously experience something without in some way being aware of or being acquainted with the experience in question. They then argue that this first-personal awareness of one's own experiences amounts to a form of self-consciousness. Secondly, they reject the suggestion that we are *attentively* conscious of everything that we experience, including our own experience, i.e. they would argue that there are unnoticed or unattended experiences. For example, I may be driving my car in traffic and paying close attention to the car in front of me, which is weaving in and out of traffic lanes. By attending to that car, however, there are many things that I am not attending to, including the precise way that I am perceiving the car. I could start to do that by reflecting on my perceptual experience, although it might be dangerous to do so in this kind of circumstance. But the point is that, even if at some level I am aware that I am watching the car in front of me, I am not aware of it in the manner of paying attention to the watching. That phenomenal consciousness entails a minimal or thin form of self-consciousness doesn't imply that I in daily life am aware of my own stream of consciousness in a thematic introspection, as a succession of immanent marginal objects. After these two alternatives are rejected, the notion of pre-reflective self-consciousness seems to be the only feasible way to explain how experience works.

Another indirect line of argument for the existence of pre-reflective self-consciousness has been that the higher-order account of consciousness generates an infinite regress. This is, on the face of it, a rather old idea. Typically, the regress argument has been understood in the following manner: if an occurrent mental state is conscious only because it is taken as an object by an occurrent second-order mental state, then the second-order mental state, if it is to be conscious, must also be taken as an object by an occurrent third-order mental state, and so forth *ad infinitum*. The standard reply to this argument has been that the premise – that the second-order mental state is a conscious one – is false and question begging. In other words, the easy way to halt the regress is to accept the existence of non-conscious mental states. Needless to say, this is precisely the position adopted by the defenders of a higher-order theory. For them, the second-order perception or thought does not have to be conscious. It will be conscious only if it is accompanied by a (non-conscious) third-order thought or perception (see Rosenthal 1997). However, the phenomenological reply to this 'solution' is rather straightforward. The phenomenologists would concede that it is possible to halt the regress by postulating the existence of non-conscious mental states, but they would maintain that such an appeal to the non-conscious leaves us with a case of explanatory vacuity. That is, they would be quite unconvinced by the claim that the relation between two otherwise non-conscious mental processes can make one of them conscious; they would find it quite unclear how a mental state without subjective or phenomenal qualities can be transformed into one with such qualities, i.e. into a subjective experience with first-personal *mineness*, by the mere relational addition of a non-conscious meta-state having the first-order state as its intentional object.

To sum up, higher-order theorists and phenomenologists all seek to account for intransitive consciousness in terms of some form of self-consciousness. But whereas the higher-order theorists view self-consciousness as a form of meta-awareness that obtains between two distinct non-conscious mental states, the phenomenologists argue that we best understand intransitive consciousness in terms of a primitive form of self-consciousness that is integral and intrinsic to the mental state in question.

The claim that intransitive consciousness (and by implication self-consciousness) is an intrinsic feature has come under attack by Rosenthal, who has argued that calling something intrinsic is to imply that it is unanalysable and mysterious, and consequently beyond the reach of scientific and theoretical study: 'We would insist that being conscious is an intrinsic property of mental states only if we were convinced that it lacked articulated structure, and thus defied explanation' (1993b, p. 157). Although Rosenthal acknowledges that there is something intuitively appealing about taking intransitive consciousness to be an intrinsic property, he still thinks that this approach must be avoided if one wishes to come up with a non-trivial and informative account, that is, one which seeks to explain conscious mental states by appeal to non-conscious mental states, and non-conscious mental states by appeal to non-mental states (Rosenthal 1993b, p. 165; 1997, p. 735).

In our view, however, it is a mistake to argue that one puts an end to any subsequent analysis the moment one considers the explanandum intrinsic and irreducible. A good demonstration of this can be found precisely in the highly informative analyses of various aspects of consciousness provided by phenomenologists (see, for example, the analysis of time-consciousness in Chapter 4). But what about the issue of naturalization? Is a one-level account of consciousness committed to some kind of supernatural dualism? Not at all. One can defend the notion of pre-reflective self-consciousness while remaining quite neutral vis-à-vis the issue of naturalization. More specifically, nothing in the rejection of a relational account of consciousness rules it out that the emergence of consciousness requires a requisite neural substratum. One should consequently avoid conflating two different issues. One concerns the relation between the neural level and the mental level, the other the relation between different mental processes. The one-level account doesn't address the bottom-up issue concerning the relation between brain processes and consciousness, it merely denies that a mental state becomes conscious by being taken as an object by a relevant higher-order mental state. From the perspective of naturalism, it might even be argued that the one-level account is simpler and more parsimonious than the relational higher-order account, and that it is also in better accordance with a popular view in neuroscience, according to which consciousness is a matter of hitting a certain threshold of neural activity.

Phenomenologists, as we have seen, claim that pre-reflective self-consciousness is non-objectifying (that is, not to be construed as a form of object-consciousness) and therefore not the result of any self-directed intentionality. It is true, however, that the plausibility of this claim to a large extent depends on what we mean by 'object' (see Cassam 1997, p. 5). To understand the phenomenological point of view, it is at this point crucial to avoid conflating issues of ontology with those of phenomenology. The claim is not that the object of experience must always differ ontologically from the subject of experience, as if the subject and the object of experience must necessarily be two different entities. Rather, the claim is simply that the experience itself is not pre-reflectively *experienced* as an object. On our understanding, for something to be an object is for that something to consciously *appear* in a specific manner. More specifically, for x to be considered an object is for x to appear as transcending the subjective consciousness that takes it as an object. It is to appear as something that stands in opposition to or over against the subjective experience of it (consider the German term *Gegen-stand*). It is against this background that it has been denied that an experience is pre-reflectively given as an object. For whereas in reflection we are confronted with a situation involving two experiences, where one (the reflected upon) can appear as an object for the other (the reflecting), we are on the pre-reflective level only dealing with a single experience, and one experience cannot appear as an object to itself, cannot be experienced as transcending itself, cannot stand opposed to itself, in the requisite way.

An additional argument (found already in several of the post-Kantian German philosophers) for why an experience cannot pre-reflectively be an object, if, that is, the experience in question is to be considered my experience, was more recently revived by Shoemaker. He has argued that it is impossible to account for first-personal self-reference in terms of a successful object-identification. To identify something as oneself one obviously has to hold something true of it that one already knows to be true of oneself. This self-knowledge might in some cases be grounded in some further identification, but the supposition that every item of self-knowledge rests on identification leads to an infinite regress (Shoemaker 1968, p. 561). This holds even for self-identification obtained through introspection. That is, it will not do to claim that introspection is distinguished by the fact that its object has a property which immediately identifies it as being me, and which no other self could possibly have, namely, the property of being the private and exclusive object of exactly *my* introspection. This explanation will not do, because I will be unable to identify an introspected self as myself by the fact that it is introspectively observed by me unless I know it is the object of my introspection, i.e. unless I know that it is in fact me who undertakes this introspection, and this knowledge cannot itself be based on identification, on pain of infinite regress (Shoemaker 1968, pp. 562–63).

Indeed, in complete support of Shoemaker's point, the phenomenologist claims that this sort of intimate acquaintance that tells me that it is I myself who is introspecting, or more generally that it is I myself who is experiencing, is provided precisely by the pre-reflective self-consciousness that is implicit in experience.

BLINDSIGHT

Higher-order theorists often refer to the case of blindsight as evidence in support of their theory, so it will be helpful to consider blindsight to see if it offers an objection to the idea of a pre-reflective self-consciousness and truly supports the higher-order representational view.

The condition of blindsight is a form of blindness caused, not by damage to the eyes, but by damage to the primary visual cortex (V1), an area of the brain functionally defined for early processing in pattern recognition. For example, as Weiskrantz et al. (1974) has shown, damage to V1 and the connections from the dorsal lateral geniculate nucleus which relay signals from the retina to V1 can cause blindsight. In most real cases, only part of the visual field is blinded (the blind areas are called 'scotomas'), and this has to be taken into consideration in experiments (see the box overleaf, "Blindsight Experiments"). To simplify matters, let's assume that the patient is totally blind in this fashion (see e.g. the case of the patient, TN, reported in de Gelder 2010). A blindsight patient's eyes will deliver visual information to his brain, but he will not have conscious visual perception because of the brain damage. The information delivered by the eyes, however, may still register and be processed in other parts of the brain. For example, a route from the retina to the mid-brain, which is different from the route through V1, has been hypothesized as being a second pathway of visual information.

Unfortunately, information travelling this other route does not allow the patient to have the conscious experience of vision. The curious and unique thing about blindsight is that the patient can nonetheless detect and locate visual stimuli if he is made to do so. If presented with visual stimuli, the patient will say that he cannot see them, because, of course, he is blind. But if he is made to guess about where precisely the stimuli are presented, or about the nature of the stimuli – shape, position, etc. – he is correct in his guesses at a rate that is above chance. So the patient reports that he is blind and cannot see anything, but his tested behaviour indicates that there is some visual information informing his cognitive experience.

Blindsight subjects can also reach and grasp objects located in their blind field at around 80 per cent of normal accuracy. They can even catch a ball thrown at them, all without conscious awareness (see Weiskrantz 1997). They are thus said to be non-consciously perceiving the visual stimuli (Marcel 1998; Weiskrantz 1986). Recent studies have shown abilities for non-conscious visual discrimination in blindsight apply not only to relatively simple object discriminations, but also to emotionally salient stimuli (Hamm et al. 2003).

The significance of blindsight for higher-order theorists is that the blindsight patient is in a non-conscious mental state with regard to the stimulus that he cannot consciously see. The question is then, what is it that makes this mental state different from a conscious mental state? Higher-order theorists will supposedly claim that the non-conscious mental state of the blindsight subject is the same as a conscious mental state of the normally sighted person, except that in the latter case the subject has become aware of it through either an HOP or an HOT. The non-conscious sensory state is intentional, in the sense that it is directed at a particular object (the presented stimulus). Rosenthal (1993c) even argues that non-conscious mental states have qualitative properties that make them one kind of state rather than another (e.g. perceptual state versus belief state, or perhaps visual state versus

Blindsight experiments

Weiskrantz et al. (1974) tested a 34-year-old man, DB. DB began to experience headaches at age 14, preceded by the experience of a bright flashing, oval-shaped light. This light could be seen only in certain areas of his visual field. When he was 26, a test showed that he had a malformation at the right occipital lobe. The malformation was removed along with a portion of his visual cortex. The removal resulted in partial blindness with a small field of vision remaining at the periphery of the upper quadrant. After the surgery the headaches subsided.

All experiments involved the testing of various stimuli in the blind field of the patient. The patient was asked to guess to the best of his ability about the visual stimuli with which he was presented. During the course of the experimentation, DB was not told the test results.

- The first experiment tested whether DB could perceive the location of a visual stimulus in his blind field. He was told that a spot of light was going to be flashed in his blind field. On verbal command, he was to move his eyes, but not his head, in the direction from which he guessed the spot of light was coming.
- The second experiment also involved locating visual stimuli. This time DB was asked to point with his hand in the direction that he believed a spot of light was located on a horizontal meridian. His eyes and head were to remain motionless throughout the duration of this experiment.
- The third experiment involved the identification of images on a screen. The images varied in size, contrast, duration, and type. Each test consisted of 30 trials, 15 with one pair of stimuli and 15 with the other pair. A different random order of projections was used in every test. DB was asked to distinguish between horizontal and vertical lines, diagonal and vertical lines, and the letters X and O. He was asked to guess or to report what he thought he might have seen on the screen.
- In the fourth experiment the task was to distinguish between images containing diffraction gratings and those where there were no lines present. Testing was done on DB's intact vision field for a control.
- In the final experiment, DB underwent five tests of 30 trials each. He was asked to guess the colour of the light that was being projected in each of the tests. Brightness levels of the stimulus were varied throughout the 30 trials.

Results

DB was able to locate stimuli in the frontal plane, differentiate orientation of lines and at least one pair of shapes in his defective field. Larger stimuli and longer exposure time yielded better results in the blind field. The accuracy in some of the experiments was remarkable. DB scored well over 50 per cent on each test, ruling out a chance phenomenon. The patient's reaction, after he was given the results of his testing, was that of astonishment. He stated that he was surprised and insisted that he was just 'guessing'. He stated that he saw nothing at all; however, sometimes he had a 'feeling' about a certain stimulus. He was very accurate in the experiment where he was directed to point to the stimulus, however not so accurate when told to move his eyes in the direction of the light. He was able to differentiate between a vertical and horizontal line and the letters *X* and *O*. He was successful in distinguishing the grating of vertical bars from a homogeneous field, when the lines were wide. There was, however, not enough evidence to show the ability to differentiate between red and green.

auditory state) and that if the mental states are made conscious, the qualitative properties are what give them their particular 'what it's likeness'.

For higher-order theory there is nothing intrinsic about the mental state that makes it conscious rather than non-conscious. Rather, something other than the mental state itself must be responsible for making it conscious. For Rosenthal, as we saw, this is the role of an HOT. Of course the problem here is that if the mental or sensory state in question is more or less the same in either case, it is not clear why the blindsight subject cannot simply direct an HOT at it and make it conscious. It is curious (or it must seem so to the HOT theorist) that the blindsight subject, who is certainly capable of HOTs, continues to complain that he cannot see the stimulus. Indeed, one might argue, this complaint is itself an HOT that is directed at the non-conscious sensory state, and yet, this does not make that sensory state conscious. One could imagine the blindsight subject, having read up on blindsight theory in the latest braille publication, saying, 'I know I have this non-conscious sensory state, but no matter how much I think about it, I don't seem to be able to make it conscious'. So the real question is: What is it about the non-conscious sensory state that prevents higher-order access to it? There must be something that differentiates it from a conscious sensory state, other than an HOT.[3]

Does the experience of the blindsight subject cause similar trouble for the phenomenological account of pre-reflective self-consciousness? First, let's note that the account of pre-reflective self-consciousness was never meant to provide a causal account of what makes a mental state conscious. It is not that there are mental states waiting to become conscious, and requiring only the addition of pre-reflective self-consciousness. Rather, the account of pre-reflective self-consciousness is a description of a constitutive aspect of a conscious mental state. If a mental state is conscious, that mental state will involve a pre-reflective self-consciousness. So the claim is not that if we simply add a pre-reflective self-consciousness to the non-conscious mental state, it will suddenly become conscious.

Second, what precisely do we mean by a non-conscious perception, non-conscious sensory state, or non-conscious mental state, as these terms are used in reference to blindsight? Here, perhaps to the surprise of phenomenologists and non-phenomenologists alike, the phenomenologists are better off appealing to the neuroscience of blindsight. After all, the most reasonable explanation of the blindsight subject's lack of visual experience is likely to be found on the neuronal level rather than on the level of an HOT. In the case of blindsight, the subject has brain damage in an area that is in some way essential for the generation of visual consciousness, even though other brain areas continue to function in the processing of visual information, which still informs the subject's motor behaviours and his guesses. We are faced with a kind of non-conscious perception not unrelated to the one we also find in subliminal priming effects.[4] Information about the world is being processed in the brain, but in a way that does not result in conscious experience. Indeed, we don't have to appeal to the exotic cases of blindsight or experimental studies of masked priming effects, because these kinds of processes go on all the time in our everyday existence. Many aspects of motor control are the result of this kind of non-conscious processing of information about the world. When I reach to grasp a glass, the visual information that controls the shape of my hand is processed non-consciously (see Jeannerod 1997). This is certainly a case of non-conscious visual perception. Should we call this a non-conscious mental state? Perhaps in this case it is even clearer that we are talking about neurological processes that are not organized in a way that would generate a consciousness of this motor control. I am simply not conscious of the visual information that shapes my grasping action; nor can I make this process transparent by directing an HOT toward the process. At best, I can become aware, by observing my own behaviour, that my hand shapes itself, and I can come to understand that it is guided by the visual information that is processed non-consciously – but my real knowledge about this can only be found through third-person scientific accounts and experiments. And such accounts, if they do generate HOTs, do not do so in a way that could then allow me to experience the neurological processes as conscious mental states.

Indeed, in cases of conscious mental states, I don't have to go looking for a mental state to think about. I'm already there, so to speak. Being pre-reflectively self-conscious of my own experience – for example, that I am getting a drink by picking up the glass – is not a qualitative property that might change from one kind of experience to another; it is the common structural feature of any conscious state. If indeed different kinds of conscious states have different qualitative properties that may be due to differences in their modalities or intentional content, it is precisely the feature of pre-reflective self-consciousness that makes it possible for these differences in qualitative properties to express themselves in qualitative feels of 'what it's like' *for me*, to see, to hear, to remember, to judge, etc., about a shape, a colour, a sound, an event, etc.

SELF-CONSCIOUSNESS AND REFLECTION

In contrast to pre-reflective self-consciousness, which provides us with an implicit sense of self at the experiential level (we will return to the notion of self in Chapter 10), reflective self-consciousness is an explicit, conceptual, and objectifying awareness that takes a lower-order consciousness as its attentional theme. I am able at any time to attend directly to the cognitive experience itself, turning my experience itself into the object of my consideration. Whereas pre-reflective self-consciousness is an intrinsic and non-relational dimension of the experience, reflection is a complex form of self-consciousness that operates with a duality of moments and which involves a kind of self-fission. Reflection occasions a certain kind of inner pluralization. It makes subjective life thematic in a way that involves self-division or self-distanciation (see Asemissen 1958/59, p. 262).

In reflection we can distinguish the reflecting experience and the experience reflected-on. The first takes the latter as its object. The experience reflected-on is already self-conscious prior to reflection, and as we have seen, this prior self-consciousness is of a non-reflective and non-positional (non-observational) kind, i.e. it does not have a reflective structure, and it does not posit what it is aware of as an object. As Sartre wrote: '[T]here is no infinite regress here, since a consciousness has no need at all of a reflecting consciousness in order to be conscious of itself. It simply does not posit itself as an object' (1957, p. 45).

We could say, following Sartre, that consciousness has two possible modes of existence, pre-reflective and reflective. The former has priority since it can exist independently of the latter, whereas reflective self-consciousness always presupposes pre-reflective self-consciousness. As Sartre wrote, 'reflection has no kind of primacy over the consciousness reflected-on. It is not reflection which reveals the consciousness reflected-on to itself. Quite the contrary, it is the non-reflective consciousness which renders the reflection possible' (1956, p. liii).

Point of clarification

Sartre occasionally writes that we are pre-reflectively aware of our experiences and that there is a pre-reflective consciousness of self (in French, the term for self-consciousness – *conscience de soi* – literally means consciousness of self). He thereby seems to suggest that even pre-reflective self-consciousness takes an object. But as Sartre explicitly points out, it is only the necessity of syntax that compels him to use such phrasings. Thus, Sartre readily admitted that the use of the 'of' (or 'de') is unfortunate since it suggests that self-consciousness is simply a subtype of object-consciousness, as if the manner in which we are aware of ourselves is structurally comparable with the manner in which we are aware of apples and clouds. We cannot avoid the 'of', but in order to show that it is merely there to satisfy a grammatical requirement, Sartre placed it inside parentheses, and frequently speaks of a '*conscience (de) soi*' and of a '*conscience (de) plaisir*', etc. (Sartre 1956, p. liv). Thus, Sartre was quite keen to avoid any phrasing that might misleadingly suggest that we, in order to have conscious mental states, must be aware of them as objects.

This preliminary differentiation between reflective and pre-reflective is not a sufficient account of reflection. A more detailed examination of the precise relation between reflective and pre-reflective self-consciousness is called for. The methodological pertinence of this issue should be obvious: to what extent will reflection enable us to disclose the structures of lived experience? Phenomenological method depends on reflection, as we saw in the previous chapter. If, for example, reflection distorts first-order, pre-reflective experience, then we need to take this into consideration. This is an important issue for both phenomenologists and cognitive scientists in regard to using phenomenological (reflective) methods to get at a veridical description of experience.[5]

Husserl and the phenomenologists hold that our experiences are tacitly self-conscious, but they are also available for us to reflect upon. They can be reflected upon and thereby brought to our attention only because we are pre-reflectively conscious of them. An examination of the particular intentional structure of this process can substantiate this claim. Reflective self-consciousness is often taken to be a thematic, articulated, and intensified self-consciousness, and it is normally initiated in order to bring the primary intentional experience into focus. As Husserl points out, it is in the nature of reflection to grasp something which was already being experienced prior to the grasping. Reflection is characterized by disclosing, and not by producing its theme:

> When I say 'I', I grasp myself in a simple reflection. But this self-experience [*Selbsterfahrung*] is like every experience [*Erfahrung*], and in particular every perception, a mere directing myself towards something that was already there for me, that was already conscious, but not thematically experienced, not noticed.
>
> (Husserl 1973b, pp. 492–93)

The experience to which we turn attentively in reflection becomes accentuated (*herausgehoben*); reflection, as Husserl suggests, discloses, disentangles, explicates, and articulates all those components and structures which were contained implicitly in the lived experience (Husserl 1966a/1991, p. 129; 1966b/2001b, p. 205; 1984, p. 244; also, for example, see the various analyses in Chapters 4 and 6 of this book). Reflection reveals not a formless or structureless fluctuating unity of lived experiences but on the contrary, a morphological structure and internal differentiation which are accessible to conceptual articulation. Of course, by paying attention to something, by accentuating or articulating it, we do change the way in which it appears. This also holds true when it comes to reflection. Reflection does not merely copy or repeat the original experience; rather, it transforms it. This transformation, however, does not necessarily introduce elements or aspects that are not already present in the first-order experience, even if it changes the way in which those aspects appear. Reflective articulation is not necessarily imposed from without; it is not necessarily foreign to the experience in question. As Husserl puts it, in the beginning we are confronted with a dumb experience, which must then – through reflection – be made to articulate its own sense (Husserl 1950/1999, p. 77). This articulation requires a practised interpretation that is informed by the phenomenological method (see Chapter 2).

Heidegger argues in a similar fashion. He also insists that our lived experience is imbued with meaning. It has an inner articulation and rationality and is, importantly, in possession of a spontaneous and immediate self-understanding, which is why it can ultimately be interpreted from itself and in terms of itself. Phenomenological investigation must build on the familiarity that the experiential dimension already has with itself; it must draw on the implicit, pre-reflective self-referential dimension that is built into the very stream of consciousness. A true phenomenological description does not constitute a violation of experience, or attempt to impose a foreign systematicity on the experiential dimension, rather it is something that is rooted in and motivated by experiential life itself (Heidegger 1993, p. 59; 1994, p. 87).

How should one appraise the reflective appropriation of lived consciousness? Can reflection make the pre-reflective dimension accessible to us or does it rather distort it radically? Does the reflective modification involve a necessary supplementation or an inevitable loss? On the one hand, we have the view that reflection merely copies or mirrors pre-reflective experience faithfully, and on the other, we have the view that reflection distorts lived experience. The middle course is to recognize that reflection involves a gain and a loss. For Husserl, Sartre, and Merleau-Ponty, reflection is constrained by what is pre-reflectively lived through. It is answerable to experiential facts and is not constitutively self-fulfilling. At the same time, however, they recognized that reflection qua thematic self-experience does not simply reproduce the lived experiences unaltered and that this is precisely what makes reflection cognitively valuable. This is not to say that phenomenologists would claim that reflection is always trustworthy. Rather, the point they are making is merely that reflection does not necessarily have to be untrustworthy.

One way to put this is to say that the relation between reflection and the pre-reflective experience that is reflected upon involves a back-and-forth interpretive process. Since the experience that is reflected upon already involves pre-reflective self-consciousness, it has resources to confirm or disconfirm our reflective reading of it. A misreading of experience can be corrected by further experience and renewed reflection. In this regard there is nothing guaranteed or facile about reflection. In addition, to the extent that phenomenological reflection can be balanced with intersubjective reports and empirical investigations, a variety of techniques can help to confirm or disconfirm the particular results of reflection, including convergences (or dis-convergences) between reflective reports and behavioural and physiological measures (see, for example, Schooler and Schreiber 2004, pp. 22ff., who review evidence from studies of imagining tasks, mind-wondering, and assessment of one's own pleasure or pain).

For example, we can note that reflective self-consciousness involves a form of *self-division* or *self-fragmentation* that we do not encounter on the level of pre-reflective self-consciousness. This observation has at least three significant implications that span ontological, methodological, and normative dimensions:

- If reflection involves a kind of self-fission, it remains necessary to explain how such a fractured self-consciousness can arise out of a supposedly unified pre-reflective self-consciousness. As Sartre poignantly reminds us: the problem is not to find examples of pre-reflective self-consciousness, they are everywhere, but to understand how one can pass from this self-consciousness that constitutes the being of consciousness to the reflective knowledge of self, which is founded upon it (Sartre 1967). Thus, it will not do to conceive of pre-reflective self-consciousness in such a manner that the transition to reflective self-consciousness becomes incomprehensible. Sartre was, by no means, trying to deny the difference between a reflective and a pre-reflective self-consciousness, yet he insisted that the two modes of self-consciousness must share a certain affinity, a certain structural similarity. Otherwise, it would be impossible to explain how pre-reflective experience could ever give rise to reflection. It is a significant feature of our lived experience that it allows for reflective appropriation; a theory of self-consciousness that can *only* account for pre-reflective self-consciousness is not much better than a theory that only accounts for reflective self-consciousness. To phrase it differently, it is no coincidence that we speak of a pre-*reflective* self-consciousness; the very choice of words indicates that there remains a connection. The reason why reflection remains a permanent possibility is precisely that pre-reflective self-consciousness already entails a *temporal* articulation and differentiated infrastructure (Sartre 1956, pp. 153–55). Thus, most phenomenologists (Michel Henry is a notable exception) would argue that pre-reflective self-consciousness must be conceived not as a static self-identity, but as a dynamic and temporal self-differentiation. We will return to the issue of temporality in the next chapter.

- If reflection is characterized by a kind of self-fragmentation, there will always remain an unthematized spot in the life of the subject. Every reflection will contain a moment of naïveté since it is necessarily prevented from grasping itself (Husserl 1962, p. 478). Experiential life can thematize and disclose itself, but it can never do so exhaustively and completely. This insight was repeated by Merleau-Ponty, when he wrote that our temporal existence is both a condition for and an obstacle to our self-comprehension. Temporality contains an internal fracture that permits us to return to our past experiences in order to investigate them reflectively, yet this very fracture also prevents us from fully coinciding with ourselves. There will always remain a difference between the lived and the understood (Merleau-Ponty 1962, pp. 344–45). Thus, both Husserl and Merleau-Ponty questioned the absolute power of reflection.

- Reflection is a precondition for self-critical deliberation. If we are to subject our different beliefs and desires to a critical, normative evaluation, it is not sufficient simply to have first-personal experience of the states in question. It is not enough to be immediately and implicitly aware of them. Rather, when we reflect, we step back from our ongoing mental activities and, as Richard Moran has pointed out, this stepping back is a metaphor of distancing and separation, but also one of observation and confrontation. This reflective distancing is what allows us to relate critically to our mental states and to put them into question; it ultimately forces us to act for reasons (Moran 2001, pp. 142–43).[6]

CONCLUSION: DRIVING IT HOME

Finally, let's get back in our car and see if we can understand how we got here:

> If you have driven for a very long distance without a break, you may have had experience of a curious state of automatism, which can occur in these conditions. One can suddenly 'come to' and realize that one has driven for long distances without being aware of what one was doing, or, indeed, without being aware of anything. One has kept the car on the road, used the brake and the clutch perhaps, yet all without any awareness of what one was doing.
>
> (Armstrong 1981, p. 12)

It is often the case that Armstrong's example of the driver who seemingly drives unconsciously (Armstrong would say that the driver non-consciously perceives the road) and forgets how he got home is mentioned as a case that is similar to blindsight (see, for example, Carruthers 2005). But the kinds of experiences involved are clearly different. If we can say that in the case of blindsight we find non-conscious perception, and the justified claim by the subject that he is simply not conscious of the visual stimuli, this is not so in the case of driving home. When I drive, I do not do so unconsciously (*pace* Armstrong, Carruthers et al.). If my friend in the passenger seat asks whether I see that car weaving in and out of traffic, my response is not likely to be, 'No, sorry, I'm not conscious of any cars; I'm not really aware of the traffic.' Had I answered like this, it is rather unlikely that I would ever have obtained a driving licence.

As we drive home we are clearly conscious of the traffic, and even if we are lost in thought we are not necessarily lost *en route*. So why can't we remember how we got home? One way to explain this is to appeal to evidence that shows that in some circumstances it is quite possible to be conscious but to quickly forget that of which one has been conscious (Wider 1997, p. 167). The driving case can consequently be explained as one of consciousness-plus-quick-forgetting.

What about self-consciousness? Armstrong denies that the driver is self-conscious. But as we have suggested in this chapter, if the driver is conscious, she is also pre-reflectively self-conscious. When driving home, I know what I am doing and I can easily respond to questions about the traffic. But why don't I remember the details of my trip? This is not a matter of a lack of attention. Rather, it is an essential aspect of pragmatic action that if we are self-conscious of what we are doing our awareness and what we remember are specified at the most appropriate reportable pragmatic level. We'll see (in the chapter on embodiment) that for some aspects of our actions we are not aware of the perceptual-motor details involved, for example the shape my hand takes in reaching from the steering wheel to the gearstick. For other aspects of our actions we are necessarily aware of environmental objects (e.g. cars and roads) and minimally self-conscious of our own movement. The latter type of awareness, which is specified at a much lower level of description, is necessarily forgotten, and the quicker the better. It is a natural component of most motor (and motoring) behaviour that we quickly forget the details. Consider what would happen if we did not. Our attention could easily drift back to the details of what we have previously accomplished in the driving process. For example, I manoeuvre a difficult overtaking of another vehicle on a curve. Having accomplished that, I don't want to rehearse or reconsider my actions in the following minutes. Rather I need to attend to new traffic patterns. If I had to process every detail of my actions along the route for episodic memory, my mind would be full of useless information that could interfere with my current driving activity. For best performance I need to let the details of my previous experience go, and I need my cognitive energy to keep my attention fixed on the current situation. There is no doubt that I will be able to tell you that I have just driven home from the office (the most appropriate pragmatic level for that action), but there is good reason that I will be unable to tell you the details, how many cars I passed, or even to remember traversing my normal route. This is a level of conscious and self-conscious experience that exists at the time of my actions, but that I do not keep in mind for purposes of recollection.

It would be a mistake to think that the defence of the existence of a primitive form of pre-reflective self-consciousness constitutes the entirety of the phenomenological investigation of consciousness and self-consciousness. On the contrary, the phenomenological investigation of the relation between consciousness and self-consciousness is characterized by the fact that it is integrated into and can be found in the context of a simultaneous examination of a number of related issues, such as the nature of intentionality, embodiment, action, selfhood, temporality, attention, sociality, etc. As part of their analysis of the structure of consciousness, the phenomenologists also discuss – to mention just a few of the topics – (1) whether one should opt for an egological or non-egological account of consciousness, i.e. whether or not every episode of experiencing always involves a subject of experience; (2) how to understand the temporality of the stream of consciousness; (3) whether pre-reflective self-consciousness is characterized by an internal differentiation or infrastructure; (4) to what extent self-consciousness is always embodied and embedded; (5) how social interaction might change the structure of self-consciousness; (6) whether reflection can disclose the structure of pre-reflective consciousness or whether it necessarily distorts its subject matter; and (7) to what extent self-consciousness, although not being itself a form of object-consciousness, nevertheless presupposes the intentional encounter with the world. We will return to many of these issues in subsequent chapters.

NOTES

1   For some critical comments on the more specific details of Kriegel's account, see Zahavi 2004c.
2   For an informative comparison of the HOT and HOP models, see Van Gulick 2000, whose own HOGS (Higher-Order Global State) model could arguably be seen as a hybrid between standard higher-order accounts and a more phenomenologically oriented account.
3   Rosenthal (1997, p. 737) stipulates that we should regard mental states as conscious only if we are conscious of them in some suitably unmediated way, namely directly or non-inferentially. Otherwise, an unconscious mental process would qualify as conscious, simply because we could

infer that we would have to have it. Whether this is a justifiable move – a move fully warranted by the HOT framework – is a question we can leave for the HOT and HOP theorists to discuss.

4   Subliminal priming effects refer to the effects of stimuli presented in such a way that they do not reach the threshold of consciousness. Visual stimuli presented momentarily and removed extremely fast do not register consciously, but can still have an effect on the subsequent behaviour of subjects. A well-known experiment in the auditory domain is known as the two-channel experiment. Subjects wear headphones and are presented with two simultaneous streams of information, one in the left ear and one in the right. They are then asked to attend to only one of these, and to shadow it, that is, to repeat aloud whatever they hear in that ear. This calls for such high demands on attention that the subjects apparently remain unaware of what is presented to the other ear. Thus, they cannot identify, report, or recall anything being said in this other ear. However, various findings seem to demonstrate that even in the absence of any conscious awareness of these non-attended stimuli, their meaning can affect the hearer and even influence the interpretation of the attended messages. For instance, in what sounds like a somewhat barbaric experiment, certain words previously associated with electric shocks continued to produce changes in galvanic skin response when presented to the non-attended ear. This even occurred with words which were semantically related to the conditioned words (Velmans 2000, p. 199; also see Marcel 1983, for some classic experiments).

5   For an excellent discussion of this issue from an empirical standpoint, see Schooler and Schreiber (2004). See also the contributions in *Journal of Consciousness Studies* 18/2 (2011).

6   We have in the previous paragraphs talked of pre-reflective self-consciousness and contrasted it with the kind of self-consciousness that can be obtained through reflection. One slightly confusing factor is the presence in the current debate of another set of terms, namely, the concepts of reflexivity and reflexive self-consciousness. In a recent article, for instance, Van Gulick writes that some degree of reflexive intentionality seems inescapably required by the experiential presence of phenomenal consciousness, and that the unity of world and the unity of self are mutually interdependent, for which reason both unities must involve a substantial degree of reflexive higher-order intentionality and self-understanding (2006, pp. 28–30). Are reflection and reflexivity the same thing? As far as we can judge, whereas the term 'reflection' is used pretty much in the same way by most authors, the term 'reflexivity' is by no means unequivocal and is in fact used by some to designate completely different phenomena. Some use the terms reflexive and reflective synonymously. Others use the term reflexivity – and this is obviously what is confusing, particularly since reflection is called *Reflexion* in German – to designate the kind of pre-reflective self-awareness that we have been discussing. This is how the term is used by Mohanty, who defines reflexivity as the pre-reflective transparency of consciousness, and distinguishes it from reflection which is a higher-order intentional act (1972, pp. 159, 164, 168). We suspect this is also how Frankfurt is using the term in the passage quoted earlier. In his recent book, *The Idea of Self*, Jerrold Seigel writes that whereas reflexivity has to do with something automatic, something involuntary, something like a reflex, reflection is usually considered something intentional and wilful (something that can also establish a distance between consciousness and its content). Thus, in his view, the two terms indicate two distinct forms of self-reference, one passive and one active (2005, pp. 12–13). We find this clarification helpful, but ultimately no consensus on the issue seems forthcoming. To some extent, one simply has to be aware of this ambiguity.

FURTHER READING

José Luis Bermúdez, *The Paradox of Self-Consciousness*. Cambridge, MA: MIT Press, 1998.

Natalie Depraz, *La conscience: Approches croisées des classiques aux sciences cognitives*. Paris: Armand Colin, 2001.

Henry Ey, *Consciousness: A Phenomenological Study of Being Conscious and Becoming Conscious*. Bloomington: Indiana University Press, 1978.

Manfred Frank (ed.), *Selbstbewußtseinstheorien von Fichte bis Sartre*. Frankfurt am Main: Suhrkamp, 1991.

Uriah Kriegel and Kenneth Williford (eds.), *Self-Representational Approaches to Consciousness*. Cambridge, MA: MIT Press, 2006.

Jean-Paul Sartre, *Being and Nothingness*. Trans. H. E. Barnes. New York: Philosophical Library, 1956.

Jean-Paul Sartre, Consciousness of self and knowledge of self. In N. Lawrence and D. O'Connor (eds), *Readings in Existential Phenomenology*. Englewood Cliffs, NJ: Prentice Hall, 1967, pp. 113–42.

Evan Thompson (ed.), *The Problem of Consciousness: New Essays in Phenomenological Philosophy of Mind*. Calgary: University of Calgary Press, 2003.

Max Velmans and Susan Schneider (eds.), *The Blackwell Companion to Consciousness*. Oxford: Blackwell, 2007.

Dan Zahavi, *Self-Awareness and Alterity: A Phenomenological Investigation*. Evanston: Northwestern University Press, 1999.

Philip D. Zelazo, Morris Moscovitch, and Evan Thompson (eds.), *The Cambridge Handbook of Consciousness*. Cambridge: Cambridge University Press, 2007.

4 Time

Think about how we experience the world. In our everyday activities we move through the world without bumping into things. For example, I may see an attractive person walking towards me in a narrow hallway. I anticipate that there will be a point at which we will need to avoid bumping into each other; we seem capable of anticipating each other's movements and we usually have no problem in smoothly passing each other by. At the same time, I may be thinking that this person looks very familiar. Where have I seen her before? Yes, of course, I remember that she was at the philosophy lecture last night. As she has just now moved past me, I stop and turn around and say, 'Hey, weren't you at the philosophy lecture last night?' She actually seems to understand my sentence, stops and answers, 'Why do you want to know?' I immediately start to wonder where this conversation will lead.

This kind of everyday encounter, and indeed any and every sort of activity in which we engage, is permeated with aspects of temporality. We anticipate certain things that are about to happen – for example, the point at which we will manoeuvre around an oncoming person in the hallway. We remember certain things that happened in the past – e.g. at the philosophy lecture last night. But we also have to maintain a working sense of what has just occurred – e.g. I know that this person, having just passed me, is now just behind me, and I still have a perceptual sense of what she looks like. When I turn to speak, I anticipate that she will still be there. The formulation of my sentence, and her ability to understand it and respond, require the abilities to produce and to grasp units of meaning that are spread out over short amounts of time. My expectations, if I have any in regard to this person, and whether they are fulfilled or dashed, are projected into a future that has not yet taken shape.

We live in a coherent and meaningful world precisely because we are able to navigate through a stream of experience without getting lost – and our other abilities, like our ability to move through space, or to find our way into relationships in the social world, fully depend on our temporal navigations. Consider what would happen if the temporal structures of our experience were disrupted. Let's consider a disruption that would be similar to this in a very narrowly circumscribed area of our experience – vision. Neuronal structures in the medial temporal cortex (MT) are specialized for visual detection of motion. If this part of the cortex is damaged, by stroke for example, visual perception of form and colour may be preserved, but perception of motion is disrupted, resulting in a condition called motion blindness, akinetopsia, or motion agnosia. Someone who suffers from motion agnosia experiences the world as seemingly without motion, frozen in place, for several seconds. Things in the world may then suddenly seem to rearrange themselves in new positions. Motion agnosia patients have profound difficulty dealing with their environments, even though they may have clear vision for shape, distance, colour, etc. Imagine crossing a busy street where you see cars and know they are moving, perhaps by auditory clues, but simply can't see their movement (see Schenk and Zihl 1997; Zihl et al. 1983).

The disruption of the visual experience of movement in motion agnosia plays havoc with the person's abilities to make sense out of the world and to act in it. Aristotle noted the close connection between movement and time. And it is true that normally our perceptions of movement and our own movements have a coherence that stretches through all three temporal dimensions in a continuous and seemingly seamless flow. Temporal continuity seems absolutely essential for making sense out of our everyday experience. This is not to deny that there is discontinuity too. We can shift rapidly from one activity to another, we can move from one situation into a completely different one, and we can even experience disruptions and breakdowns where the flow of information or activity becomes quite confused. Ultimately, if we are to restore sense to these experiences, we have to take them up into a more cohesive temporal framework. Despite difficulties with the perception of motion, the motion agnosia subject is still able to function, because the greater part of her experience retains some anchor in a cohesive temporal structure.

Consider an even more profound disruption of temporal experience. What if our ongoing, present experience lacked a temporal coherence? What if, for example, I was unable to keep the just previous moment of experience in mind long enough to write it down, or was unable to anticipate events in the next second? Would my experience make any sense at all? Would I be able to, or even be motivated to, turn around and speak to the woman who just brushed past, or would she be out of sight and entirely out of mind? If she spoke to me, would I be able to hold in mind the first words of the sentence so that I could understand the sentence as a whole? Or would my experience lack meaning if it lacked temporal integration?

THE DEFAULT ACCOUNT

One of the core findings of memory research – an area of research that involves many different disciplines, including cognitive psychology, cognitive neuroscience, and neuropathology – is that memory is not a single faculty of the mind. Rather, it is composed of a variety of distinct and dissociable processes. Memory is involved when we hold information for brief periods of time, when we learn skills and acquire habits, when we recognize everyday objects, and when we retain conceptual information, and of course memory is involved when we recollect specific incidents from the past (Schacter 1996, p. 5). Standard textbooks will distinguish episodic memory, working memory, procedural memory, and semantic memory, i.e. they will distinguish our recollection of a past summer holiday, from our ability to read and retain an eight-digit phone number long enough to press the buttons on the phone, from our memory of how to ride a bike (a skill we acquired years ago), from our memory of the name of the current Secretary General of the United Nations (a name we once learned).

What motivates the distinction between different types of memory? The differentiation can be substantiated both phenomenologically and conceptually. But in standard literature the appeal is frequently made to neuropathology and to the findings of the various brain-imaging techniques. If one scans the brains of people asked to engage in diverse memory tasks, different parts of their brains appear to be particularly active depending on the type of memory task they are engaged in. More interesting is perhaps pathological findings, where people with different types of brain damage might lose one type of memory while retaining others.

In the case of anterograde amnesia or memory loss, new events are not held in mind long enough to be captured in episodic memory. A person with anterograde amnesia does not remember anything about his experience once his attention shifts to some new event. An interesting example of this was provided in the film *Memento* (2000). Leonard, the main character, is trying to solve a crime, but has to write everything down as he is experiencing it, because he is constantly forgetting what has happened, and even the fact that he is trying to solve a crime. He has important information and a list of projects tattooed on his skin so that he doesn't forget them. The disruption of his past also disrupts his future – what projects could count as important for him are determined by his past experience, so if his past experience is entirely wiped out, so is a meaningful future.

A famous real-life case concerns the patient, HM. He suffered from severe epilepsy, and as a result it was decided to remove the front two-thirds of his hippocampus as well as the amygdala. When HM woke up after the operation he couldn't remember what had happened during the previous two years (he was at that time 27). He had normal memory for events until around the age of about 25, but there was nothing after that. But not only was HM unable to remember his recent past, everything that he experienced after the operation would only stay with him for a few minutes and would then fade away.[1] So HM was in effect trapped in a small time capsule. His personal life ended when he was 25. Later in life, when asked, he tells people that he is a young man. He talks about friends and family members who have been long dead as if they were still alive. When given a mirror he is horrified to see the face of an old man looking back at him. The only consolation he has (although he does not know it) is that within a few minutes he will have forgotten the episode. Every time he meets a person, it is as if it were for the first time. He never complains about having to complete tedious psychological tests, because to him they are all new. HM, however, retains procedural memory. He is able to acquire new motor skills, although he has no recollection of ever having learnt them (Schacter 1996, pp. 137–39, 164).

A related case concerns a patient with severe retrograde and anterograde amnesia. He lacked episodic memory, but he was an avid golf player, and he not only retained semantic memory that allowed him to employ golf terms like par, birdie, and wedge, but also retained procedural memory and the ability and skill to play well. But due to his lack of episodic memory he would be unable to find the ball if the search was delayed. He would simply forget where it had landed (ibid., p. 135).

The devastating effects of various memory disorders can serve as illustration of a more fundamental point, namely that temporality, and certain temporal structures, are absolutely essential to experience, to perception, and to action. Indeed as Merleau-Ponty would put it, by analysing time we will gain access to the concrete structures of subjectivity (1962, p. 410). If we are to do justice to the dynamic character of our experiences, we cannot ignore the role of time. What is this temporal structure, and how does it work? In developing an answer to these questions, we need to sort out several issues. First, experiences never occur in isolation. We are not faced with a mere aggregate of temporal atoms. The stream of consciousness is an ensemble of experiences unified both at any one time, and over time, both synchronically and diachronically. We have to account for this temporal unity and continuity. Moreover, not only can we recollect earlier experiences and recognize them as our own, we can also perceive enduring, i.e. temporally extended, objects and events, such as songs and sentences, and we are therefore faced with the question of how consciousness must be structured for it to be a consciousness of something like identity over time. We also have to consider that our present experiences and cognitive processes are shaped and influenced conjointly both by our past experiences and our future projects and expectations.

We can start out by quickly sketching what might be considered a simple default account of the temporality of experience, or what phenomenologists call 'time-consciousness'. In daily life, we all assume that we do have a direct experience of change and persistence. We can hear a melody, just as we can see an immobile pyramid or the flight of a bird. However, if we at any given moment were only aware of what is perceptually present to us right here and now in the narrow moment, how could we ever perceive – not to speak of imagine, remember, or judge – temporally extended objects? One natural suggestion is that we should simply recognize that our perceptions (auditory, visual, etc.) are themselves temporally extended processes. The perception of the melody starts when the melody starts, and comes to an end at exactly the same moment as the melody ends (see Figure 4.1).

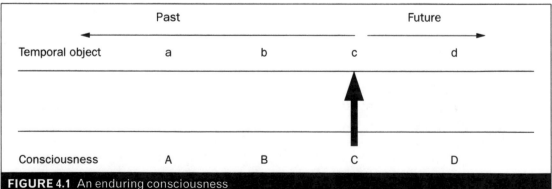

FIGURE 4.1 An enduring consciousness

Unfortunately, however, things are not quite that simple. If a perception has its own duration, it will contain temporal phases of its own. That is, there will be a time when the first couple of moments of perception (A and B) are past, when a third moment (C) is present, and a future moment (D) doesn't yet exist. So when C is present and occurring, there will be an awareness of the note c, the present slice of the temporal object (e.g. one note of a melody). But that just means that at every moment we are aware of what is present, and nothing else.

Moreover, on closer consideration, it is obvious that a mere succession of such conscious phases will not as such provide us with a consciousness of succession. To actually perceive an object as enduring over time, the successive phases of consciousness must somehow be united experientially, and the decisive challenge is to account for this temporal binding without giving rise to an infinite regress, i.e. without having to posit yet another temporally extended consciousness whose task is to unify the first-order consciousness, and so forth *ad infinitum*. In order to avoid this problem, many theorists have been tempted to adopt what Dainton has recently called the principle of simultaneous awareness (2000, p. 133). According to this principle, I am simultaneously aware of more than just the present slice of a temporal object; indeed, a sequence or succession of temporal slices of the object is experienced only as a sequence or succession if it is apprehended simultaneously by a single momentary act of consciousness (Figure 4.2). This is an idea developed by a number of nineteenth-century psychologists (e.g. Lotze 1887) and taken up also by William James (1890/1950).

The principle of simultaneous awareness is usually accompanied by the claim that the perception of the temporal object is not itself stretched out in time, but is momentary. Why do we need to postulate a momentary act of perception which embraces the full temporal sequence? We need a momentary act because, if it were extended, we would once again be confronted with the problem that an enduring consciousness is not as such a consciousness of duration. When we are aware of something temporally extended, something that includes the immediate past, the awareness itself must consequently be located in the present; it must be point-like and momentary (Dainton 2000, p. 133). The principle of simultaneous awareness obviously doesn't deny that there is a difference between hearing three succeeding tones and hearing the three tones simultaneously. The principle simply claims that the succession, in order to be apprehended as a succession, must be apprehended as

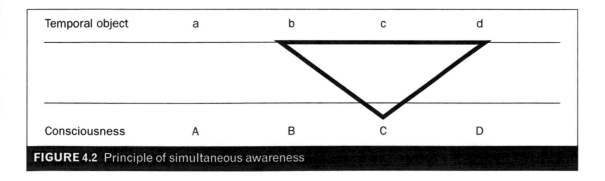

FIGURE 4.2 Principle of simultaneous awareness

a whole in a single momentary awareness; an awareness that is located in the pure now understood as an indivisible point or instant.

If one opts for this model, one has to make a choice between different versions of it. One option is to hold that a momentary act of awareness directly apprehends a succession of content with real temporal extension. On this view, an act of awareness may be momentary, but its scope is not. But this version is faced with a difficulty that has been dubbed the problem of repeated contents. Because the scope of any act of awareness must be limited, let us suppose for the sake of argument that it is limited to the apprehension of two succeeding notes, and let us then take the awareness of the sequence of the three tones Do–Re–Mi as an example. First, we will have an act (C) that apprehends Do–Re and then another act (D) that apprehends Re–Mi. If in line with the principle of simultaneous awareness we suppose that these two momentary acts are distinct, the same content ends up being experienced twice, once in C and once in D (Figure 4.3). But that of course is not true to experience. We don't hear Re twice, we only hear it once (ibid., p. 141).

Another option is to take the view that the contents apprehended by momentary acts of awareness are themselves simultaneous with the momentary act. But this is obviously problematic since the different temporal slices of a temporally extended object are not given simultaneously. We are led, then, to the following idea. Whereas the current slice of the object can be given perceptually, the former slice of the object is no longer present, and must therefore instead be re-presented when the current slice occurs. Thus, whereas we *seem* to be directly aware of temporally extended occurrences, we are in reality only aware of the *representations* of such occurrences (Dainton 2003, p. 8). One conclusion drawn by many advocates of this position is that a genuine perception of a temporal process is impossible. Our awareness of a temporal sequence is always representational. It is based on the simultaneous givenness of a manifold of contents that function as representations of a temporally extended object. The representation of a temporally distributed object consequently lacks the directness and immediacy that characterize perceptual presentations. This version of the principle of simultaneous awareness can then avoid the problem of repeated content by appealing to temporal modes of givenness. One and the same content is never given twice in the same manner; rather, every time it is given in different temporal modes, first as now, then as just-past, then as further-past, etc. Thus, rather than repeatedly experiencing the same

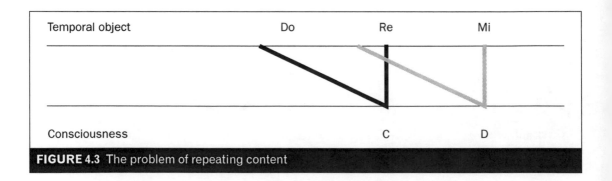

FIGURE 4.3 The problem of repeating content

content in the same temporal mode of presentation, we experience it as sinking smoothly into the past. However, despite this attempt at a solution, the question is ultimately whether an account that denies that we have a direct experience of change and succession can be satisfactory. Keep in mind that any perceptually experienced slice of an object will itself necessarily have a certain, if ever so short, temporal extension – e.g. one note of a melody itself has duration. So ultimately the position just outlined seems forced to deny the very possibility of perception of anything but an instantaneous present. We would not even be able to hear a full musical note. This seems to contradict our experience (see Gallagher 2003c).

So far the suggestions considered don't seem too promising. Let's take a look at an alternative model, one that was worked out by Husserl, who, in his phenomenology, attempts to do justice to the way we experience things.

A PHENOMENOLOGY OF TIME-CONSCIOUSNESS

It is close to standard practice to begin any discussion of time by quoting Augustine's famous words from his *Confessions* (bk 11, ch. 14): 'What, then, is time? If no one asks me, I know what it is. If I wish to explain it to him who asks me, I do not know.' Husserl follows this practice when he lectured on the problem of time-consciousness, and then added that 'we get entangled in the most peculiar difficulties, contradictions, and confusions' the moment we seek to account for time-consciousness (1966a/1991, p. 4). In fact, the analysis of time-consciousness is frequently considered to constitute one of the most difficult topics in phenomenology.

Husserl's main claim is that a perception of a temporally extended object as well as the perception of succession and change, would be impossible if consciousness provided us only with a momentary or pure now-slice of the object and if the stream of consciousness itself was a series of unconnected points of experiencing, like a line of pearls. If our perception were restricted to being conscious of what exists right now, it would be impossible to perceive anything with temporal extension and duration, for a succession of isolated, punctual, conscious states does not, as such, enable us to be conscious of succession and duration. Since we obviously do experience succession and duration, we must acknowledge that our consciousness, one way or the other, can encompass more than what is given right now – it must be co-conscious of what has just been, and what is just about to occur. The crucial question remains: how can we be conscious of what is no longer or not yet? Some have suggested that imagination or memory might play a crucial role, and that these faculties allow us to transcend the punctual now. We perceive what occurs right now, and remember what is no longer and imagine what has not yet occurred. But according to Husserl, we need to distinguish between directly experiencing change and duration and merely imagining or remembering it. In his view, we have an intuitive presentation of succession. Thus, Husserl would insist that there is a manifest phenomenological difference between seeing a movement (that necessarily extends in time) or hearing a melody, and remembering or imagining either. Moreover, he would deny that the apprehension of a present *representation* of the just-past can provide us with an intuitive awareness of something just-past.

In his own analysis, Husserl emphasized the 'width' or 'depth' of the presence: when I experience a melody, I don't simply experience a knife-edge presentation of one note, which is then completely washed away and replaced with the next knife-edge presentation of the next note. Rather, consciousness retains the sense of the first note as I hear the second note, a hearing that is also enriched by an anticipation of the next note (or at least, in case I do not know the melody, of some next auditory event). To illustrate: let us imagine that we are hearing a sequence consisting of the tones C, D, and E. If we focus on the last part of this perception, the one that occurs when the tone E sounds, we do not find a consciousness which is exclusively conscious of the tone E, but a consciousness which is still conscious of the two former notes, D and C. This does not mean that there is no difference between our consciousness of the present tone E and our consciousness of the tones D and C. D and C are not simultaneous with E; on the contrary, we experience a temporal succession. D and C are tones which *have been*, they are perceived as sinking into the past, which is why, rather than experiencing isolated tones that replace each other abruptly, we can actually experience the sequence in its temporal duration.[2] In other words, according to Husserl, the reason we can perceive melodies is that consciousness is so structured as to allow for this temporal presentation. When I am experiencing something, each occurrent moment of consciousness does not simply disappear at the next moment but is kept in an intentional currency, thereby constituting a coherency that stretches over an experienced temporal duration. To adopt some Jamesian terms, the basic unit of lived presence is not a 'knife-edge' present, but a 'duration-block', i.e. a temporal field that comprises all three temporal modes of present, past, and future (see James 1890/1950). See Figure 4.4.

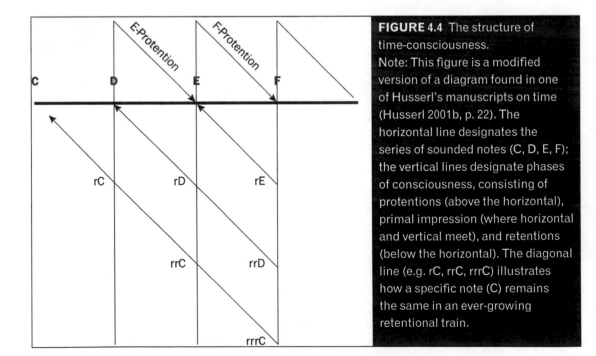

FIGURE 4.4 The structure of time-consciousness.
Note: This figure is a modified version of a diagram found in one of Husserl's manuscripts on time (Husserl 2001b, p. 22). The horizontal line designates the series of sounded notes (C, D, E, F); the vertical lines designate phases of consciousness, consisting of protentions (above the horizontal), primal impression (where horizontal and vertical meet), and retentions (below the horizontal). The diagonal line (e.g. rC, rrC, rrrC) illustrates how a specific note (C) remains the same in an ever-growing retentional train.

Husserl employs three technical terms to describe this temporal structure of consciousness. There is (1) a 'primal impression' narrowly directed toward the strictly circumscribed now-slice of the object. The primal impression never occurs in isolation and is an abstract component that by itself cannot provide us with a perception of a temporal object. The primal impression is accompanied by (2) a 'retention', or retentional aspect, which provides us with a consciousness of the just-elapsed slice of the object thereby furnishing the primal impression with a past-directed temporal context, and by (3) a 'protention', or protentional aspect, which in a more-or-less indefinite way intends the slice of the object about to occur thereby providing a future-oriented temporal context for the primal impression (Husserl 1962/1977, p. 202). If we listen to a conversation, it is the retentional aspect which keeps the intentional sense of the words of a sentence available even after the auditory signals are no longer there. Furthermore, when I utter a sentence, I have some anticipatory sense of where the sentence is going, or at the very least, that the sentence is heading to some kind of ending. This sense of knowing where the sentence (the thought) is heading, even if not completely definite, seems essential to the experience I have of speaking in a meaningful way. It is the protentional aspect of consciousness which provides us with this intentional anticipation of something about to happen. As Husserl also points out, it is protention which allows for the experience of surprise. If I am listening to a favourite melody and someone hits the wrong note, I am surprised or disappointed. If someone fails to complete a sentence, I experience a sense of incompleteness, in part because consciousness involves an anticipation of what the imminent course of experience will provide, and in these cases, what actually happens fails to match my anticipation. The content of protention, however, is not always completely determinate, and may approach the most general sense of 'something has to happen next'.[3]

According to Husserl's account, retention is not a particular thing in consciousness that we perceive; rather, we hear the just-past tone as just-past because consciousness has a retentional structure. There is no simultaneity between the retentional aspect of consciousness (which is current) and what is retained (which is just-past). The just-past tone doesn't remain present in consciousness, like some reverberation; rather, it is presented to consciousness as just-past. This is not the retention of real contents (the just-past tone is in no sense physically present); rather, consciousness retains it as part of an intentional structure. It retains the sense of what has just consciously passed, that is, of what I have just been conscious of. Thus, retention is a specific form of intentionality. Unlike primal impression, retention intends the past. Unlike episodic memory, retention presents the past; it does not merely re-present it. In short, it provides us with a direct intuitive grasp of the just-past, and is not a special apprehension of something present. As Husserl writes, 'retention is not a modification in which impressional data are really [reell] preserved, only in modified form: on the contrary, it is an intentionality – indeed, an intentionality with a specific character of its own' (1966a/1991, p. 118). To emphasize this once again, being retentionally aware of the just-past slice of the object or event doesn't entail having the just-past slice sensuously co-present in some strange distorted way.

Let's take a concrete example: if we look at a pedestrian who is crossing the street, our perception will not be restricted to capturing the durationless now-slice of his movement.

Perceptually, it is not as if the pedestrian suddenly appeared as out of nowhere; and further, we do not have to engage in an explicit act of remembering in order to establish the temporal context of his current position. Nor, however, will it be the case that all the previous slices of his movement are perceptually present in the same way as his current position. If that were the case, the pedestrian would perceptually fill the entire space he has just traversed. But we also have to avoid the idea that the past slices of his movement remain visually present in some vague ghostly manner. Temporal 'fading' into the past is not equivalent to the fading of a fading image that remains perceptually present. Retention retains the sense of my just-past experience of seeing the pedestrian, but it does not do so by keeping a faded image in consciousness. Rather, what we mean by retention is that at any moment what we perceive is embedded in a temporal horizon. Its meaning is influenced by what went before, which still intentionally registers in our awareness. For the just-past tone to be intentionally retained is for its *meaning* or *significance* to be retained as just-past.

Rather than being a memory that re-presents the object in question, retention provides us with an *intuition* of the just-past sense of the object (Husserl 1966a/1991, p. 41). This is precisely what is required if perception of succession is to be possible. Husserl would agree that the mere succession of conscious states doesn't guarantee consciousness of succession, but this doesn't entail the impossibility of a perception of duration and succession unless one also accepts the idea that perception is reduced to the grasping of a mere now-point, and that is precisely the idea that Husserl rejects. A perception cannot merely be a perception of what is now; rather, any perception of the present slice of an object includes a retention of the just-past slice and a protention of what is about to occur (1966b/2001, p. 315). Perceptual presence is therefore not punctual; it is a field in which now, not-now, and not-yet-now are given in a horizonal gestalt. This is what is required if perception of an enduring object is to be possible.

Given that retention constitutes the temporal horizon of the present – given that it constitutes what might be metaphorically considered the temporal equivalent of the visual periphery – it should be considered as part of perceptual consciousness rather than as a form of memory as typically understood. The just-past moment is not recollected. As James once put it, an 'object which is recollected, in the proper sense of that term, is one which has been absent from consciousness altogether, and now revives anew. It is brought back, recalled, fished up, so to speak, from a reservoir in which, with countless other objects, it lay buried and lost from view' (1890/1950, I, p. 646). We can only remember something which has been present and now has become past. Given this definition, retention cannot be said to be a form of memory, since it is involved in the very process of making something present for the first time. Admittedly, however, this argument presupposes a rather narrow definition of what memory amounts to. On a more liberal reading, memory is involved whenever information is retained over time, and on such a reading retention would constitute a form of (working) memory.

According to Husserl's analysis, experience of any sort (perception, memory, imagination, etc.) has a common temporal structure such that any moment of experience contains a retentional reference to past moments of experience, a current openness (primal impression) to what is present, and a protentional anticipation of the moments of experience that are just about to happen. Consciousness is the generation of a field of lived presence. The concrete and full structure of this field is determined by the *protention–primal impression–retention structure of consciousness*. Although the specific experiential contents of this structure from moment to moment progressively change, at any given moment this threefold structure is present (synchronically) as a unified whole. This analysis provides an account of the notion of the extended now found in James, Broad, and others. In the latter authors, the fact that we experience more than just a knife-edge present is offered as a solution to the problem of temporal perception, but is not itself explained. Husserl's analysis is an improvement on this since, rather than simply considering the lived presence as a brute given, it offers a phenomenological account of the dynamics involved in its constitution through a detailing of the retentional–primal impressional–protential structure of consciousness (see Gallagher 1998).

THE MICROSTRUCTURE OF CONSCIOUSNESS AND SELF-CONSCIOUSNESS

As we have mentioned, it is important to distinguish retention and protention, which are structural features of any conscious act, from recollection and expectation understood as specific types of mental acts. There is a clear difference between, on the one hand, retaining notes that have just sounded and protending notes about to sound while listening to a melody, and on the other hand, remembering a past holiday or looking forward to the next vacation. Whereas recollection and expectation presuppose the work of retention and protention, protention and retention are intrinsic components of any occurrent experience (be it a perception, a recollection, a fantasy, etc.) one might have. Unlike recollection and expectation, they are passive (involuntary) and automatic processes that take place without our active or deliberate contribution. If we compare retention with recollection, retention is an intuition, but an intuition of something which has just been but is not yet absent from our awareness, whereas recollection is a making present of a completed past event. When I recollect, the past event is reproduced in my present experience, but the recollected event is not presented as occurring at this time. It is exactly given as past – over and done with in relation to the present. If it is to be experienced as past, it must be given as past together with and in contrast to what is now present. The experience of this distance or difference is essential for recollection. If it is missing, if the past event is relived as if it were present, we would not be recollecting, but hallucinating.

Retention and protention are invariant structural features that make possible the temporal flow of consciousness as we know and experience it. In other words, they are a *priori* conditions of possibility of there being 'syntheses of identity' in experience at all: if I move around a tree, for instance, in order to gain a fuller perceptual presentation of it, then the various profiles of the tree – its front, sides, and back – do not appear as disjointed fragments, but are perceived as synthetically integrated moments. Temporal synthesis is a precondition for the perceptual synthesis with its entailed semantic integration. Thus time-consciousness must be regarded as a formal condition of possibility for the perception of any object.

Husserl's analysis of the structure of inner time-consciousness serves a double purpose, however. It is not only meant to explain how we can be aware of objects with temporal extension, but also how we can be aware of our own stream of experiences. To put it differently, Husserl's investigation is not only meant to explain how we can be aware of temporally extended units, but also how consciousness unifies itself across time.[4] As we have seen, the retention of, say, past notes of a melody is accomplished, not by a 'real' or literal re-presentation of the notes (as if I were hearing them a second time and simultaneously with the current note), but by retaining my just-past experience of the melody. Each phase of consciousness retains the previous phase of consciousness. Since the previous phase includes its own retention of a previous phase, there is a retentional continuum that stretches back through prior experience. At the same time that I am aware of a melody, for example, I am co-aware of my ongoing experience of the melody through the retentional structure of that very experience (see Zahavi 2003b).

There are thus two important aspects to this retentional continuity. The first, the 'longitudinal intentionality' (*Längsintentionalität*) of retention, provides for the intentional unification of consciousness itself, since retention is the retention of previous phases of consciousness. Second, since the prior phases of consciousness contain their respective primal impressions of the experienced object, the continuity of that experienced object is also established. Husserl refers to this as the 'transverse intentionality' (*Querintentionalität*) of retention (1966a/1991, p. 85). Although protention is asymmetrical with retention in many regards (Gallagher 1979; Varela 1999), there is clearly a longitudinal aspect to protention. That is, my anticipatory sense of the next note of the melody, or of where my sentence is going, or that I will continue to think, etc., is also, implicitly, an anticipatory sense that these experiences will be experiences for me, or that I will be the one listening, speaking, or thinking. In effect, protention involves an anticipatory sense of what I am about to do or experience.

It is this implicit, non-observational, pre-reflective self-consciousness, constituted in these basic intentional processes of time-consciousness, which allows the experience to be felt as part of my stream of consciousness. The sense of ownership or mineness for the experience thus involves no reflective, second-order, metacognition. On the contrary, Husserl's account of the temporal structure of consciousness is precisely to be understood as an analysis of the (micro)structure of pre-reflective self-consciousness (see Chapter 3 and Zahavi 1999, 2003b). It is called inner time-consciousness because it belongs to the innermost structure of the act itself. Moreover, this is why no infinite regress is generated:

> The flow of the consciousness that constitutes immanent time not only exists but is so remarkably and yet intelligibly fashioned that a self-appearance of the flow necessarily exists in it, and therefore the flow itself must necessarily be apprehensible in the flowing. The self-appearance of the flow does not require a second flow; on the contrary, it constitutes itself as a phenomenon in itself.
>
> (Husserl 1966a/1991, p. 83)

TIME-CONSCIOUSNESS AND DYNAMICAL SYSTEMS THEORY

To relate the phenomenological analysis of time-consciousness to the cognitive sciences, several theorists have explored the idea that the protentional–retentional process might be best explained in terms of a self-organizing dynamical system (Van Gelder 1999; Varela 1999). A dynamical system cannot be explained (or its behaviour predicted) based on the behaviour of the separate components that make up the system or in terms of synchronic, static, or purely mechanical interactions of parts within an isolated slice of time. For static models, time is a mere medium in which a mechanistic system operates, but is not intrinsic to the operation of the system. In a dynamical system parts interact in a non-linear fashion, reciprocally determining each other's behaviour through a process of self-organization in which the parts remain dynamically coordinated to each other over a period of time. With respect to cognitive experience, different processes in the brain, body, and environment become temporally coupled in dynamic coordination. According to this approach, then, every cognitive experience, from perceptual-motor behaviour to human reasoning, arises through the concurrent participation of several functionally distinct and topographically distributed regions of the brain and their sensorimotor embodiment (Varela et al. 2001). The integration of these different neuronal contributories involves a process that can be understood as an integration of three different scales of duration (Pöppel 1988; Varela 1999; Varela et al. 1981), the first two of which are directly relevant to protentional–retentional processes.

(1) the elementary scale (the 1/10 scale, varying between 10 and 100 milliseconds)
(2) the integration scale (the 1 scale, varying from 0.5 to 3 seconds)
(3) the narrative scale involving memory (the 10 scale).

Evidence for the first scale is found in the minimum amount of time needed for two stimuli to be consciously perceived as non-simultaneous, a threshold which varies with each sensory modality. Neurophysiologically this time frame corresponds to the intrinsic cellular rhythms of neuronal discharges within the range of 10 milliseconds (the rhythms of bursting interneurons, i.e. neurons that connect afferent and efferent neurons) to 100 milliseconds (the duration of an excitatory post-synaptic potential (EPSP)/inhibitory post-synaptic potential (IPSP) sequence in cortical pyramidal neurons which, for example, are implicated in cognitive processes in the prefrontal cortex). Such rhythmic processes are then integrated into the second scale, corresponding to the experienced living present, the level of a fully constituted, basic cognitive operation. At the neurophysiological level, this involves the integration of cell assemblies, distributed subsets of neurons with strong reciprocal connections (see Varela 1995; Varela et al. 2001). In terms of a dynamical systems model, the cell assembly must have a relaxation time followed by a bifurcation or phase transition, that is, a time of emergence within which an experience arises, flourishes, and subsides, only to begin another cycle.

Integration, Varela suggests, is due to neural activity forming transient aggregates of phase-locked signals coming from multiple regions. That is, neuronal firing rates become coordinated or coupled so that neuronal-level basic events that have a duration on the 1/10 scale, synchronize and thereby form aggregated neuronal activation patterns that correlate with cognitive operations on the 1-scale.[5] The synchronizing is not dependent on a fixed integration period measurable by objective time, but rather is dynamically dependent on a number of dispersed neuronal processes. The 1-scale temporal window is necessarily flexible (0.5 to 3 seconds) depending on a number of factors: context, fatigue, sensory modality, age of subject, and so on. Varela (1999) suggests that this integration–relaxation process at the 1-scale level corresponds to the living present, and is describable in terms of the protentional–retentional structure.[6]

The outcome of this neuronal integration manifests itself at a global level as a cognitive action or behaviour. The self-organization involved is not an abstract computation, but an embodied behaviour subject to initial conditions (specified, for example, as what the experiencing subject intends to do or has just done), and non-specific parameters (for example, changes in perceptual conditions or attentional modulation) (Gallagher and Varela 2003; Thompson 2007; Thompson and Varela 2001; Varela 1999). As Thompson puts it: 'the emergence of any cognitive act requires the rapid coordination of many different capacities (attention, perception, memory, motivation, and so on) and the widely distributed neural systems subserving them. The neurophysiological substrate for this large-scale coordination is assumed to be a neural assembly, which can be defined as a distributed subset of neurons with strong reciprocal connections' (2007, p. 331).

The data and the dynamical models show that the integrating synchronization is dynamically unstable and will thus constantly and successively give rise to new assemblies (these transformations define the trajectories of the system).[7] Each emerging process transitions from the previous ones in a way that is determined by its initial and boundary conditions. The preceding emergence is still present in (still has an effect on) the succeeding one as the trace of the dynamical trajectory (corresponding to *retention* on the phenomenological level). The initial and boundary conditions are important here. They are defined by the embodied-experiential context of the action, behaviour, or cognitive act. The boundary conditions shape the action at the global level and include the contextual setting of the task performed, as well as the independent modulations arising from the contextual setting where the action occurs (e.g. new stimuli or endogenous changes in motivation) (Varela 1999).

Just here, protention plays an important role in the self-movement of the flow. On the neurological level, the sort of mechanism that underlies protention is more appropriately thought of in terms of widely distributed and dynamical processes than in terms of localized functions. Protention is linked to particular subjective affective tonalities that reflect particular embodied and contextualized situations; as such, it helps to define specific boundary and initial conditions for the neurodynamics just described (Thompson 2007; Varela and Depraz 2000). In the initiation of an intentional cognitive act – for example if I decide to look for a particular object in the environment – I induce a transformation coloured by an affective disposition anticipating the change in perception. In the anticipation of a certain experience, I introduce exogenous order parameters that alter the geometry of the phase space.[8]

One important point to make is that the dynamics of the neuronal system are not closed off or isolated from the dynamics of the larger system of the body–environment, and that the further dynamical complexities that integrate brain–body–environment are reflected at the level of experience. More generally, the basic temporal (retentional–impressional–protentional) structure applies to motor control processes and bodily actions (Gallagher 2010a). It's possible to capture this more fully embodied and embedded model of cognition in 'open dynamical systems' which show how the dynamics of an experiencing agent are changed in different environments (Hotton and Yoshimi 2010). Yoshimi (2011), building on an example provided by Husserl, suggests that a set of dynamical rules can specify the anticipatory bodily movements (e.g. of the eyes) as one scans a familiar environment. What one perceives in the environment (perhaps some things that are not expected) will change the dynamics of bodily movement, the brain dynamics, and any further protentional processes.

IS CONSCIOUSNESS OF A TEMPORAL PROCESS ITSELF TEMPORALLY EXTENDED?

Is consciousness of a temporal process itself temporally extended and measurable in objective time? On the one hand, psychologists often try to measure temporal experience by the clock, even though they also recognize that time can pass slowly or quickly depending on certain cognitive aspects of the experience (see, for example, Friedman 1990). On the other hand, many phenomenologists have questioned whether the objective time of the clock can do justice to the time that we actually experience. To mention just one simple example: think of the way in which the experience of time (for instance the interplay between the three different temporal dimensions) is differently articulated in such diverse states as hope, anxiety, insomnia, and boredom. Think of the way in which the 'same' 30 minutes can be experienced differently depending on whether you are anxious, bored, or captivated. This is not to say that a stopwatch cannot measure something, but the question is what precisely it is that is being measured. Is the serial 'time of the clock' a form of temporality that is native to the experiences in question or is it derivative, the result of a subsequent objectification?

Ever since Aristotle noted an essential paradox about time, namely that the 'now' both changes and remains the same, philosophers who have considered the problem of time have been trying to resolve it. It is always *now*, and relative to this now, there is always a past and a future. That structure of time does not change. And yet each now seems to continually slip away, and we say that one now follows another, so that any particular now moves into the past, further and further. The British philosopher McTaggart (1908), writing around the same time as Husserl, tried to resolve the paradox by distinguishing between the A-series (past–present–future) – a psychological experience of succession that involves constant becoming (things constantly coming to the present and then moving into the past and then even further past), even though it maintains the same structure – and the B-series (before–now–after), a succession that maintains permanent relations among events (the Vikings discovered America before Columbus did, and that temporal relation will not change). Many theorists defend the idea that time is really a B-series, and that the A-series is not objectively real – it is rather a subjective or psychological phenomenon.

Husserl addresses this basic question differently at different points in his career. In

1904, he writes: 'the consciousness of a time itself [requires] time; the consciousness of a duration, duration; and the consciousness of a succession, succession' (1966a/1991, p. 192; see also 1966a/1991, p. 22). But if the experiential duration and unity of a melody is constituted by consciousness, and if our consciousness of the melody is itself experienced with duration and unity, are we then not forced to posit yet another consciousness to account for the experience of this duration and unity, and so forth *ad infinitum* (Husserl 1966a/1991, p. 80)? Husserl eventually became aware of these problems, and as he wrote:

> Is it inherently absurd to regard the flow of time as an *objective movement? Certainly!* On the other hand, memory is surely something that itself has *its now*, and the same now as a tone, for example. *No.* There lurks the fundamental mistake. *The flow of the modes of consciousness is not a process; the consciousness of the now is not itself now*. The retention that exists 'together' with the consciousness of the now is not 'now,' is *not simultaneous* with the now, and it would make no sense to say that it is.
> (Husserl 1966a/1991, p. 333)

Temporal experience is not an object occurring in time, but neither is it merely a consciousness of time; rather, it is itself a form of temporality, and ultimately the question is whether it makes sense to ascribe temporal predicates to time itself. Perhaps this worry can explain some of Husserl's somewhat enigmatic statements. Even if we ascribe some kind of temporality to the stream of consciousness due to its dynamic and self-differentiating character, we should not conflate the temporality that is intrinsic to consciousness itself with the kind of temporality that pertains to the objects of consciousness. Husserl would reject the claim that there is a temporal match between the stream of consciousness and the temporal objects and events of which it is conscious. The relations between protention, primal impression, and retention are not relations among items located within the temporal flow; rather, these relations constitute the flow in question. In short, we have to distinguish the objects that are constituted as temporal objects by the way they are structured by protention, retention, and primal impression from the relation between the constituting structures of consciousness. Just as my experience of a red circle is neither circular nor red, there is a difference between the temporal givenness of the intentional object and the temporal givenness of the experience itself. They are not temporal in the same manner. It makes, as Husserl writes, no sense to say of the time-constituting phenomena (the primal impressions, retentions, protentions) that they are 'present', 'past', or 'future' in the way empirical objects are (1966a/1991, pp. 75, 333, 375–76). Rather, it is their very conjunction which makes possible the senses of present, past, and future.

Occasionally, Husserl speaks of time-consciousness as an unchangeable form of presence (as a *nunc stans*) (2002, p. 384). It stands – to use James' phrase – permanent like the rainbow on the waterfall with its own quality unchanged by the events that stream through it (James 1890/1950, I, p. 630). But it is noteworthy that Husserl explicitly denies that this standing presence is to be understood as referring to merely one of the three temporal modalities (Husserl 2002, p. 384) – rather, it encompasses all three temporal modes. And while from a first-person perspective it certainly makes sense to say that I had an experience of joy, or a perception of a flower, and that these experiences endured and have now ceased and become past – after all, it would otherwise hardly make sense to say that I can remember a former experience. The very structure of protention–primal impression–retention, and hence the very field of experiencing that allows for presence and absence, cannot itself become past and absent *for me*.

Given the task of describing the stream of consciousness, a certain way of expressing it either captures it or does not, sinks or swims, so to speak, and this is something to be worked out, in part, in an intersubjective way. In our view, the notion of retention is a phenomenologically legitimate descriptive abstraction rather than a theoretical solution. The phenomenology of listening to a piece of music is such that when a series of notes in a melody are played, for example, I hear the melody and not just one note and now another, and now another, etc. Previously sounded notes are retained in the intentional experience so that as I hear the note that is now being sounded I hear it as part of a continuity of notes. This happens without persisting sense-data and without my having to activate a memory of previous notes. We find, in Husserl's texts, phenomenological descriptions of just such experience, which seem to be very much on the mark. Based on the experience and the descriptions of it, Husserl proposes the idea of retention as an attempt to characterize just such aspects of experience. It's a descriptive abstraction, and the only relevant question for the phenomenologist is whether it captures or distorts the experience. Occasionally, Husserl does describe things in a way that is too reified – the cross section of consciousness, and individual retentions and protentions as if they were elements that we could directly experience. In such cases the task is to try to pull such abstractions back closer to the experience by finding a more appropriate way of phrasing it, or by introducing various qualifications. This might be the beginning of a theorizing process, but it is one that is phenomenologically rooted. In any case, Husserl always intended phenomenology to be an intersubjective enterprise, open to corrections. In that spirit, he would welcome any improvements.

HISTORICITY

Our everyday experiences are normally permeated with a kind of temporal superglue – they are held together in the very short term by a strong and pragmatically important structure. As I walk down a hallway my experience of my own movement through the environment is coherent, as is my encounter with another person and our short conversational exchange. This is what the retentional–primal impressional–protentional structure of consciousness explains. But there is more to our lives than brief encounters and passing experiences, and there is more to the temporality of human existence than the interplay between protentions and retentions.

Memory, for example, with a weaker sort of glue, provides, sometimes explicitly and sometimes implicitly, a larger but sometimes less coherent framework for making sense out of our experiences. Our past knowledge of situations and events is activated continually and effortlessly as we make sense of what we experience. We may, however, remain unaware of inferences based on this knowledge, and sometimes they creep into our recollections and distort our memories. In fact, it is obvious that our memories can be distorted. This is why many psychologists and cognitive scientists, from Bartlett (1932) to Schacter (1996), have urged us to abandon the myth that memories are passive or literal recordings of reality. They are, as Schacter (ibid., p. 5) puts it, not like 'a series of family pictures stored in the photo album of the mind'.

One important source of error is due to impaired source memory. You might be right in remembering having seen or heard or experienced a certain event before, but you are wrong about the source of your recollection. You might for instance see a headline about a well-known person in a dubious magazine in a supermarket. Several months later you discuss the person's honesty and you remember the negative story, but no longer what its source was. The fact that you have forgotten that it came from a dubious source makes you more inclined to believe the story. So failures in source memory can open the door for the formation of unwarranted beliefs (Schacter 1996, pp. 116–17). This is just one example of how our cognitive systems are shaped (and sometimes mis-shaped) both by the limitations and by the effects of our past experiences.

Phenomenologists have certainly recognized the influence of implicit memory, i.e. those situations where people are influenced by past experience without any explicit awareness that this is the case. Even what appears as the most immediate experience may be permeated and influenced by earlier experiences and by acquired knowledge, as well as by a background knowledge that is shaped by the larger forces of culture and language. As Dilthey once put it, we are historical beings first, before we are observers of history, and only because we are the former do we become the latter (Dilthey 1992, pp. 277–78). Continuing along the same line, Dilthey would also claim that the richness of human nature only unfolds in history. To say that we are historical is to say that we are in history as we are in the world. I don't simply exist in the present and happen to have the capacity to envisage the future and remember the past. Rather, human reality is characterized by a kind of temporal stretch. The past continually serves as the horizon and background of our present experience, and when absorbed in action, our focus, the centre of our concern, is not on the present, but on the future goals that we intend or project. The future is salient while the present and the past constitute its background. To be human is already to be situated in the world, born (or thrown – as some phenomenologists say) into it without having chosen to be so, to be present to my surroundings, to be ahead of oneself in future projects (see Heidegger 1986/1996).

Human existence is characterized by historicity in the sense that the temporal horizon forms and shapes the present. Historicity means not simply that I am located at a certain point in history, but that I carry my history around with me; my past experience has an effect on the way that I understand the world and the people I encounter in the world. I have been among others as long as I remember, and my anticipations are structured in accordance with inherited forms of apperception and comprehension (see Husserl 1973a, pp. 117, 125; 1973b, p. 136). I see things the way others see them. I learn what is normal from others, and I thereby partake in a common tradition which stretches back through a chain of generations into a dim past. Normality is reflected in a set of norms that is set by a tradition. This is why Husserl claims that any normal person is historical as a member of a historical community (1973b, pp. 138–39, 431). The social world is not made up only by overlapping pasts belonging to individuals, but also by shared pasts belonging to groups and communities. Just as we inhabit a world made up in part of persons and things that are older than we are, so we participate in groups, communities and institutions that have been ongoing since before our birth. I understand myself as the inheritor and continuer of a tradition, or as Husserl puts it:

> I am a 'child of the times'; I am a member of a we-community in the broadest sense – a community that has its tradition and that, for its part, is connected in a novel manner with the generative subjects, the closest and the most distant ancestors. And these have 'influenced' me: I am what I am as an heir.
>
> (Husserl 1973a, p. 223)

Human time, in this sense, is neither the subjective time of consciousness, nor the objective time of the cosmos. Rather, it bridges the gap between phenomenological and cosmological time. Human time is the time of our life stories. It is a narrated time, a time structured and articulated by the symbolic mediations of narratives (Ricoeur 1988, p. 244). The beginning of my own story has always already been made for me by others, and the way the story unfolds is only in part determined by my own choices and decisions. In fact, the story of any individual life is not only interwoven with those of others (parents, siblings, friends, etc.), it is always embedded in a larger historical and communal meaning-giving structure. We will return to the issues of sociality and narrative in Chapters 9 and 10.

NOTES

1   One can encounter the same type of symptoms in massive cerebral tumours and in what is known as Korsakoff's syndrome (a profound destruction of neurons due to excessive intake of alcohol).

2   The precise span of perception can vary and depends upon our interest. If we are listening to a (short) melody we can claim to perceive the entire melody in its temporal extension, but if we are paying attention to the individual notes, one tone will cease being perceived the moment it is replaced by a new one (Husserl 1966a/1991, p. 38).

3   Husserl's analysis of the role of retention is much more detailed than his analysis of the role of protention, which is one reason why the secondary literature has mainly focused on the former. For recent overviews and discussions of Husserl's actual treatment of protention, however, see Rodemeyer (2006).

4   A more detailed account can be found in Husserl (1966a/1991). For an extended analysis of Husserl's model and its similarities and differences from James' notion of the specious present, see Gallagher (1998).

5   This currently has the status of a working hypothesis in neuroscience. Thompson summarizes: 'integration happens through some form of temporal coding, in which the precise time at which

individual neurons fire determines whether they participate in a given assembly. The most well-studied candidate for this kind of temporal coding is *phase synchrony*. Populations of neurons exhibit oscillatory discharges over a wide range of frequencies and can enter into precise synchrony or phase-locking over a limited period of time (a fraction of a second). A growing body of evidence suggests that phase synchrony is an indicator (perhaps a mechanism) of large-scale integration... Animal and human studies demonstrate that specific changes in synchrony occur during arousal, sensorimotor integration, attentional selection, perception, and working memory' (2007, p. 332). It is also important to note that there are no fixed time relations between neuronal events and correlated experience. This point has been made clear by Dennett and Kinsbourne (1992).

6   Grush (2006) points out that the dynamical analyses offered by Varela and others are not a perfect fit for Husserl's analysis of temporality. It is not clear, however, as Grush further claims, that such analyses confuse vehicle and content. For Grush dynamic processes are equivalent to neural vehicles; he equates retention with 'aspects of the current contents of awareness' (p. 425). Retention, however, is not an aspect of the content of awareness, but a structural feature of experience. The important correlation here is a structural one. If the dynamical processes described by Varela and others are processes that register information about what has just been happening in the system, that is just to say that the dynamical processes are retentional.

7   Here is a simple example of the kind of transition. If you place your hands flat on a table in front of you and start tapping your index fingers up and down so that they are in an alternating (antiphase) pattern (right finger up while left finger down, etc.) and you speed up this movement and do it as fast as you can, the back and forth alternating pattern will suddenly transition into a non-alternating (in-phase) synchronous movement, which is the optimal mode of synchronization at the higher frequencies (Kelso and Engstrøm 2006).

8   Empirical evidence for this can be found in studies of intentional movement. The intention to carry out a movement is coupled with a change in affective tone that varies in degree. One well-known case involves the readiness potential that precedes an intentional movement. For an intended finger movement, for example, a large slow electrical potential can be measured over the entire scalp, preceding by a fraction of a second the beginning of the motion. This is not necessarily a correlate of an intention (the intention may be much more complex than moving one's finger), but it gives some indication of how vast a reconfiguration of a dynamical landscape is involved in the anticipation of a fully constituted act. Such diffuse effects are in accord with mechanisms associated with neurotransmitters that condition the modes of response at the neuronal level (Gallagher and Varela 2003).

FURTHER READING

David Carr, *Time, Narrative, and History*. Bloomington: Indiana University Press, 1986.

Barry F. Dainton, *Stream of Consciousness: Unity and Continuity in Conscious Experience*. International Library of Philosophy. London: Routledge, 2000.

William J. Friedman, *About Time: Inventing the Fourth Dimension*. Cambridge, MA: MIT Press, 2000.

Shaun Gallagher, *The Inordinance of Time*. Evanston: Northwestern University Press, 1998.

Martin Heidegger, *Being and Time*. Trans. J. Stambaugh. Albany: SUNY Press, 1996.

Edmund Husserl, *On the Phenomenology of the Consciousness of Internal Time (1893–1917)*. Trans. J. Brough. Collected Works IV. Dordrecht: Kluwer Academic Publishers, 1991.

Toine Kortooms, *Phenomenology of Time*. Dordrecht: Kluwer Academic Publishers, 2002.

Paul Ricoeur, *Time and Narrative*, vol. 3. Transl. K. Blamey and D. Pellauer. Chicago: Chicago University Press, 1988.

5 Perception

The Primacy of Perception, the title of one of Merleau-Ponty's most famous essays, gives us a hint as to how most phenomenologists view perception. It is considered to be primary. The phenomenological dictum 'to the things themselves' can be seen as a call for a return to the perceptual world that is prior to and a precondition for any scientific conceptualization and articulation. As both Merleau-Ponty and Husserl point out, there is a more original relation to the world than the one manifested in scientific rationality. In our pre-scientific perceptual encounter with the world, the world is given concretely, sensuously, and intuitively. In daily life, we do not interact with ideal theoretical objects, but with tools and values, with pictures, statues, books, tables, houses, friends, and family (Husserl 1952/1989, p. 27), and our lives are guided by practical concerns. Phenomenologists remind us that our knowledge of the world, including our scientific knowledge, arises primarily from a first- and second-person perspective, and that science would be impossible without this experiential dimension.

The attempt to highlight pre-scientific perception can consequently be interpreted as an implicit criticism of scientism, as a rejection of the view that 'science is the measure of all things, of what is that it is, and of what is not that it is not' (Sellars 1963, p. 173). This criticism is by no means to be interpreted as a rejection of scientific rationality. The idea is not that a scientific exploration of reality is false, invalid, or superfluous. The target of the criticism is not science itself, but a certain inflated self-interpretation of science. Scientific discourse is embedded in the world of experience, in the experiential world, and if we wish to comprehend the performance and limits of science, we have to investigate the original experience of the world of which science is a higher-order articulation (Merleau-Ponty 1962, pp. viii–ix). Even the most exact and abstract scientific results presuppose the intuitively given subject-relative evidence of the lifeworld – a form of evidence which does not merely function as an unavoidable, but otherwise irrelevant, waypoint towards scientific knowledge, but as a permanent and quite indispensable source of meaning and justification (Husserl

1970, p. 139). The standardizations of procedures and the development of instruments that provide precise measurements have facilitated the generation and accumulation of third-person data and the establishment of intersubjective consensus. But without perceiving and embodied agents to manipulate, interpret and discuss them, meter settings, computer printouts, fMRI images, and the like remain meaningless. Scientific knowledge depends (although, of course, not exclusively) on the actions and experiences of individuals: it is knowledge that is shared by a community of experiencing subjects.

With regard to cognition and action generally, perception is basic and primary. Because of that, it is always first on the phenomenologist's list. Husserl, for instance, frequently distinguishes between *signitive*, *imaginative* (*pictorial*), and *perceptual* ways of intending an object or state of affairs: I can talk about a withering oak which I have never seen, but which I have heard is standing in the backyard; I can see a detailed drawing of the oak – or I can perceive the oak myself.[1]

Similarly, I can talk about how terrible it must be for homeless people to sleep on the streets; I can see a television programme about it – or I can become homeless myself and experience it. For Husserl, these various ways of intending are not unrelated. On the contrary, there is a strict hierarchical relation between them, in the sense that the modes can be ranked according to their ability to give us the object as directly, originally, and optimally as possible. The object can be experienced more or less directly, that is, it can be more or less *present*.

The lowest and most empty way in which the object can be intended is in the signitive act. These (linguistic) acts certainly have a reference, but apart from that, the object is not given in any fleshed out manner. On the basis of a signitive act, or perhaps someone else's speech act, I can believe that something is the case, but that's a far cry from perceiving that it is the case. Imaginative (pictorial) acts have a certain intuitive content, but like signitive acts, they intend the object *indirectly*. Whereas signitive acts intend the object via a contingent representation (a linguistic sign), pictorial acts intend the object via a representation (picture) which bears a certain resemblance to the object as seen from a certain perspective. It is only the actual perception, however, which gives us the object directly. This is the only type of intention which presents us with the object itself in its bodily presence (*leibhaftig*), or, as Husserl says, *in propria persona*. Thus, on the phenomenological account, perception does not confront us with pictures or images of objects – except, of course, in so far as we are perceiving paintings or photographs – but with the objects themselves. Consequently, when we say that something *appears* perceptually, this should not be understood to mean that the perceptually given is a picture or sign of something else (Husserl 2003, p. 107).

We can also speak of diverse epistemic levels. To talk about my notebook, to see an image of it, or to write in it, is not to be confronted with three different notebooks but with one and the same notebook given in three different ways. If I am looking for my notebook and find it, we are dealing with a situation where the found notebook, or to be more exact, the perceptually given notebook, satisfies or *fulfils* my intention. Whereas at first I had a mere signitive intention, it is now being fulfilled by a new intention, where the same object is given *perceptually*. What was first thought is now also seen. Husserl likens the relation between the empty linguistic intention and its fulfilment in perception to the classical relation between concept/thought and intuition (Husserl 2001a, II, p. 184).

The idea of perceptual fulfilment has a large scope. It is not the case of an either/or. Either there is (absolute) fulfilment, or there is none. On the contrary, there can be various degrees of fulfilment. Its range can vary, but so can its clarity. If I see a withering oak from afar, then I am certainly confronted with the oak itself; the oak is intuitively present. But it is not as optimally given as if I stood closer by and could discern more details (Husserl 2001a, II, p. 238; 1976/1982, pp. 143–44). At the same time it should also be emphasized that Husserl does not define the optimal perception by means of parameters like light and spatial presence. It might be difficult to see most things in the dark, but stars are among the exceptions. Husserl usually understands optimal perception as the kind of perception that offers us the object with as much information and in as differentiated a manner as possible (Husserl 1966b/2001, p. 205).

Husserl and Merleau-Ponty both consider linguistic reference to be less original and fundamental than perceptual intentionality. They would both claim that the former is rooted in a prelinguistic and prepredicative encounter with the world, and they would consequently counter the suggestion that all meaning is propositional in nature.[2] To detach sense and the sensuous (*Sinn* and *Sinnlichkeit*) from each other, to deny the continuity between the perception of an object and its predicative expression, would be the product of an intellectualistic abstraction that would make it incomprehensible how the perceived could ever function as a guideline for linguistic articulation. To deny the existence of prelinguistic cognition, and to claim that every apprehension of something as something presupposes language use would make it incomprehensible how we ever acquire language in the first place. The prefix pre- in this context refers not only to the fact that the experiences in question are temporally prior to language (or language acquisition), but also to the fact that our perceptual acquaintance with the world is a permanent condition of and a source for linguistic meaning. Even though a person might know terms like 'crimson', 'scarlet', and 'vermillion', he would lack a proper knowledge of the involved colours if he were blind.

Another characteristic feature of the phenomenological approach to perceptual intentionality is the emphasis on its direct or unmediated nature. The directness of perception means that there is no intermediary (image or representation) between perceiver and object perceived. There is no internal thing that stands in for the object in the world. Phenomenologists have consequently been critical of representational theories of perception. According to one classical formulation of this representational view, our mind cannot on its own reach all the way to the objects themselves, and the typical claim has therefore been that we need to introduce some kind of interface between the mind and the world if we are to understand and explain perception. Our cognitive access to the world must be mediated by some kind of mental representations relating to the everyday objects we ordinarily claim to perceive, as inner effects to external causes. To perceive the world is to generate a representational structure within the mind – something like a picture or a map that represents external reality. At the extreme, perception is viewed as a kind of point-for-point descriptive representation of the world generated in the mind, a coherent reorganization of the collection of atomistic sensations, or as something that does not go beyond an internal isomorphic neural collation generated by the constantly changing patterns of retinal stimulations.

To illustrate, let us assume that I am looking at a red rose. In this case, I have an experience of the rose, but of course, this cannot mean that the rose *qua* physical object is physically present in my consciousness. The representational theory of perception claims that the rose affects my sensory apparatus, and that this causes a mental representation of the rose to arise. According to this theory, then, every perception implies (at least) two different entities, the extramental object and the intramental representation. First, let's consider the classical expression of this kind of representationalism:

> I pretend not to teach, but to inquire; and therefore cannot but confess here again that external and internal sensations are the only passages that I can find of knowledge to the understanding. These alone, as far as I can discover, are the windows by which light is let into this *dark room*. For, methinks, the *understanding* is not much unlike a closet wholly shut from light, with only some little opening left, to let in external visible resemblances, or *ideas* of things without; would the pictures coming into such a dark room but stay there, and lie so orderly as to be found upon occasion, it would very much resemble the understanding of a man in reference to all objects of sights and the *ideas* of them.
>
> (Locke 1975, pp. 162–63)

How would phenomenologists appraise this attempt to clarify the mind–world relation? We can admit that nothing might seem more natural than to say that the objects I am aware of are outside my consciousness. And when my experiences, be they perceptions or other kinds of mental acts, present me with objects, how could this possibly happen except by way of some representational mediation? The objects of which I am conscious are outside my consciousness, but inside my consciousness I find representations (pictures and signs) of these objects, and these internal objects enable me to be conscious of the external ones. But as Husserl points out, this theory is not only empirically false, it is completely nonsensical. It conceives of consciousness as a box containing representations that resemble external objects, but it forgets to ask how the subject is supposed to know that the representations are in fact representations of external objects. Some have argued that a picture is something that resembles what it depicts, and that it is the resemblance which imbues the picture with its representational quality. This is known as the resemblance theory of pictorial representation. But in order for me to understand that x represents y by resembling it, I must have an access to y that is not mediated by x, so that I can compare the two in order to see the resemblance. If I know only the representation, I cannot know that it resembles the object represented. In addition, if one conceives of the mental representations as being like everyday representations (photos, paintings, symbols), one is immediately faced with the so-called homunculus problem:

> The ego is not a tiny man in a box that looks at the pictures and then occasionally leaves his box in order to compare the external objects with the internal ones, etc. For

such a picture-observing ego, the picture would itself be something external; it would require its own matching internal picture, and so on *ad infinitum*.

(Husserl 2003, p. 106)

At the limit, for a representation to operate as a representation, we have to assume a kind of non-representational perception. Husserl, considering external (i.e. non-mental) representations, denies that a picture or a sign is an object, which in addition to its other qualities, such as form, size, and colour also has an intrinsic representational, picture quality or sign quality. According to Husserl, a picture or a sign must be apprehended as a picture or a sign in order to function as a representation of something else (2003, pp. 106–7). It only acquires its representational quality by means of a special cognitive apprehension. If x is to represent y, x needs to be interpreted as being a representation of y. It is exactly the interpretation, i.e. a particular form of intentionality, which confers x with its representative function. More specifically, if x (a painting, a photo, an icon, a symbol, etc.) is to serve as a representation of something else, we first need to perceive x in order then to confer its representational quality upon it. In tandem with the homunculus problem, this is yet another reason why the representational theory of perception must be rejected. It presupposes what it seeks to explain.

One could object, however, that this classical and rather crude theory of representation is not the contemporary version of representationalism. After all, the Lockean account of perception, with its reference to internal pictures, has to a large degree been abandoned. In reply, however, we might add, *mainly by philosophers*. Some version of this view (mediated through the work of Hermann von Helmholtz) is still endorsed by numerous neuroscientists. Compare for instance the following quote by Damasio:

> When you and I look at an object outside ourselves, we form comparable images in our respective brains. We know this well because you and I can describe the object in very similar ways, down to fine details. But that does not mean that the image we see is the copy of whatever the object outside is like. Whatever it is like, in absolute terms, we do not know.

(Damasio 1999, p. 320)[3]

Similar ideas have been propounded by Francis Crick, who in his description of the so-called *binding problem* claims that one of the striking features of our internal picture of the visual world is how well organized it is (1995, p. 232), and that although we know how the visual parts of the brain take the picture (the visual field) apart, we still don't know how the brain puts it all together (ibid., p. 22). More generally, many vision scientists still conceive of vision as a process where we, on the basis of what is proximally present, namely images in the head or eye, seek to discover (by way of inference) what is present out there, in the world. As Richard Gregory writes: 'We are given tiny distorted upside-down images in the eye, and we see solid objects in surrounding space. From patterns of stimulation on the retinas we perceive the world of objects, and this is nothing short of a miracle' (1997, p. 9).

As long as this kind of view is meant to suggest that we actually perceive internal pictures, it is open to phenomenological criticism; not only is it not in accordance with phenomeno-logical evidence, but the view also entails a highly problematic use of the notions of both 'perception' and 'picture'. Rather than saying that the perceiving brain constructs an internal representation of the perceived world, it would be far less controversial simply to claim that our brain enables us to see a visual scene.

In contrast, however, if the claim is that in order to explain our perceptual experience of external objects we must make reference to various representational processes on the subpersonal level, the phenomenological criticism might at first seem to lose hold. After all, how could phenomenologists possibly be in a position to specify what goes on at the subpersonal level? But perhaps this underestimates some of the force of the phenomeno-logical arguments. Not only is there the question of what precisely representation might mean on the subpersonal level, but more importantly, even if one were to (reluctantly) accept that it is coherent to speak of subpersonal representations, it is still an open question whether the existence of such entities would count in favour of a representationalist account of perception. It is one thing to argue that subpersonal representations (which may mean simply, neuronal activation patterns) are among the internal enabling conditions for perception, and something quite different to argue that perception itself is representational in character.

In Chapter 6, which deals more broadly with the concept of intentionality, we will consider further arguments against the representationalist account of the mind. For now, let it simply suffice to say that phenomenologists conceive of perception as a direct embodied involvement with the world. A rather neat articulation of such an alternative non-represen-tionalist view of perception has recently been offered by Alva Noë:

> This claim about the world-involving character of perceptual experience – that experience is an encounter with things and situations – is not compatible with any old metaphysical or empirical picture of perception and its nature. For in presenting perceptual experience as a kind of *involvement* with or *entanglement* with situations and things, the phenomenology presents experience as something that could not occur in the absence of situations and things. Phenomenology reveals perceiving, then, to be a condition whose nature depends *essentially* on the presence and involvement of the world encountered. If there were no object, or no situation, then there could be no contact with or involvement with them, which is just to say that there could be no perceptual experience.
>
> (Noë 2007b, p. 235)

Noë is here developing an *enactive* account of perception first enunciated in these terms by Varela et al. (1991) who, in turn, were building on aspects of Merleau-Ponty's phenom-enology of perception. This also makes it clear that when the phenomenologist talks about direct perception, this does not mean context-free perception; perception is always situated in some physical environment, and normally within social and cultural environments. It is also a temporal process in which meaning, including our recognition of the thing perceived, is constrained by our past experience and our present intentions. Nor does this view deny that there are complex subpersonal processes, embodied processes that include brain processes, forming part of the perceptual whole. More specifically, for this kind of enactive phenomenology, perception should be understood in terms of its direct and holistic involvement with motor action.

PERCEPTUAL HOLISM

Phenomenology's emphasis on the *primacy of perception* might remind one of empiricism, but on closer examination it should be clear that there are numerous differences. In the eighteenth century, the French philosopher Condillac proposed a thought experiment. He suggested that we think of a statue bereft of any perceptual abilities, and then add one sensory modality at a time in order to consider the effects of perceptions in the visual, tactile, auditory, etc., domains. The question however is whether a statue, i.e. an immobile entity, without the capacity to move, would ever be able to enjoy perceptual experiences. Moreover, Condillac presupposed that it would make sense to construct sensory experience one modality at a time. As an empiricist, he thought that we could make sense out of sensing by considering how isolated sensory data organized themselves into object perception. Both phenomenology and science tell us that this is not the way it works. We should not think of perception as being built up out of small atoms of sense data; nor can we think of it as a collection of separate sense modalities. Indeed, we have good reason to think that perception is itself part of a larger whole. Let us look at each of these claims in turn.

In *Phenomenology of Perception*, Merleau-Ponty criticized the empiricist idea that perception is composed of sensations, taken as units of experience. As he points out, we simply do not experience sensations per se – 'this notion corresponds to nothing in our experience' (1962, p. 3). Or, as Heidegger points out,

> We never really first perceive a throng of sensations, e.g. tones and noises, in the appearance of things ... rather we hear the storm whistling in the chimney, we hear the three motored plane, we hear the Mercedes in immediate distinction from the Volkswagen. Much closer to us than all sensations are the things themselves. We hear the door shut in the house and never hear acoustical sensations of even mere sounds. In order to hear a bare sound we have to listen away from things, divert our ear from them, i.e. listen abstractly.
>
> (Heidegger 1964, p. 656)

Rather than being true elementary components of perceptual experiences, sensations are theoretical constructs. Consider the simplest experience of a patch of white colour against a background:

> All the points in the patch have a certain 'function' in common, that of forming themselves into a 'shape'. The color of the shape is more intense, and as it were more resistant than that of the background; the edges of the white patch 'belong' to

it, and are not part of the background although they adjoin it: the patch appears to be placed on the background and does not break it up. Each part arouses the expectation of more than It contains, and this elementary perception is therefore already charged with a meaning.

(Merleau-Ponty 1962, pp. 3–4)

It might be objected that each point of the patch contributes to, adds to, the final composition, and so it is only by sensing each point that we achieve a perception of the whole. As Merleau-Ponty points out, however, this is to ignore the fact that we perceive a gestalt, where each point, and the object itself, are against a background – 'the perceptual "something" is always in the middle of something else, it always forms part of a "field"' (Merleau-Ponty 1962, p. 4). In addition, empiricism also forgets the subject of perception. The perceived object is always contextualized, not just by its physical surroundings, but by the particular projects and interests of the perceiver, the particular actions and potential actions that the perceiver is engaged in or could be engaged in, and other aspects of experience that are constituted across sense modalities and emotional dimensions. Only in relation to such intermodal experiences, emotions, actions, and contexts can we capture the nature of perception.

The role of perceptual and pragmatic contexts, along with the 'collaboration' of sensory and motor systems in a complex and variable neurophysiological processing, is to generate stability within the instabilities of perception. In that stability and in the processes of integration we find, not the isolated datum of sensation, but 'a formation already bound up with a larger whole, already endowed with a meaning' (ibid., p. 9). This phenomenological critique of sensation theory – a theory that ignores the context and pragmatic purposes of the perceiver – implies a larger set of questions about how to do cognitive science. As we experiment and build theories, we run the risk of positing theoretical mechanisms that aren't really there. A science that tries to account for experience in objective terms 'introduces sensations which are things, just where experience shows that there are meaningful patterns. ... It requires that two perceived lines, like two [objectively measurable] lines, should be equal or unequal ... without realizing that the perceived, by its nature, admits of the ambiguous, the shifting, and is shaped by its context' (ibid., p. 11).[4]

Think of the well-known Müller-Lyer lines (Figure 5.1). Why do these lines, which are objectively of equal length, appear to be of different lengths? The fact that they are drawn

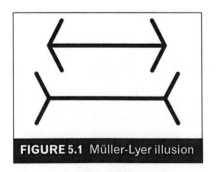

FIGURE 5.1 Müller-Lyer illusion

with arrows or tails changes them so that they are not perceptually equal. If these lines were physical objects that I could pick up and use, iron rods for example, I would necessarily treat them as unequal, both in terms of how I would grab them, and in terms of what I could do with them. My perception reads these pragmatic aspects into its visual estimations. If we erased the arrows and tails, we would have two identical things, and could easily see their equal lengths. 'That is to say, an isolated, objective line, and the same line taken in a figure, cease to be, for perception [which means, for action, and for pragmatic purposes] the same line' (ibid.).

In the 'Ebbinghaus illusion' (Figure 5.2), the centre circle to the left is perceived as smaller than the centre circle to the right. They are, however, objectively of equal diameters. How should we describe and interpret this finding? It is usually presented as an example of a robust visual illusion, and in that sense, we might say that we perceive incorrectly. But an alternative interpretation would be that we perceive these circles in precisely the right way, and that we are simply confronted with a vivid illustration of the classical gestalt principle according to which the context influences our perception of the parts. Indeed, if one were to perceive the two centre circles as being of equal size, this would be a misperception, a failure of perception, rather than an accurate and veridical one, because one would fail to perceive the available perceptual gestalt.[5] This is precisely what happens in some individuals with schizophrenia whose perceptual processes are not properly constrained by gestalt effects; they see the two circles as being the same size (Horton and Silverstein 2011).

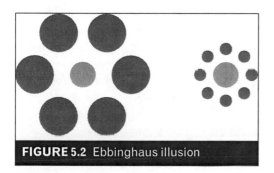

FIGURE 5.2 Ebbinghaus illusion

Another reason why the attempt to explain perception in terms of an amalgam of sensory data fails, is that we perceive both more and less than what is sensorially given. This is a curious thought, but one we find developed in the basic analysis of perception provided by Husserl. When I see an object, say an armchair, the object is never given in its totality but always incompletely, in a certain restricted profile or adumbration. It is never the entire armchair, including its front, backside, underside, and inside, which is given intuitively, not even in the most perfect perception. The same applies to tactile perception. Despite this, the object of my perception is exactly the appearing object and not the adumbration. I perceive the chair, for example, and not the perspectively given surface of the front or the back, seat, and legs of the chair. Of course, I can change my focus to intend the surface of the leg (instead of the whole chair), but that will be given in profiles as well. Our perceptual consciousness is consequently characterized by the fact that we persistently transcend the perspectively appearing profile in order to grasp the object itself. That is, perception furnishes us with a full object consciousness, even though only part of the perceived object is intuitively given (Husserl 1973c/1997, pp. 49–50).[6] The central question is: How is this possible? According to Husserl, the reason why we perceive the armchair itself, although it is actually only a single profile which is intuitively present, is because of the contribution of what he terms *horizonal intentionality*. Husserl claims that our intuitive consciousness of the present profile of the object is always accompanied by an intentional consciousness of the *object's horizon* of *absent* profiles (Husserl 1970, p. 158). Were we only directed towards the intuitively given, no perceptual consciousness of the very object would be possible:

The improperly appearing objective determinations are co-apprehended, but they are not 'sensibilized,' not presented through what is sensible, i.e. through the material of sensation. It is evident that they are so apprehended, for otherwise we would have no objects at all before our eyes, not even a side, since this can indeed be a side only through the object.

(Husserl 1973c/1997, p. 55)

Every spatiotemporal perception (ordinarily termed 'external perception') can be deceptive, although it is a perception that, according to its own meaning, is a direct apprehension of the thing itself. According to its own meaning it is anticipatory – the anticipation [*Vorgriff*] concerns something cointended – and, in such a radical fashion, that even in the content of that which is perceptually given as itself, there is, on closer inspection, an element of anticipation. In fact, nothing in perception is purely and adequately perceived.

(Husserl 1959, p. 45)

The meaning of the presented profile depends upon its relation to the absent profiles of the object, and no perceptual awareness of the object would be possible if our awareness were restricted to the intuitively given. In other words: in order for a perception to be a perception-of-an-object, it must be permeated by a horizonal intentionality which intends the absent profiles, bringing them to a certain *appresentation* (Husserl 1970, p. 158; 1962/1977, p. 183; see below for more on this concept of appresentation). This is not only the case in vision but also in, say, tactile perception. When, without looking, I hold an object larger than my hand, the surface of my hand covers only part of the object, but I nevertheless have the sense that the object is composed of more than just the surfaces that I touch (Noë 2004, p. 60). Moreover, my perception of an object is also influenced by other objects in the background, by what can be called the outer horizonal structure.

We not only see more than we see, in the sense just outlined, we also see less than we think we see. If someone holds a bright red apple behind me and gradually moves it into the periphery of my visual field, my ordinary assumption might be that I would certainly be able to identify the colour of the object as it enters my peripheral field. In fact, as Dennett (1991) points out, we are unable to discern colour in the peripheral visual field, and it is only when the apple is moved closer to the focal point of vision that we are able to perceive the colour, and the apple as such. Our visual awareness is consequently not as fully detailed as we may think it is. Focus your visual attention on this word: gorilla. If you don't move your eyes (no peeking, please) you will not be able to process many other words on the page (including these), although they certainly seem to be there in your visual field (ibid., p. 49). One possible interpretation of this finding is that we have to go after the information, and that we do so as we need it. It's not all there in our mind. If it were we could close our eyes and read the rest of the page off of the representation that we supposedly have. Try it and see how far you get. Other experiments show that we are often incapable of seeing things happen right before our eyes. This is referred to as change blindness or inattentional blindness.[7] In these experiments, we discover that in observing a scene that gradually changes, or even one that dramatically changes, whether we are attending to some feature in specific, or even looking for what precisely is changing, our ability to notice changes is extremely poor.

We are pragmatic perceivers. We don't have to clutter up our minds with representations or internal models that we would need to constantly update, since the information we need is easily available all around us.[8] Of course, we do have to go after it, selectively. We have to move our eyes; we have to turn our heads; we have to reposture our bodies; we have to reach and grab and pull things closer to us and manipulate them so we can examine them, or if they are too big to grab, we have to walk over to them and around them. In this regard the body is the active perceiver, and not a mediator between mind and world. The role of the body in perception is not properly or fully captured by the claim, for example, that it is by virtue of bodily sensations that we tactilely perceive objects in the environment (e.g. Richardson 2011). This explanation ignores the role of the perceiver's motor and action capacities. A heavy piece of exercise equipment feels different – different to the touch – for the trained athlete than it does to the trained philosopher who spends most of her day tapping on her laptop.

The phenomenology of perception supports what has become known as the enactive theory of perception. The idea of enactive perception has been around for some time, although recently it has drawn on both scientific and phenomenological resources to make it a viable alternative to representationalist views. John Dewey, in his 1896 essay, 'The Reflex Arc Concept in Psychology', maintained against sensation theory that in perception we begin

> not with a sensory stimulus, but with a sensorimotor coordination ... it is the movement which is primary, and the sensation which is secondary, the movement of body, head and eye muscles determining the quality of what is experienced. ... [In audition] the sound is not a mere stimulus, or mere sensation; it again is an act. ... It is just as true to say that the sensation of sound arises from a motor response as that the running away is a response to [a scary] sound.
>
> (Dewey 1896, p. 358)

In effect, perception is not a passive intake of information. Perception involves activity – for instance, the movement of our body. As Gibson (1986, pp. 53, 205) points out, we see with mobile eyes set in a head that can turn and is attached to a body that can move from place to place; a stationary point of view is only the limiting case of a mobile point of view. What we see and hear and touch and taste and smell (or avoid smelling, etc.) is shaped by what we do, and what we are capable of doing – our pragmatic possibilities and the sensorimotor capacities of our bodies. In ordinary experience, perception and movement are always united. I touch something by moving the arm. I see something by moving the head and eyes. What is perceived is perceived as nearby and perhaps reachable, or further way, as something that can be approached and explored.

Husserl, for example, pointed to the close connection between perception and kinaes-thesia (sense of movement). Our embodied movement participates in seeing, touching, hearing, etc. thereby informing our perceptual grasp on the world. Our perceptual organs (eyes, hands, ears, etc.) function together with our body's kinaesthetic experience. My movement, my doing something, is 'bound together in a comprehensive unity'. The way that objects appear in perception is not independent of the kinaesthetic dimension; they work together to produce the fulfilled meaning of the objects (see Husserl 1970, p. 106).

We can illustrate Husserl's idea with a concrete example. I am taking a look at my friend's new dual-fuel vehicle, and am standing in front of it. Whereas the front of the car is correlated with my particular bodily position, the horizon of the co-intended but momentarily absent profiles of the car (its back, sides, bottom, etc.) is correlated with my kinaesthetic horizon, i.e. with my capacity for possible movement. The absent profiles are linked to an intentional 'if–then' connection. If I move in this way, then this profile will become visually or tactually accessible. The back of the car which I do not see has the meaning of 'the back of the same car I am currently perceiving' because it can become present through the execution of a quite specific bodily movement on my part. One should consequently say that perceptual intentionality presupposes a moving and therefore embodied subject (Husserl 1973c/1997, p. 176). In short, the crucial point made by Husserl is not that we can perceive movement, but that our very perception presupposes movement (see Husserl 1970, p. 161; 1966b/2001, p. 15). To understand perception is to understand the intentionality of our own body (Husserl 1962/1977, pp. 196–97).

Perceptual experience is not determined simply by neuronal states that are activated by sensory input. Nor is it fully determined by neuronal processes in the dorsal visual pathway that perceptually prime the body for movement and action. It also depends on the sensorimotor skills of the perceiver and the possibilities afforded by the environment. As a rule, perception is an embodied coping with the environment. Merleau-Ponty claims that vision and perception more generally are forms of action (1962, p. 377), and this is just the view expressed by proponents of enactive perception. Consider, for instance, the following programmatic statement by Alva Noë, in the very start of his book, *Action in Perception*:

> Perception is not something that happens to us, or in us. It is something we do. Think of a blind person tap-tapping his or her way around a cluttered space, perceiving that space by touch, not all at once, but through time, by skilful probing and movement. This is, or at least ought to be, our paradigm of what perceiving is. The world makes itself available to the perceiver through physical movement and interaction. ... [A]ll perception is touch-like in this way: Perceptual experience acquires content thanks to our possession of bodily skills. *What we perceive* is determined by what we do (or what we know how to do); it is determined by what we are *ready* to do. In ways I try to make precise, we enact our perceptual experience; we act it out.
>
> (Noë 2004, p. 1)

Where the action is, for enactive theorists, isn't in the brain. Vision isn't a representation that emerges in a network of neurons. Rather, it's the action of the organism as a whole, exploring the environment. If we are in the world and can access the environmental detail relevant to our needs, there is no need to create an internal representation that would be a redundant copy of that detail. Just as when I need to talk to a friend, and she is standing right in front of me, it would be odd to call her on the phone, so it is odd to think that although the environment is immediately present, we need a representational model of it to perceive it. A nice illustration of how the environment can aid our cognitive capacities is found in a recent study comparing novice and expert bartenders. When receiving the cocktail order, the experts would select and array distinctively shaped glasses. They would then use these persistent cues to help recall and sequence the order. In tests where uniform glassware are used, the performance of the experts plummets, whereas the performance of novices remains unaffected (Gibbs 2006, p. 143). For a more sober example, just think of how you determine whether you need to purchase more milk: by remembering the number of bottles you have bought, and subtracting all the ones you have emptied, or simply by looking in the refrigerator? (Haugeland 1998).

To emphasize that perception is action, however, should not exclude consideration of more passive aspects of perception. Perception is not entirely action, although it certainly always involves my possible action. There are passive aspects of perception that are due to the fact that the environment is not neutral in regard to how my body gears itself into the world. Our perception of the world, as Heidegger's notion of the 'ready-to-hand' and Gibson's notion of affordances show, is of an environment that affects us and elicits our action. This is consistent, too, with the concept of 'forcible presence', as explicated in the enactive theory of perception:

> *Forcible presence* is the fact that, contrary to other mental states like my knowledge of history, for example, a sensory experience imposes itself upon me from the outside, and is present to me without my making any mental effort, and indeed is mostly out of my voluntary control.
>
> (Myin and O'Regan 2002, p. 30)

The world is experienced, not as a fully formed presence, but as a set of possibilities determined by an ongoing dynamic interplay of environmental opportunities and sensori-motor abilities. This is another way of saying that I am *in-the-world*, and that my experience is shaped by the insistence of the world as much as it is by my embodied and enactive interests.

Husserl distinguishes between activity and passivity. Activity, making a positive cognitive move, is apparent in acts of attending, judging, valuing, wishing, and so forth. Passivity concerns the experience of involuntary influence, when things happen to me. But Husserl makes a second distinction between *receptivity* and *affectivity*. Receptivity involves responding to something that is passively affecting me; it presupposes a prior affection (see Zahavi 1999, p. 116). Affection concerns affect and the feeling of being influenced or perturbed. In perception, whatever becomes noticeable to you must already have been affecting you; it must have pre-established an affective force that manifests itself as it captures your attention. Movements and loud noises in the environment are like this. They are perceptually salient; they capture our attention whether we want them to or not.

CONCEPTUALITY AND AMBIGUITY

If we orient our discussion of perception to questions about how perception justifies belief, then we are led immediately to the further question about whether perception is conceptual in nature. This is a question extensively explored by John McDowell (1996). On the position defended in his early work, perception must be conceptual (in a strong propositional sense) if it is to serve as a reason to believe. That is, if perceptual information is to serve as a basis for such beliefs, according to McDowell it needs to have the same kind of content as our beliefs, namely conceptual or propositional content. To have a reason to believe something, or to seek a justification for one's belief, one needs to be able to take a critical perspective on its rationality. A succinct summary of McDowell's guiding idea is provided by Thomas in the following quote:

> McDowell's account of concept possession involves both self-consciousness and the capacity for critical reflection. Both of these ideas express the common intuition that the mind must be able to reflect on its own operations, by reflexively applying those operations to itself, if it is to enjoy the full normativity which for McDowell is the essence of mentality.
>
> (Thomas 1997, 285)

McDowell also denies that that there is a basic level of non-conceptual experience. In experience one takes in 'that things are thus and so' (McDowell 1996, 9), that is, that they fit into some conceptual framework. Consequently he claims that experience always has conceptual content and that conceptual capacities are at work in the experiences themselves (and not just in our judgements based on them) (McDowell 1996, 24).

Given such a view, it shouldn't be too surprising that McDowell eventually denies that non-human animals and infants (and for McDowell infants are mere animals, distinctive only in their potential) have experiences (McDowell 1996, 50, 123). Animals and infants have sentience and can feel pain, but their pain and the pain of language users are two different kinds of pain. By denying that animals and infants have experiences, McDowell is consequently not trying to reduce them to automatons; rather his main aim is to deny that there is a common substratum to non-conceptual sentience and to conceptual experience. Conceptuality is not to be seen as a layer added on top of an existing structure, but as something that radically transforms that pre-existing structure.

It should be obvious that infants present a more pressing challenge to McDowell than non-human animals in general. The reason for this is that infants do not remain in a merely animal mode of living; at some point, they are transformed into full-fledged subjectivities (McDowell 1996, 125). It is rather urgent to understand how this transformation occurs and how it is possible. We must avoid a two-tiered account that leaves us with an unbridgeable dualism between the non-conceptual sentience of the infant and the conceptualized mind of the adult. How does McDowell make the developmental connection between the two intelligible? The answer supplied by McDowell is revealing. He describes the initiation into conceptual capacities as a question of *Bildung*, and argues that the transformation occurs as a result of being initiated into a language (McDowell 1996, 84, 125). Indeed, it is language that for McDowell constitutes the prior embodiment of mindedness (McDowell 1996, 125). As he puts it in the very conclusion of *Mind and World*:

> The feature of language that really matters is rather this: that a natural language, the sort of language into which human beings are first initiated, serves as a repository of tradition, a store of historically accumulated wisdom about what is a reason for what. The tradition is subject to reflective modification by each generation that inherits it. Indeed, a standing obligation to engage in critical reflection is itself part of the inheritance. ... But if an individual human being is to realize her potential of taking her place in that succession, *which is the same thing as acquiring a mind*, the capacity to think and act intentionally, at all, the first thing that needs to happen is for her to be initiated into a tradition as it stands.
>
> (McDowell 1996, 126; emphasis added)

One obvious question to ask is how McDowell can explain the very process of language acquisition, given that he takes infants to be mindless.

If, as for McDowell, as for others (e.g. Bermúdez 1998), conceptuality is tied to language, then it would be difficult to say that young, prelinguistic infants, as well as non-human animals, perceive. Yet the behaviour of animals and infants clearly suggests that they do perceive, and respond to what they perceive. Indeed, as shown in recent so-called 'false-belief' experiments 15-month-old infants can seemingly understand where someone will look for an unseen object (see e.g. Baillargeon et al. 2010). On most accounts of this behaviour, infants perceive certain events (e.g. agent A putting a toy in a box and leaving the room), and they **see a** related, subsequent situation (i.e. they see that person A returned to the room and that now A is ready to look for that toy). The fact that the infant looks at the box where she expects the agent to look (anticipatory looking), or that she looks longer at unexpected behaviour by the agent (violation of expectations) suggests that there is some kind of understanding, if not of the false belief of the agent, then at least of the situation. If this understanding is conceptual in some sense, it does not seem to be strongly linguistic, at least in the sense that it does not require what is traditionally called 'language acquisition'.

From a phenomenological perspective, however, we need some further qualifications. First, it can be noted that language does not wait around until the child reaches an appropriate age (around two years) to acquire it. As Merleau-Ponty (1964, 40) suggested, language tends to acquire the infant even before the infant speaks. The infant is surrounded by language (the language of others) from the beginning and is caught up in the 'whirlwind of language' since caregivers speak to the infant (and sing, and tell stories, etc.) and most infants hear or overhear speech even when it is not directed to the infant. Very young infants can discriminate the voice of their mother from others, and this may even be the case in prenatal auditory experience (Fifer and Moon 1988). One- to two-day-old newborns who prior to birth had been read stories by their mothers preferred to hear the same stories that were read to them during pregnancy (DeCasper and Spence 1986). Setting aside the question of what is innate versus fast developing, perhaps we should call this a proto- or preliminary linguistic (rather than prelinguistic) capacity. It's clear that this capacity leads infants to some understanding of language (speech as well as gesture) long before they utter their first word.

In some of the early false-belief experiments just mentioned, agent A is informed by speech or gesture that the toy has been moved, and the infant then shows surprise when A goes to the original location where the toy is not located (Song et al. 2008). That is, the infant no longer expects A to go to the original location since A now has linguistically communicated information about the location of the toy. In another study with 17-month-old infants (Southgate et al. 2010), A hides two toys in separate boxes, and then leaves. Unknown to A another person switches the contents of the two boxes. A returns and points to one of the boxes, announcing that the toy hidden inside is a 'sefo'. When the infants are then asked to retrieve the 'sefo' most of them approach the other box where it is really located, indicating that they must have understood what the agent intended.

One can give a strong mentalistic interpretation of such behaviour, or an interpretation that stays closer to perceptual and behavioural aspects. Baillargeon et al. (2010), following the first kind of interpretation, suggest that the infant not only *infers* that the agent's mental state consists of a false belief, but that the child can reason about a complex set of mental states, including dispositional preferences, intended goals, knowledge about the situation, inferences, and false beliefs. This would involve a rather sophisticated (metarepresentational) conceptual ability. One might rightly ask whether the kind of pre-(liminary) linguistic capacity that the infant has at this point is sufficient to subtend that kind of higher-order cognitive ability. It is possible, however, to consider a less mentalistic, more perceptual-based, account that involves a weaker (non-propositional) notion of conceptuality which would go along with this more pre-(liminary) linguistic capability.

The weaker notion of conceptuality is one based on the ability to differentiate, which is something characteristic of perception from the very beginning. On an ecological view of perception, for example, perception involves differentiation between self and non-self. We can also think that to perceive anything in particular – that is, if anything is to stand out in the perceptual field as a unitary something, e.g. a face or a toy or a mother's voice – it must be differentiated from other things and from a background. Neonates are able to attend to faces and are soon able to differentiate one (e.g. the mother's face) from all others. Differentiation is essential to perception, and one can consider such differentiation as one important aspect of conceptuality. Another aspect of conceptuality is also to be found in perception, namely, the ability to register (be affected by) similarity. Infants respond selectively to faces in ways they do not respond to other objects. Faces are similar, not only in general appearance (two eyes, nose, mouth), but also in motivating similar responses. For example, faces are salient and infants tend to look to faces before looking to other body parts; they can also imitate facial gestures shortly after birth.

The kind of differentiation and response to similarity that accompanies perceptual ability, we note here, as we noted above, is tied directly to action possibilities. The very young infant sees X in terms of it being something she can grab, or suck, or imitate. In this regard, we can say that the rationality that belongs to perception serves action and is a kind of *practical* (and, as we'll soon see, intersubjective) *rationality*, rather than something which comes to exclusively serve belief justification. This is not to say that perception cannot be put to use in the kind of rationality involved in justifying beliefs, something that comes along later on the developmental line when children attain the concept of belief and the practice of giving reasons. To think that this is its primary purpose, however, is to put into question the kind of perception that infants and non-human animals have, and that we, as adults, continue to have. We might say, then, that perception is more about the *landscape of actions* (to use Bruner's phrase) than about the *space of reasons* (to use Sellars' phrase for the logical space in which we justify our beliefs or actions). Again, this is not to deny that perception can serve to justify beliefs, but only that perception primarily (and pre-reflectively) serves action, and only derivatively (through reflection) the giving of reasons or evaluation. Intentional action can still be for reasons without the giving of reasons. As McDowell puts it, 'Acting for a reason ... does not require that one reflects about whether some consideration is a sufficient rational warrant for something it seems to recommend' (McDowell 2006, 2).

The debate surrounding the question of the conceptuality of perception is a critical one from the perspective of the enactive view of perception as action oriented. The issue at stake concerns nothing less than the very nature of the mind. To say that the world as perceived is conceptually structured (as McDowell suggests) does not necessarily entail, for the phenomenologist, a strong epistemological or justificatory claim about how our beliefs match up to reality. Rather, it means simply that we can make sense out of the world in terms of the differentiations and similarities that inform our actions. Perception, however, remains inherently ambiguous according to Merleau-Ponty. This can be seen in what Charles Siewert (2005, 283) has called 'phenomenally corrigible illusions'. Merleau-Ponty provides an example.

> The difference between illusion and perception is intrinsic, and the truth of perception can be read off only from perception itself. If, on a sunken path, I think I can see, some distance away, a broad, flat stone on the ground, which is in reality a patch of sunlight, I cannot say that I ever see the flat stone in the sense in which I am to see, as I draw nearer, the patch of sunlight. The flat stone, like all things at a distance, appears only in a field of confused structure in which connections are not yet clearly articulated. In this sense, the illusion, like the image, is not observable, which means that my body has no grip on it, and that I cannot unfold it before me by any exploratory action. And yet, I am capable of omitting this distinction and of falling into illusion. ... I see the illusory stone in the sense that my whole perceptual and motor field endows the bright spot with the significance 'stone on the path'. And already I prepare to feel under my foot this smooth, firm surface. ... I say that I perceive correctly when my body has a precise hold on the spectacle, but that does not mean that my hold is ever all-embracing. ... In experiencing a perceived truth, I assume that the concordance so far experienced would hold for a more detailed observation. ...
>
> (1962, 296–97)

McDowell has recently acknowledged that animals, as well as humans, respond to non-conceptual affordances (McDowell 2007, 344–45; see Jensen 2008 for a good discussion of disjunctivism and the differences between McDowell and Merleau-Ponty). McDowell is here responding to Dreyfus' argument that human bodily engagement ('coping'), since it is similar to animal bodily engagement, cannot be conceptual (Dreyfus 2005, 12n38; but see Dreyfus 2007b and Zahavi, forthcoming-b). It may be, as McDowell suggests, that humans can integrate such non-conceptual affordances into a conceptual framework of meaning, in order to justify their beliefs and actions, but, for the phenomenologist, this does not mean that they do so in every case, or that this is a basic process involved in perception. We suggest that it's enough that human bodies engage with their environment in ways different from those of animals with different kinds of bodies. Affordances are relative to bodies. What affords a place to sit for a human may not be the same thing that affords a place to sit for an elephant. Some meaning is constituted on this bodily level, tied directly to the enactively perceived affordances of the environment.

The ability of infants demonstrated in the early 'false-belief' experiments is a case in point. The enactive-phenomenological alternative to the higher-order (theory theory) explanation offered by Baillargeon et al. stays closer to the perception–action level. In each case we can say that the infant expects a certain action; that expectation is formed by the infant's perception of the situation in which the agent sees or does not see something. The infant is aware, for example, that the agent has not seen where the toy has been placed, anticipates that the agent will look one place, but is surprised that the agent looks in a different location. The surprise is related to the logic of perception and action. The agent (A) has not seen the toy's movement from one location to the other. If the agent's actions are guided by what she has seen, then one would expect her to look in the original location and be surprised when she looks in the other.

The enactive phenomenological view, without appealing to conceptual rationality, theoretical inference, simulation or behavioural rules,[9] suggests that infants are applying perception–action principles. Specifically, the infant perceives others in terms of *how he or she can interact with them*, or in terms of the infant's (possible) engagement in what the other is doing or expressing or feeling. As Merleau-Ponty (1964, 119) puts it, 'the other's intentions somehow play across my body' as a set of possibilities for my action. Accordingly, the infant sees the other's action as aimed at the world in ways that offer social affordances for interacting. This applies even when the infant is observing rather than actually interacting with the agent. The agent's involvement in the world, which the infant can see, influences its expectations.

Consider, for example, some of the more interactive experimental designs that address this issue. In a study by Buttelmann, Carpenter and Tomasello (2009) 18-month-olds are allowed to interact with the agent (A); they try to help A retrieve a toy while taking into account the fact that A doesn't know about a switched location (the 'false-belief' situation). In that situation, when A focuses on the wrong container (at the original location), the infant is ready to lead him to the other (correct) box, but not in the situation when A does know about the switch, i.e. the 'true-belief' situation, but nonetheless goes to the original location. In the latter case the infant goes to offer assistance to A at that location. In this study when A goes to the original location, the infant sees exactly the same thing in the case of true belief (when A knows the toy has been shifted) as in the case of false belief (when A does not know about the shift). Again, the fact that the infant has perceived either that A has seen the switch or has not seen the switch, plus A's behaviour with respect to the box at the original location (e.g. moving there and attempting to open it), is enough to specify the difference in A's intention. For the infant, that signals a difference in affordance, i.e. a difference in how the infant can act, and thereby interact with A. The infant does not have to make inferences to mental states since all of the information needed to understand A's action, and to interact with A is already available in what the infant has seen of the situation.

What the infant does in experimental situations where the infant is allowed to interact with the agent (also see the study by Southgate et al. 2010 cited above) suggests that the violation of expectations in the less interactive setting may be a violation of affordance expectations. It is not at all clear that the infant has to engage in higher-order (conceptual–propositional) inferences about A's beliefs since all of the relevant information is available perceptually, and is sufficient to inform the infant's action. Our point here is that perception has a primacy and delivers sufficient information for the infants' actual or potential response. We will return to questions about theory of mind and social cognition in a later chapter.

THE ROLE OF OTHERS

My perception of an object as within a context is not a perception of an object plus perception of a context; it is always perception of an object-in-context. But is perception something that can be accomplished by a single moving subject, or is the context in question always also social? Is perception a process that by definition also involves other subjects?

This question has been pursued by a number of phenomenologists. Some have tried to find a place for sociality in the public nature of perceptual objects. As Merleau-Ponty argues, the perceptual world is not only experienced as my world, as the correlate of my own consciousness, but as the correlate of any consciousness I may ever encounter (1962, p. 338). If I enter into conversation with someone else, I am not conversing with 'a flow of private sensations indirectly related to mine through the medium of interposed signs'; rather, I am speaking with someone who 'has a living experience of the same world as mine', who is present together with me in this world, and 'with whom I am in communication through that world' (p. 405). Hence it is not the case that each of us has her own private world. Instead, if I were over there where the other is, then I would experience what the other experiences, and conversely, the other would experience what I experience if she were here at this moment. Thus my own perspective on the world does not have determinate boundaries, but spontaneously slips into and overlaps that of the other (Merleau-Ponty 1968, pp. 61, 142). This observation eventually motivates Merleau-Ponty's claim that I, the experiencing subject, have no perceptual monopoly on being; rather, the objects only display themselves to me partially, and thus have a right to 'many other witnesses besides me' (Merleau-Ponty 1964, pp.15–16, 170). In other words, my perceptual objects are not exhausted in their appearance for me; rather, each object always possesses a horizon of coexisting profiles, which although being momentarily inaccessible to me – I cannot see the front and the back of a chair simultaneously – could very well be perceived by other subjects. Since the perceptual object is always there for others too, whether or not such other subjects do, in fact, appear on the scene, the object refers to those other subjects, and is for that very reason intrinsically intersubjective. It does not exist solely for me, but refers to intersubjectivity, and so does my intentionality whenever I am directed at intersubjectively accessible objects.[10]

Let us try to clarify the argument. As we have already seen, in perceiving an object we appresent or co-intend the absent profiles; they are correlated to possible perceptions. If one attempts to follow up on this systematically, two possible accounts seem viable:

(1) The absent profiles are appresented as profiles correlated with my past or possible future perceptions. Thus, the back of the lamp is appresented as the side which I either have seen or which I would be able to perceive in a future perception.
(2) A different possibility is that the absent profiles are appresented as the correlates of fictitious *co-present* perceptions. They are correlated with the perceptions which I would have, if it were possible for me to be there now (instead of here). Thus, the co-intended back of the lamp is fictitiously given as the side that I would see, if I were facing the back now. In this case we are dealing with a fictitious and not an actualizable possibility, since the front and the back of the lamp are in principle incapable of being given perceptually for the same consciousness simultaneously.

On closer examination, it should be clear, however, that neither of these accounts is really satisfying. The first account conceives of the object as a unity in a series of temporally separated profiles. This conception, however, does not match with our experience. When I perceive the lamp, I am not perceiving something which at that very moment possesses one actual profile, and which previously possessed and will subsequently possess various others. The present front is not a front with respect to a past or future back, but is determined through its reference to a present coexisting back. Consequently, it belongs to the very notion of the transcendence of the object that it, at any given moment, possesses a plurality of *coexisting* profiles.

This objection also affects the second account, however. Although perception only gives us a partial presentation of the object, the entire object is experienced as real, and we do not do justice to this reality if we let the object be composed of a number of fictitious slices.

Is there any alternative account? Consider the following: the absent co-intended profiles are correlated with possible perceptions. As we have seen, these possible perceptions must be compatible with my own actual perception, since they must be simultanously actualizable; my horizonal appresentation of the absent profiles of the object must preserve their character as actual *coexisting* profiles. Yet, both my fictitious as well as my previous or subsequent perceptions lack this compatibility. As a consequence, the absent profiles cannot be correlated with my possible perceptions. But as Husserl then suggests, the absent profiles can be correlated with the possible perceptions of others (see Zahavi 1997). As Sartre writes, summing up Husserl's view:

Thus each object [e.g. a table, a wall] far from being constituted as for Kant, by a simple relation to the *subject*, appears in my concrete experience as polyvalent; it is given originally as possessing systems of reference to an indefinite plurality of consciousnesses; it is [by this object,] the table, the wall, that the Other is revealed to me as that to which the object under consideration is perpetually referred – as well as on the occasion of the concrete appearances of Pierre or Paul.

(Sartre 1956, p. 233; translation revised)

Thus, the basic idea is that an analysis of the horizonal incompleteness of perceived objects refers us to the perceptions (intentions) of a plurality of possible subjects, or as Husserl calls it, to an 'open intersubjectivity':

Thus everything objective that stands before me in experience and primarily in perception has an apperceptive horizon of possible experience, own and foreign. Ontologically speaking, every appearance that I have is from the very beginning a part of an open endless, but not explicitly realized totality of possible appearances of the same, and the subjectivity belonging to this appearance is open intersubjectivity.

(Husserl 1973a, p. 289; see also 1973b, p. 497)

But isn't perception always an activity undertaken by a *factual*, individual subject? This seems difficult to deny. When I perceive an object on my own, the object is perceived by me alone. The claim is, however, that I am able to perform this activity only because my horizonal intentionality entails structural references to the perceptions of possible other perceivers, and precisely for that reason, the structure of my horizonal intentionality is incompatible with any solipsism which, in principle, would deny the possibility of a plurality of subjects. As Merleau-Ponty declares: 'Into each perception and into each judgement I bring either sensory functions or cultural settings which are not actually mine' (1962, p. 358). The objects that I perceive and intend are characterized by a transcendence and a horizonal manner of appearance that reveal their being for other subjects. Since my object of perception always possesses profiles that can be perceived by other subjects, it refers to them continually and is, as a result, intrinsically intersubjective:

The perceived world is not only *my* world, but the one in which I see the behavior of other people take shape, for their behavior equally aims at the world, which is the counterpart not only of my consciousness, but of any consciousness *which I can possibly encounter*.

(Merleau-Ponty 1962, p. 338)

If there are important differences between perceiving another person and perceiving an object (see Chapter 9), it is nevertheless also the case that these two kinds of perception are interdependent. When I perceive someone, I am not only perceiving another living body situated 'there', but also perceiving her as a perceiver of the same world that I inhabit. Sartre gives this a dramatic formulation when he writes that my relationship to things undergoes a fundamental change when I experience somebody else observing these very same things:

> Thus suddenly an object has appeared which has stolen the world from me. Everything is in place; everything still exists for me; but everything is traversed by an invisible flight and fixed in the direction of a new object. The appearance of the Other in the world corresponds therefore to a fixed sliding of the whole universe, to a decentralization of the world which undermines the centralization which I am simultaneously effecting.
>
> (Sartre 1956, p. 255)

As soon as the other appears on the scene, the world appears to me as alienated, for it is given to me as already looked at – indeed, as 'furrowed, explored, worked over' on all fronts. In this way the presence of the other has the function of revealing complexes of sense that are already *given* (Sartre 1956, p. 520). But at the same time, when the world centred on me is experienced by an other, it is decentred as well, since the other imposes on the instrumental things of my world an order that points back to the other as a new centre of reference (ibid., p. 255). The other is experienced not simply as another object in the world, but as a subject for the world.

From a developmental perspective, others are present from the very start. When we first perceive objects we learn to perceive them in joint attention, and we learn to perceive them as being involved in some purpose. Something is ready-to-hand or an affordance not only because of how it is relative to our embodied possibilities for action, but because we have learned our actions and what things are for, from others. Something is ready to hand, something affords me possibilities, only because I have seen some of those possibilities actualized by others; others who pick things up and use them, and others who offer me things for play or for work. My perception is then shaped by these experiences; the others do not cease to exist when I am alone, and although they may not be perceptually present, they are potentially and implicitly involved in the very structure of my perception. The world that we perceive is contextualized not only physically (characterized by inner and outer horizons) but also socially.

For this reason, it would not be enough to give Condillac's statue all of the standard sense modalities. If the statue were *suddenly* made better than a sophisticated robot, that is, if it were suddenly transformed to have an animal nature and could see and hear and touch and taste and smell as well as sense its own body and its movement through the world, would it be able to perceive the world as anything more than a facade, or a representation, or a grand illusion generated within its own system? Humans are born and are raised by others who already act and perceive in the world. Our sense of the reality of the world, and of the things that we perceive, depends on this.

NOTES

1 We discuss these three modes, but other important forms are imaginative fantasy and recollection. Although pictorial consciousness and fantasy both imply a consciousness of something absent, there remains an obvious difference between the two. In pictorial consciousness I intend something via something else. This *representative* function is not a part of fantasy. If I imagine a dancing faun, this faun is not taken to be a representation of a real faun. On the contrary, we are dealing with an intentional object which is not taken to be real, but which merely appears *as if* it were real (Husserl 1959, pp. 112–13).

2 One objection often voiced against Husserl's idea of prelinguistic experience is that in seeking an immediate level of experience prior to every interpretation, Husserl overlooked the fact that all experience involves interpretation. This hermeneutical criticism itself, however, makes the mistake of thinking that all interpretation is linguistic. But, as both Husserl and Heidegger have shown, interpretation itself can be prelinguistic (see Heidegger 1976, pp. 144–45); it might for instance manifest itself in our practices. One and the same object can be used in various ways; this difference in use, this difference in how we take the object, amounts to a form of practical interpretation. But even more fundamentally, whenever we perceive objects, we co-intend the absent profiles of the object, and thereby go beyond the merely given. This is why every perception according to Husserl entails an aspect of '*Hinausdeutung*' or interpretation (1966b/2001, p. 19); see below for more on this aspect of perception.

3 To take this to the extreme and to say that all we know are representations and that they are generated by a causal influence on our sense organs and brain, is to overlook, not only the non-phenomenological and speculative character of this account, but also the circularity implied. If such an extreme representationalism is to be consistent, it must naturally claim that our sense organs and brain (which are after all only known to us through perception) are also only known as representations, wherefore the origins of representations are explained by the causal impact of something unknown on representations. As an explanation this will hardly do.

4 Although today only a very few people in philosophy or psychology support a sense-data theory of perception (but see Maund 1995; O'Shaughnessy 1985; Robinson 1994), the more general point about the problem of conceiving of subjective experience in objective terms is still relevant given the various mechanistic, reductionist, computationalist, and representationalist approaches in cognitive science.

5 We should note that in this case, and in contrast with how our motor system would treat the Müller-Lyer illusion, the gestalt effect in the Ebbinghaus illusion does not bias our ability to reach and grab the two circles, which our motor system treats as being of equal size. The difference has to do with precisely the elements that we would grasp and manipulate; in the first case the lines of equal length come with their tails and arrows, and in the second case, the centre circles are grasped without the surrounding circles.

6 For a fuller presentation of Husserl's early concept of perception, see Zahavi 1992.

7 Simons and Chabris' (1999) 'gorillas in our midst' experiment may be the most well-known example of inattentional blindness. They show that when subjects are asked to perform a task that requires visual attention on specific dynamical events in the environment (in this case, a video

of a group of people throwing or playing catch with a ball), other events that should be extremely apparent (such as someone dressed in a gorilla suit walking through the ball-playing group and waving at the camera) are rarely noticed. Change blindness is the failure to notice significant changes occurring in full view.

8 The claim here is a phenomenological one and does not justify any particular inference to what happens on the subpersonal level. In this regard it remains an open question whether one should interpret what goes on in the brain in terms of representations, or what precisely representation would mean on that level. For a critical discussion of the use of the concept of representation in cognitive sciences, see Ramsey (2007).

9 The *behavioural-rules* approach appeals to the infant's grasp of behavioural rules (e.g. 'people look for objects where they last saw them') gained via statistical learning abilities (Ruffman and Perner 2005).

10 For a more extensive presentation of this line of argumentation, see Zahavi 1997, 2001b, and 2003c.

FURTHER READING

P. Sven Arvidson, *The Sphere of Attention: Context and Margin*. Dordrecht: Springer, 2006.

Susan L. Hurley, *Consciousness in Action*. Cambridge, MA: Harvard University Press, 1998.

Edmund Husserl, *Thing and Space: Lectures of 1907*. Trans. R. Rojcewicz. Dordrecht: Kluwer Academic Publishers, 1997.

Maurice Merleau-Ponty, *Phenomenology of Perception*. Trans. C. Smith. London: Routledge & Kegan Paul, 1962.

Maurice Merleau-Ponty, *The Primacy of Perception*. Trans. W. Cobb. Evanston: Northwestern University Press, 1964.

Alva Noë, *Action in Perception*. Cambridge, MA: MIT Press, 2004.

A. David Smith, *The Problem of Perception*. Cambridge, MA: Harvard University Press, 2002.

6 Intentionality

As you read these words you are conscious of something. Maybe you are conscious of the words, or maybe you are mainly conscious of the meaning of the words as your eyes skim over the lines of the text. If you look up you will find yourself in some kind of environment. Perhaps you are sitting with this book at your desk; or maybe you are reading this book as you soak in the tub sipping a glass of champagne. Indeed, you may be studying your philosophy in extraordinary style. In any case, if you look up you will see something. For our purposes, it doesn't matter what. We know that whether you are reading the text or looking around the room or tasting your champagne or hearing a noise in the next room, you are conscious of something, because that is the way consciousness works. If you were conscious of nothing, as Sartre once put it, you would be unconscious. In the phenomeno-logical tradition, this idea, that consciousness is always consciousness-of-something, is referred to as the intentionality of consciousness. In this chapter we want to make clear why this is an important concept for understanding cognition.

Let's start with this question: must a theory of consciousness include a concept of intentionality, and if so, why? In his book *The Conscious Mind*, David Chalmers introduced what has become a much discussed distinction between the 'hard problem' and the 'easy problems' of consciousness. The easy problems are those concerned with the question of how the mind can process information, react to environmental stimuli, and exhibit such conscious capacities as discrimination, categorization, and introspection (Chalmers 1996, p. 4; 1995, p. 200). All of these abilities are impressive, but they are, according to Chalmers, not metaphysically baffling, since they can all be tackled by means of the standard repertoire of cognitive science and explained in terms of computational or neural mechanisms. This task might still be difficult, but science has the means to address it. In contrast, the hard problem – also known as the problem of consciousness (Chalmers 1995, p. 201) – is that of explaining the phenomenal or experiential aspect of the mind.

Chalmers later clarified his position by suggesting that such notions as attention, memory, intentionality, etc., contain both easy and hard aspects (Chalmers 1997, p. 10). A full and comprehensive understanding of intentionality, for example, would consequently entail solving the hard problem, or to put it differently, an analysis of thoughts, beliefs, categorizations, etc., that ignored the experiential side would merely be an analysis of what could be called pseudo-thoughts or pseudo-beliefs (ibid., p. 20). This clarification fits well with an observation that Chalmers made already in *The Conscious Mind*, namely, that one could operate with a deflationary and an inflationary concept of belief, respectively. Whereas the first concept is a purely psychological (functional) concept that does not involve any reference to conscious experience, the second concept entails that conscious experience is required for true intentionality (Chalmers 1996, p. 20). In 1997, Chalmers admits that he is torn on the issue, and that over time he has become increasingly sympathetic to the second concept, and to the idea that consciousness is the primary source of meaning. He is thus led to the idea that intentional content may in fact be grounded in phenomenal content, but he thinks the matter needs further examination (Chalmers 1997, p. 21).

We welcome this clarification, but we also find it slightly surprising that Chalmers is prepared to concede this much since the very distinction between the easy problems and the hard problem of consciousness becomes questionable the moment one opts for the inflationary concept. Given this concept, there would in effect be no easy problems of consciousness. The truly easy problems would all be problems about pseudo-intentional states, that is, about non-conscious information processing. A treatment of these issues should not be confused with an explanation of the kind of conscious intentionality that we encounter in human beings. In other words, we will not understand how human beings consciously intend, discriminate, categorize, react, report, and introspect, etc., until we understand the role of subjective experience in those processes (see D. Hodgson 1996).

Although Chalmers' discussion of the hard problem identifies an aspect of consciousness that cannot be ignored, the original way of defining and distinguishing the hard problem from the easy problems is indebted to the very reductionism that Chalmers opposes. If one thinks that cognition and intentionality are basically a matter of information processing and causal covariation that could in principle just as well go on in a mindless computer – or to use Chalmers' own favoured example, in an experienceless zombie – then one is left with the impression that all that is really distinctive about consciousness is its qualitative or phenomenal aspect. But this suggests that with the exception of some evanescent qualia everything about consciousness, including intentionality, can be explained in reductive (computational or neural) terms; and in this case, one might easily end up embracing epiphenomenalism – the idea that consciousness is just a by-product and has no causal role to play in behaviour or cognition.

Chalmers' distinction between the easy problems and the hard problem of consciousness shares a common feature with many other recent attempts in analytic philosophy to defend consciousness against the onslaught of reductionism: they all grant far too much to the other side. Reductionism has typically proceeded with a classical divide-and-conquer strategy. Accordingly, one should distinguish two sides to consciousness: intentionality and phenomenality. We don't currently know how to reduce the latter aspect, so let us separate the two sides, and concentrate on the first. If we then succeed in explaining intentionality reductively, the phenomenal or experiential aspect cannot be all that significant. Many non-reductive materialists have uncritically adopted the very same strategy. They have marginalized subjectivity by identifying it with epiphenomenal qualia and have then claimed that it is this aspect which eludes reductionism.

The dominant tendency in phenomenology has been to question the partition and to argue that the problems of experience and intentionality are intimately connected. Indeed, as we will see in the following, according to phenomenologists it is not possible to investigate intentionality properly without taking experience, the first-person perspective, first-person meaning, etc., into account. And vice versa: it is not possible to understand the nature of subjectivity and experience if we ignore intentionality. To think otherwise is to run the risk of reinstating a Cartesian subject–world dualism that ignores everything captured by the phrase 'being-in-the-world'.

WHAT IS INTENTIONALITY?

The concept of intentionality has a long history that stretches back at least as far as Aristotle. It played a central role in medieval scholastic epistemology, but the modern revival of the term 'intentionality' is due to Brentano. In his influential work *Psychology from an Empirical Standpoint*, 1874, Brentano sought to establish a clear demarcation between the realm of psychology and the realm of natural science. As he writes, psychology is the science of the *psychical* phenomena, whereas natural science is that of the *physical* phenomena (1973, pp. 97–100). What is the difference between these two classes of phenomena?

> Every mental phenomenon is characterized by what the Scholastics of the Middle Ages called the intentional (or mental) inexistence of an object, and what we might call, though not wholly unambiguously, reference to a content, direction toward an object (which is not to be understood here as meaning a thing), or immanent objectivity. Every mental phenomenon includes something as object within itself, although they do not all do so in the same way. In presentation something is presented, in judgement something is affirmed or denied, in love loved, in hate hated, in desire desired and so on.

> This intentional in-existence is characteristic exclusively of mental phenomenon. No physical phenomenon exhibits anything like it. We can, therefore, define mental phenomena by saying that they are those phenomena which contain an object intentionally within themselves.

> (Brentano 1973, pp. 88–89)

According to Brentano, all psychical, i.e. mental, phenomena exhibit intentionality, no physical phenomena do, which is why he can claim not only that intentionality is the defining mark of the mental, but also that the physical and the psychical are distinct realms. The sense of 'intentional' in this context should not be confused with the more familiar sense of having a purpose in mind when one acts, which is only one kind of intentionality in the phenomenological sense. Rather, 'intentionality' is a generic term for the pointing-beyond-itself proper to consciousness (from the Latin *intendere*, which means to aim in a particular direction, similar to drawing and aiming a bow at a target). Intentionality has to do with the directedness or of-ness or aboutness of consciousness, i.e. with the fact that when one perceives or judges or feels or thinks, one's mental state is about or of something.

Brentano's thesis has been influential. His description and characterization of intentionality, however, are not only somewhat puzzling; they are also rather unfortunate. As Chisholm later argued, Brentano's description contains a tension between an *ontological* and a *psychological* thesis (Chisholm 1967, p. 6). On the one hand, Brentano apparently adopts a scholastic terminology and speaks of the object's intentional '(in)existence' in consciousness, where 'inexistence' should be read as 'existence within' or 'inner existence'. The object of consciousness is contained immanently in the psychical act, and the *existential mode* of this object, its ontological status, is therefore called intentional. On the other hand, Brentano also claims that the psychical phenomenon is characterized by its *directedness* at or *reference* to an object (1973, p. 97). Thus we can alternatively speak of the intentional inexistence of the object, and of the intentional directedness of the mental act. Although these two features are by no means identical, they are nevertheless brought together in Brentano's (early) theory of intentionality, insofar as he claims that consciousness is intentionally directed at an intentionally (in)existing object. Thus, Brentano seemed to focus on the mind's ability to refer to or be directed at objects existing solely in the mind.

We will return to this tricky issue concerning the ontological status of the intentional object in a moment, but for now, one can simply observe that Brentano's discussion has given rise to heated debate.

Brentano regarded intentionality as an irreducible feature of the mind and sought on this basis to establish psychology as an autonomous science. By contrast, one can roughly discern three distinct approaches to intentionality in analytic philosophy and cognitive science:

- The first language-philosophical approach tried to throw light on the intentionality of consciousness through a careful examination of the logical properties that characterize sentences used to describe psychological phenomena.[1]
- The second approach, which has been dominated by such figures as Quine, Dennett, Fodor, Dretske, the Churchlands, etc., has mainly been occupied with the question of how to naturalize intentionality, i.e., with the question of how to account for intentionality in terms of non-intentional mechanisms. As Fodor writes, 'It's hard to see ... how one can be a Realist about intentionality without also being, to some extent or other, a Reductionist. ... If aboutness is real, it must be really something else' (1987, p. 97). The assumption has consequently been that you either naturalize intentionality by downward reduction of intentional states to behaviour, neurophysiology, and ultimately physics, or you argue that such reduction is impossible and then conclude that the intentional vocabulary is empty talk and should be eliminated from our scientific discourse.

- The final approach is one that can be found in recent work by, for instance, Searle, Strawson, Siewert, and Crane. They all consider it necessary to include the first-person perspective in their investigation and argue that a careful description of the structures of intentionality is an indispensable part of a philosophical investigation of consciousness.

The phenomenological account of intentionality differs from the first two ways of approaching the issue of intentionality. Phenomenologists are primarily interested in intentionality as a decisive feature of consciousness. Moreover, they specifically focus on an account of intentionality from the first-person perspective, that is, from the subject's point of view. In fact, none of the phenomenologists are engaged in a naturalization of intentionality, if that is understood as an attempt to explain intentionality reductively by an appeal to non-intentional mechanisms and processes. If one thinks that a theory of intentionality must result in a reductive account one will be bound to find the phenomenological treatment of intentionality disappointing.

What is the aim of the phenomenological account of intentionality, then? First and foremost, to provide a descriptive analysis of the structures of conscious intentionality. In doing so, however, the phenomenologists also seek to clarify the relation between mind and world (rather than the relation between mind and brain). This latter investigation, which basically intends to demonstrate the world-involving character of the mind and rejects the view that consciousness is a subjective sphere that exists independently of the world that is revealed through it, has some more, overarching philosophical implications. We will discuss those in the last part of the present chapter.

RESEMBLANCE, CAUSATION, AND MENTAL REPRESENTATION

Before going into more detail about the phenomenological account of intentionality, let us briefly consider some of the non-phenomenological alternatives. To clear away a potential misunderstanding, we need to start out with some remarks about the term 'representation'. Both analytic philosophy and the cognitive sciences make frequent references to so-called mental representations. How does this use of the term 'representation' relate to the phenomenological use of the term – *Vergegenwärtigung* in German, which is usually translated as re-presentation and literally means 'making present'? When phenomenologists use this term, they typically put the emphasis on the first syllable. A *re*-presentation is something that *re*-presents; it is something that provides us with a derivative and mediated contact with the object represented. As illustration, consider the difference between perceiving the Eiffel Tower, and looking at a photo of the Eiffel Tower. In both cases, arguably, we are intentionally directed at the same object, namely the Eiffel Tower, but whereas in the first case we are directly confronted with the tower itself, the second case exemplifies a form of indirect intentionality; we are directed at the Eiffel Tower through an intermediate entity, namely a picture or pictorial re-presentation of the tower.

As we saw in our discussion of perception in the previous chapter, some authors have indeed posited a kind of intermediate mental entity when they talked of 'a mental representation', but today many researchers simply use the term to designate a mental state that exhibits intentionality. Although the term might indeed have somewhat confusing connotations, nothing in this use of the term 'representation' as such commits one to the idea that our cognitive contact with the world involves some intermediate entities, be they mental images, sense data, or the like.

As mentioned above, much effort has been devoted to the attempt to naturalize intentionality, that is, to provide a reductive explanation of how a mental state can be about something. The aspiration has been to explain intentionality in terms of non-intentional mechanisms, and to reduce mental states to complex information-processing events housed in the brain. There are currently a number of highly technical proposals on the market – though none that so far has managed to gain general acceptance. Since it would lead too far afield if we were to attempt to do justice to all the various suggestions,[2] we will instead quite briefly outline the two standard proposals – which in fact have a long ancestry – namely, the attempt to explain intentionality in terms of either *resemblance* or *causation*.

Resemblance might at first seem a rather likely candidate for a natural form of representation. Think of the way in which a mirror image represents what it reflects, or a picture or photo represents what it depicts. But contrary to appearance, resemblance is not a sufficient condition for representation. (It is obviously not necessary either, since words can represent without resembling what they represent.) A forest contains numerous trees that resemble each other, but that does not make one tree represent the other. Every object resembles itself, but every object does not represent itself. Furthermore, whereas resemblance is a reciprocal relation, representation is not; that is, whereas the Danish queen might resemble her portrait, she is not a representation of it.

If we want to naturalize intentionality, if we want to reduce it to naturally occurring forms of representation, causation seems another promising candidate. Think of how smoke represents fire, and red spots represent rubella. In both cases, we are not dealing with a mere conventional relation between the representation and what is represented. Rather, something about the smoke and the red spots naturally relates them to fire and rubella, respectively. Indeed, in both cases there is a causal relation between the represented and the representation (which, by the way, is why it might be more appropriate to designate both as signs *of* something, rather than as signs *for* something). Couldn't it be that causality is also the glue that connects mind and world, so that a conscious state can be said to represent (be directed at) an object if, and only if, it is connected to the object in question by 'a causal chain of the appropriate type'. If so, it would indeed be possible to naturalize intentionality. However, this rather crude causal account faces some obvious difficulties. One problem has to do with specifying what is meant by 'appropriate' (or 'relevant') without begging the question. When I look at a distant hill through binoculars, we would ordinarily say that the object of my perception is the hill. However, although (light reflected from) the hill might be causally influencing my visual system, it would certainly not be the only cause, but merely a rather distal one. Why don't I perceive (represent) the lenses of the binoculars, not to speak of the proximal stimulation of my retina? Another problem is that the notion of causality seems too coarse grained to capture the aspectual nature of intentional reference. One is never conscious of an object simpliciter, one is always conscious of an object in a particular way, be it from a certain perspective, or under a certain conception or particular description.

Furthermore, real existing spatial objects in my immediate physical surrounding, things that seem to have real causal force, only constitute a very small part of what I can be conscious of. When I am sitting at my desk, I can think not only about the backside of the moon, I can also think about square circles, unicorns, next Christmas, or the principle of non-contradiction. But how are these absent objects, *impossible* objects, *fictive* objects, *future* objects, or *ideal* objects supposed to have causal influence on my thinking? The fact that it is possible to intend objects which do not exist seems a decisive argument against a theory which claims that an object must influence me causally if I am to be conscious of it. Finally, it is crucial for a theory of representation to account for misrepresentation and the possibility of error as well, since one of the central features of representations is that they have truth values and truth conditions. They can be true or false, and there are conditions under which they are true and others under which they are not. But this presents a problem for the causal theory. If x represents y if and only if x has been caused in the appropriate way by y, misrepresentation is pretty much ruled out. More sophisticated forms of causal theories have subsequently been developed in order to tackle these various difficulties, but so far there is no general agreement that they have succeeded in doing so.

THE POSITIVE ACCOUNT

Husserl's *Logical Investigations* contains the first proper phenomenological investigation of intentionality. Like Brentano, Husserl argues that one does not merely love, fear, see, or judge; one loves a beloved, fears something fearful, sees an object, and judges a state of affairs. Regardless of whether we are talking of a perception, thought, judgement, fantasy, doubt, expectation, or recollection, all of these diverse forms of consciousness are characterized by intending objects, and cannot be analysed properly without a look at their objective correlate, i.e. the perceived, doubted, expected object. The converse is also true: the intentional object cannot be analysed properly without a look at its subjective correlate, the intentional act. Neither the intentional object nor the mental act that intends it can be understood apart from the other. Acts of consciousness and intentional objects, even if the latter do not exist, are essentially interdependent: the relation between them is an internal rather than an external one. That is to say, one cannot first identify the items related and then explore the relation between them. Rather, one can identify each item in the relation only by reference to the other item to which it is related. Husserl would consequently argue that we cannot philosophically comprehend what it means for something to be a perceived object, a remembered event, a judged state of affairs, if we ignore the intentional states (the perception, the remembering, the judging) that reveal these objects to us. Although in daily life we tend to ignore such subjective states, the task of phenomenology was from the beginning to break with the naivety of daily life and call attention to and investigate the correlation between *cogito* and *cogitatum*, between act and object.

Brentano considered intentionality a *dyadic relation* holding between an experience and an object. His assumption was that the intentional relation is what we might call an ordinary relation that presupposes the existence of both *relata*, and he specifically introduced the notion of intentional in-existence in order to solve the problem of our directedness towards non-existing entities. When I am imagining a faun, or when I am hallucinating a pink elephant, I remain intentionally directed, but neither the faun nor the pink elephant exists in reality. The dyadic approach is consequently forced to claim that the faun and the pink elephant are objects with a very peculiar form of (intentional in-)existence. In itself this is not a very satisfying solution, and given the need for a unified theory of intentionality, it also causes grave problems when we are to account for veridical perceptions. For example, when seeing a blooming apple tree, am I then in reality seeing an intentional object with a very peculiar ontological status (something with the same status as the object that I would be seeing if I were merely hallucinating the apple tree)? And is the only difference between hallucinating and perceiving the apple tree the (phenomenally undetectable) fact that, in the latter case, the extraordinary intentional object corresponds to a real ordinary object?

Husserl develops a concept of intentionality that does not run into this problem. For him, intentionality is not an ordinary relation to an extraordinary object, but a special kind of relation to the intended object, be it spatio-temporal or ideal; a special 'relation' that can hold, even if the object doesn't exist; and that can persist even if the object ceases to exist. There might be particular types of intentional states that cannot exist unless their objects exist and vice versa. Perceptions are a case in point. Perceptions do entail the existence of their objects. If you seem to perceive a red tomato and it turns out that the tomato doesn't really exist, then you didn't really perceive it. But one cannot in general infer from the fact that a certain act exists that its object exists as well. When it comes to intentions that are directed towards 'unreal' objects, they are in his view just as much characterized by their *directedness* as are ordinary perceptions. In contrast to normal perceptions, however, the referent does not exist, neither intramentally nor extramentally. In the case of a hallucination, the pink elephant exists neither inside nor outside of consciousness, but the hallucination is still about a pink elephant. This account dispenses with the need for ascribing a special kind of existence (or intentional in-existence) to the hallucinated object in order to preserve the intentionality of the act. As Husserl writes:

> If I represent God to myself, or an angel, or an intelligible thing-in-itself, or a physical thing or a round square etc., I mean the transcendent object named in each case, in other words my intentional object: it makes no difference whether this object exists or is imaginary or absurd. 'The object is merely intentional' does not, of course, mean that it exists, only in an intention, of which it is a real (*reelles*) part, or that some shadow of it exists. It means rather that the intention, the reference to an object so qualified, exists, but not that the object does. If the intentional object does exist, the intention, the reference, does not exist alone, but the thing referred to exists also.
>
> (Husserl 2001a, II, p. 127)

In short, although one of the peculiar features of the mind is its ability to think about objects that do not exist, we shouldn't accept the reality of non-existent objects. To claim that some intentional objects do not exist is not to say that there are *non-existing* objects, i.e. that some non-existent intentional objects exist; rather, it simply means that intentional states can refer to – be about – something, even when the referent doesn't exist.[3]

To rephrase, even if the referent of an intentional state doesn't exist, the intentional state has a reference. Not in the sense that some other object with a mysterious form of existence steps in instead, but merely in the sense that the intentional state keeps referring, keeps being about something; it retains – to use a different terminology – certain conditions of satisfaction that could be fulfilled if the object had existed, but which in the present state of affairs remain unfulfilled.

The intentional object is not a special kind of object, but rather the answer to the question of what a certain intentional state is about. If the answer refers to some non-existing object, the intentional object doesn't exist. If the answer refers to some existent thing, then the intentional object is that real thing. So if I look at my fountain pen, then it is this real pen which is my intentional object, and not some mental picture, copy, or representation of the pen (Crane 2001, p. 26; Husserl 1976/1982, pp. 207–8; 1979, p. 305). By arguing in this manner, Husserl distanced himself from various mediator theories – those that take our intentional relation to spatio-temporal objects such as stones and lamps to be mediated by a relation to some intermediary entities – as well as from theories which argued that when we intend objects that do not really exist, such as the elixir of life or the perpetual motion machine, we are nevertheless standing in a relation to some object which possesses some kind of existence (like those suggested by Meinong) – otherwise we couldn't be directed at them.

We can specify the features of the intentional directedness further. It is customary to speak of intentional 'relations' as being aspectual or perspectival. One is not simply conscious of an object, one is always conscious of an object in a particular way. One always has a certain perspective or point of view on the object; the object is always presented in a certain way or under a certain aspect for the subject. More specifically, however, we can distinguish the intentional object in 'the how of its determinations' and in 'the how of its givenness' (Husserl 1976/1982, pp. 303–4). To take a simple example, consider a perception of a red sports car. As we discussed in the previous chapter, we always see the car from one perspective or another; we never see it in its totality all at once. Furthermore, the car always appears to us in a certain illumination and with a certain background. Moreover, it also appears in a certain context with a determinate meaning. Depending on my previous experiences and current interests, I might see the car as a necessary means of transportation, as a source of enjoyment, as a headache and economic drain (because it is not working and I have to take it to my mechanic), as a vicious product of late capitalism, as contributing to the problem of global warming, etc. Rather than portraying this as a case where raw perceptual content is completed by additional thoughts that, so to speak, are added on top of it, phenomenologists have stressed the continuity between perception and thinking. The fact that perception is inherently meaningful makes the transition from perception to thinking an easy one. In the above cases, it is consequently better to say that my perception of the car is in various ways informed by valences, feelings, past experiences, and frameworks of reference and interest, and that these factors shape the way I actually see things. But apart from intending different properties of the object, or the object in its different meanings, apart from varying what the object I am intending is presented as, I might also vary the very form of intentionality itself. Instead of perceiving the car, I can also imagine it, judge about it, remember It, etc.

In effect, every intentional experience possesses two different, but inseparable, moments. Every intentional experience is an experience of a specific type, be it an experience of perceiving, judging, hoping, desiring, regretting, remembering, affirming, doubting, wondering, fearing, etc. Husserl called this aspect of the experience, the *intentional quality* of the experience. Every intentional experience is also directed at something, it is about something, be it a deer, a cat, or a mathematical state of affairs. Husserl called the component that specifies, not only which object is intended, but also what the object is apprehended or conceived as being, the *intentional matter* of the experience (Husserl 2001a, II, pp. 119–20). Husserl's distinction between the intentional matter and the intentional quality consequently bears a certain resemblance to the contemporary distinction between propositional content and propositional attitudes (though it is important to emphasize that Husserl by no means took all intentional experiences to be propositional in nature).

Needless to say, the same object can be combined with different intentional qualities, and the same intentional quality can be combined with different intentional matters. It is possible to doubt that 'inflation will continue', to doubt that 'the election was fair', or to doubt that 'one's next book will be an international best-seller', just as it is possible to deny that 'the lily is white', to judge that 'the lily is white', or to question whether 'the lily is white'.

Interestingly, Husserl furthermore considered these cognitive differences to be experiential differences. There is an experiential difference between *affirming* that Hegel was the greatest of the German idealists, and *denying* that same idea, just as there is an experiential difference between *expecting* and *doubting* that Denmark will win the next FIFA World Cup. What it is like to be in one type of conscious intentional state differs from what it is like to be in another type of conscious intentional state.[4] Similarly, the various intentional objects, as they are experienced, contribute to the phenomenal character of the experience. There is an *experiential* difference between denying that 'the Eiffel Tower is higher than the Empire State Building' and denying that 'North Korea has a viable economy', just as there is an *experiential* difference between believing that 'justice will prevail' and believing that 'When an equal amount is taken from equals, an equal amount results'. Husserl would consequently reject the currently widespread view that only sensory and emotional states have phenomenal qualities. In his view, there is something it is like to be in a conscious state, regardless of whether it is sensory or cognitive. In fact, to reduce phenomenality to the 'raw feel' of sensation marginalizes and trivializes phenomenal consciousness, and is detrimental to a correct understanding of its cognitive significance.[5]

Someone may deny, however, that there is a distinct phenomenality to thoughts. The argument might go like this. Abstract thoughts are accompanied by mental imagery and the phenomenal qualities to be encountered in abstract thought are in fact constituted by this imagery and not by the thoughts themselves. However, from time to time, the thoughts we are thinking, for instance a thought like 'every algebraic equation of uneven grade has at least one real root', will in fact not be accompanied by any imagery whatsoever, but this doesn't entail that the thought in question completely lacks phenomenality. Moreover,

consider the case where we first listen to a certain string of meaningless noises, and compare this to the case where we hear the very same string but this time understand and grasp
its meaning. Who would deny that there is a marked phenomenal difference between the
two. As Husserl suggests,

> Let us imagine that certain arabesques or figures have affected us aesthetically, and
> that we then suddenly see that we are dealing with symbols or verbal signs. In what
> does this difference consist? Or let us take the case of an attentive man hearing
> some totally strange word as a sound-complex without even dreaming it is a word,
> and compare this with the case of the same man afterwards hearing the word, in the
> course of conversation, and now acquainted with its meaning, but not illustrating it
> intuitively. What in general is the surplus element distinguishing the understanding of
> a symbolically functioning expression from the uncomprehended verbal sound? What
> is the difference between simply looking at a concrete object A, and treating it as a
> representative of 'any A whatsoever'? In this and countless similar cases it is the
> act-characters that differ.
>
> (Husserl 2001a, II, p. 105; see 2001a, I, pp. 193–94)[6]

Throughout this kind of analysis, phenomenology contends that consciousness is characterized by an intrinsic intentionality, and resists the attempt to provide a reductive account
of intentionality, for example trying to explain it by appeal to non-intentional factors such as
causality. But how exactly does intentionality work? How do we intend objects? This is where
the notion of meaning becomes central (we return to this in the final section of this chapter).
For the phenomenologists, intentionality is a question of meaning. We intend an object by
meaning something about it (Husserl 2001a, I, p. 201).[7]

INTENTIONALISM

We have so far been considering object-directed intentionality, but many experiences are
not object-directed – for example, feelings of pain and nausea, and moods such as anxiety,
depression, and boredom. Philosophers whose conception of intentionality is limited
to object-directedness deny that such experiences are intentional (e.g. Searle 1983).
Phenomenologists, however, in distinguishing between intentionality as object-directedness
and intentionality as a pointing-beyond, as an openness to what is other than the subject,
have a broader conception. It is true that pervasive moods such as sadness, boredom,
nostalgia, and anxiety must be distinguished from intentional feelings such as the desire
for an apple or the admiration for a particular person. Nevertheless, moods are not without
a reference to the world. They do not enclose us within ourselves, but are lived through
as pervasive atmospheres that deeply influence the way the world is disclosed to us.
Moods such as curiosity, nervousness, or happiness disclose our embeddedness in the
world and articulate or modify our existential possibilities. They are taken up into the intentional structure of our experiences. As Heidegger argued, moods, rather than being merely

attendant phenomena, are fundamental forms of disclosure: 'Mood has always already disclosed being-in-the-world as a whole and first makes possible directing oneself toward something' (Heidegger 1986/1996, p. 129).

What about pain? Sartre's classic analysis of eye strain in *Being and Nothingness* is illuminating in this case. Imagine that you are sitting late at night trying to finish reading a book. You have been reading most of the day and your eyes hurt. How does this pain originally manifest itself? According to Sartre, not initially as a thematic object of reflection, but by influencing the way in which you perceive the world. You become restless, irritated, and have difficulties in focusing and concentrating. The words on the page become blurry. The pain is not yet apprehended as an intended object, but that does not mean that it is either cognitively absent or unconscious. It manifests itself as an aspect of the intentional quality or as an affective atmosphere that influences and informs your intentional interaction with the world (see Sartre 1956, pp. 332–33). As Buytendijk writes,

> [W]hen the eyes become tired in reading, the reader does not perceive his fatigue first, but that the light is too weak or that the book is really boring or incomprehensible. ... Patients do not primarily establish *which* bodily functions are disturbed, but they complain about the fact that 'nothing works right anymore,' 'the work does not succeed,' that the environment is 'irritating,' 'fatiguing.'
>
> (Buytendijk 1974, p. 62)

Recently a number of analytical philosophers have criticized the view that phenomenal qualities are in and of themselves non-intentional, and have instead defended what might be called an *intentionalistic* interpretation of phenomenal qualities. Pain is a favourite example in this discussion. The point of departure has been the observation that it can often be quite difficult to distinguish a description of certain objects from a description of the experience of these very same objects. Back in 1903, G. E. Moore called attention to this fact, and dubbed it the peculiar *diaphanous* quality of experience: when you try to focus your attention on the intrinsic features of experience, you always seem to end up attending to what the experience is of. And as Tye argues, the lesson of this transparency is that '*phenomenology ain't in the head*' (1995, p. 151). To discover what it is like, you need to look at what is being intentionally represented. Thus, as the argument goes, experiences do not have intrinsic and non-intentional qualities of their own; rather, the qualitative character of experience consists entirely, as Dretske writes, in the qualitative properties objects are experienced as having (1995, p. 1). The loudness of a sound, the smoothness of a surface, the sweetness of a taste, the pungency of a smell are not qualities of experiences, they are qualities of things represented. Differences in what it is like are actually intentional differences. Thus an experience of a red apple is subjectively distinct from an experience of a yellow sunflower in virtue of the fact that different kinds of objects are represented. Experiences simply acquire their phenomenal character by representing the outside world. As a consequence, all phenomenal qualities are as such representational. There are no non-intentional experiences. Thus, for Tye pain is nothing but a sensory representation of bodily damage or disorder (1995, p. 113).

Dretske's and Tye's interpretation of phenomenal qualities has the great advantage of staying clear of any kind of sense-data theory. As already mentioned, it also bears a certain resemblance to views found in phenomenology. As Merleau-Ponty points out, colours, like red or green, 'are not sensations, they are the sensed, and quality is not an element of consciousness, but a property of the object' (1962, p. 4). To think that the sensed are components of consciousness is to commit the 'experience error', and to make perceptions out of things perceived (ibid., p. 5). A particularly radical criticism of this mistake can be found in Sartre's interpretation of intentionality. To affirm the intentionality of consciousness is, according to Sartre, to deny the existence of any kind of mental content (including any kind of sense-data or qualia) (1956, p. lix). There is nothing in consciousness, neither objects nor mental representations. It is completely empty. Thus, for Sartre, the being of intentional consciousness consists in its revelation of transcendent being (ibid., p. lxi). Sartre consequently takes phenomenal qualities to be qualities of worldly objects, and certainly not to be located within consciousness. However, from the fact that consciousness is nothing apart from its revelation of transcendent being (or as Tye and Dretske would probably say, from the fact that it exhausts itself in its representation of external reality), Sartre would never infer that intentional consciousness is therefore no problem for scientific reductionism.

Both Tye and Dretske explicitly criticize the attempt to draw a sharp distinction between the intentional or representational aspects of our mental lives and their phenomenal or subjective or felt aspects. But interestingly enough, their reason for attacking the separation is exactly the opposite of ours. By proposing an intentionalistic or representationalistic interpretation of phenomenality they hope to avoid the hard problem altogether. Why? Because if phenomenality is basically a question of intentionality, and if intentionality can be explained reductively in terms of functional or causal relations, one can accept the existence of phenomenality (neither Dretske nor Tye is an eliminativist) and still remain a physicalist (Tye 1995, pp. 153, 181).

This conclusion seems wrong. The decisive difficulty for reductionism is not the existence of epiphenomenal qualia, qualia in the sense of atomic, irrelational, ineffable, incomparable, and incorrigible mental phenomena. And the hard problem does not disappear if one (rightfully) denies the existence of such entities, and if one, so to speak, relocates the phenomenal 'outside' rather than 'inside'. The hard problem is not about the existence of non-physical objects of experience, but about the very existence of subjective experience itself; it is about the very fact that objects are *given* to us (see Rudd 1998).

Furthermore, Tye and Dretske fail to realize that there are two sides to the question of the 'what it is like'. There is a difference between asking about the property the object is experienced as having (what does the object feel like to the perceiver, e.g. how does the surface of a table feel differently from the surface of an ice cube) and asking about the property of the experience of the object (what does the perceiving feel like to the perceiver, e.g. how does perceiving the ice cube feel differently from imagining the ice cube). Both questions pertain to the phenomenal dimension, but whereas the first question concerns a worldly property, the second concerns an experiential property.[8] Contrary to what both Dretske and Tye are claiming, we consequently need to distinguish between (1) what the object is like for the subject, and (2) what the experience of the object is like for the subject (see Carruthers

1998; R. McIntyre 1999). It is worth noticing that even G. E. Moore seems to have recognized this. After stating that consciousness seems to vanish if we try to fix our attention upon it, and that if we try to introspect the sensation of blue all we can see is blue since the sensation itself is as if it were diaphanous, Moore continues: 'Yet it can be distinguished if we look enough, and if we know that there is something to look for' (1903, p. 450).

As phenomenologists would argue, we are never conscious of an object simpliciter, but always of the object as appearing in a certain way, as judged, seen, described, feared, remembered, smelled, anticipated, tasted, etc. We cannot be conscious of an object (a tasted lemon, a smelt rose, a seen table, a touched piece of silk) unless the experience through which this object is made to appear (the tasting, smelling, seeing, touching) is self-given. This is not to say that our access to, say, the lemon is *indirect*, or that it is mediated, contaminated, or blocked by our awareness of the experience, since the experience is not, itself, an object on a par with the lemon, but instead constitutes the very access to the appearing lemon. But the same object, with the exact same worldly properties, can present itself in a variety of manners. It can be given as perceived, imagined, or recollected, etc. When I am phenomenally acquainted with various objects, I am not mind- or self-blind. The objects are there *for me* in different modes of intentional experience (as imagined, perceived, recollected, anticipated, etc., or informed by my different moods, or distorted by the pain involved in eye strain), and it makes little sense to suggest that this 'for me' quality, this mineness of experience, is an external feature of the object presented. Indeed, contrary to the claim of Tye and Dretske, we should recognize that phenomenality is not merely world-presenting, it is also self-involving.

In short, the wrong conclusion to draw from an intentionalistic interpretation of phenomenal qualities is that there is no hard problem of consciousness but only the easy problem of intentionality (considered as reducible to information processing). The right conclusions to draw are that intentionality has a first-person aspect to it that makes it part of the hard problem, and that it resists reductive explanation to the same extent as phenomenality does.

INTENTIONALITY AND CONSCIOUSNESS

Even if it is true that intentionality and phenomenality are related, the nature of this relation still remains open for discussion. Is it intrinsic or extrinsic? Is it essential or merely contingent? To claim that it is contingent, that is, to claim that intentionality is indifferent to whether it takes place in a conscious or unconscious medium is to subscribe to something McGinn has called the *medium conception*. According to this view, the relation between consciousness and intentionality is like that between a medium of representation and the message it conveys. On one side, we have the medium of sound, shape, or experience, and on the other, the content of meaning and reference. Each side can be investigated separately from the other since their relation is completely contingent. Thus, according to this view, consciousness is nothing but a (rather mysterious) medium in which something relatively mundane, namely intentionality, is contingently embedded (McGinn 1991, p. 35). But is this really convincing?

On the face of it, *what the experience is like* and *what it is of* are by no means independent properties. Phenomenologists have typically argued that every appearance is an appearance of something for someone. McGinn makes the same point, and argues that experiences are *Janus-faced*: they have a world-directed aspect, they present the world in a certain way, but at the same time they also involve presence to the subject, and hence a subjective point of view. In short, they are of something other than the subject and they are like something for the subject, and as McGinn then continues:

> But these two faces do not wear different expressions: for what the experience is like is a function of what it is of, and what it is of is a function of what it is like. Told that an experience is as of a scarlet sphere you know what it is like to have it; and if you know what it is like to have it, then you know how it represents things. The two faces are, as it were, locked together. The subjective and the semantic are chained to each other.
>
> (1991, pp. 29–30)

In other words, the intentional/semantic aspect of an experience stands in an intimate relation to its phenomenal character and vice versa. But if what we are aware of is inextricably bound up with how it *appears* to us, phenomenal consciousness is not epiphenomenal, but rather cognitively indispensable.

This raises the question about the possibility of non-conscious intentionality. If the intimate relation between intentionality and phenomenality entails that all conscious states display some form of intentionality, does it also entail that consciousness is not only sufficient but also necessary for true intentionality? Does that mean it is impossible to have an unconscious belief? Of course, it is possible to find a variety of different views on the matter. Some would say that only consciousness is in possession of genuine intentionality, and that any other ascription of intentionality is either derived or metaphorical (Searle 1998, pp. 92–93). According to such a view, pictures, signs, symbols, posters, words do refer. They are about something. But the intentionality they display is not original or intrinsic to the pictures or signs; it is derived. They owe their intentionality to the fact that they are interpreted by conscious minds. Their intentionality is bestowed upon them by consciousness. On some views, the reason why consciousness is able to accomplish this is that it – by contrast – possesses an intrinsic or underived form of intentionality. Its intentionality is not merely a manner of speech or derived from others' interpretative stance towards it (otherwise, we would face an infinite regress). One line of argumentation in favour of such a view would be a line stressing the intrinsic connection between *experience*, *meaning*, and *intentionality*. As Galen Strawson puts it:

> [M]eaning is always a matter of something meaning something to something. In this sense, nothing means anything in an experienceless world. There is no possible meaning, hence no possible intention, hence no possible intentionality, on an

> experienceless planet ... There is no entity that means anything in this universe. There is no entity that is about anything. There is no semantic evaluability, no truth, no falsity. None of these properties are possessed by anything until experience begins. There is a clear and fundamental sense in which meaning, and hence intentionality, exists only in the conscious moment ...
>
> (1994, pp. 208–9)

Strawson consequently claims that experience is a necessary condition for genuine aboutness, and he suggests that there is an analogy between the sense in which a sleeping person might be said to be in possession of beliefs, preferences, etc., and the sense in which a CD might be said to contain music when it is not being played by a CD player. Considered merely as physical systems, neither of them is intrinsically about one thing rather than another, neither of them has any intrinsic (mental or musical) content. Strictly speaking, 'it is no more true to say that there are states of the brain, or of Louis, that have intrinsic mental content, when Louis is in a dreamless and experienceless sleep, than it is true to say that there are states of a CD that have intrinsic musical content as it sits in its box' (ibid., p. 167). A phenomenologist like Husserl would concur with this view, and would also consider consciousness to be the source of intentionality and meaning.

However, apart from outright denying the existence of genuine non-conscious intentionality, another option is also open. One might accept the existence of a non-conscious form of intentionality, but still argue that non-conscious intentionality and conscious intentionality have nothing (or very little) in common, for which reason an elucidation of the first type of intentionality throws little light upon the kind of intentionality that we find in conscious life. It is not possible to account for the intentionality of my experience without accounting for the phenomenal aspect of the experience as well, and it is impossible to account for the phenomenal aspect of the experience without referring to its intentionality. Any discussion of intentional consciousness that left out the question of phenomenal consciousness (and vice versa) would be severely deficient. In short, when it comes to conscious intentionality we need an integrated approach.

There are of course many additional problems that have been left untouched. To mention a few: there is the question about the existence of the unconscious, and about so-called dispositional beliefs. How do they fit into the framework presented above?[9] What about the objection that the attempt to argue for an intimate relation between intentionality and experience implies some subtle form of psychologism? To claim that there is a special experience of understanding is bound to provoke the Wittgensteinians. How should one defuse their criticism? Finally, a huge discussion is also taking place concerning internalism and externalism with respect to mental content. Externalists typically claim that differences in thought can be extraphenomenally defined. If this is true, what implications does it have for the relation between intentionality and experience? Then there is the question of how an intentionalistic interpretation of phenomenal qualities can handle cases of hallucinations. All of these questions are topics in need of further treatment, but to bring this chapter to a conclusion we will confine our considerations to how the phenomenological account of intentionality relates to the debate between internalists and externalists.

PHENOMENOLOGY, EXTERNALISM, AND METAPHYSICAL REALISM

'Internalism' and 'externalism' are umbrella terms. It is consequently not enough to ask in general whether somebody is an internalist or an externalist, since the answer will depend on the specific kind of internalism or externalism one has in mind. In the present context, however, internalism will be understood as the view that a subject's beliefs and experiences are wholly constituted by what goes on inside the mind of that subject, so that factors in the subject's natural and cultural environment have no bearing on their content. Thus, according to this view, mental states depend for their content upon nothing external to the subject whose states they are, i.e. the mind is taken to have the referential powers it has quite independently of how the world is. This is not to deny that some of our mental states, for instance our perceptions, might be causally dependent upon external factors; the point is simply that the internal states – regardless of how they are being caused – determine what we are conscious of. By contrast, externalism argues that mental states are externally individuated. What we think about, what we refer to, depends upon what actually exists in the (physical, social, and cultural) environment; our experience depends upon factors that are external to the subject possessing the mental states in question.

Where should one place phenomenology on the internalism–externalism scale? A widespread tendency has been to argue that whereas Husserl was a classical Cartesian internalist, existential phenomenologists like Heidegger, Sartre, and Merleau-Ponty favoured a form of externalism since they were all fully committed to the view that the mind is essentially determined by its intentional relationship to the world (see Dreyfus 1991; Keller 1999; McClamrock 1995; Rowlands 2003). Although it is quite true that later phenomenologists to a somewhat larger extent than Husserl emphasized the importance of practical and bodily forms of intentionality – as we will see in some of the subsequent chapters, Heidegger speaks of a form of directed comportment towards entities that are ready-to-hand, and Merleau-Ponty stresses the importance of motor-intentionality and argues that consciousness is not primarily an 'I think', but an 'I can' – this interpretation remains too simplistic. It ignores plenty of evidence suggesting that Husserlian phenomenology has affinities with a certain kind of externalism (see Zahavi 2004a, 2008a). At the same time, however, it is by no means obvious that Heidegger or Merleau-Ponty can be classified as straightforward externalists. Although Heidegger, for instance, by using the term 'being-in-the-world' wished to stress the fundamental world-involvement of the self – Dasein (human existence) is in the world, not by being in it like water in a glass, but ecstatically by means of a fundamental form of self-transcendence – he also spoke repeatedly of the self-sufficiency (*Selbstgenügsamkeit*) of (experiential) life (see Heidegger 1993, p. 261), and denied that a perception only becomes intentional if its object somehow enters into a relation with it, as if it would lose its intentionality if the object didn't exist. As a perception it is, as Heidegger writes, *intrinsically intentional* regardless of whether the perceived is in reality on hand or not (Heidegger 1979, p. 40). Heidegger later adds that it is a decisive error to interpret intentionality as a relation between a psychical subject and a physical object. The truth of the matter is that Dasein is intentionally structured within itself. Intentionality does not first arise through the actual presence of objects but lies in the perceiving itself, whether veridical or illusory (Heidegger 1975/1982, pp. 83–85). As we understand Heidegger, the underlying assumption behind these statements is (1) that even misperceptions, illusions, and hallucinations remain world-involving intentional acts, and (2) that the world-involvement in question, rather than being added from without, is something intrinsic to the acts themselves.

But this brief outline leaves us with something of a puzzle. Should we conclude that phenomenological accounts of the mind–world relation are in general characterized by features that point in the directions of both internalism and externalism? Does that reflect a confusion, or does it suggest that phenomenologists opt for a dual component theory that seeks to reconcile internalist and externalist intuitions? Or rather, does it point to the fact that the very alternative between internalism and externalism – an alternative arguably based on the division between inner and outer – is inapplicable when it comes to phenomenological conceptions of the mind–world relation?

To get closer to an answer, let us return to the issue of meaning. If externalism denies that intentionality is determined by meaning and conditioned by subjectivity, but rather holds that it is reducible to some kind of causal covariation, none of the phenomenologists would count as externalists. But this is not the only way to define externalism. Just like internalism, externalism can hold that meaning determines reference as long as the meaning in question is externally embedded or world-involving. McDowell has explicitly argued that an externalist account of meaning should be complemented by an externalist account of the mind. Putnam is famous for having argued that meanings 'just ain't in the head' (1977, p. 124), but as McDowell adds, neither is the mind (1992, p. 36). The moment both mind and meaning are taken to be environmentally embedded, there is nothing mysterious in ascribing an intrinsic referentiality or world-directedness to the mind: 'The need to construct a theoretical "hook" to link thinking to the world does not arise, because if it is thinking that we have in view at all – say being struck by the thought that one hears the sound of water dripping – then what we have in view is *already* hooked on to the world; it is already in view as possessing referential directedness at reality' (ibid., p. 45). One can find a comparable view in McCulloch, who has argued that we need to reject the dualism between a self-contained mind and a mindless world. The subjective is not inside the mind and the objective is not *outside* of it. Echoing McDowell, McCulloch writes that meanings ain't in the head, they are in the mind, but the mind just ain't in the head (2003, pp. 11–12). In his view, there is no tension between phenomenology and externalism as long as both are understood properly (ibid., p. 12).

Although it 'ain't' correct grammar, there is some truth to this. Phenomenologists (and that includes Husserlian phenomenologists) would be sympathetic to some of the ideas espoused by McDowell and McCulloch, and it is clear that they all have common enemies. Not only do they reject the kind of internalism known as *Cartesian materialism*, i.e. the view that the mind can be identified with the brain, and that the brain is a self-contained organ that can be understood in isolation from the world, but they would also oppose the kind of externalism that seeks to reduce intentionality and reference to brute causal mechanisms.

Although Husserl does argue that meaning determines reference, it would be a mistake to think that his theory is only geared towards handling those types of reference where the meaning–content prescribes a certain object by detailing its properties descriptively. On the contrary, Husserl claims that the available meaning includes components that allow us to refer to particulars independently of definite descriptions. This is precisely the case for demonstrative reference. So, already early on, Husserl was aware that the word 'this' refers directly, rather than attributively, and what is even more important, he also realized to what extent perception involves a demonstrative content of sense. When I see a red ball, the ball is my intentional object, not because it satisfies the general meaning 'the red ball', but because it satisfies the demonstrative content '*this* red ball'. To perceive an object is not simply to perceive a certain type of object, that is, any object having the type of properties prescribed by the content, rather it is to perceive *this* particular object. Some would argue that the directionality of demonstrative reference is due to the fact that it is based not on meaning but on causality. That assumes that the only way for meaning to 'capture' particulars is by doing so attributively, i.e. on the basis of definite descriptions. But Husserl's point is exactly that 'this' is a non-descriptive meaning, and that it refers directly and non-attributively. For him, the directedness of demonstrative reference is founded on the immediacy of *intuition*.

A natural way to present the choice between internalism and externalism is by asking the following question: Is intentionality determined by factors *internal* to the mind or by factors *external* to the mind? However, this apparently straightforward way of presenting the available options is, on closer inspection, quite inadequate, for whereas internalism typically postulates a gap between mind and world, externalism argues precisely that the world is not external to the mind. But the moment externalism is seen as arguing that mind and world are inseparable, it could also quite easily be defined as a position that takes intentionality to be determined by factors *internal* to this whole. Thus defined, externalism is difficult to distinguish from the kind of internalism that insists that intentionality is determined by factors internal to the mind, but which conceives of the mind in sufficiently broad terms. On one reading, Husserl's philosophy might be said to constitute exactly such an attempt to undermine any commonsensical divide between mind and world. As we saw in our discussion of introspection in Chapter 2, already in the *Logical Investigations* Husserl rejected the facile divide between inside and outside as being pertinent for an understanding of intentionality, and as he writes in a later text, 'Thus, object, objective being, and consciousness belong *a priori* inseparably together' (Husserl 2003, p. 73).[10]

A related point can be found in Heidegger, who denies that the relation between Dasein and world can be grasped with the help of the concepts 'inner' and 'outer':

> In directing itself toward ... and in grasping something, Dasein does not first go outside of the inner sphere in which it is initially encapsulated, but, rather, in its primary kind of being, it is always already 'outside' together with some being encountered in the world already discovered. Nor is any inner sphere abandoned when Dasein dwells together with a being to be known and determines its character. Rather, even in this 'being outside' together with its object, Dasein is 'inside' correctly understood; that is, it itself exists as the being-in-the-world which knows. Again, the perception of what is known does not take place as a return with one's booty to the 'cabinet'

of consciousness after one has gone out and grasped it. Rather, in perceiving, preserving, and retaining, the Dasein that knows *remains outside as Dasein*.

(1986/1996, p. 62)

The notions of internalism and externalism remain bound to the inner–outer division, but this is a distinction that phenomenology puts into doubt.

Considering the way in which phenomenologists conceive of intentionality, of the mind–world relationship, it is questionable whether it really makes much sense to classify their views as being committed to either internalism or externalism. Avoiding the two terms obviously won't solve all the problems, but it might at least permit us to avoid letting our investigation be guided by misleading metaphors. The mind is neither a container nor a special place. Hence it makes little sense to say that the world must be either inside or outside of the mind. Ultimately, we should appreciate that the phenomenological investigations of the structures and conditions of possibility for phenomena are antecedent to any divide between interiority and exteriority, since they are investigations of the dimension in which any object – be it external or internal – manifests itself (see Heidegger 1986/1996, p. 419; Waldenfels 2000, p. 217). Rather than committing the mistake of interpreting the phenomena mentalistically, as being part of a mental inventory, we should see the phenomenological focus on the phenomena as an attempt to question the very subject–object split, that is, as an attempt to stress the co-emergence of mind and world. The take-home message might be precisely that phenomenology can teach us that the forced choice between internalism and externalism is misguided. There are other options available.[11]

In his book *Expressing the World*, Anthony Rudd introduced a distinction between *realist externalism* and *Kantian externalism* (2003, p. 44). Both forms of externalism take intentionality seriously. Both deny the self-contained nature of the mind and argue that it is tied to the world. But Kantian externalism then adds a twist by arguing that the reverse also holds true. In his refutation of idealism, Kant argued that I can be aware of myself only when I am aware of the world around me. But the world to which the mind is bound is the phenomenal world, which is equally bound to the mind. This move allowed Kant to reject the scepticism that sought to drive a wedge between mind and world, but since Kant – at least according to a standard interpretation – went on to distinguish the phenomenal world and the noumenal reality of the things in themselves, he might be said to have simply relocated the sceptical problem (Rudd 2003, p. 5). A more radical move was made by the phenomenologists, who rejected the notion of the noumenal *Ding an sich* as unintelligible and nonsensical (see Heidegger 1975/1982, p. 422; Husserl 1950/1964, p. 38). In their view, mind and world are not distinct entities; rather, they are bound constitutively together. As Merleau-Ponty puts it:

The world is inseparable from the subject, but from a subject which is nothing but a project of the world, and the subject is inseparable from the world, but from a world which the subject itself projects. The subject is a being-in-the-world and the world remains 'subjective' since its texture and articulations are traced out by the subject's movement of transcendence.

(1962, p. 430)

In other words, phenomenologists would typically argue that the relation between mind and world is an internal relation, a relation constitutive of its *relata*, and not an external one of causality (see Rudd 2003, pp. 53, 60). Not surprisingly, the phenomenological account bears some rather obvious similarities to the one proposed by the enactive view of cognition, since the latter has the explicit goal of negotiating a middle path between the Scylla of cognition as a recovery of a pregiven outer world (realism), and the Charybdis of cognition as the projection of a pregiven inner world (idealism) (Varela et al. 1991, p. 172).

To insist on the interdependence of mind and world doesn't amount to any form of phenomenalism, metaphysical idealism, or panpsychism. If we look closer at reality, we won't find consciousness all over the place. If we analyse a physical object, it does not dissolve into consciousness, it dissolves into atoms and molecules. Thus, it is not as if statements about botanical or geological states of affairs are henceforth to be reinterpreted as statements about mental content. But any claim to the effect that 'there is a real object' or 'that there is a reality' refers back to certain epistemic connections, to certain conscious operations, and it is in reference to these that the being of objects and all objective states of affairs acquire their meaning (Husserl 2003, pp. 28–29). What we find in phenomenology – and this brings us back to some of the more overarching philosophical implications discussed in Chapter 2 – is a deliberate blurring of the distinction between ontology and epistemology, and by implication a clear rejection of metaphysical realism.

To summarize the two main results from our survey: Phenomenological accounts of intentionality are those that specifically seek to examine intentionality from the first-person perspective (rather than by appeal to various non-intentional mechanisms), and accounts of the mind–world relations are not easily captured and categorized as being either internalist or externalist in nature.

NOTES

---

1 It was discovered that the ordinary principles of 'substitutivity of ordinarily coreferential expressions' and 'existential generalization' don't hold true in a number of sentences involving psychological verbs. Whereas the following two arguments are valid:

> Fido is a dog
> There exists a dog

and

> Fido is a dog
> Fido is owned by the butcher
> The butcher owns a dog.

The two following arguments are invalid:

> John thinks that Fido is a dog
> There exists an object which John thinks is a dog

and

> John thinks that Fido is a dog
> Fido is owned by the butcher
> John thinks that the butcher owns a dog.

2 A popular and much discussed recent theory is the so-called teleosemantic account, which, according to a standard reading, argues that the semantic content of a mental representation is determined by its proper function or purpose, i.e. what through evolution or learning it has been designed to represent. However, according to one of its foremost defenders, the teleosemantic account doesn't actually explain intentionality, if understood as the property of 'ofness' or 'aboutness'. As Ruth Millikan writes, 'When the bare teleosemantic theory has been spent, the central task for a theory of intentional representation has not yet begun. Teleosemantic theories are piggyback theories. They must ride on more basic theories of representation, perhaps causal theories, or picture theories, or informational theories, or some combination of these' (2004, p. 66).

3 This view might superficially resemble internalism – the view that the mind has the referential powers it has quite independently of how the world is, since mental states depend for their content upon nothing external to the person whose states they are. But as we will see shortly, things are more complicated, and one should not conflate the view that we can refer to objects that do not exist with the view that we can refer to objects quite independently of whether or not there is a world.

4 Using a decidedly Husserlian *jargon*, Siewert has recently spoken of *noetic phenomenal features* (1998, p. 284). Sticking to the distinction between propositional content and attitude, one could argue that there are distinctive qualitative feels to the different propositional attitudes.

5 For further attempts to argue in defence of a broader notion of phenomenal consciousness, see Smith 1989, Flanagan 1992, Van Gulick 1997, and Siewert 1998.

6 For a more recent similar line of argument, see Galen Strawson 1994, pp. 5–6.

7 Let us here introduce Husserl's technical term 'noema'. A huge amount of scholarly discussion has taken place about the proper way to interpret the Husserlian notion of the noema (see Drummond 2003, for an overview). The discussion concerns the relation between the *object-as-intended* (the noema) and the *object-that-is-intended* (the object itself) – the wine-bottle-as-perceived (as felt and seen) and the bottle itself. According to one reading, the noema is a type of representational entity, an ideal sense or meaning that mediates the intentional relation between the mental act and the object. On this reading, consciousness is directed towards the object by means of the noema and thus only achieves its openness to the world in virtue of this intermediary ideal entity (Smith and McIntyre 1982, p. 87). According to a competing interpretation, intentional experiences are intrinsically self-transcending; their being is constituted by the being *of* something else, and they do not first achieve a reference to the world by virtue of some intermediate representational entity. As a consequence, it is argued that the noema is to be understood neither as an ideal meaning, nor as a concept, nor as a proposition; it is not an intermediary between subject and object; it is not something that bestows intentionality on consciousness (as if consciousness prior to the introduction of the noema would be like a closed container with no bearing on the

world) – rather, it is the object itself considered in the *phenomenological* reflection, i.e. precisely as experienced. The noema is the perceived object as perceived, the recollected episode as recollected, the judged state of affairs as judged, etc. This does not imply, however, that there is no distinction (within the reflective stance) between the object-as-it-is-intended and the object-that-is-intended, but this distinction is exactly a structural difference *within* the noema (Drummond 1990, pp. 108–9, 113). In so far as an investigation of the noema is one of any kind of object, aspect, dimension, or region, considered in its very manifestation, in its very significance for consciousness, the object and the noema turn out to be the same, though differently considered. Against this background, the first interpretation has been criticized for confusing what is an ordinary object considered abstractly, and with a non-ordinary (phenomenological) attitude, with a non-ordinary abstract entity (Drummond 1992, p. 89). It would take us too far afield to review the twists and turns of this debate, so we shall simply state for the record that we, for a variety of reasons, think the first representationalist interpretation of the noema to be mistaken (see Zahavi 2003a, pp. 53–68; 2004a).

8 To speak of worldly properties in this context should not be misunderstood; it does not entail any metaphysical claims concerning the subject-independent existence of the said properties. The claim being made is merely that the properties in question are properties of the experienced objects and not of the experience of the objects.

9 Flanagan has proposed a distinction between 'experiential sensitivity' and 'informational sensitivity'. Somebody may be experientially insensitive but informationally sensitive to a certain difference. When we are merely informationally sensitive to something, we are not conscious of it, that is, pure informational sensitivity, or to use a better expression, pure informational pickup and processing, is non-conscious. It is a processing without phenomenal awareness (Flanagan 1992, pp. 55–56, 147). One could think of blindsight as an example in a specific sensory domain. Subjectivity has to do with experiential sensitivity, and it is only the latter that lets us have phenomenal access to the object. But although it might be appropriate to operate with a notion of non-conscious informational processing, one should be careful not to assume that the informational sensitivity provides us with a non-phenomenal version of the exact *same* information as the experiential sensitivity. To suggest something like that is once again to flirt with the view that consciousness is cognitively epiphenomenal.

10 Let us anticipate an obvious objection. Isn't Husserl (in)famous for not having ruled out the existence of a worldless mind? As Husserl writes in the notorious §49 in *Ideas I*, 'pure' consciousness can be considered an independent realm of being, and even though consciousness would be modified if the world of objects were annihilated, it would not be affected in its own existence (1976/1982, pp. 104–5). But one should note that Husserl's imagined annihilation of the world has nothing to do with global scepticism. Husserl is not trying to drive a wedge between the world as we experience it and the real world. He is not claiming that it makes sense to suppose that the phenomenologically given could remain the same while the world itself ceased to exist. Quite to the contrary, in fact, since he quite explicitly states that such a proposal is nonsensical (Husserl 2002, p. 402). Husserl's point is rather that our experiences might conceivably cease to be ordered in a harmonious and coherent fashion; further, he argues that we, in such a case, would no longer have any reason to believe in the existence of a coherent world. Thus, Husserl is certainly not arguing that every type of experience is compatible with the absence of the world

or that every type of experience would remain the same even if the world didn't exist. All he is saying is that some form of consciousness might be possible even in the absence of an ordered and objective world.

11 For further discussions of internalism and externalism in phenomenological perspective, see the special issue of *Synthese* (Zahavi 2008a).

FURTHER READING

Franz Brentano, *Psychology from an Empirical Standpoint*. Trans. A. C. Rancurello, D. B. Terrell and L. L. McAlister. London: Routledge & Kegan Paul, 1973.

Tim Crane, *Elements of Mind*. Oxford: Oxford University Press, 2001.

John J. Drummond, *Husserlian Intentionality and Non-foundational Realism*. Dordrecht: Kluwer Academic Publishers, 1990.

Edmund Husserl, *Logical Investigations*. 2 vols. Trans. J. N. Findlay. London: Routledge & Kegan Paul, 2001.

Edmund Husserl, *Ideas Pertaining to a Pure Phenomenology and to a Phenomenological Philosophy, First Book*. Trans. F. Kersten. The Hague: Martinus Nijhoff, 1982.

William Ramsey, *Representation Reconsidered*. Cambridge: Cambridge University Press, 2007.

John Searle, *Intentionality: An Essay in the Philosophy of Mind*. Cambridge: Cambridge University Press, 1983.

David W. Smith and Ronald McIntyre, *Husserl and Intentionality*. Dordrecht: D. Reidel, 1982.

7 The embodied mind

Let's start with a fully cognizing human being who is complete in body and mind, and ask what we could subtract while still retaining a cognizing mind. Such thought experiments may help us to home in on precisely what a cognitive system or mind actually is.

Let's take as our example any one of us who happens to be complete in body and mind, understanding that in an ordinary and everyday way. Now we can ask, would it make any difference in regard to her ability to think or imagine or remember, or to engage in most cognitive exercises if she were missing one or even several of her limbs? Right, it doesn't seem that we need all our limbs to engage in cognizing. So let's get rid of them. While we're at it, we may as well get rid of all the other extraneous body parts – those that we don't seem to need in order to do our thinking. As these kinds of thought experiments go, we usually end up with just our brains, since even sensory input can be provided artificially. For example, we can directly stimulate the parts of the brain responsible for registering sensory information and thereby, supposedly, have exactly the same experience we would have if our sensory organs were delivering that information. This common thought experiment is referred to as the brain-in-a-vat, and the image is of a brain floating around in a vat of chemicals, kept alive by artificial nourishment, and kept informed by various electrodes that carry information about the world, or about whatever the mad scientist running this experiment wants to feed it.

Dennett (1981) has taken this thought experiment one step further. He tells the story of being sent on a mission that involved removing his brain, storing it in a vat, but remaining connected with the body via radio waves. Dennett's mission, however, is a dangerous one, and in the process his body ceases its biological functioning and, in effect, dies. His brain, however, is still alive in the vat. Understandably, he gets upset:

> Waves of panic and even nausea swept over me, made all the more horrible by the absence of their normal body-dependent phenomenology. No adrenaline rush of

tingles in the arms, no pounding heart, no premonitory salivation. I did feel a dread sinking feeling in my bowels at one point, and this tricked me momentarily into the false hope that I was undergoing a reversal of the process that landed me in this fix – a gradual undisembodiment. But the isolation and uniqueness of that twinge soon convinced me that it was simply the first of a plague of phantom body hallucinations that I, like any other amputee, would be all too likely to suffer.

(1981, p. 225)

As time goes on, Dennett is provided with a new body, which he finds difficult to master, but which, after a period of adjustment, seems just fine. He thinks perhaps this is similar to undergoing extensive plastic surgery or a sex-change operation. Dennett then learns that the technicians had copied his brain's functional structure and all of the information in it to a computer program, and that he is doubly and wirelessly connected – to his brain still in the vat, and, with the flick of a toggle switch, to the computer running his artificial brain. When he flips the switch between brain and computer, he is unable to tell the difference in his experience.

The moral of this story, if we were to follow Dennett's line of reasoning and put this story together with the standard line of thought about brains-in-vats, is that not only is the body unnecessary for experience and cognition, but we don't even need the brain, as long as we have the program and information running on the right kind of hardware. This constitutes a functionalist perspective according to which a sophisticated computational program or an artificial neural-network can generate the same mental experiences as can be generated by the brain alone. What's important is not the physical instantiation (although this is certainly a consideration, since it would likely make a difference if we tried to run the software on a Mac or a PC rather than on a sophisticated neural-net computer); rather, what is important is the software program and the information that constitutes the essential part of a system required to generate me, and my cognitive life. Once we have the right information and the proper brain-replicating syntax, we should be able to generate your cognitive experience in any machine that can run the program.

Does this mean that the body contributes nothing of importance to the cognitive system? Of course, we can say that the brain is important in all normal cases where we do not have a back-up artificial brain. And even Dennett suggests that to *do* anything, to take action in some way, one might need some kind of body. But we could think that a robotic body could do just as well, as long as it were properly connected (by radio transmitters) to the artificial brain.

The image of the brain-in-a-vat is surprisingly influential even for opponents of functionalism. Thus, Searle, who takes an anti-functionalist view, and emphasizes the importance of neurobiology, nonetheless, in defending a radical form of internalism, appeals to the same image:

Even if I am a brain in a vat – that is, even if all of my perceptions and actions in the world are hallucinations, and the conditions of satisfaction of all my externally referring Intentional states are, in fact, unsatisfied – nonetheless, I do have the Intentional content that I have, and thus I necessarily have exactly the same Background that I would have if I were not a brain in a vat and had that particular Intentional content.

> *That* I have a certain set of Intentional states and that I have a Background do not logically require that I be in fact in certain relations to the world around me. ...
>
> (Searle 1983, p. 154)

This kind of denial of the cognitive significance of the body is part of a long philosophical tradition. Compare the following statement in Plato's dialogue, *Phaedo*:

> It seems that so long as we are alive, we shall continue closest to knowledge if we avoid as much as we can all contact and association with the body, except when they are absolute necessary, and instead of allowing ourselves to become infected with its nature, purify ourselves from it until God himself gives us deliverance.
>
> (Plato 1985, p. 67a)

Such a disembodied view on the mind was also found in classical cognitive science, since it examined intelligent behaviour as if it were independent of any specific bodily form. Indeed, until recently, insofar as neuroscientists considered the body, it was only *qua* its representation in the somatosensory cortex.

Now one might think that it is incumbent on the phenomenologist, or on the theorists of embodied cognition, to prove that there cannot be cognition without embodiment. But there are two questions here. First, the in-principle question of whether the notion of a cognizing disembodied brain (a brain in a vat) is at all intelligible; and second, regardless of what the answer is to the first question, we can ask whether human cognition is de facto disembodied. We can answer the second question (in the negative) without having to demonstrate that the brain-in-a-vat thought experiment is incoherent. It just is an empirical fact that we are indeed embodied, that our perceptions and actions depend on the fact that we have bodies, and that cognition is shaped by our bodily existence. This is, we might say, a 'no-brainer'. But we can note the following in response to the first question. The brain-in-a-vat thought experiment actually shows that perception and action do require some kind of embodiment. Even the pure brain-in-a-vat requires absolutely everything that the body normally provides – for example, sensory input and life support. Indeed, the importance of the body can be measured in considering precisely what it would take to sustain a disembodied brain and the supposed experience that goes along with it. What is possible for a brain-in-a-vat is only possible if it is provided with a properly balanced nutrition, a properly balanced mix of hormones and neurotransmitters, and a complex stream of sensory information, properly adjusted for the temporal differentiations that are in fact involved in intermodal binding. If we consider only the visual input, we would have to assume that any poking around in the visual cortex that would replicate our human visual experience would have to be so specified in its details, that an analogue or digital input mechanism would have to be as complicated, as chemically complex, and as enactive as the human eye. That is, the full and extraordinary support system that would be required to allow a brain-in-a-vat to experience things as we experience them, or in other words, to allow a brain-in-a-vat to be phenomenologically in-the-world and not just physically in-a-vat, would have to replicate the bodily system that already supports our ordinary existence (see Damasio 1994, p. 228; Gallagher 2005b).

Whether or not a brain-in-a-vat is a real possibility, it is certain that *our* cognitive experience is shaped by an embodied brain and that the brains we have are shaped by the bodies we have, and by our real world actions. Cognition is not only embodied, it is situated and, of course, it is situated because it is embodied.

The fact that we stand upright, for example, is distinctive for the human species, and this biological fact, which comes along with many other biological facts, has far-reaching consequences with respect to perceptual and action abilities, and by implication, with respect to our entire cognitive life. Erwin Straus, for example, points out that 'the shape and function of the human body are determined in almost every detail by, and for, the upright posture' (1966, p. 138). Consider a brief list:

- First, in regard to *human anatomy and skeletal structure*, the upright posture requires a specific shape and structure of the human foot, ankle, knee, hip, and vertebral column, as well as the proportions of limbs, and all of this demands a specific musculature and nervous system design. In terms of evolution, the shaping of the body for the upright posture also permits the specifically human development of shoulders, arms, hands, skull, and face. The important point here is that these anatomical structures define our capabilities and therefore define what counts as the world. Gibson (1986) developed the idea that objects in the environment can afford different kinds of action, given the kind of body that we have. Such affordances are closely tied to our bodily shape and our action capabilities. A chair affords sitting precisely because the human body bends at the knees, hips, etc. Capabilities to sit or to adopt some other posture are first of all motor; but they arguably extend to the most abstract and rational capacities for cognition, such as counting and the development of mathematics (see M. Johnson 1987; Lakoff and Johnson 1980; Lakoff and Núñez 2001; Sheets-Johnstone 1990).
- Second, in terms of *development*, attaining the upright posture is delayed in humans. The infant is required to learn it in a struggle against gravity. This calls for a basic conscious wakefulness: if you fall asleep, you fall. Posture and movement are directly related to biological states of sleep and wakefulness. Prior to standing, early crawling behaviour influences the development of perception and cognition (Campos et al. 1992). The change of posture that comes with standing and walking equally affects what we can see, what we can attend, what we can grasp and manipulate.
- Third, in terms of *how we are related to things and other people*, with the upright posture we maintain distance and independence – distance from the ground; distance from things; and some degree of independence from other people. In standing, the range of vision is extended, and accordingly, the environmental horizon is widened and distanced. The spatial frameworks for perception and action are redefined. Standing frees the hands for reaching, grasping, manipulating, carrying, using tools, and pointing. Both phylogenetically (with respect to evolution) and ontogenetically (with respect to individual development), these changes introduce complexities into brain structure, complexities that eventually help generate rational thought (Paillard 2000).
- With respect to our *perceptual abilities*, which in turn shape all other cognitive abilities, in evolutionary terms, attaining the upright posture means that the olfactory sense declines

in importance; seeing becomes primary. We are able to see far ahead of where we are currently located, and this grants foresight and allows for planning. While our hands are liberated for more proficient grasping and catching, our mouths are liberated for other purposes, since olfactory mechanisms (required for finding our way around when close to the ground) shrink and no longer dominate facial structure. The jaw structure not only defines what we eat, but along with the development of the more subtle phonetic muscles, enables the development of vocal language. And if you ask Aristotle, he'll tell you that this means the development of both politics and rationality.

Add to this the idea that the body 'pre-processes' and filters incoming sensory signals, and 'post-processes' and limits efferent signals that contribute to motor control. Comparative anatomy shows that the shape and relative locations of the ears, for example, allow us to determine the direction of a sound (Chiel and Beer 1997). Bodily movements are not fully determined at brain level; rather, they are re-engineered by the design and flexibility of muscles and tendons, their geometric relations to other muscles and joints, and the prior history of their activation (Zajac 1993). Thus, 'the nervous system cannot process information that is not transduced by the periphery, nor can it command movements that are physically impossible for that periphery' (Chiel and Beer 1997, p. 554). These observations are part of a larger story about what shapes the body and how that also shapes cognition. But they are sufficient to indicate that the biological body (what it enables and excludes by its structure, basic posture, and motor capacity) is the body that shapes the way that we humans perceive and think about the world.

ROBOTIC AND BIOLOGICAL BODIES

These are lessons hard won, not by means of thought experiments, where you seemingly can think many aspects of the system away, but in the 'real world' of the biological sciences, as well as in advanced robotics. Roboticists, like Rodney Brooks at MIT, have discovered that the traditional approaches of trying to develop robots from the top down, i.e. starting with a disembodied syntax and trying to add a functional artificial body that would heed the commands from a central intelligence computer, just don't work. Rather, their more recent initiatives are attempts to design robots from the bottom up, building simple, pragmatically ordered, biologically inspired, sensorimotor machines that can move around environments by using information gathered in real time from the environments themselves. Such robots are 'physically grounded', which means they are physical entities embedded in their physical environments, but in a way in which their representations pragmatically reference the real world; they are enactive perceiving machines, grasping the world in terms of projects to be accomplished.

Nouvelle AI is based on the physical grounding hypothesis. This hypothesis states that to build a system that is intelligent it is necessary to have its representations grounded in the physical world. Our experience with this approach is that once this commitment is made, the need for traditional symbolic representations soon fades entirely. The key observation is that the world is its own best model. It is always exactly up to date. It always contains every detail there is to be known. The trick is to sense it appropriately and often enough. To build a system based on the physical grounding hypothesis it is necessary to connect it to the world via a set of sensors and actuators.

(Brooks 1990, p. 5)

Brooks comes to this important realization, however, not by thinking of robots as bodies, but by thinking of bodies as robots:

The body, this mass of biomolecules, is a machine that acts according to a set of specifiable rules. ... We are machines, as are our spouses, our children, and our dogs. ... I believe myself and my children all to be mere machines.

(Brooks 2002, pp. 173–75)

The philosophical background to this particular way of conceiving of the body is clearly Cartesian. Descartes inspired the view of animals as purely physical automata – robots devoid of conscious intelligence. This was extended to humans by a variety of philosophers, including La Mettrie (1745) and Cabanis (1802), and was further explicated by S. Hodgson (1870) and Huxley (1874). Brooks seems bound to follow in this tradition, perhaps topping it off by proposing that conscious or conscious-like intelligence should emerge from this kind of system. An alternative philosophical backdrop supporting the concept of embodied cognition, however, is alive and well. This is worked out in the phenomenological views of Husserl and Merleau-Ponty, and updated by philosophers and scientists like Clark (1997), Varela et al. (1991), Thompson (2007), Thompson and Varela (2001), Sheets-Johnstone (1990, 1999), Michael Wheeler (2005), and others. This alternative approach follows Merleau-Ponty in rejecting the idea that the body is simply a 'highly polished machine' (1962, p. 76). So let's dig deeper into the meaning of embodiment, how it situates us and how it shapes our cognitive experience.

Phenomenology of the body – a very short history

The best-known philosopher of embodiment is undoubtedly Merleau-Ponty. But Merleau-Ponty was certainly not the only phenomenologist who devoted time and energy to a painstaking analysis of the lived body. Not only have other French phenomenologists written extensively on the body, Sartre and Michel Henry, for example, but it would even be a mistake to identify phenomenology of embodiment with French phenomenology. Already in Husserl's lecture course *Thing and Space* from 1907 one can find far-reaching phenomenological analyses of the moving and sensing body. And it is well known that Husserl's analysis of the body in the second volume of his *Ideas* served as a decisive inspiration for Merleau-Ponty's *Phenomenology of Perception*. Husserl's manuscript was only published posthumously in 1952, but Merleau-Ponty visited the Husserl archives shortly before the outbreak of the Second World War – as one of its first foreign visitors – and had on that occasion a chance to read Husserl's unpublished manuscript (see Zahavi 1994, 2006). But even Husserl might not have been the first. Michel Henry has argued that one can find an implicit theory about the lived body in the most famous dualist of them all, namely Descartes (Henry 1975, p. 139). And if one moves forward in history, to the Napoleonic Wars, one will encounter the work of another French philosopher Maine de Biran who – and this is still according to Michel Henry – provides a phenomenological account of the body that is superior to the ones subsequently to be found in the writings of Husserl, Sartre, and Merleau-Ponty.

The phenomenological investigation of the body is not the analysis of one object among others. That is, it is not as if phenomenology in its investigation of a number of different ontological regions (the domain of logic, mathematical entities, utensils, works of art, etc.) also stumbles upon the body and then subjects it to a close scrutiny. On the contrary, the body is considered a constitutive or transcendental principle, precisely because it is involved in the very possibility of experience. It is deeply implicated in our relation to the world, in our relation to others, and in our self-relation, and its analysis consequently proves crucial for understanding of all these relations.

The phenomenological emphasis on the body obviously entails a rejection of Cartesian mind–body dualism. But it should be just as obvious that this does not entail an endorsement of some kind of Cartesian materialism. It is not as if the phenomenological way to 'overcome' dualism is by retaining the distinction between mind and body, and then simply getting rid of the mind. Rather, the notion of embodiment, the notion of an embodied mind or a minded body, is meant to replace the ordinary notions of mind and body, both of which are derivations and abstractions. Merleau-Ponty famously speaks of the ambiguous nature of the body, and argues that bodily existence is a third category beyond the merely physiological and the merely psychological (1962, p. 350). The lived body is neither spirit nor nature, neither soul nor body, neither inner nor outer, neither subject nor object. All of these contraposed categories are derivations of something more basic.

Phenomenologists object to the metaphysical division between *res extensa* and *res cogitans*. If one accepted such a division, the only place for the body would seem to be on the side of the *res extensa*. But phenomenologists deny that the body is a mere object in the world. The body is not merely an object of experience that we see, touch, smell, etc. Rather, the body is also a principle of experience, it is what permits us to see, touch, and smell, etc. Obviously, the body can also explore itself. It can take itself (or the body of another) as its object of exploration. This is what typically happens in physiology or neurology, etc. But such an investigation of the body as an object is not exhaustive. As Sartre famously points out, we should be careful not to let our understanding of the lived body be determined by an external perspective that ultimately has its origin in the anatomical study of the corpse (1956, p. 348; see also Merleau-Ponty 1962, p. 351). As he continues in *Being and Nothingness*:

> The problem of the body and its relations with consciousness [are] often obscured by the fact that while the body is from the start posited as a certain *thing* having its own laws and capable of being defined from outside, consciousness is then reached by the type of inner intuition which is peculiar to it. Actually if after grasping 'my' consciousness in its absolute interiority and by a series of reflective acts, I then seek to unite it with a certain living object composed of a nervous system, a brain, glands, digestive, respiratory, and circulatory organs whose very matter is capable of being analyzed chemically into atoms of hydrogen, carbon, nitrogen, phosphorus, etc., then I am going to encounter insurmountable difficulties. But these difficulties all stem from the fact that I try to unite my consciousness not with *my* body but with the body of *others*. In fact the body which I have just described is not *my* body such as it is *for me*.
>
> (Sartre 1956, p. 303)

The phenomenological contribution to a solution of the mind–body problem does not take the form of a metaphysical theory of mental causation, nor does it consist in an explanation of how the body interacts with the mind; rather, it seeks to understand to what extent our experience of the world, our experience of self and our experience of others are formed by and influenced by our embodiment. But through this change of focus, it also rethinks and questions some of the distinctions that define the mind–body problem in the first place.

The first and most basic phenomenological distinction to be made, and the one that allows us to see that Brooks may be working with the wrong concept of the body, is between the *objective body* and the *lived body* (Husserl's distinction between *Körper* and *Leib*, respectively; Merleau-Ponty's distinction between the *Le corps objectif* and the *corps proper* or *corps vécu*). This is a phenomenological distinction rather than an ontological one. It is not meant to imply that each of us has two bodies: one objective and one lived. Rather, it is meant to explicate two different ways that we can experience and understand the body (Husserl 1973a, p. 57). Whereas the latter notion captures the body understood as an embodied first-person perspective, the former focuses on the body as seen from an observer's point of view, where the observer may be a scientist, a physician, or even the embodied subject herself. I can view my own body as if from the outside. I can look at my hand and think, 'Hmm, how truly odd that this thing has five wiggling digits'. The objective body is, in varying degrees of abstraction, and defined in a variety of perspectives (neurological, physiological, anatomical), a perceived body; it is the objectification of a body which is also, nonetheless, lived. Looking at the body as a thing that can be analysed, dissected, objectively understood, in the way that we might understand a machine or a robot, is clearly important for making progress in the biological sciences, in medicine, and perhaps in robotics. If we are taking this perspective on the body, we are taking a third-person perspective – examining the body as something that we, as subjects, can observe as an object.

In contrast, of course, the only way we can make such observations, or any observations, is if we are in fact an experiencing, sensorimotor, living body – if we have eyes that see, hands that are capable of haptic touch, ears that hear, and so forth. In this regard I do not observe or contemplate my hand, I reach out with it and grab something. The body as subject, as experiencer, as agent, rather than the body as object, as thing experienced – this is a basic distinction missed by the Cartesian tradition. When Descartes – according to the standard interpretation – insists that he is a thinking thing, and is not his body, which is an extended thing, he thinks that he can think without his body thinking. In fact, however, Descartes was able to think such thoughts only because he was a living body that included a highly inter- and intraconnected brain. As far as we can tell, Descartes stopped thinking these thoughts in the early morning of 11 February 1650 when he died. An autopsy on his objective body would have shown a serious respiratory infection as cause of death.

A description of the lived body is a description of the body from the phenomenological perspective. On the one hand, it is the way the body appears in experience. On the other hand, it is much more than that – it is the way the body structures our experience. The body is not a screen between me and the world; rather, it shapes our primary way of being-in-the-world. This is also why we cannot first explore the body by itself and then subsequently examine it in its relation to the world. On the contrary, the body is already in-the-world, and the world is given to us as bodily revealed (Husserl 1971/1980, p. 128). Indeed, as Sartre points out, the body is operative in every perception and in every action. It constitutes our point of view and our point of departure (1956, p. 326):

> The case could not be otherwise, for my being has no other way of entering into contact with the world except to be *in the world*. It would be impossible for me to realize a world in which I was not and which would be for me a pure object of a surveying contemplation. But on the contrary it is necessary that I lose myself in the world in order for the world to exist and for me to be able to transcend it. Thus to say that I have entered into the world, 'come to the world,' or that there is a world, or that I have a body is one and the same thing.
>
> (Sartre 1956, p. 318; see also Merleau-Ponty 1962, p. 82)[1]

We have a sense of the body in what it accomplishes. I have a tacit sense of the space that I am in (whether it is crowded, whether it is wide open, or whether it is closing in). Likewise, I have a proprioceptive sense of whether I am sitting or standing, stretching or contracting my muscles. Of course, these postural and positional senses of where and how the body is tend to remain in the background of my awareness; they are tacit, recessive. They are what phenomenologists call a 'pre-reflective sense of myself as embodied'.[2]

This sense of embodiment is not simply spatial. I can feel sluggish (after eating a heavy dinner, for example) or clumsy; or I can feel energetic and fully attuned to my surroundings (after exercising or yoga, for example). If I am depressed by some bad news, I can feel that in my body; if I am elated by good news or buoyed up by an impending challenge – these are feelings and moods that I feel bodily. If I am angry or fearful or happy and comfortable, these are emotions that I feel bodily. Moreover, all of these aspects of embodiment shape the way

I perceive the world. If I'm depressed, the world seems depressing; if I am elated, the world seems promising; if I am hungry, as William James noted, an apple appears larger than when I am satiated. A recent study by Danziger et al. (2011) shows that judgement, specifically the application of legal reasoning, is affected by whether the judge is hungry or satiated. On average, lenient rulings drop gradually from around 65 per cent to nearly 0 per cent between breakfast and lunch, and then abruptly return to around 65 per cent just after lunch.

Since this is the lived body with which I, as experiencing agent, perceive and act, it is in constant connection with the world. This connection is not a mere surface-to-surface contact, as a corpse might lie on the surface of a table; rather, my body is integrated with the world. To be situated in the world means not simply to be located someplace in a physical environment, but to be in rapport with circumstances that are bodily meaningful. It means something if the drink that I want is out of reach; and it means something different if I am unable to sprint as fast as I need to when I am being chased by a ferocious animal, or in danger of being run down by a bus. The possibilities that my body enables, and that define the environment as a world of affordances, just as much as those activities that my body prevents or limits – these are aspects of embodiment that I live with, and live through, and that define the environment as situations of meaning and circumstances for action.

Much more could be said about the body–environment relation, since the environment is not simply a place where we perform our actions. The environment directly and indirectly regulates the body, so that the body is in some sense the expression or reflection of the environment. The environment calls forth a specific body style so that the body works with the environment and is included in it. The posture that the body adopts in a situation is its way of responding to the environment. The body finds itself already with feelings, drive states, kinaesthetic sensations, etc., and they are partially defined by the environment in which it must function. The 'internal environment' of the body, which functions homeostatically and automatically, and is constituted by innumerable physiological and neurological events, is simply an internalized translation and continuation of the 'external' environment. Changes in the 'external' environment are always accompanied by changes in the 'internal' one, e.g. 'changes induced in the blood by alterations in the [external] environment, such as increased carbon dioxide or decreased oxygen tension in the inhaled air, and alterations in the temperature of the environment are minimized by appropriate alterations in circulation, respiration, and endocrine activity' (Gellhorn 1943, p. 15). All of these automatic regulations take place and are lived in bodily performances that are subpersonal and anonymous, although the results of this anonymous living are surely reflected, directly or indirectly, in the experience of the subject. It is also the case that when changes occur in the 'internal' environment, the 'external' environment can suddenly take on a different significance – i.e. the environment can become experientially different. The onset of eye strain is a good example, as is the phenomenon of hallucination (see Gallagher 1986).

Nothing in this conception of embodiment should lead us to conceive of the body as something static, as if it has a fixed set of skills and abilities. The situation is quite different. Not only can the body expand its sensorimotor repertoire by acquiring new skills and habits, it can even extend its capacities by incorporating artificial organs and parts of its environment (Leder 1990, p. 30). In acquiring new skills, for example, we may begin by paying close attention to certain rules of performance, and when doing so we typically focus on and monitor our own bodily performance to an unusually high degree. But a successful acquisition of this new ability will lead to performance without explicit monitoring of bodily movement; the skill becomes fully embodied and embedded within the proper context. As Leder has pointed out, 'A skill is finally and fully learned when something that once was extrinsic, grasped only through explicit rules or examples, now comes to pervade my own corporeality. My arms know how to swim, my mouth can at last speak the language. ... A skill has been incorporated into my bodily "I can"' (1990, p. 31). This process of incorporation also has a marked temporal significance. 'Practice makes perfect' because it makes a skill habitual. What has been practised in the past has become embedded in my present bodily repertoire, and allows me to cope skilfully with new arising situations.

It is also possible to extend the capacities of the lived body by means of artificial extensions. Or to put it differently and perhaps even more strikingly, the lived body extends beyond the limits of the biological body. It doesn't stop at the skin. The classical example is the blind man's cane (a frequent example in the literature since Head (1920) first mentioned it). When first employing such a cane one experiences it as an external object exerting an impact upon the hand. But as the tool is mastered, one begins to feel through it to the experiential field it discloses (Leder 1990, p. 33). As Merleau-Ponty writes: 'The blind man's stick has ceased to be an object for him, and is no longer perceived for itself; its point has become an area of sensitivity, extending the scope and active radius of touch, and providing a parallel to sight' (1962, p. 143). Something similar can happen with the use of far more complex technologies. Consider, for example, the well-known experiments of Bach-y-Rita with sensory substitution and the technology known as tactile-vision sensory substitution (TVSS) (see Bach-y-Rita et al. 1969, 2003; González et al. 2005). The TVSS was designed to provide vision to blind subjects. It maps images from a video camera to a vibrotactile belt worn on the back or abdomen. Because of the intermodal nature of sensory perception, we can, with some learning, 'see' the environment using tactile or auditory prostheses. The stimulation of the skin generates a quasi-visual experience of the environment. In recent development of this technology similar experience is generated by an electro-tactile tongue display unit. The intermodal sensory system of the body translates tactile signals on the skin into something like a visual experience of the external environment. Once the subject is habituated to the tactile stimulation the technology itself ceases to be an object and is incorporated into the body in a way that discloses the world. Such technologies, which are clearly objective pieces of engineering, can capitalize on sensorimotor contingencies and brain plasticity and become part of the body that we live.

Cole et al. (2000) provide another example by describing a virtual reality set-up that links a human agent to a remote NASA robot, allowing the agent to steer the robot's arms by moving his own, and to see the robot's visual field through cameras mounted in the robot's head. After a few minutes of practice with this technology, the agent starts to have a strong sense of embodiment with the robot (Figure 7.1). That is, the agent begins to have a sense of agency for the robotic arms. He begins to feel and to use them as if they were his arms, and as if he were occupying the robot's perspective. As far as we know, and this is in contrast to Brooks's claim that our bodies are simply robots, this would not work the other way around, from robot to human.

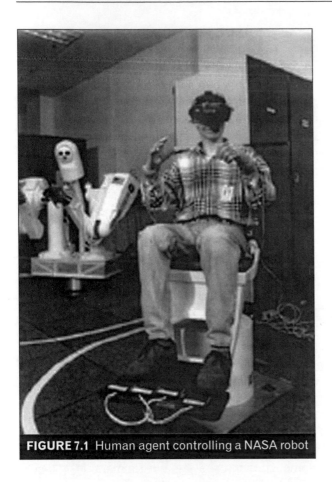

FIGURE 7.1 Human agent controlling a NASA robot

Thus, I can extend my set of skills and potential actions. I can do this through practice (as we can see in dance, athletics, etc.) or through artificial augmentation (as we see in sensory substitution technologies or robotics). What we describe as the lived body from the phenomenological perspective is exactly the same body as the biological one that we study from an objective perspective. The lived body clearly has a physiological basis, and as such it can be defined as 'a certain power of action within the framework of the anatomical apparatus' (Merleau-Ponty 1962, p. 109). Accordingly, it can suffer losses as well as experience gains. Thus brain lesions can occasion various forms of bodily self-alienation. One example is provided by the condition known as *anosognosia for hemiplegia*. Many right-hemisphere stroke patients deny their left-side paralysis. This denial typically remains despite the manifest demonstration of the paralysis. In one case, a patient with left paralysis claimed that she could walk, could touch the doctor's nose with her left hand, and could clap, when instead all she was doing was making motions with only her right hand (Ramachandran and Blakeslee 1998). When pressed, the patients may venture completely out of the realm of reality in defending their ability to move, stating that the immobile limb belongs to someone else, or is not a limb at all. One famous story tells of a patient who claimed that his paralysed hand belonged to the doctor. When the doctor showed the patient his own two hands and asked how it was possible that he should have three hands, the patient calmly replied, 'A hand is the extremity of an arm. Since you have three arms, it follows that you must have three hands' (Bisiach 1988, p. 469).

A stroke in the right hemisphere of the brain might result in symptoms of unilateral neglect. Patients fail to attend to the left side of their own body, or to respond to stimuli, objects, and even people located to their left side. This neglect finds astonishing manifestations. For instance, when served food, the patients will only eat the food that is on the right side of the plate, and will then complain that the hospital is starving them, and that they are not given enough to eat. If asked to copy a drawing, they will only copy one half of it. Furthermore, it was recently shown that this neglect not only affects our visual power, but also our power of imagination and recollection, thereby stressing the intricate interplay between these different forms of intentionality. During a two-minute period, patients were asked to mention as many French cities as they could remember. If these city names were subsequently marked on a map, it was discovered that all the mentioned cities were located in the eastern part of France. No cities in the western part (or left side of the map) of France were mentioned. In another experiment, patients from Milan were asked to think of the Piazza del Duomo, a place they knew very well. They were asked to imagine first that they were standing at the steps of the cathedral looking away from it, and they were then asked to describe what they were visualizing. They would describe only the right side of the square. They were then asked to imagine moving to the opposite side of the piazza and face the cathedral. When asked to describe what they were then visualizing, they would still describe only the right side of the square from their new imagined perspective. In effect they now described the parts of the square that they had 'forgotten' a moment ago, whereas the parts of the square that they had just previously described were now lost to them (Bisiach and Luzzatti 1978).

These examples point to the important insight that core features of subjectivity can be sharply illuminated through a study of their pathological distortions. Pathological cases can function heuristically to make manifest what is normally simply taken for granted. They serve as a means of gaining distance from the familiar, in order better to explicate it. This is something phenomenology has long insisted upon, and it is no coincidence that especially the area of clinical psychopathology has attracted a lot of attention from phenomenologists, and that there exists a long-standing tradition of phenomenological psychiatry in France and Germany. Important figures include Minkowski, Binswanger, Tatossian, Tellenbach, and Blankenburg (see Parnas and Zahavi 2002; Parnas et al. 2002).

Thus, we can best come to understand our form of embodied life as it exists for us not in hypothetical or far-fetched thought experiments, but precisely in the ordinary cases of habit formation, and in the extraordinary cases of sensory substitution and pathological loss. To understand how the lived body works and how it shapes our cognition, we may be able to use high technology and robotics, but we clearly need both phenomenology and biology.

HOW THE BODY DEFINES THE SPACE OF EXPERIENCE

One influential conception of knowledge, as we mentioned in Chapter 2, takes knowledge to be a question of faithfully mirroring a mind-independent reality. If we want to know true reality, we should aim at describing the way the world is, not just independently of its being believed to be that way, but independently of all the ways in which it happens to present itself to us human beings. What we have been suggesting, however, is that this goal is illusory and unattainable. Even when doing science we have to start from an embodied perspective that we never fully escape. As Merleau-Ponty (1962, p. 67) puts it, in response to a proposal for attaining a view from nowhere made by Leibniz, 'Is not to see always to see from somewhere?'

The 'somewhere' is a zero-point set by the perceiving body. Out of it a perspectival spatiality opens up. Although the objective body can be given a position in this perspectival space, the lived body cannot. 'The outline of my body is a frontier which ordinary spatial relations do not cross. This is because its parts are interrelated in a peculiar way: they are not spread out side by side, but [are] enveloped in each other' (ibid., p. 98). This is something that we need to further explore. The claim seems to be that the body inhabits its own kind of space, while at the same time being the origination point for the perceptual space within which the things of the world appear. Are these two different kinds of space?

In fact, we need to distinguish three kinds of spatial frames of reference. The standard distinction between allocentric and egocentric spatial frames of reference names two of them. Allocentric space is purely objective space that can be defined in terms of latitude and longitude (the global positioning system operates in allocentric terms) or in terms of compass directions, as when we say that Copenhagen is north of Rome, for example. Once you adopt the canonical mapping of the earth, it doesn't matter where you happen to be standing, in Copenhagen, or Rome, or New York, or in the space lab; Copenhagen is always north of Rome. *Egocentric space*, in contrast, is the perspectival space of perception and action that is defined relative to the perceiving or acting body. My computer is in front of me; the window through which I hear the church bell is to my left, and the door of my office is to my right. If I turn 180 degrees, then all of this changes. My computer is then behind me; the window is to the right and the door is to the left. This egocentric frame of reference is really a body-centred frame of reference. Kant recognized the practical importance of this egocentric, experiential spatial frame of reference:

> ... [T]he most precise map of the heavens, if it did not, in addition to specifying the positions of the stars relative to each other, also specify the direction by reference to the position of the chart relative to my hands, would not enable me, no matter how precisely I had it in mind, to infer from a known direction, for example the north, which side of the horizon I ought to expect the sun to rise. The same thing holds of geographical and, indeed, of our most ordinary knowledge of the position of places. Such knowledge would be of no use unless we could also orientate the things thus ordered, along with the entire system of their reciprocal positions, by referring them to the sides of our body.
>
> (1755–70/1992, pp. 367–68)

Simply put, even if I know that Copenhagen is to my north, if I don't know where north is relative to the way I am facing, then I don't know which way Copenhagen is. Even closer to home, so to speak, I perceive the world as organized around my body – some things to the left, some things to the right, some are up and some are down, some are in front of, and some behind me. When I reach for something, I have to reach forward or backward, to my right or to my left, at a certain angle relative to where my hand is currently positioned. Both perception and action are calibrated in egocentric space, sometimes referred to by phenomenologists as lived space. But egocentric space is still not the space of the body that Merleau-Ponty mentions.

As perceivers and agents we are embedded and embodied agents. All perception and action involves a component of bodily self-experience. I am sitting in a restaurant. I wish to begin to eat, and so I need to pick up my fork. But how can I do that? In order to pick up the fork, I need to register its position in relation to myself. That is, my perception of the fork must contain some information about me, otherwise I would not be able to act on it. On the dinner table, the perceived fork is on *my* left, the perceived knife is on *my* right, and the perceived plate and wine glass in front of *me*. This self-referencing in perception registers subpersonally in the sensorimotor system, but it also shapes my experience. Every perspectival appearance implies that the embodied perceiver is herself the experiential origin, the indexical 'here' in relation to which every appearing object is oriented. As an experiencing, embodied subject I am the point of reference in relation to which all of my perceptual objects are uniquely related. I am the centre around which and in relation to which (egocentric) space unfolds itself, or as Merleau-Ponty would put it, when I perceive the world, the body is simultaneously revealed as the unperceived term in the centre of the world toward which all objects turn their face.

According to Merleau-Ponty, 'the spatiality of the body must work downwards from the whole to the parts, the left hand and its position must be implied in a global bodily design and must originate in that design' (1962, p. 99; translation modified). He cautions, however, that this description is inadequate insofar as it remains tied to a static geometrical perspective. He suggests that we flesh this out in terms of pragmatic action: since my body is geared towards existing or possible tasks, its spatiality 'is not, like that of external objects or like that of "spatial sensations", a *spatiality of position*, but a *spatiality of situation*' (ibid., p. 100).[3] We should say, then, that in connection with perception and action, there is a bodily spatial frame of reference that is innate and, in its own way absolute. It is neither allocentric nor egocentric, but a frame of reference that applies to the lived body as perceiver and actor. In precise terms, this is a non-perspectival, proprioceptive frame of reference. Let's try to map out this bodily space in further detail.

The body, as Merleau-Ponty already indicated, is the origin of phenomenally experienced spatiality: 'far from my body's being for me no more than a fragment of space, there would be no space at all for me if I had no body' (1962, p. 102). If one accepts the premise that sense perception of the world is egocentrically organized by reference to the perceiver's bodily position, the basis for that reference cannot itself be in an egocentric frame of reference without the threat of infinite regress. I could not say, for example, that my body is to my right or to my left.[4] This point is closely tied to the notion of the experiential transparency of the body (the fact that when I experience the world my experience of my body is highly attenuated), and is accurately stated by Merleau-Ponty:

> I observe external objects with my body, I handle them, examine them, walk around them, but as for my body, I do not observe it itself [in action or in the act of perception]: in order to be able to do so, I should need the use of a second body which itself would be unobservable.
>
> (1962, p. 91; translation modified)

Whereas I can approach or move away from any object in the world, the body itself is always here as my very perspective on the world. That is, rather than being simply another object that I experience in a perspectival manner, the body itself is precisely what allows me to perceive objects perspectivally (see Sartre 1956, p. 329). In a primary sense, I am not conscious of my body as an intentional object. I do not perceive it; *I am it*. As a perceiver and actor, I do not have observational access to my body in perception or in action. I neither stand outside nor inside my own body – indeed, whatever inside and outside mean in this case, they depend on me being my body (see Legrand 2006).

Although I do not have observational access to my body in action, I can have non-observational proprioceptive and kinaesthetic awareness of my body in action.[5] Proprioception is the innate and intrinsic position sense that I have with respect to my limbs and overall posture. It's the 'sixth sense' that allows me to know whether my legs are crossed, or not, without looking at them. It is literally innate insofar as the proprioceptive system develops prenatally. What kind of spatial frame of reference is involved in proprioceptive awareness? It is not egocentric since proprioceptive awareness does not organize the differential spatial order of the body around a perspectival origin. For example, whereas it may be that this book is closer to me than that book over there, it is not the case that my foot is closer to me than my hand. As José Luis Bermúdez points out, there is a 'fundamental disanalogy between the bodily space of proprioception and the egocentric space of perception and action. ... In contrast with vision, audition, and the other canonically exteroceptive modalities, there are certain spatial notions that do not seem to be applicable to somatic proprioception' (1998, pp. 152–53). Specifically he mentions distance and direction. That is, we can ask about the distance and direction of a perceived object in terms of how far away it is, and in what direction. But these spatial parameters are meaningful only in relation to a frame of reference that has a perspectival origin. This does not apply to proprioception.

Of course it is possible to read egocentric registers into the body, and to say that bodily sensation A is to the left of bodily sensation B, or that sensation A is further away from sensation B than is sensation C. Relative to a certain task (e.g. scratching an itch) my hand may be further away from my foot than from my knee, depending on posture. Someone might tell me to hold my hands out in front of me, and I might comply by extending my arms so that my hands are in front of my chest. But this is simply to adopt a certain convention or to make my chest something like a temporary origin; quite literally, one cannot put one's hands in front of one's body since they are part of the body and cannot be put in front of themselves. Being located on the front side of my body (my nose, my toes, etc.) is not equivalent to being in front of my body. Left, right, centre, and distance are spatial parameters that are completely relative in egocentric spatial perception. What is to my right may be to your left. And what is to my right now will be to my left if I turn 180 degrees. But intrabodily, my right hand is proprioceptively just so, and always at the end of my right arm, whether my right side is located to your left, or whether I turn from north to south. If I move my left hand to touch my right shoulder, it does not become a second right hand because it happens to move to that side of my body. If sensation A is just this distance from sensation B, I cannot make them closer on the intrabodily map even if I contort my body to make them closer objectively or pragmatically (in order to scratch one of them, for example). So intrabodily spatiality is not egocentric.

One might think, then, that the proprioceptive frame of reference is an allocentric one. It is certainly possible to conceive of body parts being located on an allocentric map, but to the extent that allocentric means something like 'independent of the perceiver's position', it is difficult to think of the proprioceptive mapping in those terms since it is precisely the perceiver's body that is at stake. Brian O'Shaughnessy (1995) suggests that proprioception is a system of spatial ordering that is unique in that it is framed by and applies to only the body itself. He attributes this to the immediacy of proprioception: the fact that proprioceptive awareness does not attentively mediate the perception of the body; for if it did, it would require an ordering system, a spatial frame of reference that would have to be independent of the body. Proprioception thus involves neither an allocentric nor an egocentric frame of reference, but a non-perspectival awareness of the body in an implicit spatial frame of reference.[6]

This proprioceptive frame of reference, then, is the necessary embodied basis for the egocentric frame of reference. I perceive that something is to my right or to my left only by having a proprioceptive sense of where my right is and where my left is, 'knowing' my right hand from my left hand, my right leg from my left leg. Egocentric spatial order, then, always runs back to the body of the perceiver/actor. As Merleau-Ponty tells us: 'for us to be able to conceive space, it is in the first place necessary that we should have been thrust into it by our body, and that it should have provided us with the first model of those transpositions, equivalents and identifications which make space into an objective system and allow our experience to be one of objects, opening out on an "In itself"' (1962, p. 142). Moreover, this bodily space, in contrast to perceived space, is like 'the darkness needed in the theatre to show up the performance' (ibid., p. l00).

THE BODY AS EXPERIENTIALLY TRANSPARENT

Let's shine a little light into this 'darkness', or what we might call the disappearing act of the body. We have indicated that in action, when we are engaged in some project, sensory feedback about our own body is attenuated.

> The bodily mediation most frequently escapes me: when I witness events that interest me, I am scarcely aware of the perceptual breaks which the blinking of the eye-lids imposes on the scene, and they do not figure in my memory. ... [T]he body proper and its organs remain the bases or vehicles of my intentions and are not yet grasped as 'physiological realities'.
>
> (Merleau-Ponty 1963, p. 188, also see p. 217)

The body tries to stay out of our way so that we can get on with our task; it tends to efface itself on its way to its intentional goal. We do not normally monitor our movements in an explicitly conscious manner, although, as we indicated in Chapter 3, we have a pre-reflective awareness of our body in very general terms. I can say whether I am running, walking, sitting, standing, and what kind of effort or posture I am putting forth. But this pre-reflective awareness is not very detailed. I can say that I am reaching to grasp a cup; but my sense of this is oriented toward the goal or intentional project that I am involved in, and not toward the specifics of my movement. I can't say very much at all about how I shape my hand to pick up the cup. As Sartre puts it, when I reach out to grasp something that has caught my attention, 'my hand has vanished; it is lost in the complex system of instrumentality in order that this system may exist' (1956, p. 323). He suggests that the lived body is invisibly present, precisely because it is existentially lived rather than known (ibid., p. 324). When I play ping-pong, my movements are not given as intentional objects. My limbs do not compete with the ball for my attention. If that were the case, I would be unable to play efficiently. As we will elaborate in the next chapter, our attention, our intentional focus, is normally on the task to be performed, the project to be accomplished, or on some worldly event that seems relevant to our action. Our attention is not on our bodily movement. Much of the action is controlled by body-schematic processes below the threshold of consciousness. Our hand shapes itself when we are grasping, and it does so automatically and without our explicit awareness. Our gait automatically adjusts itself to the terrain of the environment. This kind of automaticity, however, is not simple reflex movement. It is part of our intentional action which involves grasping something for some purpose, or choosing to stroll or to rush to our destination. Furthermore, when I execute movements, even if certain details of the control processes remain non-conscious, the movements themselves are not non-conscious, or merely mechanical, or involuntary; rather, they are part of my functioning intentionality, and are immediately and pre-reflectively felt (Henry 1975, p. 92; Merleau-Ponty 1962, p. 144).

Body image and body schema

Two concepts frequently used across a number of disciplines (both scientific and philosophical) are the concepts of *body image* and *body schema*. Unfortunately the usage of both concepts has been rather ambiguous and confusing. In the phenomeno-logical literature this situation has not been improved by the fact that Merleau-Ponty's term *schéma corporel* has been rendered as 'body image' in the English translation of *Phenomenology of Perception* (see Merleau-Ponty 1962, p. 98). We propose the following characterization. A body image is composed of a system of experiences, attitudes, and beliefs where the object of such intentional states is one's own body. Studies that involve body image frequently distinguish among three intentional elements:

(1) A subject's *perceptual* experience of his/her own body.
(2) A subject's *conceptual* understanding (including folk and/or scientific knowledge) of the body in general.
(3) A subject's *emotional* attitude toward his or her own body.

Conceptual and emotional aspects of body image are no doubt affected by various cultural and interpersonal factors, but in many respects their content originates in perceptual experience.

By contrast, the concept of *body schema* includes two aspects: (1) the close-to-automatic system of processes that constantly regulates posture and movement to serve intentional action; and (2) our pre-reflective and non-objectifying body awareness. So, on the one hand, the body schema is a system of sensorimotor capacities and activations that function without the necessity of perceptual monitoring. Body-schematic processes are responsible for motor control, and involve sensorimotor capacities, abilities, and habits that enable movement and the maintenance of posture. Such processes are not perceptions, beliefs, or feelings, but sensorimotor functions that continue to operate, and in many respects operate best, when the intentional object of perception is something other than one's own body. On the other hand, however, the body schema (and this reflects Merleau-Ponty's usage of the term) also includes our pre-reflective, proprioceptive awareness of our bodily action. In either case, the emphasis is on the fact that the normal adult, in order to move around and act in the world, neither needs nor has a constant body percept that takes the body as an object. Rather, in the self-movement of most intentional activities the body-in-action tends to efface itself and to be experientially attenuated (see Gallagher 1986; Leder 1990; Tsakiris and Haggard 2005). To the extent that one does become explicitly aware of one's own body in terms of monitoring or directing perceptual attention to limb position, movement, posture, pleasure, pain, kinaesthetic experience, and so on, such awareness constitutes aspects of a body image and presupposes the tacit contribution of the body schema.

This can be seen clearly in pathologies that involve body schematic processes. The case of IW is a dramatic example. At the age of 19, due to illness, he lost all sense of touch and proprioception from the neck down (Cole 1995; Gallagher and Cole 1995). Shortly after the onset of his disorder, when IW tried to move a limb or his entire body, he could initiate the movement, but had no control over where the moving part ended up. If he reached for something the hands would miss or overshoot wildly, and unless he kept an eye on his hands, they started 'wandering' without his knowledge. His hands would no longer be where IW thought they were and could only be located through vision. IW's lack of proprioceptive feedback has two effects. First, the ordinary pre-reflective proprioceptive awareness of one's bodily movement is no longer operative in IW. Second, his body-schematic system, responsible for motor control, is never updated, and in effect, his body cannot gain the motor control it needs to perform action in the ordinary way. Subsequently IW learned to control his movements, but only through intense mental concentration and constant visual vigilance. That is, he learned to rely on a combination of *visual kinaesthesia* (that is, visual feedback about our own movement generated by our own movement through the environment) and *visual perception* of limb movements; this enabled him to move around in a controlled way. His awareness of his own body remains completely transformed, however. It is a reflective awareness rather than a pre-reflective one. Every single movement has to be done attentively. Even to sit in a chair without falling out of it requires constant attention. He can only initiate a standing position if he looks at his feet, and, unless he freezes in place, he can easily fall if he closes his eyes or if the lights go out. If he sneezes while walking his mental concentration is disrupted, and he could fall over. IW demonstrates how much we depend on our pre-reflective, proprioceptive–kinaesthetic awareness of our bodily movement, and on body-schematic processes for the performance of action.

This body schematic aspect of embodiment constitutes what Husserl called the 'I can', that is, the embodied capabilities for action that correlate with the affordances of the world. As we saw in the chapter on perception, the hidden sides of objects can become present if certain *movements* are executed. Whereas the profile currently presented by the object is correlated with my present bodily position, the absent profiles are all correlated with positions that I could adopt, and this means, Husserl indicates, that they are correlated with my kinaesthetic (sensorimotor) system. I would be unable to intend the absent profiles of the object, and consequently be unable to perceive objects per se, if I were not in possession of a bodily, kinaesthetic, self-awareness in the form of an 'I can'. I 'know' my body first as a set of abilities which are not fully present to consciousness (Buytendijk 1974, p. 25) – certainly a prelinguistic and non-conceptual form of knowledge, or know-how – the limits of which become more explicitly known when things go wrong.

Imagine that you are playing tennis. Your attention is directed at the ball, which is heading towards you with high speed, as well as on the position of your opponent. Your body tightens in order to return the ball in a masterful smash, but suddenly you feel a sharp and intense pain in your chest. Your smashing opportunity is lost, and the pain is now demanding all your attention. It attracts your attention whether you want it to or not. Those things that were important a moment ago – the ball, the match, your opponent – lose significance. There is nothing that reminds us of our embodiment (our vulnerability and mortality) as much as pain. Moreover, the painful body can occasionally be experienced as alien. This is so because in pain we often lose control over the body; the 'I can' suddenly dissipates, and this disturbs the projects which define who we are (Leder 1990). Something similar is also true for various forms of illness, whether they require us to stay in bed, or observe a strict diet, or force us to visit the hospital for daily treatments.

As is frequently the case in life, it is the privation which teaches us to appreciate what we take for granted. It is when it no longer functions smoothly that we realize the importance of the body. Bernard Toussaint makes this point clearly:

> The body shows itself precisely when my body limits do not accord with the possi-
> bilities I project. ... In such cases my body calls attention to itself as an obstacle, or
> as Plato would say, a prison. Thus my body becomes like an object, something alien to
> my intention. There arises a dichotomy between aspiration and my facticity, between
> project and limit. This dichotomy, I suspect, may well be the phenomenological basis
> for the development of the mind–body dualism.
>
> (1976, p. 176)

The lived body does not live this dualism, but when this dualism is generated – when action breaks down and our body suddenly seems to be an object in our way – we gain some phenomenological access to what generally goes unnoticed – the smooth functioning of our body in perception and action as the constant and pervasive support system for our cognitive life.

EMBODIMENT AND SOCIAL COGNITION

We will have more to say about the relation between embodiment and intersubjectivity in Chapter 9, but let us end this chapter with at least some indications of the link. It should be obvious that my bodily self-apprehension and the way I live my body can be influenced by my social interaction, and by the way my body is perceived and apprehended by others – just think of broad categories like gender and race, or more specific experiences of shame or embarrassment. But perhaps even more basically, social interaction is as such an embodied practice.

To exist embodied is to exist in such a way that one exists under the gaze of the other, accessible for the other. My bodily behaviour always has a public side to it. Thus the standard question posed as 'the problem of other minds' – 'How do I gain access to the other person's mind?' – is mistaken. It suggests that I am enclosed in my own interiority, and that I then have to employ methods to reach the other who is hidden away in her own interiority. But this way of framing the problem fails to recognize the nature of embodiment.

Bodily behaviour, expression, and action are essential to (and not merely contingent vehicles of) some basic forms of consciousness. What we call mental states (intentions, beliefs, desires) are not simply or purely mental. That is, they are not ethereal shadows floating around inside our heads; they are bodily states that are often (even if not always) manifested in bodily postures, movements, gestures, expressions, and actions. As such, they can be directly apprehended in the bodily comportment of people whose mental states they are. As Peter Hobson has recently put it: 'We perceive bodies and bodily expressions, but we do so in such a way that we perceive and react to the mental life that those physical forms express' (2002, p. 248; see also 1993, p. 184).

When presented with behaviour, it is not as if we are faced with mere bodily processes that can then be interpreted any way one likes. When you see somebody use a hammer, or feed a child, or clean a table you don't have a problem understanding what is going on. You may not necessarily understand every aspect of the action, but it is immediately given as a meaningful action (in a shared world). It is not as if you are first confronted with a perceived exterior, and then have to infer the existence of an interior mental space. In the face-to-face encounter, for example, we are neither confronted with a mere body, nor with a hidden psyche, but with a unified whole. When I see another's face, I see it as friendly or angry, etc., that is, the very face expresses these emotions. This does not rule out that some mental states are covert, of course, but not all mental states can lack an essential link to behaviour if intersubjectivity is at all to get off the ground.

To take embodiment seriously is to contest a Cartesian view of the mind in more than one way. Embodiment entails birth and death. To be born is not to be one's own foundation, but to be situated in both *nature* and *culture*. It is to possess a physiology that one did not choose.

It is to find oneself in a historical and sociological context that one did not establish (see Merleau-Ponty 1962, p. 347). Birth is essentially an intersubjective phenomenon, not only in the obvious sense, because I was born by somebody, but because this very event only has meaning for me through others. My awareness of my birth, of my commencement, is intersubjectively mediated; it is not something I can intuit or remember on my own. I do not witness my coming into being, but I always already find myself alive (Merleau-Ponty 1962, p. 215; Ricoeur 1966, pp. 433, 438, 441). I know of my own mortality only through others. Ultimately, the issues of birth and death enlarge the scope of the investigation of embodiment. They call attention to the role of historicity, generativity, and sexuality.[7] Indeed, rather than being simply a biological given, embodiment is also a category of sociocultural analysis. What this means, however, is that to gain a more comprehensive understanding of the embodied mind, one needs to take a much wider scope, and the first step in developing this expanded concept of the mind is to consider the complexities of the circumstances in which more than one body is involved and where there is intersubjective interaction. Before we look at interaction, however, it will be helpful to look at action itself. Intersubjectivity is not found simply in the proximity of two or more passive subjects, but is primarily an encounter between agents.

NOTES

1   For an illuminating discussion of Sartre's analysis of the body, see Cabestan (1996).
2   This pre-reflective sense of our own embodiment contributes to our ability to identify our body in an objective fashion. Subjects who view videos of moving figures wearing point-light displays in the dark (the bodies are marked by lights positioned at joints so that when walking their gait is clearly visible) are better at identifying themselves than they are at recognizing friends and colleagues. The puzzle is how they are able to do so, since what they see is how their gait looks 'from the outside'. And this cannot be something they are perceptually well acquainted with, since people obviously see the gaits of friends and colleagues more than they see their own (Gibbs 2006, p. 51). One suggestion is that their pre-reflective proprioceptive sense of their own embodiment cross-modally informs their perception of the visual gestalt of their gait. For more on the pre-reflective awareness of one's body, see Legrand (2006).
3   In his lectures at the Collège de France in the mid-1950s, for example, Merleau-Ponty describes perception in this context in the following terms. When I perceive an object, I am aware of it in terms of my implicit motor possibilities: 'The thing appears to me as a function of the [actual and potential] movements of my body. ... My body is the absolute "here." All the places of space proceed from it. ... The Absolute in the relative is what my body brings to me' (2003, pp. 74–75).
4   Cases of out-of-body experiences (OBEs) or autoscopy (AS), where an awake person apparently sees his body from a position outside of it, are special cases where, to get the phenomenology correct, one needs to distinguish between the lived or perceiving body and the objective or perceived body. Blanke et al. (2004) suggest that OBE and AS involve a failure to integrate proprioceptive, tactile, and visual information with respect to one's own body, and a vestibular dysfunction that leads to an additional disintegration between personal (vestibular) space and extrapersonal (visual) space.

5   Phenomenologists take pre-reflective body awareness to be a question of how (embodied) consciousness is given to itself not as an *object*, but as a *subject*. Whereas Bermúdez claims that 'somatic proprioception is a form of perception' that takes 'the embodied self as its object' (1998, p. 132), the phenomenologists would argue that *primary* body awareness is not a type of object consciousness; it is not a perception of the body as an object at all (see Gallagher 2003b; Zahavi 2002).

6   The proprioceptive register is thus not independent of the subject's experience. The grid of a global positioning system might map out my body as I lay in the sun at Cocoa Beach, but this is not the system I use when I need to scratch my foot; nor do I have to figure out whether my foot is to the east or west of my hand, even if in some languages I would have to figure out whether the foot was on my south leg. '[S]peakers of Guugu Yimithirr (Australia) use only the last kind of description; ... even to describe the location of an object on a body part – a Guugu Yimithirr speaker would say "There's an ant on your south leg"' (Majid et al. 2004, pp. 108–9). Majid et al., however, ignore the question of how this knowledge is possible. Compass directions can only be dead-reckoned from the 'here' of my lived body in relation to some landmark. Directions are always directions away from *me*, where my 'here' defines the 'first coordinates'. Phenomenologically, I triangulate north, pointing to it from here, with some implicit or explicit reference point of which I know the relative location, e.g.the beach is on the east coast. Looking at the ocean I know which way north is. How do I know whether the foot I want to scratch is on my south leg or my north leg? I have to determine whether my right leg is to the north or south of my left leg, and to do that I first have to know whether the northerly direction is to my right or to my left (see Gallagher 2006).

7   Heidegger, who is not exactly known as a philosopher of the body, chose a neuter, '*das Dasein*', as the central term for human existence. And as Heidegger points out in the lecture course *Metaphysische Anfangsgründe der Logik im Ausgang von Leibniz* ("The metaphysical foundations of logic in the philosophy of Leibniz") from 1928, the neutrality of *Dasein* entails an asexuality (*eine Geschlechtslosigkeit*) (Heidegger 1978, p. 172). Subsequent thinkers have questioned the validity of this move, and have argued that the basic structures of our embodiment would not remain the same if we were asexual creatures.

FURTHER READING

José Luis Bermúdez, Anthony Marcel, and Naomi Eilan (eds), *The Body and the Self*. Cambridge, MA: MIT Press, 1995.

Andy Clark, *Being There: Putting Brain, Body, and World Together Again*. Cambridge, MA: MIT Press, 1997.

Shaun Gallagher, *How the Body Shapes the Mind*. Oxford: Oxford University Press/Clarendon Press, 2005.

Michel Henry, *Philosophy and Phenomenology of the Body*. Trans. G. Etzkorn. The Hague: Martinus Nijhoff, 1975.

Edmund Husserl, *Ideas Pertaining to a Pure Phenomenology and to a Phenomenological Philosophy, Second Book*. Trans. R. Rojcewicz and A. Schuwer. Dordrecht: Kluwer Academic Publishers, 1989.

Drew Leder, *The Absent Body*. Chicago: Chicago University Press, 1990.

Maxine Sheets-Johnstone, *The Primacy of Movement*. Amsterdam: John Benjamins, 1999.

Francisco Varela, Evan Thompson, and Eleanor Rosch, *The Embodied Mind: Cognitive Science and Human Experience*. Cambridge, MA: MIT Press, 1991.

Bernard Waldenfels, *Das leibliche Selbst: Vorlesungen zur Phänomenologie des Leibes*. Frankfurt am Main: Suhrkamp, 2001.

Kathleen V. Wider, *The Bodily Nature of Consciousness: Sartre and Contemporary Philosophy of Mind*. Ithaca: Cornell University Press, 1997.

8 Action and agency

To set the stage for the following discussion we begin by pointing out that our way of being in the world, according to many phenomenologists, is characterized primarily in terms of practical action. Our lives are not driven by theoretical wondering, although some philosophers have considered this as our ultimate talent. It is driven by practical concerns. In our everyday lives we are pragmatists. To put it differently, our primary way of encountering worldly entities is by using them rather than by theorizing about them or perceiving them in a detached manner.

In his analysis of our being-in-the-world, Heidegger frequently emphasizes that the world, rather than being simply a complex unity of objects characterized by substantiality, materiality, and extension, is in fact a network of meaning. More precisely the world we live in, and the world as we perceive it, is a world saturated by practical references of use. That the knife is lying there on the table means that I can reach and grasp it. Indeed – and following up on our discussion in the previous chapter – the spatiality of the lifeworld – of the world we live in – is a spatiality captured not by geometrical measures, but structured by contexts of use. Whether something is present or absent, near or remote is something that is determined by our practical concerns. What is nearest is not necessarily what is closest in geometrical terms, but what we are concerned with, what we can reach for and use. A couple of examples can illustrate this idea:

- Measured in centimetres I am closer to the glasses I wear than to the picture I inspect, just as I am closer to the phone I am using than to the person I am talking to. But phenomenologically speaking (in terms of meaning or significance) the relation is the reverse.
- A village which is 20 kilometres away and which can be reached on foot might be much nearer than an inaccessible mountain top which is only a few kilometres away. An

'objectively' long but easily traversed way can be much shorter than an 'objectively' short but difficult way (Heidegger 1986/1996, p. 106). Geometrical measures are very exact, but their exactness doesn't guarantee that they are relevant and useful when it comes to capturing the spatiality of practical concerns.

More generally speaking, Heidegger is famous for having argued that we are not first and foremost occupied with perceptual objects in a theoretical way, but with 'handling, using, and taking care of things' (ibid., pp. 67, 68–69). The entities we encounter in this 'taking care of things' Heidegger calls 'useful things', 'gear', or 'equipment' (each of these expressions has been used to translate Zeug), and their unique mode of being he characterizes as readiness-to-hand. Worldly entities are first of all things we can grab or manipulate or use, or are such that they resist usage. It is only because of this coping engagement with the ready-to-hand that something like a theoretical exploration of such entities is possible. It is only because we use the hammer that circumstances can arise where the hammer is dysfunctional, and it is precisely then that we start to notice and scrutinize it as an object that possesses extension, weight, colour, etc. According to Heidegger, it is consequently not in theoretical observation but in practical use that worldly entities show themselves as what they are. More fundamentally speaking, it is not cognition – understood in a narrow intellectual sense as a theoretical detached observation – that establishes the relation between self and world. Rather, in cognition, the self acquires a new relation to entities in an already disclosed world. Cognition is a secondary modification of our primary being-in-the-world, and is only possible and attainable because we already are in the world.

In daily life we do not interact with ideal theoretical objects, but with tools and objects of practical or emotional or aesthetic or personal value (Husserl 1952/1989, p. 27). Our interest is guided by practical and social concerns, just as our actions are guided and shaped by patterns of normality, by how others act. When I use equipment or instruments, my goals are intersubjectively structured. When I use anything, a natural object or a manufactured piece of equipment, my use is guided by the fact that there are right and wrong ways to use such things; my use is guided by norms. How I use things is influenced by how I have seen others use them and by what other people expect me to do. More generally, action is always action in a particular environment that is both physical and social, and such factors shape our intentions.[1] The meaning of action, therefore, is contextually complex and cannot be reduced to a mere stimulus–response aggregate.

Consider the following examples. You are sitting comfortably in your seat:

(1   For no apparent reason, I ask you to get up and open the door. You do.
(2)   I ask you to open the door if you have a question. Perhaps this is a little silly, but then you have a question, and you get up and open the door.
(3)   You hear a knock at the door and you are expecting a friend to visit, so you get up, walk to the door and open it.

Are these three actions of yours equivalent? We think that the answer is obviously 'yes' and 'no'. In some narrow sense, yes, assuming that your physical starting point is the same in all three cases, and you make the same movements to get the job done. We could say, yes, these movements are 'mechanically' or motorically the same; they are the same in terms of the movements involved. But, *no*, they are clearly different actions if we try to specify them in terms of contexts and goals, or more generally, intentions. Under an intentional description we would say that in (3) you are opening the door for a friend; in (1) you are simply following an abstract instruction; and in (2) you are indicating that you have a question. The intentional action is different in each case, but also the intentionality of consciousness – what you are aware of when you are acting – is different.

In all of these actions you are acting for a reason. If I asked you why you are opening the door, you could respond, 'Because you asked me to', or 'Because I have a question', or 'Because I want to let my friend in'. In (3), you want to do something or get something done. In (1), you have been asked to do it, and perhaps you simply want to be cooperative, but there is nothing meaningful in the movement itself; and in the case of (2), you are actually expressing or communicating something by your movement. Discussions going back as far as Aristotle distinguish between actions that have no goal other than themselves, and actions that have goals that are more than the action itself. Unless you really enjoy getting up and opening the door, (1) comes close to an action without a goal, although you may claim that the goal is simply to respond to my request or to keep me happy. Clearly (2) and (3) are actions with goals that go beyond simple movement: opening the door in order to ask a question, or opening the door in order to let a friend in. It is clearly possible to distinguish actions like these from mere movements. For example, if I hit your knee with a small rubber hammer and your leg kicks out, we would not call that an action on your part. This reflex movement was actually caused by me knocking on your knee. 'Knee knocking' leads to movement, but such movement is something short of action. So what is it that makes a movement an action?

Before we answer that, let's take a closer look at the different kinds of movements that can be discerned in the range between reflex movement and intentional action. There are some movements that are neither reflex nor intentional. O'Shaughnessy (1980, II, pp. 60ff.) describes a class of movements that he calls 'subintentional'. For example, I may be sitting listening to you tell an exciting story about your last visit to Cincinnati and my foot may be wagging (not unlike the wag of a dog's tail) with enjoyment or anticipation, or whatever it is one wags a foot at. This is neither a reflex movement nor an intentional action on my part. Further, it has no goal, nor does it support anything like an intentional action. Nothing would be lost in regard to my intentional action (of attending to your story) if I did not wag my foot, although it may serve some purpose such as reducing some kind of tension; or it may be generated by a kind of restlessness. Other movements are intentional movements even if they are not part of the proper description of the full-blown intentional act, or what we might call the organizing intention. For example, I can describe (3) as an intentional action of answering the door and letting my friend in. In performing this action, of course, I have to get up out of my chair, walk across the room, and twist the doorknob. All such movements subtend and support the intentional action of letting my friend in; in that sense, they are organized by the intentional action; and as such they are all intentional movements. If you stop me before I reach the door and ask me if I knew that I was walking across the room and if I intended to do so, I would surely say yes – I have to do so to get to the door.

Another class of movements is located somewhere between subintentional and intentional movement. It is somewhat difficult to get at these movements because they resemble intentional movements insofar as they serve and support an organizing intentional action, but they differ in that if you stop me in the action I will likely not know that I was doing any such movement, and I would be hard pressed to say that I intended to do the movement. Mark Rowlands (2006, pp. 102ff., following Anscombe 1957) calls these 'preintentional' movements; we might also call them 'prenoetic' because they happen without our knowledge or awareness. The difficulty in deciding whether a movement is preintentional or intentional can be found in one of Rowlands' examples. He claims, we think mistakenly, that the movement of a pianist's fingers as they play, for example, Chopin's *Fantasie Impromptu in C# Minor* are preintentional movements. Clearly it is the case that the profoundly proficient and practised pianist does not have detailed awareness of everything that her fingers are doing as she is playing the piece. But if we stopped the pianist in midstream and asked whether she knew that her ring finger had hit the C#, I think that she would say, 'Yes, of course, since I am trying to finish this *Fantasie*', in the same way that I would say 'Yes, of course I'm walking across the room; I want to answer the door'. Finger action on the piano is clearly intentional movement.

That even very habitual or practised movements, which we don't single out for attention, such as walking or playing a musical instrument are intentional is also clear from those cases where their execution is inhibited or in other ways fail to match our intentions. More generally speaking, we are normally prepared to describe our habitual or practised movements as actions. I would say that 'I hit the ball' or 'I played one of Beethoven's sonatas', rather than 'the arm (or fingers) changed position in space'. But in this case the movements are at some level conscious. They are teleological *actions* which contain a reference to the objects at which they aim (Merleau-Ponty 1962, p. 139). To comprehend these actions, we cannot simply give a description of some objective changes in geometrical space; we have to take account of the lived situation in which they occur (Straus 1966, p. 44). Such movements display an original intentionality. It is original, both in the sense that it is intrinsic to the movements (it is not simply a question of interpreting the movements *as if* they were intentional), but also in the sense that it is a very basic form of intentionality, a form of our being-in-the-world, which is more original and fundamental than the one encountered in our theoretical attitude (Merleau-Ponty 1962, p. 387).

Rowlands provides a much better example of preintentional movement: saccadic eye movements. It's been shown that such movements do serve and subtend intentional action. Rowlands cites the work of Yarbus (1967), who showed that saccades are specified by the task one is engaged in. If you are asked to view a certain group of people with the task of judging how old the people are, versus remembering the clothing they are wearing, versus locating them vis-à-vis certain objects in the room, etc., it turns out that your eyes saccade differently for each task. These different ways of scanning the environment relative to task are not reflex, although they are automatic and non-conscious. As a result, the eye movement happens in a way that totally escapes my awareness so that if you stopped and asked me whether I knew that my eyes were moving this way or that, and whether I intended them to move in such ways, I would certainly say no. This kind of movement falls short of intentional movement, but it nonetheless serves my intention to perform a specific task, in a way that subintentional movements do not.

For a movement to be an action it has to be goal-directed and intentional. A movement that is a reflex, or passive, or subintentional, or preintentional is not an action, although it might be interpreted as an action from the outside, that is, by some other person. If my finger slips on the trigger, someone might suggest that I committed an act of murder, if the bullet kills someone. I could claim that I did not do it intentionally, and under some legal systems I could be convicted of accidental homicide or manslaughter, but not murder. Under some circumstances I might be mistakenly sentenced for a movement rather than for an action (although in other circumstances my sentence might be based on a rightful charge of negligence). Notice that on this view, there is no such thing as an unintentional action, although there could be unintentional movement or unintentional consequences of my action.

Now, let's dig a little deeper, philosophically. And let's note that a consideration of human action will illustrate how the different themes we are considering in this book are interconnected, since to understand the phenomenology of action, it will be necessary to draw on our previous discussions of the phenomenology of pre-reflective consciousness, temporality, embodiment, perception, and intentionality (just as we will also have to return to and amplify our treatment of action in our subsequent chapters on sociality and selfhood).

What makes a movement intentional – what makes it an action? What does it mean to have an intention to act? We said: all intentional movements – all actions – are goal directed, even if the goal is the action itself. So to have an intention to act means that we have some kind of goal in mind. But this raises other questions. Where precisely do we locate the goal? If, as you start to get up to answer the door for your friend, I stop you and ask, 'Why are you pressing your hand against the arm of that chair?', you could respond, 'Because I'm getting up'. It would be wrong-headed, however, to suggest that the goal of your action is simply to rise out of the chair. As you start to move toward the door I could ask: 'What are you doing?', and you could answer in any number of ways: 'I'm getting the door', or 'I'm letting my friend in', or you could express a goal beyond that, assuming that your friend is visiting for a reason. You could say, 'Thor and I are going to practise our song'. So obviously you have to open the door to let Thor in. You might be able to identify more distant goals: you may want to enjoy making music, or you and Thor may want to become pop singers, because you want to make lots of money, because you really want to buy a house at the beach, because you ultimately want to be happy, etc. The more distant one gets from the actual movement in question, however, the less satisfying the answer is as an answer to the question. Just as the most appropriate question about the goal of your action lies somewhere between 'Why are you pressing your hand against the arm of that chair?' and 'What do you ultimately want from life?' the most appropriate answer lies somewhere between 'Because I am getting up' and 'Because I want to be happy'.[2]

But are we assuming too much when we talk in this ordinary way about action? The assumption is that action is intentional if I am acting with a goal in mind, or, to say it another way, if I am in some sense deciding to act for a reason.

This implies that to understand an action is to know not what caused it in a purely physical sense, but rather what motivated or justified it, either in general or in the eyes of the agent. One could explain the cause of an action in a number of different ways. For example, one could explain the action in terms of its subpersonal causes – the neuronal processes that underpin motor control and perception. When we ask someone why she did something, however, we don't expect this sort of explanation:

'Why did you buy that dress?'
'Because the neurons in my right prefrontal cortex were firing!'

No. Rather, we expect something of a personal explanation, where the person gives some good (or even not so good) reasons that we can count as motivation for acting as she does:

'Because the style is perfect for the dance tonight.'

Explanations at the personal level, in terms of reasons, can be complicated by a good deal of context shared by people living in the same cultural setting. For example, to understand what happens when A hands B a small round metal disc, we need to know what money is and why it is used. And if A is bribing B (or repaying a debt, or making a loan), we need to know a fair amount about socio-economic arrangements in human society. No amount of neuro-physiology will contribute to that kind of explanation, just as no amount of neuroscience will explain why Neville Chamberlain after the Munich Agreement in 1938 declared that peace had now been preserved. The rationality of behaviour is not given a deeper explanation by specifying the involved neural facts.

THE PHENOMENOLOGY OF AGENCY

The fact that there is a phenomenology of agency has been disputed by some phenomenologists. Dreyfus, for instance, has spoken of subjectivity as the lingering ghost of the mental, and denies that there is any immersed or implicit ego in absorbed coping. Indeed, in total absorption one ceases to be a subject altogether (2007b, 373). In fact, on his account, our immersed bodily life is so completely and totally world engaged, that it is entirely oblivious to itself. In some places, Dreyfus likens absorbed coping to an airport radio whose beacon doesn't give a warning signal unless the plane strays off course. And as he then writes, 'when the pilot is on the beam there is no experience at all' (Dreyfus 2007a, 358). As long as everything goes smoothly there is only silent guidance. It is only deviation that occasions a warning signal, and it is this signal that is then registered experientially. As Dreyfus puts it, a coper must have the capacity to enter a monitoring stance if the brain sends an alarm signal that something is going wrong (Dreyfus 2007b, 374). When reading statements like these, and when comparing them to those where Dreyfus writes that consciousness is only called into action once the brain has detected something gone wrong (2007b, 377), that features of the environment that are available to the perceptual system needn't be available to the mind (Dreyfus 2005, 54), and that adults, infants, and animals in their direct dealing with affordances can cope without thinking at all simply by taking 'input energy' and processing it appropriately (Dreyfus 2005, 49, 56), one gets the impression that the relevant processing takes place non-consciously. But if the coping is indeed completely unconscious, it is difficult to understand how one can meaningfully speak of a *phenomenology* of mindless coping – as Dreyfus repeatedly does. Unless of course, he is thinking of a quite different kind of phenomenology. It is revealing that Dreyfus in a recent paper, co-authored with Sean Kelly, writes that Dennett's heterophenomenology might be an improvement and better alternative than the phenomenologies of Husserl and Sartre (Dreyfus and Kelly 2007, 47).

In contrast to this view, we understand agency, in its proper sense, to depend on the agent's consciousness of agency. That is, if someone causes something to happen, that person is not an agent (even if they are a cause) if they do not know that they have caused it to happen. A hurricane may cause the electric system to fail, but we would not attribute agency to the hurricane in what we take to be the normal use of the term 'agency'. The kind of conscious knowledge involved in agency, however, does not have to be of a very high order; it could be simply a matter of a very thin, pre-reflective awareness, and in most cases it is just that. An expert skier schussing down the slope may not be reflecting on anything, but that does not mean he is not conscious of what he is doing at some level, even if his doing is a form of absorbed coping. If the skier is also considering the possible changes in the snow conditions as he moves down the hill, this is not something that necessarily interrupts his absorbed coping, but may in fact be an important part of what keeps him in the flow. Sometimes, however, in other circumstances, there may be an explicit consciousness of acting for reasons. It certainly seems that in many cases I act for a reason, and that sometimes such actions are preceded by a decision-making process. And in such cases, I have a developed awareness that I am the person in charge, the agent, of my actions. The *sense of agency* (or self-agency) for my actions, then, may involve a thin, pre-reflective awareness of what I am doing as I am doing it, or it may involve a more explicit consciousness filled with well-developed reasons. Let's take a close look at the sense of agency and how it relates to the experience of having an intention to act.

In a previous chapter we discussed the concept of intentionality, in the sense of consciousness always being *of* or *about* something. One should be careful not to confuse this concept of intentionality with the concept of having an intention to act. Having an intention to act is usually associated with an exercise of the will. I intend to go shopping this afternoon, and when this afternoon comes, I actually go shopping; *ceteris paribus*, it can be said that actually going was the result of my wilful decision to do it. Of course, the intentionality of consciousness seems to be fully involved in such intentional action, so although we want to distinguish between the intentionality of consciousness (its being *about* something) and the kind of intention that leads to wilful action, we also want to ask what the relationship is between these two aspects of experience.

When I am engaged in intentional action, what precisely am I conscious of? Part of the problem involved in answering this question concerns the parsing of action. For example, if I decide to go shopping at my favourite shop, I have to leave my office, and to leave my office I have to open the door; and to do that I first have to get up out of my chair. Now it seems clear that I might engage in some deliberation about the best time to go shopping, and as an outcome decide that it would be best to go in about an hour, around 2 p.m. When my clock indicates 2 p.m., I get up from my chair, open the door, leave my office, and walk down the street to my favourite shop. I might do all of this without much more than the thought that it's time to go shopping. Yet my action has to have some connection with the deliberative decision that I made an hour before. If, for no reason at all, or without the thought of going shopping, I suddenly exited my office and walked toward the shop, in the manner of an automaton, that is, without being conscious of what I was doing, then none of it would be intentional action, although it might look like intentional action from the outside. Something like this may happen in pathological fugue states or in epileptic automatism. Perhaps, finding myself now at the shop, I would say, 'I hadn't intended to go shopping, but since I'm here, I may as well do some shopping'. From that point on, one might say, my shopping action would be intentional, because I would have made a decision to shop.

If there is deliberation and decision to do something, then it seems a clear-cut case of intentional action. The intentionality involved – I am deliberating about something, I am thinking of doing something – is apparent. But not all intentional actions are clearly predated by deliberative decision. I might act before I have a chance to decide to act. If, upon approaching the bus stop, I see the bus pulling away, I might start running to catch it. If you stop me and ask, 'Are you trying to catch the bus?' my answer would be yes, that was my intention. But it is not clear that I had made any deliberation or conscious decision to run after the bus. I might say, 'I decided with my feet', meaning, my decision was in my action, not something separate from it. John Searle (1983) calls this 'intention-in-action'. But this kind of intention-in-action is pervasive, even in action that involves an explicit decision. I had decided to go shopping, and when the time came, I didn't actually make a further explicit decision to get up from my chair, open the door, leave my office, and so on. Rather, my intention is in my action; and for anyone who is observing me, they would see part of my intention expressed in the action.

There is still the question of parsing. I intend to go shopping, and this is clear from my previous decision and the intentionality of that decision making. But do I also intend to open the door on my way out of the office? Obviously I do, even though I did not make any explicit decision to open the door. Opening the door involves an intention-in-action. We would still say it is intentional, and I would certainly answer in the affirmative if you asked me whether I intended to open the door just then: 'Of course, because I'm going shopping.' I can give my reasons retrospectively, if I need to. But I don't explicitly (or even implicitly) think about why I am opening the door. So what is the intentional content of my consciousness as I am engaged in an intentional action?

As I open the door to leave my office, I am likely thinking about what I need to buy when I get to the shop. The one thing that I am likely *not* thinking about is the way that I am moving my feet across the carpet, or the way that I am reaching for the doorknob. To be precise, I am not attending to my movement, although I am certainly conscious that I am moving, opening the door, leaving my office, etc. I have a pre-reflective sense that I am moving, even as I am reflecting on what I need to buy at the shop. What is the nature of this pre-reflective awareness? It is recessive and rather lacking in detail, in the sense that it does not involve attention. I am not paying attention to the way that I am putting one foot in front of another; I am not attending to the way my arm is reaching for the door, or the way my grasp is shaping itself to conform to the shape of the knob. If you stop me in the process of opening the door, and ask what I am doing, my answer would likely be, 'I'm going shopping'. My attention is mainly directed toward the highest appropriate pragmatic level of description – the level of my larger project. I would probably not say 'I am reaching my arm to grasp the knob'. Nor would I say 'I am extending my arm muscles and shaping my grasp'. Although in some sense all of these statements might be true.

All of these issues – how we normally parse our actions, at what level of description we can provide reasons for our actions, the intentional content of our awareness during our action, both at the reflective and the pre-reflective level, and what makes our actions intentional – are connected. In regard to the sense of agency, we also need to distinguish two ways in which the notion of agency enters into intentional action. First, there is an *experiential sense of agency* that comes along with action at the pre-reflective level, the first-order level of consciousness – the level at which I have a sense that I am moving, even if I am not aware of the precise details of my movement. Second, there is the *attribution of agency* that I can make if asked about my action. If I am asked whether I did something (Did you go shopping today?) I can respond, 'Yes'. I thereby attribute a certain action to myself. I might make the attribution on the basis of memory, but the memory would not be there if originally I did not have an experiential sense of agency for the action. So the experiential sense of agency is more basic than the attribution of agency, which depends on it.

One way to get at the concept of an experiential sense of agency is to distinguish it from a sense of ownership for movement. In Chapter 2 we introduced the distinction between the sense of agency for action and the sense of ownership (or mineness) for movement. We indicated that in the normal experience of intentional action, these two aspects are close to indistinguishable. We should note also that the sense of ownership for the movement of my hand, for example, may be conceptually distinguished from the sense of ownership for my hand as part of my body, but that these two are practically intertwined in the sense that movement of my hand never happens without my hand and normally the sense that the movement is mine is tied to the sense that this is my hand. It is possible to experience myself moving and to have a sense of ownership for it, i.e. experience it as my movement, but have no sense of agency for the movement, for example in normal reflex or involuntary movements. If someone is moving my arm, or the doctor is knocking my knee, I experience the movement as mine, although I am not the author of that movement. This is clear in the case of reflex movement. Even in the case of involuntary movement, as when someone pushes me from behind, the loss of the sense of agency holds, at least, for the first moment of the movement. De Haan and de Bruin (2009) are right to point out that almost immediately I can respond and in this response my sense of agency is re-established, perhaps even in a stronger and more conscious way as I struggle to control what is happening to me. There are also different ways to think about the sense of ownership for movement. Clearly, if someone takes my hand and uses it to hit someone else, before I can prevent it, I do not experience this as my action, and I have no sense of agency for this action, but do I not experience this as *my* movement? De Haan and de Bruin suggest that I don't. If that were the case, it's not clear why the movement would matter to me. If a movement occurs for which I have no sense of agency or sense of ownership, then it would have nothing to do with me and I couldn't really complain about the movement. If someone grabs my hand and moves it, and assuming I can feel this, for example, proprioceptively, then this is a feeling (experience, sense) that I (rather than, for example, the person my hand hits) am the one moving. When it comes to attributing movement, I may be tempted to say that this is not *really my* movement in any strong sense, but it would be difficult to deny that I felt *my* hand move and thereby felt that it was *my* movement and have a sense of ownership for it in this minimal sense.

We can throw further light on this by referring to pathological cases (e.g. anarchic hand syndrome or schizophrenia) to disentangle certain aspects of agency that are less clear in non-pathological cases. In the anarchic hand syndrome, patients find one of their hands performing complex, apparently goal-directed movements that they are unable to suppress. These often unwanted and socially unacceptable movements might include undoing the shirt buttons a moment after the other hand has done them up, throwing uncracked eggs and unpeeled onions into the frying pan, or taking leftovers off a neighbouring diner's plate. Although the patient is kinaesthetically aware of the movements of the hand and although the hand itself is felt as the patient's own, the movements it performs are explicitly disavowed by the patient.

In schizophrenic symptoms of delusions of control or thought insertion, the sense of ownership is retained in some form, but the sense of agency is missing. The schizophrenic who suffers from these delusions will claim that *his* body is moving but that someone else is causing the movement; or that there are thoughts in *his* mind, but that someone else is putting them there.

Distinctions between the sense of self-agency and sense of ownership of bodily movement may be found both in first-order phenomenal experience and higher-order, attributional levels of consciousness. In regard to the latter, for example, Graham and Stephens (1994) work out an account of introspective alienation in schizophrenic symptoms of delusions of control in terms of two kinds of self-attribution:

- *Attributions of subjectivity* (ownership): the subject reflectively realizes and is able to report that he is moving. For example, he can say, 'This is my body that is moving'.
- *Attributions of agency*: the subject reflectively realizes and is able to report that he is the author of his action. For example, he can say, 'I am initiating this action'.

This distinction is consistent but not identical with the distinction that we have been discussing, which is made in regard to the level of first-order phenomenal consciousness (see Gallagher 2000a, 2000b).

- *Sense of ownership*: the pre-reflective experience or sense that I am the subject of the movement (e.g. the kinaesthetic experience of movement).
- *Sense of agency*: the pre-reflective experience or sense that I am the author of the action (e.g. the experience that I am in control of my action).

The first-order experiences of ownership and agency are embodied, non-conceptual experiences, and are closely tied to the temporal structure of consciousness. For example, if I reach to pick up a glass, there is information in my motor system that specifies something about the present and immediate history of my hand position, and an anticipation that is built into my movement as my hand shapes its grasp. This temporal structure of movement is mirrored in my sense of control over the movement and so in my sense of self-agency. Furthermore, it seems reasonable to say that the higher-order, conceptually informed attributions of ownership or agency may depend on this first-order experience of ownership or agency. So, having picked up the glass, if I am then asked, did I pick up the glass, I can correctly attribute agency to myself: 'Yes, I was the one who picked up the glass', although, to be sure, this question is not one I usually pose to myself. Graham and Stephens (1994; Stephens and Graham 2000), however, suggest that the sense of agency may in fact be generated at the higher (conceptual) level of attribution. Following Dennett, they propose an explanation of the sense of agency in terms of 'our proclivity for constructing self-referential narratives' which allow us to explain our behaviour retrospectively: 'such explanations amount to a sort of theory of the person's agency or intentional psychology' (Graham and Stephens 1994, p. 101; Stephens and Graham 2000, p. 161). In regard to thinking, for example, if we understand thinking to be an action on our part, then, on Graham and Stephens' account, my sense of agency for that thinking derives from the reflective attitude I take toward it:

> [W]hether I take myself to be the agent of a mental episode depends upon whether I take the occurrence of this episode to be explicable in terms of my underlying intentional states.
>
> (1994, p. 93)

This 'radical top–down' account[3] depends on an approach according to which we reflectively make sense of our actions in terms of our beliefs and desires. So, if a subject does or thinks something for which she has no intentions, beliefs, or desires – mental states that would normally explain or rationalize such actions – the first-order movements or thoughts would not appear as something she intentionally does or thinks. Thus, whether something is to count for me as my action

> ... depends upon whether I take myself to have beliefs and desires of the sort that would rationalize its occurrence in me. If my theory of myself ascribes to me the relevant intentional states, I unproblematically regard this episode as my action. If not, then I must either revise my picture of my intentional states or refuse to acknowledge the episode as my doing. ... [T]he subject's sense of agency regarding her thoughts likewise depends on her belief that these mental episodes are expressions of her intentional states. That is, whether the subject regards an episode of thinking occurring in her psychological history as something she does, as her mental action, depends on whether she finds its occurrence explicable in terms of her theory or story of her own underlying intentional states.
> (Graham and Stephens 1994, p. 102; see Stephens and Graham 2000, pp. 162ff.)

On this approach, non-schizophrenic first-order phenomenal experience appears the way it does because of properly ordered second-order interpretations, and schizophrenic first-order experience appears the way it does because of a second-order *misinterpretation*. It would follow, on this view, that the sense of agency results from an inference made on the basis of higher-order introspective or perceptual self-observations: 'what is critical [in the case of delusions of control or thought insertion] is that the subject find her thoughts [or actions] inexplicable in terms of beliefs about her intentional states' (Graham and Stephens 1994, p. 105).

An alternative, 'bottom–up' explanation starts with the first-order phenomenology. As previously indicated, the pre-reflective experience of agency can be distinguished from the pre-reflective sense of ownership. I experience myself moving, even if the movement is involuntary – e.g. if I am pushed from behind. So for involuntary movement, I have a sense of ownership in that I sense my body moving, but I have no sense of self-agency for it. Part of what makes my movement intentional, and therefore an action, is that I have a sense of self-agency for it, in addition to a sense of ownership. That is, I feel that I am in some sense the author or the cause of my action.

EXPERIMENTING WITH THE SENSE OF AGENCY

In contrast to the radical top–down account, a radical bottom–up approach would suggest that the sense of agency originates in neural processes responsible for the motor aspects of action. One version of such an account proposes that efferent signals (the signals the brain sends to the muscles to make them move) or certain forward motor control mechanisms (i.e. processes that keep our actions on track as they develop, and prior to getting any sensory feedback about them) generate a phenomenal experience of agency (e.g. Blakemore et al. 2002; Frith et al. 2000; Gallagher 2000a, 2000b; Marcel 2003; Wolpert and Flanagan 2001). On this account, problems that develop at the neuronal level could lead to (1) the loss of the actual experience of agency, and (2) the generation of an actual experience of the movement or thought as alien (i.e. as caused by someone or something else), as in schizophrenic delusions. The latter may be tied to disruptions in specific processes that underpin self–other distinctions for action (e.g. Georgieff and Jeannerod 1998). In support of this kind of account, a number of neuroscientists have attempted to find the neural correlates of the sense of agency (e.g. Chaminade and Decety 2002; Farrer and Frith 2002; Farrer et al. 2003). Their brain-imaging experiments are examples of 'front-loaded' phenomenology (see Chapter 2) insofar as the experimental designs are based on the phenomenological distinction between the sense of agency and the sense of ownership (as defined in Gallagher 2000a).

A close reading of these experiments, however, raises some *troubling*, but nonetheless *interesting*, questions. Troubling in the sense that the experimenters sometimes seem confused about what they are testing. Interesting, nonetheless, because the experimental designs raise a question about how we should understand the first-order, pre-reflective sense of agency. The question we want to explore here is this: should we think of the pre-reflective sense of agency as belonging to the realm of motor control and body movement, or as belonging to the realm of intentional action?

The distinction between the sense of agency and sense of ownership, which is referenced in all of these experiments, relies on the logic of involuntary movement. Since in the case of involuntary movement there is a sense of ownership and no sense of self-agency, and because my awareness of my involuntary movement comes from afferent sensory feedback (visual and proprioceptive/kinaesthetic information that tells me that I'm moving), but not from motor commands issued to generate the movement (so, no efferent signals), it seems natural to suggest that in ordinary voluntary movement the sense of ownership might be generated by sensory feedback, and the sense of agency might be generated by efferent signals that send motor commands to the muscle system. Tsakiris and Haggard (2005; also see Tsakiris 2005) provide empirical evidence to support this division of labour. Their research also raises a question about the three experiments that attempt to identify the neural correlates of the sense of agency. In all three, the experimental design was meant to discriminate the sense of self-agency from the sense that someone else is the agent of an action. In these experiments, however, subjects are required to move in each trial in order to accomplish a task. What we can call the Tsakiris–Haggard objection is that since the subjects are moving in each trial, efferent processes must be generating a sense of agency for that movement, as well as a sense of ownership. What becomes clear is that whereas Tsakiris and Haggard think of the sense of agency as closely tied to bodily movement and motor control, the experimenters think of the sense of agency as tied to the intentional accomplishment of a task.

For example, in the PET study by Chaminade and Decety (2002), subjects moved a joystick to control an icon on a computer screen in order to accomplish one of two tasks.

> *Task A* (Leader): Subject moved their own icon, and observed another subject's icon following it.
> *Task B* (Follower): Subject followed another subject's icon with their own.

The authors describe the experiment as involving 'a computerized environment free of explicit reference to body parts', to indicate that the sense of agency is related to the intentional aspect of the action, and not to motor control aspects (Chaminade and Decety 2002, p. 1977). One assumption in the experiment is that A (leading) would generate a sense of agency, while B (following) would not. One obvious objection is that in both cases (A and B) the subject may have a sense of agency for the intentional aspect – i.e. accomplishing the task. The subject might say, 'My task in A is to lead, and I have done so, and my task in B is to follow, and I have done so. I am the agent of both of these actions, respectively (leading and following)'. So differential activation of the brain areas shown to be involved in this experiment (the pre-supplemental motor area and the right inferior parietal cortex as putatively responsible for generating the sense of self-agency, and in contrast, activation of the left inferior parietal cortex and the right pre-central gyrus as putatively responsible for other-agency) may be activated for something other than the difference between self-agency and other-agency. The Tsakiris–Haggard objection, however, is somewhat different. It is that the subject will necessarily have a sense of agency in both A and B because in both tasks the subject moves his hand to control the joystick. Tsakiris and Haggard understand agency to be directly tied to motor control, and in that regard, to efferent signals, and this in contrast to Chaminade and Decety who associate the sense of agency with the intentional aspect of action – the accomplishment of the task.

This same issue can be raised in regard to the other two experiments as well. So even if we think that the sense of agency is present already in first-order experience rather than at a higher-order cognitive level, there is still a question about whether it is generated by motor processes or by some awareness of the intentional aspect of action.

In a very similar experiment, Farrer and Frith, like Chaminade and Decety, associate the sense of agency with the intentional aspect of action, i.e. whether I am having some kind of effect with respect to the goal or intentional task. They find that the anterior insula is activated in correlation to the sense of self-agency. Once again, the Tsakiris–Haggard objection is that since in each task the subject is required to move the joystick, a sense of agency for that movement must result. Since Farrer and Frith clearly think of the sense of agency as something tied to the intentional aspect of action and not to mere bodily movement, they could easily claim to sidestep the Tsakiris–Haggard objection. Curiously and confusingly, however, when it comes to *explaining why* the anterior insula should be involved in generating the sense of agency, Farrer and Frith revert to an explanation more consistent with the Tskaris–Haggard objection, that is, they explain the involvement of the anterior insula in terms of motor control:

> The sense of agency (i.e. being aware of causing an action) occurs in the context of a body moving in time and space. Damasio (1999) [in *The Feeling of What Happens*] has suggested that the sense of agency critically depends upon the experience of such a body. There is evidence that both the inferior parietal lobe and the anterior insula are representations of the body ... the anterior insula, in interaction with limbic structures, is also involved in the representation of body schema. ... One aspect of the experience of agency that we feel when we move our bodies through space is the close correspondence between many different sensory signals. In particular there will be a correspondence between three kinds of signal: somatosensory signals directly consequent upon our movements, visual and auditory signals that may result indirectly from our movements, and last, the corollary discharge [efferent signal] associated with motor commands that generated the movements. A close correspondence between all these signals helps to give us a sense of agency.
>
> (Farrer and Frith 2002, pp. 601–2)

They also cite well-known evidence that the inferior parietal cortex, which they are associating with a sense of other-agency, is responsible for a sense of body ownership – 'patients with right parietal lesion do not recognize their limbs as their own and perceive them as belonging to others' (p. 601). If this is the case, then the fact that for each task the subject moves does indeed complicate things – as the Tsakiris–Haggard objection contends.

The third study (Farrer et al. 2003) involved a different paradigm – subjects moved their own hand, but saw a virtual hand projected on screen at veridical or non-veridical angles. The less the subject felt in control, the higher the level of activation in the right inferior parietal cortex. The more the subject felt in control (the stronger the sense of agency), the higher the level of activation in the right posterior insula. Notice here that there seems to be a clear shift away from the assumption made in the previous experiments, in which the sense of agency was construed in terms of an intentional task that went beyond mere bodily movement; rather, in this experiment, the sense of agency is construed in terms of bodily movement and motor control. In this case the Tsakiris–Haggard objection seems to hold. If the sense of agency is generated by mere bodily movement rather than task-related action (at least a kind of purposive action that goes beyond simply moving one's hand for the sake of an experiment) – and bodily movement does seem to be the only thing at stake in this experiment – then the fact that the subject moves his own hand in all trials in this experiment certainly does not provide any way to discriminate the sense of ownership from the sense of agency, and suggests that the subject should have a sense of agency for all movements of his body.

In explaining their results, the authors seem to add a further confusion between sense of agency and sense of ownership: 'Lesions of the inferior parietal cortex, especially on the right side, have been associated with delusions about the patient's limb that may be perceived as an alien object or as belonging to another person' (Farrer et al. 2003, p. 329). Such delusions are about ownership rather than agency, despite the fact that the authors are offering their findings as relevant for an understanding of the sense of agency. In addition, in Tsakiris and Haggard (2005), activity in the insula was also found in the absence of movement, which implies that this area may in fact reflect body ownership rather than agency.

Finally, note that the results of this experiment, which indicate the involvement of the right posterior insula, are not fully consistent with those of Farrer and Frith (2002), which indicate involvement of the anterior insula bilaterally. Noting this, Farrer et al. (2003, p. 331) seem unable to explain the discrepancy: 'We have no explanation as to why the localization of the activated areas differ in these studies, except that we know that these two regions are densely and reciprocally connected.' Yet it seems clear that there were significant differences in experimental design, task, and foci of attention (that is, phenomenologically, between focusing on a task and focusing on the virtual representation of one's own movement) that may explain the differences in neural activity.

Where does all of this leave us? Primarily, we want to note that the sense of agency is not reducible to awareness of bodily movement or to sensory feedback from bodily movement. Consistent with the phenomenology of embodiment, in everyday engaged action afferent or sensory-feedback signals are attenuated, implying a recessive consciousness of our body (see, for example, Merleau-Ponty 1962; Tsakiris and Haggard 2005). I do not attend to my bodily movements in most actions. I do not stare at my hands as I decide to use them; I do not look at my feet as I walk; and I do not attend to my arm movements as I engage the joystick. Most of our motor-control and body-schematic processes are non-conscious and automatic. It still may be the case, however, since action is embodied, that just such processes contribute to a sense of agency, and without the feeling of the embodied nature of action our sense of agency would be very different. In addition, however, if our descriptions and explanations of what we are doing in action are cast at the highest appropriate pragmatic level of description ('I'm helping my friend', or 'I am on my way to the pub', or whatever, rather than 'I'm moving my hand', or 'I am walking'), then our sense of agency for the action will be tied to that intentional aspect, and that aspect will be where our attention is directed – in the world, in the project or task that we are engaged in. So clearly a form of *intentional feedback*, which is not afferent feedback about our bodily movements, but some perceptual sense that my action is having an effect, must contribute to the sense of agency.

We suggest, then, that the sense of agency, at the first-order level of experience, is complex because it is the product of several contributory elements: efferent signals, sensory (afferent) feedback, and *intentional* feedback, which is perceptual in nature. If any of these contributory elements fail, or fail to be properly integrated, then we can get a disruption in the sense of agency.

In general, then, we can identify three aspects of the sense of agency that are normally integrated with each other:

- Sense of agency as first-order experience linked to intentional aspect (task, goal, etc.) (Chaminade and Decety 2002; Farrer and Frith 2002).
- Sense of agency as first-order experience linked to bodily movement (Farrer et al. 2003; Gallagher 2000a, 2000b; Tsakiris and Haggard 2005).
- Sense of agency as second-order, retrospective attribution (Graham and Stephens 1994).

It is also clear that a fuller and more complicated sense of agency is affected by prospective intention formation at the second-order, reflective level. The fact that I may engage in the formation of prior intentions can certainly contribute to a feeling that I am in control of my subsequent action (Gallagher 2010b). This also suggests that the loss of the sense of agency in various cases – including schizophrenia, anarchic hand syndrome, obsessive-compulsive behaviour, narcotic addiction, etc. – may in fact be different sorts of loss. In any particular case the sense of agency might be disrupted in different ways depending on what contributory element is disrupted. In this regard there are four possibilities for explaining the pathological loss of the sense of agency:

- **Radical top–down:** the sense of agency may be disrupted by problems with retrospective or prospective higher-order cognition – this may very well be the case in advanced and involuted symptoms of schizophrenia.
- **Radical bottom–up:** the sense of agency may be disrupted by problems with motor control mechanisms – efferent signals (Tsakiris and Haggard 2005) or the integration of sensory and motor signals in the insula (Farrer et al. 2003).
- **Intentional theory:** perceived lack of concordance between intention and effects of action may generate a disturbance in the sense of agency (Chaminade and Decety 2002; Farrer and Frith 2002).
- **Multiple aspects:** the sense of agency is complex, and based on the integration of efferent, afferent, and intentional feedback (some sense that my action is having the

intended effect on the world), as well as a coherent higher-order sense of self, so a disturbance in any one contributory may lead to a disturbance in the sense of agency.

The multiple aspects option would integrate the first three and may provide the best way to understand a range of pathological disruptions in the sense of agency.

MY ACTIONS AND YOURS

These experiments pursue the distinction between self-agency and other-agency, between my actions and the actions of others. Just as my intentions are explicit in my actions, I understand your intentions to be explicit in yours. Intentions are not completely hidden in the mind, but also expressed in behaviour, and this – to anticipate discussions in a subsequent chapter – has implications for intersubjective understanding.

A customary answer to the question of how we know what we are doing has been that we need to recognize the difference, the epistemic asymmetry, between our knowledge of our own actions and our knowledge of the actions of others. Whereas the latter knowledge is based on observation and 'outer' sensory awareness, agents typically have knowledge of what they are doing 'from within'. What precisely does this amount to, however? Is it a question of having direct access to my mental events of intending or trying, or a matter of being aware of my bodily movements from within, that is, proprioceptively? And is it at all possible to divide action into two components, a psychological component of trying, and a non-psychological component of bodily movement, or is action on the contrary an indivisible unity? Does our knowledge of it bridge or deconstruct the divide between inner and outer?

The attempt to explicate how we are aware of our own actions is heaped with difficulties. The situation is not much different if we instead turn to the question of how we acquire knowledge about the actions of others. Does perception present us only with information about bodily movements, and do we then have to rely on inference? Do we have to postulate the existence of hidden mental happenings, if we are to interpret someone's bodily movement as, for example, buying a ticket, gesturing goodbye, or expressing joy, or is it rather the case that intentions are manifested directly in goal-directed movements? Contrary to what is being claimed by some theorists, there is much to suggest that we do in fact directly and non-inferentially understand other people acting with intent. When I am playing football, I do not need to draw any inferences to see that you and I are fighting for the same ball. Without the benefit of such an immediate recognition, action coordination – and survival – would be much more cumbersome than it actually is (Dokic 2003, p. 332).

One thing to stay clear about in any such discussions is the difference between different kinds of explanations. We indicated above that causal or neuronal explanations cannot give us an adequate account of actions. The same can be said for neuronal accounts of action awareness – my awareness of my own action or my awareness of yours. Georgieff and Jeannerod (1998), for example, have offered the 'who system' as a neuronal model of action identification. The issue is an important one in terms of subpersonal processes that could account for how my cognitive system identifies my action as distinguished from your action. This is cashed out in neurological terms in the kinds of experiments we discussed in the previous section. One question arises in the realization that the same areas of my brain that are activated when I engage in intentional action are also activated when I see you perform the same or similar intentional action (not just mirror neurons in the promotor cortex, but 'shared representations' in several areas; see Chapter 9 for further discussion of mirror neurons). It has on this background been claimed that the activation is neutral in regard to who is doing the action (see, for example, de Vignemont 2004; Gallese 2005; Hurley 2005; Jeannerod and Pacherie 2004). But if so, one requires an additional subpersonal mechanism to specify who the agent is. This is precisely what the 'who system' does. If we are able to point to specific areas of the brain that are activated when I am the agent, in contrast to areas of the brain activated when you are the agent, this can add to our understanding of how the brain specifies action in regard to agency.

Difficulties arise, however, if we try to project what may be important subpersonal distinctions onto the level of consciousness. Jeannerod and Pacherie (2004), for example, propose that the stepwise distinctions found on the subpersonal neuronal level are also apparent on the experiential level. They characterize the neutrality of shared representations as 'naked intentions' – that is, intentions or intentional actions for which agency is yet to be determined – and they assume that an articulation at the level of neural activations, specifically between those activations responsible for (1) registering the 'naked' intention of an action, and (2) specifying the agent for the action, means that there is an articulation *in experience* between the perception of intention and the perception of agency. They thus claim that we 'can be aware of an intention, without by the same token being aware of whose intention it is. [And that] ... something more than the sole awareness of a naked intention is needed to determine its author' (ibid., p. 140). If in fact the brain can process information about intentions without assigning agency to the intentions, is it legitimate to say that our experience is similarly articulated? Jeannerod and Pacherie answer in the affirmative:

> We claim that it is like this with the perception of intention: when Mary watches John open the door, she is primarily aware of an intention to open the door, rather than being primarily aware that John intends to open the door. Similarly, when Mary herself intends to open the door, she is primarily aware of an intention to open the door, rather than being primarily aware that she herself intends to open the door.
>
> (2004, p. 116)

Phenomenologically (experientially), however, intentions in almost all cases come already fully clothed in agency. The idea that we perceive naked intentions in another's action, or our own, and secondarily attribute agency, seems here to be based on an unjustified supposition of isomorphism between subpersonal and personal-phenomenological levels.[4] The 'who' question, which is rightly posed at the neurological level, hardly ever comes up at the level of experience, because the neural systems have already facilitated the answer. Even if I'm wrong about who the agent of an action is (something that may happen in schizophrenic symptoms of delusions of control), I am still experiencing or perceiving the action as already specified in respect to agency. I don't experience actions without agents; I experience 'X's action' where X is either you or me. Indeed, at the level of awareness, we are highly reliable in regard to discriminating between self and non-self. Pathologies and oddly arranged experiments may reveal 'who' problems, but in normal ecological behaviour it is generally clear whose intention/action it is. As we know from philosophers like Wittgenstein, Shoemaker, and Evans, the self-identification question – 'Someone is intentionally picking up this apple, is it me?' – just doesn't come up.

In effect, it is important to realize that there is no necessary isomorphism between the phenomenological and the neuronal levels. So if the neuronal processes can be defined as involving a stepwise process, this does not mean that a stepwise process needs to show up in phenomenology.[5]

Similar things can be said concerning the role of higher-order cognition or reflective introspection of the sort proposed by Graham and Stephens (1994; Stephens and Graham 2000) in explaining the sense of agency. If actions are specified from the very start and at the first-order level of experience as belonging to particular agents, i.e. if in everyday experience we do not act and then consider whether it was our action or someone else's, this suggests that the first-order, pre-reflective, non-conceptual experience of agency is primitive relative to metacognitive self-ascriptions of actions that involve conceptual and linguistic resources. This is part of what it means to say that our way of being in the world is characterized primarily in terms of action. To be human is already to be action-situated in the world in a way that defines the organized usefulness of the things we find around us, and then lets us think about them.

NOTES

1   Normality is also a question of conventionality. As Husserl points out, there exist indeterminate general demands made by custom and tradition: 'One' judges thus, 'one' holds the fork in such and such a way, etc. (1952/1989, p. 269). As Sartre would later observe, 'To live in a world haunted by my fellowmen is not only to be able to encounter the Other at every turn of the road; it is also to find myself engaged in a world in which instrumental-complexes can have a meaning which my free project has not first given to them. It means also that in the midst of this world *already* provided with meaning, I meet with a meaning which is mine and which I have not given to myself, which I discover that I "possess already"' (1956, pp. 509–10).

2   Anscombe (1957) argues that for something to be a reason for action, one must be able to see how one's current action is going to bring it about ('bringing about heaven on earth' is not a real answer to why I pick up the fork or vacuum the carpet). To accept that 'because I want to be happy' could be an answer to the question of why I walk towards the door, we should be able to see some means–end relation between the current activity and the distal goal; my desire for the latter is what makes the former appropriate.

3   We use the term 'radical top–down' to distinguish the sort of account that involves reflectively conscious cognitive processes (as we find here in Graham and Stephens) from what are sometimes called 'top–down' processes in neuroscience. In neuroscience 'top-down' does not imply conscious processes. For example, Tsakiris (2005) speaks about non-conscious body-schematic (neural) representations as being top–down processes.

4   Matters are not helped by introducing considerations about first-person perspective in this regard, as we find in de Vignemont (2009). That the first-person perspective is self-specific does not rule out the fact that we can perceive another agent as other from that perspective. But this doesn't touch the issue of agent neutrality as proposed by Jeannerod and Pacherie. De Vignemont suggests that a representation could be both from a first-person perspective and neutral with respect to who the agent is, where the important distinction is between the descriptive content of the representation (someone acting) and its mode of presentation (my first-person perception of that action). 'The agent component of the content and the mode of presentation are therefore two separate dimensions. There is no contradiction in representing an action both with an unfulfilled parameter for the agent and from the first-person perspective' (p. 286). Our point, however, is not that there is a contradiction between the perceiving subject viewing action from a first-person perspective and the agent status of the perceived action. Rather, the problem is in the concept of a naked intention, or agent neutrality, or an action with 'an unfulfilled parameter for the agent' if this is meant to apply to an action as it is consciously experienced. The agent neutrality of certain subpersonal processes involved in this perception does not scale up to agent neutrality in the phenomenology.

5   On the question about isomorphism between subpersonal and personal levels, see Gallagher (1997), Hurley (2005), and Varela (1996).

FURTHER READING

Alain Berthoz and Jean-Luc Petit, *The Physiology and Phenomenology of Action*. Trans. C. McCann. Oxford: Oxford University Press, 2008.

Marc Jeannerod, *The Cognitive Neuroscience of Action*. Oxford: Blackwell Publishers, 1997.

Susan Pockett, William P. Banks, and Shaun Gallagher (eds), *Does Consciousness Cause Behavior?* Cambridge, MA: MIT Press, 2006.

Paul Ricoeur, *Freedom and Nature: The Voluntary and the Involuntary*. Trans. E.V. Kohák. Evanston: Northwestern University Press, 1966.

Johannes Roessler and Naomi Eilan, *Agency and Self-Awareness*. Oxford: Oxford University Press, 2003.

9 How we know others

How do we get to know and understand others? Is social cognition perceptual or infer-ential in nature? Is our understanding of others in principle like our understanding of trees, rocks, and clouds, or does it differ in fundamental ways from our understanding of inanimate objects? Do we understand others by analogy to ourselves, that is, does self-understanding have primacy over the understanding of others, or is the understanding of self and other equally primordial, basically employing the same cognitive mechanisms?

According to a prevalent but mistaken view, whatever valuable insights phenomenology might possibly offer to an understanding of the mind, an account of social cognition is not part of its repertoire. As Dennett argues, for instance, traditional phenomenology is committed to a form of methodological solipsism; rather than investigating the mental life of others, the classical phenomenologist is concerned only with his or her own mental life, and thus engaged in a process of autophenomenologizing (1987, pp. 153–54). As we shall see in the following, however, no one familiar with the phenomenological tradition can endorse the claim that phenomenology has failed to analyse the minds of others. But let us take a look at the standard options in the contemporary debate, before turning to what phenomenology has to offer.

THEORY-OF-MIND DEBATE

In recent years, much of the discussion of the nature of social cognition has taken place within the framework of the so-called theory-of-mind debate. The expression 'theory of mind' is generally used as shorthand for our ability to attribute mental states to self and others and to interpret, predict, and explain behaviour in terms of mental states such as intentions, beliefs, and desires (see Premack and Woodruff 1978, p. 515). Although it was originally assumed that it was the possession and use of a *theory* that provided the individual with the capacity to attribute mental states, the contemporary debate is split on the issue, and is generally considered to be a dispute between two views. On one side, we find the *theory theory* (TT) of mind and on the other the *simulation theory* (ST) of mind.

Theory theory is so called because it claims that our understanding of others relies on adopting a theoretical stance; it requires the appeal to a particular theory, namely, folk psychology, which offers us the common-sense explanation of why people do what they do. Simulation theory, in contrast, is the grandchild of the argument from analogy (see, for example, Gordon and Cruz 2006). It claims that our understanding of the other is based on self-simulating their beliefs, desires, or emotions. I put myself in their place and ask what I would be thinking or feeling, and then I project the results onto them. On this view, we do not need theory or folk psychology since we have our own mind to use as a model of what the other's mind must be like.

This neat division is an oversimplification, however. Not only because of the existence of several hybrid theories that combine TT and ST, but also because neither of the main positions is a theoretical monolith. Theory-theorists are basically split on the issue of whether the theory in question is innate and modularized (Carruthers, Baron-Cohen) or whether it is acquired in the same manner as ordinary scientific theories (Gopnik, Wellman). As for the simulationists, some claim that the simulation in question involves the exercise of conscious imagination and deliberative inference (Goldman), some insist that the simulation, although explicit, is non-inferential in nature (Gordon), and finally there are those who argue that the simulation rather than being explicit and conscious is implicit and subpersonal (Gallese).

Generally speaking, however, TT holds that the understanding of minded beings (be it of oneself or others) is theoretical, inferential, and quasi-scientific in nature. It views the attribution of mental states as a matter of inference to best explanation and prediction of behavioural data and argues that mental states are unobservable and theoretically postulated entities. It consequently denies that we have any direct experience of such states. Many philosophers (phenomenologists included) would claim that we need concepts in order to extract and comprehend the informational richness of what is already given, already present to us (like the connoisseur who is able to discern and differentiate aromas and flavours in the wine to which others are not sensitive). Many would also endorse the idea that our observations are influenced and enriched by former experiences. When TT claims that the attribution of mental states is theoretically mediated, however, it has something more radical in mind. The idea is basically that the employment of theory allows us to transcend what is given in experience:

> One of the most important powers of the human mind is to conceive of and think about itself and other minds. Because the mental states of others (and indeed of ourselves) are completely hidden from the senses, they can only ever be inferred.
>
> (Leslie 1987, p. 139)

> Normal humans everywhere not only 'paint' their world with color, they also 'paint' beliefs, intentions, feelings, hopes, desires, and pretenses onto agents in their social

world. They do this despite the fact that no human has ever seen a thought, a belief, or an intention. (Tooby and Cosmides, in Baron-Cohen 1995, p. xvii)

It should be noticed that TT defends a double thesis. It not only claims that our understanding of others is inferential in nature; it also argues that our own self-experience is theoretically mediated. After all, the basic idea is that *any* reference to mental states involves a theoretical stance, and thus involves the application of a theory of mind.

False-belief tests

Claims about the developmental route of theory of mind are often based on false-belief experiments. A simple version of the test involves a child finding out that a crayon box actually contains candles. Another person (or a puppet) enters the room and the child is asked what this other person (or puppet) might think is in the crayon box. The three-year-old, on average, thinks the other person will say there are candles in the box; the four-year-old, on average, will recognize that the other person (or puppet) will have a false belief, namely that because it is a crayon box, the box will have crayons in it. Why this interest in children's ability to succeed on false-belief tasks? To ascribe false beliefs to others (and to itself), the child is assumed to be able to understand that our beliefs might differ from, and thus be distinct from, real-world events and situations. The child's understanding that a person has a false belief consequently provides compelling evidence that the child is able to appreciate the distinction between world and mind, between reality and our beliefs about reality. In short, in order for the child to ascribe false beliefs to self or other, the child must have beliefs about beliefs. It must be in possession of a theory of mind.

Other false-belief tests involve narratives or small plays. For example, in Baron-Cohen et al. (1985), three groups of children were tested: 20 autistic children (mean chronological age (CA) 11 years, 11 months (11/11); mean verbal mental age (MA) of 5/5), 14 Down's syndrome children (mean CA of 10/11; mean MA 2/11), and 27 children from the general population (CA and MA 4/5). The children are seated opposite the experimenter and on the desk in front of them are two dolls, Sally and Anne. Sally has a basket; Anne has a box. Sally hides a marble in her basket and leaves the room to go for a walk. When she is away Anne takes the marble out of Sally's basket and puts it in her own box. When Sally returns, the child is asked the belief question: 'Where will Sally look for her marble?' (see Figure 9.1). The correct answer, of course, is 'in Sally's basket'; the incorrect response is 'in Anne's box'. If the child gives the correct answer, it is assumed that they have developed a theory of mind sufficient to recognize that Sally has a false belief, and a belief that differs from their own. When children four years and older are confronted with this question

continued

they will typically say that she will look inside her basket, since that is where she (falsely) believes it to be hidden. Younger children, however, will often point to the box, indicating that they think that Sally will look for the marble where it really is. They apparently fail to understand that other persons' beliefs could be false (Frith and Happé 1999, pp. 3–4). In this experiment all of the children were able to answer factual and location questions about the marble, but only 20 per cent of the autistic children were able to answer the belief question in contrast to 86 per cent of the Down's syndrome and 85 per cent of those from the general population. The conclusion drawn was that autistic children have not fully developed theories of mind (for some critical remarks, see Hobson 1993; Zahavi and Parnas 2003).

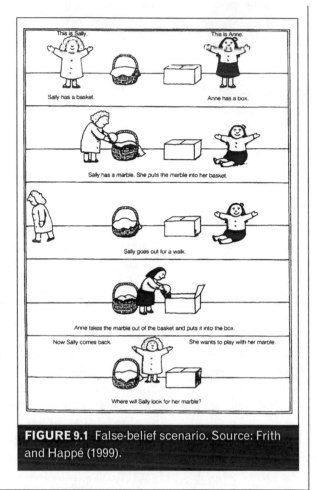

FIGURE 9.1 False-belief scenario. Source: Frith and Happé (1999).

Whereas TT argues that our understanding of others chiefly engages detached intellectual processes, moving by inference from one belief to the other, ST argues that our understanding of others exploits our own motivational and emotional resources. Thus, in contrast to the theory-theorists, the simulationists would deny that what lies at the root of our mentalizing (mind-reading) abilities is a sort of theory. In their view, we possess no such theory, or at least none complete enough to underpin all our competence with psychological notions. Thus far, the different versions of the simulation theory agree. However, when it comes to a more positive account of what the simulationist alternative amounts to, the opinions differ. We'll focus on Goldman's version of explicit simulation, since it is the one that most unequivocally relies on and refers to a routine that merits the name 'simulation'. We will later return to the question of whether our understanding of others could be based on implicit simulations.

According to Goldman, our understanding of the minds of others draws on our introspective access to our own mind; our capacity for self-ascription precedes the capacity for other-ascription. More specifically, Goldman argues that my understanding of others draws on my ability to project myself imaginatively into their situation. I literally use my imagination to put myself in the target's 'mental shoes'. If, for instance, I witness an immigrant being harassed by a desk clerk, I would be able to grasp the immigrant's mental state and predict his subsequent behaviour by means of the following procedure. By means of an explicit simulation, I would imaginatively put myself in his situation, I would imagine how I would feel and react under similar circumstances, and on the basis of analogy I would then attribute or project similar states to the person I am simulating (see Goldman 2000). Here is Goldman's stepwise description of this process:

> First, the attributor creates in herself pretend states intended to match those of the target. In other words, the attributor attempts to put herself in the target's 'mental shoes'. The second step is to feed these initial pretend states [e.g. beliefs] into some mechanism of the attributor's own psychology ... and allow that mechanism to operate on the pretend states so as to generate one or more new states [e.g. decisions]. Third, the attributor assigns the output state to the target. ...
>
> (Goldman 2005, pp. 80–81)

One might think that there would be problems with the very first step: 'the attributor creates in herself pretend states intended to match those of the target'. This suggests that the simulator already has some idea of what's going on with the other person. But where does that knowledge come from and why isn't that already the very thing we are trying to explain? Hybrid theorists who combine TT and ST suggest that folk psychology provides, not a sense of what is going on with the other person, but some general rules about how people think and behave in certain situations, and that this is what the simulationist can use to generate the pretend mental states needed for the simulation process (e.g. Currie and Ravenscroft 2002). In contrast, Goldman appeals to subpersonal mirror resonance processes (discussed below), although he then faces the problem of how to translate these processes into a conceptual grasp of propositional attitudes.

Both sides in the theory-of-mind debate are faced with difficulties. One can, for instance, question some of the empirical claims and implications associated with TT. If a theory of mind is required for the experience of minded beings, then any creature that lacks such a theory will also lack both self-experience and other-experience. According to the standard view, however, children gain possession of a theory of mind only when they are around four years old. Thus, a direct implication of TT seems to be that young children will lack any understanding of self and others during the first three to four years of life. But is that really true? When pressed on the issue, some theory-theorists refer to various mechanisms that might be regarded as precursors to a theory of mind (see Baron-Cohen 1995) and will in fact concede that children do understand (experience) psychological states such as emotions, perceptions, and desires in both self and others prior to the possession of a proper theory of mind. They then argue that what these children lack is an understanding of *representational* mental states (see Wellman et al. 2001, pp. 656, 677). However, since the term 'representational mental state' is quite ambiguous, this admission doesn't do much to clarify the situation. At times, the term is used inclusively to cover all intentional states, including perceptions; at other times, it is used much more restrictively to cover only beliefs proper (thoughts). This vacillation makes IT into something of a moving target. It also threatens to leave it with the uncomfortable choice between only two options. It can, on one of these options, defend a very strong, some would say extreme, claim, according to which the child has no first-person access to any of its own mental episodes and no experience of other minded creatures prior to the acquisition of a theory of mind. Alternatively, it can defend a much weaker, some would say trivial, claim by defining representational mental states in such narrow and conceptually complex terms that it is no wonder that it takes a relatively high level of cognitive sophistication to be able to understand and attribute them to self and other. To rephrase the criticism in slightly different terms: one can define a mental state as something purely interior and private, as something that is not visible in meaningful actions and expressive behaviour. Given such a concept of a mental state, there are good reasons to believe that children will only be able to master the concept and ascribe it to others and self at a relatively late stage. However, the obvious and crucial question is why one would want to operate with such a narrow understanding of the mind in the first place.

When it comes to ST, one might initially question whether any experiential evidence supports the claim that our understanding of others relies on conscious simulation routines. Consider that on most versions of explicit ST, the claim is that simulation is not only explicit but pervasive. That is, we use it all the time, or at least it is the default way of understanding others. Goldman thinks this is a moderate claim:

> The strongest form of ST would say that all cases of (third-person) mentalization employ simulation. A moderate version would say, for example, that simulation is the *default* method of mentalization ... I am attracted to the moderate version. ... Simulation is the primitive, root form of interpersonal mentalization.
>
> (2002, pp. 7–8)

Third-person mentalization signifies simply that one person is trying to understand another, rather than trying to understand herself (which would be first person). But if simulation is both explicit and pervasive, then one should have some awareness of the different steps that one goes through as one consciously simulates the other's mental state. Is there any phenomenological evidence for this? A simple phenomenological objection to explicit ST is that when I interact with or come to understand another person, there is no experiential evidence that I use such conscious (imaginative, introspective) simulation routines. That is, when we consult our own common experience of how we understand others, we don't find such processes. Of course, this is not to say that we never use simulations, but that in itself is telling. It may be the case that confronted with some unaccountable behaviour I do try to understand the other person by running a simulation routine. This is clearly the rare case, however. Moreover, I can easily become aware that I am in fact taking this approach, and it is all the more apparent when I do this, simply because it tends to be the exception. But this tells against the idea that I employ simulation in the usual everyday circumstance. Many of our encounters are not third-person puzzles solved by first-person procedures. They are second-person interactions in which my sense of what is going on with the other person is facilitated by my perception of the other's emotional expression and by our common pragmatic or socially contextualized interactions. Wittgenstein once raised precisely the right question in this regard: 'Do you look within yourself, in order to recognize the fury in *his* face?' (Wittgenstein 1980, §927).

Furthermore, one might ask whether it is really legitimate to cast our experience of others in terms of a first-person imaginative exercise. When we project ourselves imaginatively into the perspective of the other, when we put ourselves in his or her shoes, will we then really attain an understanding of the other or will we merely be reiterating ourselves? As Gilbert Ryle once remarked, the logic of simulation isn't correct, because the idea of imputing to a variety of others what is true of my simulated action ignores the diversity of their actions. '[T]he observed appearances and actions of people differ very markedly, so the imputation to them of inner processes closely matching [those of one's self or] one another would be actually contrary to the evidence' (1949, pp. 53–54). If I project the results of my own simulation on to the other, I understand only myself in that other situation, but I don't necessarily understand the other. As Lipps concluded after having defended a view very akin to Goldman's: 'Psychologically considered, other human beings are duplications of myself' (Lipps 1900, 418). The question, then, is whether a process of simulation will ever allow for a true understanding of the other, or merely let me attain an understanding of myself in a different situation (see below for further discussion).

PROBLEMS WITH IMPLICIT SIMULATION

Some of these same questions can be raised about the implicit version of ST. Simulation theory has gained more ground in recent years by appealing to good neuroscientific evidence involving subpersonal activation of mirror neurons (MNs), shared representations, or more generally, resonance systems. If simulation is subpersonal, and not something of which we would be aware, then phenomenology is not in a position to raise objections, since phenomenology doesn't give us access to the subpersonal domain. In this regard, however, it is important to note that the implicit version of ST is actually an argument against the explicit version of ST. That is, if our understanding of others is in fact mediated by an implicit and automatic simulation process, then we have little need for the more explicit version. Indeed, to the extent that an implicit ST would explain the phenomenological scarcity of explicit simulation, it would support the simple phenomenological argument against explicit simulation. Along this line, Gallese states: 'Whenever we face situations in which exposure to others' behavior requires a response by us, be it active or simply attentive, we seldom engage ourselves in an explicit, deliberate interpretive act. Our understanding of a situation most of the time is immediate, automatic, and almost reflex like' (2005, p. 102).

Let's take a closer look at the recent neuroscience that seemingly supports the idea of implicit simulation. The basic finding in this regard is that one's motor system reverberates or resonates in one's encounters with others. My motor system is activated when I perceive another person performing an intentional action, for example. Mirror neurons in the premotor

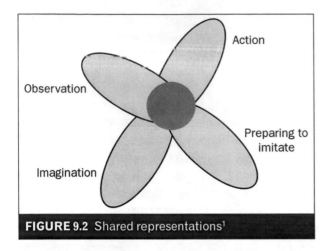

FIGURE 9.2 Shared representations[1]

cortex and in Broca's area, areas of the human brain generally associated with motor control and language, respectively, are activated both when I engage in specific instrumental actions, and when I observe someone else engage in those actions (Rizzolatti et al. 1996). Also, specific overlapping neural areas (shared representations), in parts of the frontal and parietal cortexes, are activated under the following conditions: (1) when I engage in an intentional action; (2) when I observe some other person engage in that action; (3) when I imagine myself or another person engage in that action; and (4) when I prepare to imitate another person's action (Figure 9.2) (see, for example, Grèzes and Decety 2001).

These subpersonal mechanisms are said to constitute a simulation of the other's intentions (Gallese 2001; Gallese and Goldman 1998). Gallese captures it clearly in his claim that

> Whenever we are looking at someone performing an action, beside the activation of various visual areas, there is a concurrent activation of the motor circuits that are recruited when we ourselves perform that action. ... Our motor system becomes active as if we were executing the very same action that we are observing. ... Action observation implies action simulation ... our motor system starts to covertly simulate the actions of the observed agent.
>
> (2001, pp. 37–38)

This involves subpersonal processes generated by 'automatic, implicit, and nonreflexive simulation mechanisms ... ' (Gallese 2005, p. 117). The processes themselves are very real, and there is plenty of neuroscientific evidence to support this. But is it appropriate to characterize these processes as simulations?[2]

As we saw, one possible objection to ST is that since it employs a model that is first person, or at least confined to my own system (a simulation in my own mind or motor system), nothing justifies inferring anything about what must be going on in the other person. Defenders of the implicit version of ST have an answer to this. As noted in the previous chapter, MNs (and shared representations) are said to be agent neutral – activated both for my own action and for observation of the other's action. Thus, activation of the system simulates the intentional action but not the agent (de Vignemont 2004; Gallese 2005; Hurley 2005; Jeannerod and Pacherie 2004). In this case, the subpersonal simulation process, like its explicit cousin, involves a multistep process. First, activation in primary perceptual areas, e.g. visual cortex, corresponding to our seeing an action; this is followed immediately (30–100 milliseconds later) by activation of shared representations – in neutral mode – generating an agent-neutral sense of the action; and then by a determination of agency (i.e. a specification of who did the action – me or the other person) (Jeannerod and Pacherie 2004).[3]

The neuroscientific data, however, is open to an alternative and more parsimonious interpretation. One could easily claim that the neural resonance processes of which we have been speaking, in fact are part of the processes that underlie intersubjective *perception* rather than the extra cognitive step of *simulation*. That is, we can regard these processes as underpinning a direct perception of the other person's intentions, rather than a distinct mental process of simulating their intentions. This claim requires that we conceive of perception as a temporal phenomenon, and as enactive, and thus as involving motor processes. First, MNs fire 30–100 milliseconds after appropriate visual stimulation. What is, even in neurological terms, a short amount of time between activation of the visual cortex and activation of the premotor cortex, raises the question of where precisely to draw the line between the act of perception and something that would count as a simulation. Even if it is possible to draw a line between activation of the visual cortex and activation of the premotor cortex, this does not mean that this line distinguishes between perception and simulation as a stepwise process.

Let's be careful and clear about this. Gallese and the neural simulationists are not claiming that the stepwise neuronal processes (sensory activation of visual cortex, followed by mirror system activation) generate a stepwise conscious process of perception plus simulation. Gallese contends that the simulation stays implicit or non-conscious, but that the mirror system activation itself can be read, functionally, as a simulation process. Nonetheless, we can raise two issues in this regard.

The first issue is this: if perception is an enactive process – sensorimotor, and not just sensory reception (see Chapter 5) – then it may be more appropriate to think of the resonance processes as part of the structure of the perceptual process when perception is of the other's action. Mirror activation, on this interpretation, is not the initiation of simulation; it's part of an enactive intersubjective perception of what the other is doing. At the phenomenological level, when I see the other's action or gesture, I see (I *directly perceive*) the action or gesture as meaningful. I see the joy or I see the anger, or I see the intention in the face or in the posture or in the gesture or action of the other. I see it. I don't have to simulate it. And I immediately see that it is *their* action, gesture, emotion, or intention, and it is extremely rare that I would be in a position to confuse it with my own.

Of course, the simulationist can accept the phenomenology ('Yes indeed, that is what seems to happen') and still hold to the interpretation that the specific subpersonal processes involve simulation. But what precisely justifies this interpretation? Can the simulationist offer any convincing evidence that the activation of resonance processes is in fact a simulation?

Let's set aside the fact that what the implicit simulation theorists are calling 'simulation' does not conform to the definition of simulation as found in the original versions of ST where both instrumental control over the simulation and the involvement of a certain pretence seem essential. For subpersonal processes both of these characterizations fail (Gallagher 2007). Indeed, this is a worry voiced by Goldman.

> Does [the neural simulation] model really fit the pattern of ST? Since the model posits unmediated resonance, it does not fit the usual examples of simulation in which pretend states are created and then operated upon by the attributor's own cognitive equipment (e.g. a decision-making mechanism), yielding an output that gets attributed to the target.
>
> (Goldman and Sripada 2005, 208)

To address this worry Goldman and Sripida propose a generic definition of simulation that sets aside both the instrumental and pretence conditions:

> The general idea of simulation is that the simulating process should be similar, in relevant respects, to the simulated process. Applied to mindreading, a minimally necessary condition is that the state ascribed to the target is ascribed as a result of the attributor's instantiating, undergoing, or experiencing, that very state. In the case of successful simulation, the experienced state matches that of the target. This minimal condition for simulation is satisfied [in the neural model].
>
> (Ibid.)

The proposal that simulation as matching can save the idea that MNs activate simulations, however, is undermined by a number of empirical studies that suggest that more frequently than not, MN activation does not involve matching. Dinstein et al. (2008), for example, have shown that in certain areas of the brain where MNs are thought to exist – specifically within the *anterior intraparietal sulcus* – activated for producing a particular hand action are not activated for perceiving that hand action in another. That is, even for matching gestures, there were no neuronal matching patterns found across action *versus* observation of action conditions in the MN area. Catmur et al. (2007) demonstrated that learning can work against matching. They trained subjects to move their fingers in a manner incongruent with an observed hand, for example, moving the little finger when they observed movement of the index finger. After training, motor-evoked potentials (MEPs) were greater for the little finger when index-finger movement was observed. 'The important implication of this result is that study participants who exhibited incongruent MEP responses presumably did not mistake the perception of index finger movement for little finger movement . . . ' (Hickok 2009, p. 1236). That is, the lack of matching in the motor system does not pre-empt some kind of recognition of what the other person is doing.

In addition, Csibra (2005) points out that conservatively, between 21 and 45 per cent of neurons identified as MNs are sensitive to multiple types of action; of those activated by a single type of observed action, that action is not necessarily the same action as defined by the motor properties of the neuron; approximately 60 per cent of MNs are 'broadly congruent', which means there may be some relation between the observed action(s) and their associated executed action, but not an exact match. Only about one-third of MNs show a one-to-one congruence. Newman-Norlund et al. (2007, p. 55) suggest that activation of the broadly congruent MNs may represent a complementary action rather than a similar action. In that case they could not be simulations defined on the matching hypothesis.

EMPATHY AND THE ARGUMENT FROM ANALOGY

The phenomenological tradition contains rich but also quite diverse and even occasionally competing accounts of intersubjectivity. In the following, we cannot cover all the different versions, but will focus on those that are of most immediate relevance for issues in the contemporary debate.

Let us take our point of departure in the classical attempt to come to grips with the problem of other minds known as the *argument from analogy*. The argument runs as follows. The only mind I have direct access to is my own. My access to the mind of another is always mediated by his bodily behaviour. But how can the perception of another person's body provide me with information about his mind? In my own case, I can observe that I have experiences when my body is causally influenced, and that these experiences frequently bring about certain actions. I observe that other bodies are influenced and act in similar manners, and I therefore *infer* by analogy that the behaviour of other bodies is associated with experiences similar to those I have myself. In my own case, being scalded by hot water is associated with the feeling of intense pain; this experience then gives rise to a quite distinct behaviour: screaming. When I observe other bodies being scalded by hot water and screaming, I infer that it is likely that they are also feeling pain. Thus, the argument from analogy can be interpreted as an inference to the best explanation. An inference bringing us from observed public behaviour to a hidden mental cause. Although this inference does not provide me with indubitable knowledge about others and although it does not allow me to actually experience other minds, at least it gives me more reason to believe in their existence, than in denying it.

What is the relationship between this classical argument and the contemporary theory-of-mind debate? More specifically, how does the argument from analogy relate to ST and to TT, respectively? The argument straddles the difference between the two alternatives. It has affinities with (one version of) the simulation theory in so far as it argues that we have an immediate and direct access to the content of our own minds, and in so far as it holds that this self-acquaintance serves as our point of departure when it comes to an under-standing of others, that is, in so far as it insists that we come to know others by analogy with ourselves. On the other hand, by arguing that our understanding of others is an inference to the best explanation, an inference bringing us from observed public behaviour to a hidden mental cause, the argument from analogy also shares fundamental claims with the theory theory of mind.

The phenomenologist, Max Scheler, helps to throw cold water on the argument from analogy. As he points out, the argument presupposes what it is meant to explain. If I am to see a similarity between, say, my laughing or screaming and the laughing or screaming of somebody else, I need to understand their bodily gestures and behaviour as expressive phenomena, as manifestations of joy or pain, and not simply as physical movements. If such an understanding is required for the argument from analogy to proceed, however, the argument presupposes what it is supposed to establish. In other words, we employ analogical lines of reasoning only when we are already convinced that we are observing minded creatures but are simply unsure precisely how we are to interpret the expressive phenomena in question (Scheler 1954, p. 240; see Gurwitsch 1979, pp. 14, 18).

Scheler also questions two of the crucial presuppositions that are made by the argument from analogy. First, the argument assumes that my point of departure is my own consciousness. This is what is at first given to me in a quite direct and unmediated fashion, and it is this purely mental self-experience that is then taken to make possible the recognition of others. One is at home in oneself and then has to project into the other, whom one does not know, what one already finds in oneself. Second, the argument also assumes that we never have direct access to another person's mind. We can never *experience* her thoughts or feelings. We can only infer that they must exist based on what we perceive, namely her bodily and behavioural appearances. Although both of these assumptions might seem perfectly obvious, Scheler rejects both. As he puts it, the argument from analogy underestimates the difficulties involved in self-experience and overestimates those involved in the experience of others (Scheler 1954, p. 251). We should not fail to acknowledge the embodied and embedded nature of self-experience and we should not ignore what can be directly perceived about others. That is, Scheler is pointing to the importance of embodiment on both sides of this relation: he denies that our initial self-acquaintance is of a purely mental nature and that it takes place in isolation from others, and he also denies that our basic acquaintance with others is inferential in nature. We can perceive the joy, sadness, puzzlement, eagerness of others, or that they have a question or a concern, etc., in their movements, gestures, facial expressions, and actions.

> For we certainly believe ourselves to be directly acquainted with another person's joy in his laughter, with his sorrow and pain in his tears, with his shame in his blushing, with his entreaty in his outstretched hands, with his love in his look of affection, with his rage in the gnashing of his teeth, with his threats in the clenching of his fist, and with the tenor of his thoughts in the sound of his words. If anyone tells me that this is not 'perception', for it cannot be so, in view of the fact that a perception is simply a 'complex of physical sensations', and that there is certainly no sensation of another person's mind nor any stimulus from such a source, I would beg him to turn aside from such questionable theories and address himself to the phenomenological facts.
>
> (Scheler 1954, p. 260)

It is no coincidence that we use psychological terms to describe behaviour; indeed, we would be hard pressed to describe it in terms of bare movements. Affective and emotional states are not simply qualities of subjective experience; rather, they are given *in* expressive phenomena, i.e. they are expressed in bodily gestures and actions, and they thereby become visible to others. There is something highly problematic at the phenomenological level of description about claiming that intersubjective understanding is a multistage process in which the first stage is the perception of meaningless behaviour and the final one an intellectually based attribution of psychological meaning. In the majority of cases, it is quite difficult (and artificial) to divide a phenomenon neatly into a psychological aspect and a behavioural one – think merely of a smile, a handshake, an embrace, a leisurely stroll. In the face-to-face encounter, we are confronted neither with a mere body, nor with a hidden psyche, but with a unified whole. Scheler speaks of an 'expressive unity' (*Ausdruckseinheit*). It is only subsequently, through a process of abstraction, that this unity can be divided and our interest then proceed 'inwards' or 'outwards' (Scheler 1954, p. 261).

Phenomenological views, then, emphasize non-mentalizing, embodied perceptual approaches to questions of understanding others and the problem of intersubjectivity. We begin from the recognition that the body of the other presents itself as radically different from any other physical entity, and accordingly that our perception of the other's bodily presence is unlike that of physical things. The other is given in its bodily presence as a *lived* body, a body that is actively engaged in the world. As Sartre pointed out, it would be a decisive mistake to think that I ordinarily encounter the body of another as I would the kind of body described by physiology. The body of another is always given to me in a situation or meaningful context, which is co-determined by the action and expression of that very body (1956, p. 345).

Some phenomenologists suggest that this involves a distinctive mode of consciousness which they call *empathy* (see Scheler 1954; Stein 1989). Empathy is defined as a form of intentionality in which one is directed towards the other's lived experiences.[4] Any intentional act that discloses or presents the other's subjectivity from the second-person perspective counts as empathy. Although empathy, so understood, is based on perception (of the other's bodily presence) and can involve inference in difficult or problematic situations (where one has to work out how another person feels about something), it is not reducible to some additive combination of perception and inference. The phenomenological conception of empathy thus stands opposed to any theory that claims our *primary* mode of understanding others is by perceiving their bodily behaviour and then inferring or hypothesizing that their behaviour is caused by experiences or inner mental states similar to those that apparently cause similar behaviour in us. Rather, in empathy, we experience the other directly as a person, as an intentional being whose bodily gestures and actions are expressive of his or her experiences or states of mind (for further discussion, see Thompson 2001, 2005, 2007; Zahavi 2001a, 2008c, 2010).

In several of his writings, Scheler defends the view that we are empathically able to *experience* other minds (Scheler 1954, 9). It is no coincidence that he repeatedly speaks of the perception of others (*Fremdwahrnehmung*), and even entitles his own theory a *perceptual theory of other minds* (Scheler 1954, 220). One could, however, ask whether we really enjoy as direct an access to the experiential life of others as we do to our own. This is precisely what other phenomenologists have disputed. Husserl, for instance, concedes that my experience of others has a quasi-perceptual character in the sense that it grasps the other as such. But at the same time, Husserl also says that although the body of the other is intuitively given to me *in propria persona*, this is not the case with the other's experiences. They can never be given to me in the same original fashion as my own experiences. In short, empathy is both like and unlike perception. It is like perception in being direct, unmediated, and non-inferential. It is unlike perception, however, in not offering us the fullest presence of the empathized experience – that presence is only available to the subject of the experience (Husserl 1952, 198). Even Merleau-Ponty would agree with the latter point. He suggests that, although I can perceive the grief or the anger of the other in his or her conduct, in his face or hands, and although I can understand the other without recourse to any 'inner' experience of suffering or anger, the grief and the anger of the other will never quite have the same significance for me as they have for him. For me these situations are displayed, for him they are lived through (Merleau-Ponty 1962, 356).

But does this entail that we have to choose between Scheler on the one side, and Husserl (and Merleau-Ponty) on the other? Not necessarily. One way to reconcile the different views might be as follows. When claiming that we can *experience* others, and as a consequence do not exclusively have to rely on and employ inferences, simulations, or projections, this is not meant to entail that we can experience the other in precisely the same way as she herself does, nor that the other's consciousness is accessible to us in precisely the same way as our own is. Second- (and third-)person access to psychological states *do* differ from first-person access. But we shouldn't make the mistake of restricting and equating experiential with first-person access. It is possible to experience minds in more than one way. When I experience the facial expressions or meaningful actions of another, I am *experiencing* another's subjectivity, and not merely imagining it, simulating it, or theorizing about it. The fact that I can be mistaken and deceived is no argument against the experiential character of the access.

Moreover, the fact that my experiential access to the minds of others differs from my experiential access to my own mind is not an imperfection or shortcoming. On the contrary, it is a difference that is constitutional. It is precisely because of this difference, precisely because of this asymmetry, that we can claim that the minds we experience are *other* minds. As Husserl points out, if I had the same access to the consciousness of the other as I have to my own, the other would cease being an other and would instead become a part of myself (Husserl 1950/1999: 159). To put the point differently, in order to get at interpersonal understanding, we have to reject both claims: that everything about the other is invisible, and that everything is visible. Indeed, a more precise way of capturing what is at stake might be by saying that we experience bodily and behavioural expressions as expressive of an experiential life that goes beyond the expression. Thus, the givenness of the other is of a most peculiar kind. The otherness of the other is precisely *manifest* in his elusiveness and inaccessibility. As Lévinas observed, the absence of the other is exactly his presence *as other* (1979, 89). There is, so to speak, more to the mind of the other than what we are grasping, but this does not make our understanding non-experiential.

MENTALISM AND THE CONCEPTUAL PROBLEM OF OTHER MINDS

Despite their differences, TT and ST both deny that it is possible to directly *experience* other minded creatures; this is supposedly why we need to rely on and employ either theoretical inferences or internal simulations. Both accounts consequently share the view that the minds of others are completely hidden, and they consider one of the main challenges facing a theory of social cognition to be the question of how and why we start ascribing such hidden mental entities or processes to certain publicly observable bodies. As we have seen, phenomenologists would object to the way this question is framed. They would argue that an exclusive appeal to either theory or simulation is unwarranted since it is motivated by an overly impoverished conception of what is given, of what is experientially available. It is occasionally assumed that a phenomenological account of intersubjectivity is by and large opposed to TT, whereas the relation between phenomenology and ST is much more conciliatory. This is only partially correct. In fact, by emphasizing the embodied nature of self-experience, several of the phenomenologists have called attention to a problem that in retrospect must seem particularly troublesome for Goldman's simulationist account. Whereas theory theorists such as Gopnik have traditionally emphasized the parallelism between the ascription of mental states to self and other (Gopnik 1993), Goldman has stressed the asymmetry. But if we start out by accepting the conceptual separation of the mental from the behavioural, and if my own self-experience is of a purely mental nature, whereas my experience of others is purely behavioural in nature, we need to understand why I should even so much as think that there are other minded creatures. As Davidson has put it:

> If the mental states of others are known only through their behavioral and other outward manifestation, while this is not true of our own mental states, why should we think our own mental states are anything like those of others?
>
> (2001, p. 207; see Merleau-Ponty 1962, p. 348)

If we adopt what McCulloch (2003, p. 94) has recently called a behaviour-rejecting mentalism, i.e. if we deny that embodiment and bodily behaviour have any essential role to play in experience and cognition, if we deny that embodiment and environmental embedding are essential to having a mind, we will have a hard time escaping what is known as the *conceptual problem of other minds*. If my self-experience is, in the primary instance, of a purely mental nature, i.e. if my body does not figure essentially in my self-ascription of (some) psychological states, while my ascriptions of mental states to others are based solely on their bodily behaviour, what, then, should guarantee the ascriptions of the same type of states to self and to others? How would we ever come to be in possession of a truly general concept of mind that is equally applicable to different subjects? (See Avramides 2001, pp. 135, 224.)

Merleau-Ponty's solution was to insist on the embodied character of self-experience. Were self-experience of a purely mental nature, were it only present in the form of an immediate and unique inwardness, I would not only lack the means of ever recognizing other bodies as embodied subjects, I would also lack the ability to recognize myself in the mirror, and more generally, I would be unable to grasp a certain intersubjectively describable body as myself:

> If the sole experience of the subject is the one which I gain by coinciding with it, if the mind, by definition, eludes 'the outside spectator' and can be recognized only from within, my cogito is necessarily unique, and cannot be 'shared in' by another. Perhaps we can say that it is 'transferable' to others. But then how could such a transfer ever be brought about? What spectacle can ever validly induce me to posit outside myself that mode of existence the whole significance of which demands that it be grasped from within? Unless ... I have an exterior others have no interior. The plurality of consciousness is impossible if I have an absolute consciousness of myself.
>
> (Merleau-Ponty 1962, p. 373)

> The other can be evident to me because I am not transparent for myself, and because my subjectivity draws its body in its wake.
>
> (ibid., p. 352).

Since intersubjectivity is, in fact, possible, there must exist a bridge between my self-acquaintance and my acquaintance with others; my experience of my own subjectivity must contain an anticipation of the other (ibid., pp. 353, 448). That bridge or common ground is embodied being-in-the-world. When I experience myself, and when I experience others, there is in fact a common denominator. In both cases, I am dealing with *embodiment* and one of the features of my embodied subjectivity is that it, per definition, entails acting and living in the world. When I go for a walk, write a letter, or play ball, to use Strawson's classic examples (P. F. Strawson 1959, p. 111), I am experiencing a certain way of engaging with the world that already involves others and in a way that anticipates my possible responses to others.

The proper way to respond to the sceptical challenge is consequently by abandoning the radical divide between the subject's mind and body. This is where the notions of expression and action become crucial. It could be argued, of course, that any account of the mind has to take subjectivity and the first-person perspective seriously, and that a focus on expression and action will consequently lose sight of what is essential to the mind. However, this worry is misguided. There is nothing reductive in the reference to expression and action, since subjectivity figures centrally in both concepts.

The idea is not to reduce consciousness as such to intentional behaviour. But we should recognize that the expressive relation between mental phenomena and behaviour is stronger than that of a mere contingent causal connection, though weaker than that of identity. Bodily behaviour is neither necessary nor sufficient for a whole range of mental phenomena, so one can occur without the other – which is why lying, deception, and suppression are possible – but this is not to say that this is generally the case or that it could conceivably always be the case. As a rule, we do not come to know one independently of the other. As Wittgenstein says, 'One can say "He is hiding his feelings." But that means that it is not a priori they are always hidden' (1992, p. 35e). In fact, as Rudd (2003, p. 114) has recently argued, intersubjective understanding is possible precisely because some of our mental states find a natural expression in bodily behaviour, and because the language we learn for our mental states is a language that we learn to apply to others even as we learn to apply it to ourselves.

Expression is more than simply a bridge that closes the gap between inner mental states and external bodily behaviour. In seeing the actions and expressive movements of other persons, one already sees them as meaningful. No inference to a hidden set of mental states is necessary. Expressive behaviour is saturated with the meaning of the mind; it reveals the mind to us. Certainly, it differs from the mind's direct manifestation available from the first-person perspective. We should respect and maintain the asymmetry between the first-person and the second- (and third-)person access to psychological states, but this is not a difference between an immediate certainty on the one side, and an insecure inference on the other. We should recognize that each type of access has its own strengths and weaknesses. The second- (or third-)person access only 'falls short' of the first-person access if it is assumed that the latter is privileged, and that it is the internal aspiration of the former to approximate the latter as closely as possible (R. Moran 2001, p. 157).

The idea that behaviour, considered in itself, is neither expressive nor significant, is unacceptable. The idea that behaviour is merely the outwardly observable effect of mental states is also unacceptable. If we say that behaviour is expressive, this does not mean that it expresses or externalizes something that is internal or hidden away. Such views do not merely fail to recognize the true nature of behaviour, they also present us with a misleading perspective on the mind, suggesting that the mind is a purely internal happening located and hidden in the head, thereby giving rise to the problem of other minds (see McDowell 1998, p. 393). We should avoid construing the mind as something visible to only one person and invisible to everyone else. The mind is not something exclusively inner, something cut off from the body and the surrounding world as if psychological phenomena would remain exactly the same, even without gestures, bodily expressions, etc. As Overgaard (2005) points out, psychological phenomena stretch their arms in many directions – they play many publicly observable roles – and to cut off all of these public arms would leave us with a severely distorted picture of the mental.

When somebody blushes because he is ashamed, the blush reveals and manifests the shame, it doesn't conceal it. When somebody screams in pain while the dentist drills in his tooth, it makes little sense to say that this is merely behaviour, and that the real pain is still concealed and inner. As Bennett and Hacker observe, we can speak of indirect evidence or of knowing indirectly only where it also makes sense to speak of a more direct evidence, but there is no more direct way of knowing that somebody is in pain than seeing him writhe in pain, or knowing that somebody sees something than by him showing what he sees, or knowing what he thinks than from his sincere confession. By contrast, noticing a bottle of painkillers next to his bedside together with an empty glass of water and concluding that he is in pain is an example of knowing indirectly or by way of inference (2003, pp. 89, 93).

This is not behaviourism. The idea is not to identify or reduce mental states to behaviour or to behavioural dispositions, nor does it rule out that some experiential states are covert; but not all experiences can lack a natural expression if intersubjectivity is to get off the ground.[5] To suggest that the indirect means of verifying claims about black holes or subatomic particles can 'give us a model for verifying hypotheses in the area of the study of human and animal subjectivity' (Searle 1999b, p. 2074) seems deeply confused.

One reason why the problem of other minds seems so persistent is that we have conflicting intuitions about the accessibility of the mental life of others. On the one hand, there is something right about the claim that the feelings and thoughts of others are manifest in their expressions and gestures. On the other hand, there also seems to be something right in the idea that the mental life of another is in some respect inaccessible. There are situations, where we have no reason to doubt that the other is angry, in pain, or bored. There are other situations where we have no clue as to their precise state of mind. Despite this, it seems wrong to claim that the mental life of others is essentially inaccessible, just as it seems wrong to claim that everything is open to view. The challenge is to reconcile both intuitions, rather than letting one of them go (Overgaard 2005).

It is consequently important to understand that the claim being made is not that bodily expressivity exhausts our mental life and that everything is directly visible. Rather what is being denied is that bodily expressivity lacks intrinsic psychological meaning, as if it owed whatever meaning it does have exclusively to the fact that it stands in a certain relationship to various hidden mental states.

A satisfying account of social cognition must consequently accomplish something of a balancing act. On the one hand, it won't do to overstate the difference between self-experience and the experience of others, since this will confront us with the conceptual problem of other minds. On the other hand, it won't do to downplay the difference between self-experience and the experience of others either, since this would fail to do justice to the otherness of the other.

INTERACTION AND NARRATIVE

Primary intersubjectivity

In contrast to TT and ST, more recent phenomenological approaches to the issues of social cognition have been guided by the emphasis on social interaction in developmental science. Developmental studies tell us that long before the child reaches the age of four, the supposed age for acquiring a theory of mind, capacities for human interaction and inter-subjective understanding have already been active in certain embodied practices – practices that are emotional, sensorimotor, perceptual, and non-conceptual. These embodied practices constitute our primary way of understanding others, and they continue to do so even after we attain more sophisticated abilities in this regard (Gallagher 2001; Zahavi 2004b).

From early infancy humans engage in forms of embodied interaction with others that fall under the heading of what the developmental psychologist Colwyn Trevarthen (1979) calls 'primary intersubjectivity'. Primary intersubjectivity builds on the innate or early-developing sensorimotor capacities that bring us into immediate relations with others and allow us to interact with them. These capacities are manifested at the level of perceptual experience – we *see* or more generally *perceive* in the other person's bodily postures, movements, facial expressions, directed gaze, gestures, and actions what they intend and what they feel, and we respond in a tightly coupled way with our own bodily movements, gestures, facial expressions, gaze, etc. In this respect perception is enactive; it is perception-for-action or more precisely -for-interaction, rather than mere off-line observation. From birth the infant is pulled into these interactive processes. This can be seen in the very early behaviour of the newborn. Infants from birth are capable of perceiving and imitating facial gestures presented by another (Meltzoff and Moore 1977; 1994). Importantly, this kind of interactive imitation is not an automatic or mechanical procedure; Csibra and Gergely (2009) have shown, for example, that the infant is more likely to imitate only if the other person is attending to it. Neonate imitation depends not only on a minimal embodied contrast between self and non-self, and a proprioceptive sense of one's own body, but also on a responsiveness to the fact that the other is of the same sort as oneself (Bermúdez 1995; Gallagher 1996; Gallagher and Meltzoff 1996). The fact that they imitate only *human* faces (see Legerstee 1991; S. Johnson 2000; Johnson et al. 1998) suggests that infants can parse the surrounding environment into those entities that perform human actions (people) and those 'things' that do not (Meltzoff and Brooks 2001). An intermodal tie between a proprioceptive sense of one's body and the face that one sees is already functioning at birth.

At 2 months of age, infants can follow the gaze of the other person, see that the other person is looking in a certain direction, and sense what the other person sees (which is sometimes the infant herself), in a way that throws the intention of the other person into relief (Baron-Cohen 1995; Maurer and Barrera 1981). In addition, second-person interaction is evidenced by the timing and emotional response of infants' behaviour. Infants 'vocalize and gesture in a way that seems [affectively and temporally] "tuned" to the vocalizations and gestures of the other person' (Gopnik and Meltzoff 1997, 131). Murray and Trevarthen (1985) have shown the importance of this temporal attunement in the mother's live (and lively) interaction with her 2-month-old infant. The infant will enthusiastically interact with its mother via a two-way, live video monitor. When presented with a recorded replay of their mother's previous actions, that is, the very same actions with which the infant had previously engaged, the relation fails. Because the timing of the mother's actions is not synchronized with the infant's actions and responses the infant quickly disengages and becomes distracted and upset. Similar results have been shown in Tronick's well-known still-face experiments. Infants are engaged in a normal face-to-face interaction with an adult for 1 to 2 minutes, followed by the adult assuming a neutral facial expression. This is followed by another normal face-to-face interaction. Infants between 3 and 6 months become visibly discouraged and upset during the still-face period when interaction breaks down (Tronick et al. 1978). The importance of interactive touch has also been demonstrated in the still-person effect (Muir 2002).

At 5–7 months, infants can detect correspondences between visual and auditory information that specify the expression of emotions (Walker 1982; Hobson 1993, 2002). At 6 months infants start to perceive grasping as goal directed, and at 10–11 months infants can parse some kinds of continuous action according to intentional boundaries (Baldwin and Baird 2001; Baird and Baldwin 2001; Woodward and Sommerville 2000). They follow the other person's eyes, and perceive various movements of the head, the mouth, the hands, and more general body movements as meaningful, goal-directed movements (Senju et al. 2006). Such perceptual and interactive experiences give the infant, by the end of the first year of life, a non-mentalizing understanding of the intentions and dispositions of other persons (Allison et al. 2000; Baldwin 1993; S. Johnson 2000; Johnson et al. 1998).

The early capabilities that contribute to primary intersubjectivity do not depend on what theory of mind in each case calls inferential 'mentalizing' or 'mind-reading'. Infants, notably without the intervention of theory or simulation, can see bodily movement as goal-directed intentional movement, and perceive other persons as agents. This does not require advanced cognitive abilities; rather, it is a perceptual capacity that is 'fast, automatic, irresistible and highly stimulus-driven' (Scholl and Tremoulet 2000, p. 299). Accordingly, before we are in a position to wonder what the other person believes or desires, we already have specific perceptual understandings of what they feel, whether they are attending to us or not, whether their intentions are friendly or not, and so forth. There is, in primary inter- subjectivity, a common bodily intentionality that is shared across the perceiving subject and the perceived other. As Gopnik and Meltzoff indicate, 'we innately map the visually perceived motions of others onto our own kinesthetic sensations' (1997, p. 129). The evidence from the research on MNs and resonance systems in social neuroscience supports this more enactive view of perception for interaction.[6] That is, the infant's perceptual understanding of the other's comportment serves to shape the infant's response to the other and is part of a larger interactive process that requires response on both sides of the interaction. Before we are in a position to theorize, simulate, explain, or predict mental states in others, we are already interacting with them and understanding them in terms of their expres- sions, gestures, intentions, and emotions, and how they act toward ourselves and others. Importantly, primary intersubjectivity is not primary simply in developmental terms. Rather, it remains primary throughout the life span, across all face-to-face intersubjective experi- ences, and it underpins those developmentally later practices that may involve explaining or predicting mental states in others.

Secondary intersubjectivity

In spite of the access to others that primary intersubjectivity gives us, this is certainly not sufficient to explain the full range of intersubjective understanding. If human faces are especially salient, even for the youngest infants, or if we continue to be capable of percep- tually grasping the meaning of the others' expressions and intentional movements, such face-to-face interaction does not exhaust the possibilities of intersubjective understanding.

Expressions, intonations, gestures, and movements, along with the bodies that manifest them, do not float freely in the air; we find them in the world, and infants soon start to notice how others interact with the world. When infants begin to tie actions to pragmatic contexts, they enter into what Trevarthen calls 'secondary intersubjectivity'. Around the age of 1 year, infants go beyond the person-to-person immediacy of primary intersubjectivity, and enter into *contexts* of shared attention – shared situations – in which they learn what things mean and what they are for (see Trevarthen and Hubley 1978). Behaviour representative of joint attention begins to develop around 9–14 months (Phillips et al. 1992). The child alter-nates between monitoring the gaze of the other and what the other is gazing at, checking to verify that they are continuing to look at the same thing. Indeed, the child also learns to point around this same time. Eighteen-month-old children comprehend what another person intends to do with an instrument in a specific context. They are able to re-enact to completion the goal-directed behaviour that someone else fails to complete. Thus, the child, on seeing an adult who tries to manipulate a toy and who appears frustrated about being unable to do so, quite readily picks up the toy and shows the adult how to do it (Meltzoff 1995; Meltzoff and Brooks 2001). The child can understand that the other person wants food or intends to open the door (though not necessarily why); that the other can see him (the child) or is looking at the door. This is not taking an intentional stance, i.e. treating the other as if they had desires or beliefs hidden away in their minds; rather, the intentionality is perceived in the contextualized actions of others. Others are not given (and never were given) primarily as objects that we encounter cognitively, or as entities in need of explanation. We perceive them as agents whose actions are framed in their practical activities. It follows that there is not one uniform way in which we relate to others, but that our relations are mediated through the various pragmatic circumstances of our encounters. Indeed, we are caught up in such pragmatic circumstances, and are already existing in reference to others, from the very beginning (consider, for example, the infant's dependency on others for nourishment), even if it takes some time to sort out which agents provide sustenance, and which ones are engaged in other kinds of activities.

As we noted, children do not simply observe others; they are not passive observers. Rather, they interact with others, and in doing so they develop further capabilities in the contexts of those interactions. Our understanding of others is keyed to the most relevant pragmatic (intentional, goal-oriented) level of action, ignoring possible subpersonal or lower-level descriptions, and also ignoring mentalizing interpretations. Rather than making an inference to what the other person is intending by starting with bodily movements, and moving thence to the level of mental events (desires and beliefs), we see actions as meaningful in the context of the physical and intersubjective environment. If, in the vicinity of a loose board, I see you reach for a hammer and nail, I know what your intentions are as much from the hammer, nail, and loose board as from anything that I observe about your bodily expression or postulate in your mind. We interpret the actions of others in terms of their goals and intentions set in contextualized situations, rather than abstractly in terms of either their muscular performance or their beliefs.[7] The environment, the situation, or the pragmatic context is never perceived neutrally (non-semantically), either in regard to our own possible actions, or in regard to the actions and possibilities of others. As Gibson's theory of affordances suggests, we see things in relation to their possible uses, and therefore never as disembodied observers. Likewise, our perception of the other person, as another agent, is never of an entity existing outside of a situation, but rather of an agent in a pragmatic context that throws light on the intentions (or possible intentions) of that agent.

Let us at this stage briefly return to our earlier discussion of empathy. The use of the concept is not uncontroversial. In fact, even in phenomenological circles, the notion has fallen into a certain disrepute. As Heidegger argues, if one seeks to understand intersubjectivity on the basis of empathy one will remain committed to a serious miscon-ception of the nature of the self:

> If this word [empathy] is at all to retain a signification, then only because of the assumption that the 'I' is at first in its ego-sphere and must then subsequently enter the sphere of another. The 'I' does not first break out … since it already is outside, nor does it break into the other, since it already encounters the other outside.
>
> (2001, p. 145)

According to this understanding of the concept, the notion of empathy is linked to the problem of how one (isolated) subject can encounter and understand another (isolated) subject. Even if the empathic approach does not commit the same mistakes as the argument from analogy it still misconstrues the nature of intersubjectivity, since it takes it to be first and foremost a thematic encounter between individuals, where one is trying to grasp the inner emotions or experiences of the other (this connotation is particularly obvious in the German word for empathy: *Einfühlung*). However, as Heidegger also points out, the very attempt thematic-ally to grasp the experiences of others is the exception rather than the rule. Under normal circumstances, we understand each other well enough through our shared engagement in the common world.

A similar criticism is formulated by Aron Gurwitsch. Gurwitsch readily acknowledges the importance of expressive phenomena, but he criticizes Scheler for having been too one-sided in his approach, and then argues that the realm of expressive phenomena is neither the only, nor the primary, dimension to be considered if we wish to understand what it is that enables us to encounter other human beings as humans (Gurwitsch 1979, p. 33). In his view, we do not primarily, and ordinarily, encounter others as thematic objects of cognition. Rather, we encounter them in the world in which our daily life occurs, or to be more precise, we encounter others in worldly situations, and our way of being together and understanding each other is co-determined in its meaning by the situation at hand (ibid., pp. 35–36, 95, 106).

To exemplify, Gurwitsch analyses a situation, reminiscent of an example given by Wittgenstein, where two workers are cobbling a street. In this work situation, one worker lays the stones while the other knocks them into place. Each worker is related to the other in his activity and comportment. When one worker understands the other, the understanding in question does not involve grasping some hidden mental occurrences. There is no problem of other minds. There is no problem of how one isolated ego gets access to another. Rather, both workers understand each other in virtue of the roles they play in the common situation (ibid., pp. 104, 108, 112).

It is precisely within such common, and mainly pragmatic, situations that expressive phenomena occur. When working or conversing with my partner, she might shake her head or wrinkle her brow. But these facial expressions and bodily gestures are not unambiguous. They do not reveal psychological states simply or uniformly. Each person has different counten-ances and facial habits. But this is rarely a problem, since we do not encounter expressions in isolation. They always occur in a given context, and our understanding of the context, of what comes before and after, helps us understand the expression. As Gurwitsch points out, the 'same' shaking of the head can take on different meanings in different situations. What an expressive phenomenon is and what it signifies in a particular case become comprehensible to me in the whole of the present situation (ibid., p. 114; see Sartre 1956, p. 347).

Heidegger and Gurwitsch both emphasize the social and cultural embeddedness of intersubjective understanding. However, one can accept this emphasis and still consider the notion of empathy to be useful. Consider for instance Alfred Schutz's position. Schutz argues that the most basic form of interpersonal understanding, the one we find in the face-to-face encounter, is a theoretically unmediated quasi-perceptual ability to recognize other creatures directly as minded creatures and that this amounts to an irreducible *sui generis* form of intentionality. But although Schutz would accept that certain aspects of the other's consciousness, such as his joy, sorrow, pain, shame, pleading, love, rage, or threats, are given to us directly and non-inferentially, he denies that it should follow from the fact that we can intuit these surface attitudes that we also have a direct access to the *why* of such feelings. But when we speak of understanding (the psychological life of) others, what we mean is precisely that we understand what others are up to, why they are doing what they are doing, and what that means to them. To put it differently, interpersonal understanding crucially involves an understanding of the actions of others, of their whys, meanings, and motives. And in order to uncover these aspects, it is not sufficient simply to observe expressive movements and actions, we also have to rely on interpretation, we also have to draw on highly structured contexts of meaning (Schutz 1967, pp. 23–24). However, in those cases where the other in question is one that is bodily co-present we do not have to rely exclusively on imagination, memory or theory to unearth the why of his actions. Rather a more productive focus is on the shared motivational context and situation, on the fact that we encounter each other in a shared world (Schutz 1967, p. 170).

Thus, one might acknowledge that our typical understanding of others is contextual and that empathy, properly understood, is not a question of feelingly projecting oneself into the other, but rather an ability to experience behaviour as expressive of mind, i.e. an ability to access the life of the mind of others in their expressive behaviour and meaningful action. In fact, in contrast to mentalistic theory-of-mind approaches that define the problem as trying to access the other person's mind, phenomenological approaches suggest that a more productive focus is on the other person's world. As Merleau-Ponty puts it: 'In so far as I have sensory functions ... I am already in communication with others. ... No sooner has my gaze fallen upon a living body in process of acting than the objects surrounding it immediately take on a fresh layer of significance; they are no longer simply what I myself could make of them, they are what this other pattern of behaviour is about to make of them' (1962, p. 353). In effect, to understand other persons I do not primarily have to get into their minds; rather, I have to pay attention to the world that I already share with them.

Narrative competency

How do we get the more complex and nuanced understanding of why people do what they do? Certainly we start to realize that when confronted with a loose board, one person may pick up a hammer and nail and go to work, while another person may simply talk about the looseness of the board, and a third may ignore it altogether. We start to understand that one person may know something that another person doesn't, or that others may think something very different from us. To understand others in these situations and to engage in such practices we need something more than our basic perceptions, emotions, and embodied interactions.

Tomasello has recently proposed that our social cognition takes three forms. We can understand others (1) as animate beings, (2) as intentional agents, and (3) as mental agents. In his view, the ontogenetic relevance of this tripartition is straightforward. Whereas infants can distinguish animate from non-animate beings already from birth onwards, they can only detect intentionality, in the sense of goal-directed behaviour, from around 9–12 months of age (as evidenced in phenomena such as joint attention, gaze following, joint engagement, imitative learning, etc.), and they only become aware of others as mental agents with beliefs that might differ from their own at around 4–5 years of age. Why does the last step take so much longer? The answer provided by Tomasello is twofold. On the one hand, he calls attention to the different roles of expressive behaviour. Whereas the animacy of others is directly expressed in their behaviour, intentionality is also expressed in actions, but is at the same time somewhat divorced from them, since on occasion it may remain unexpressed or be expressed in different ways. Finally, when it comes to thoughts and beliefs these might lack natural behavioural expressions altogether (Tomasello 1999, p. 179), which is what makes them so much more difficult to grasp. On the other hand, Tomasello argues that the more advanced form of social cognition emerges as late as it does because it depends on prolonged real-life social interaction (ibid., p. 198). More specifically, he argues that language use may play a crucial role in children's coming to view other people as mental agents (ibid., p. 176). To understand that other persons have beliefs about the world that differ from their own, children need to engage them in discourses in which these different perspectives are clearly apparent, be it in disagreements, misunderstandings, requests for clarification, or reflective dialogues (ibid., pp. 176, 182).

One might question Tomasello's developmental time frame (cf., for instance, Onishi and Baillargeon 2005). Moreover, it seems potentially misleading to designate the difference between an understanding of the goal-directed actions of others and that of their false or divergent beliefs as one of an understanding of others as intentional agents and as mental agents. Such a characterization might suggest both that there is nothing mindful about goal-directed actions and no intentionality to thoughts and beliefs. But Tomasello is certainly right in pointing to the fact that our understanding of others gradually becomes more sophisticated, and that there are some dimensions of the mind that are not as readily accessible as others. Moreover, he is also right in pointing to the cultural and social dimension of this developmental process. Rather than being the result of an automatic maturation of certain innate cognitive modules, it seems plausible to view these more sophisticated forms of social cognition as abilities that develop in tandem with increasingly complex forms of social interaction.

Theory-of-mind approaches, both TT and ST, or any hybrid version that combines them, miss some basic and important capacities for social cognition. Yet, the acknowledgement of capabilities for understanding others that define primary and secondary intersubjectivity – the embodied, sensorimotor (emotion informed) capabilities that enable us to perceive the intentions of others, and the perceptual and action capabilities that enable us to understand others in the pragmatically contextualized situations of everyday life – is still not sufficient to address what are clearly new developments around the ages of two, three, and four years. The 'elephant in the room' around the age of two years is, of course, language. But if language development itself is something that depends on the capabilities of primary and secondary intersubjectivity, language also carries these capabilities forward and puts them into service in much more sophisticated social contexts. Explanation and prediction of action from a third-person stance is far more infrequent and far less reliable than our normal intersubjective means of coming to understand others through dialogue and conversation and shared narratives (Hutto 2004, 2008). If someone is acting in a puzzling way, by far the easiest and most reliable way to gain further information is not to engage in detached theorizing or internal simulation, it is to employ conversational skills and ask the person for an explanation.

Importantly, the capacity for understanding narrative, which starts to develop around age two, provides a more nuanced way of understanding others. The pervasive presence of narrative in our daily lives, and the development of narrative competency, provides a parsimonious alternative to claims about the primacy of theory or simulation approaches, and an alternative way to account for the more nuanced understandings (and misunderstandings) we have of others. Competency with different kinds of narratives enables us to understand others in a variety of ways. For example, folk-psychological narratives (Bruner 1986) may facilitate our understanding of intentional actions when, as observers, we are confronted with a puzzling case. This is what Hutto suggests by his narrative practice hypothesis:

> The Narrative Practice Hypothesis (NPH) claims that children normally achieve [folk-psychological] understanding by engaging in story-telling practices, with the support of others. The stories about those who act for reasons – i.e. folk psychological narratives – are the foci of this practice. Stories of this special kind provide the crucial training set needed for understanding reasons.
>
> (Hutto 2007, p. 53)

A complementary idea is that other kinds of narrative competencies enable a less mediated interpretation of the other's actions and intentions. Normally, coming to understand another's reasons is not a matter of comprehending their discrete 'mental states' but rather their attitudes and responses as whole situated persons. I encounter the other person, not abstracted from their circumstances, but in the middle of something that has a beginning and that is going somewhere. I see them in the framework of a story in which either I have a part to play or I don't. The narrative is not primarily about what is 'going on inside their heads'; it's about what is going on in our shared world and about how they understand and respond to it. In this sense, our common-sense understanding of others can also be seen as a skilful practical reasoning that depends on a developed narrative competency.

But, one might ask, aren't narratives simply types of theories, and doesn't this heavy reliance on narratives entail an endorsement of some kind of theory of mind? As we see it, the narratives that frame our social interactions differ in two crucial ways from the kind of theories to which TT appeals. In his defence of TT, Botterill, for instance, has argued that every theory necessarily involves explanatory and predictive power along with counterfactual projection. He also mentions the introduction of unobservable entities and the implicit definition of concepts as a recurrent element. He concludes by arguing that theories are characterized by producing cognitive economy through the integration of information within a small number of general principles (Botterill 1996, 107–9). Accordingly, first, for TT, mental states are theoretically postulated entities comparable to the black holes posited by astrophysics, and many theory-theorists of an eliminativist persuasion would even argue that black holes are considerably more real than mental states such as hopes, memories, intentions, and emotions. In contrast, narratives are grounded in observable events that take place in the world. Second, this implies, as Bruner (1986) suggests, that narrative is a particular mode of thinking that relates to the concrete and particular; it takes the concrete context to be of primary importance in the determination of meaning. In contrast, theories in the proper sense of the term are concerned with the abstract and general, and in this sense they abstract away from the particular context.[8]

In the case of someone's puzzling action, a narrative can facilitate understanding by filling in a 'rationale' when this is not immediately obvious. This doesn't mean that our understanding of others requires an occurrent or explicit narrative storytelling: but it does require the ability to see and frame the other person in a detailed pragmatic or social context, and to understand that context in a narrative way. As Alasdair MacIntyre (1985) suggested, for an observer, or for a participant, an action has intelligibility when it can find a place in a narrative (see Gallagher and Hutto 2007).

Narratively framing my understanding of others may happen explicitly or implicitly. An implicit use of narrative simply means that while I interpret another person's actions, I do so without realizing that I'm understanding the other person's action in narrative terms, that is, contextualized in terms of what went before, or where I think the action is heading, what I know about this particular person or what certain typical cultural narratives lead me to expect in this particular situation. Even when an explicit knowledge of a person's story helps me to make sense out of what they are doing, there may be much more going on. I understand any particular story in terms of other narratives about relevant social practices, contexts, and characters. Such narratives may also shape my evaluative judgements about the other person's actions.

Sartre's example of being caught peeping through a keyhole is apropos. If I catch you as you are down on your knees peeping through a keyhole at some people in the next room, I may immediately assume your behaviour to be an offensive invasion of privacy. You are a 'peeping Tom' and ought to be exposed. But my understanding of your behaviour is not based on having a theory about peeping Toms, or about inferences about what you might believe or desire. After all, I caught you 'in the act', 'red handed', and my evaluation of your behaviour is fully informed by the various narratives that go along with peeping Toms. You know the same narratives and for that very reason you can immediately feel shame and the weight of my judgement.

This central role for narratives points in two directions. First, larger narratives that further contextualize the situation, either in terms of different cultural norms or the peculiarities of a person's history or values, may be needed for a fuller understanding. Such narratives are available as, and help to constitute, the shared normative practices that inform our cultural and common-sense understandings (see Brandom 1994). Together, armed with these narrative understandings, we go on to invent important institutions, create laws, and engage in complex social practices.

Second, in acquiring the narratives that we share with others, we shape our own self-understandings. Since we develop in social contexts and normally acquire the capacity for understanding in those contexts, the development of self-narrative obviously involves others. Katherine Nelson (2003) points out that narrative abilities start to emerge in two-year-olds, 'with respect to the child's own experience, which is forecast and rehearsed with him or her by parents'. Self-narrative requires building on our experiences of and with others and their narratives. Thus, at the beginning of this process we find that 'children of 2–4 years often "appropriate" someone else's story as their own' (ibid., p. 31). There is, then, another side to the story of how we understand others through narratives; we also understand ourselves through narratives. As we'll see in the next chapter, this idea lends support to a growing interdisciplinary consensus among developmental psychologists, neuroscientists, and philosophers (see Bruner, Dennett, Damasio, McIntyre, Ricoeur, Schechtman) about the importance of a socially embedded narrative self.

NOTES

1   Thanks to Peer Bundgaard for the diagrammatic suggestion.
2   Gallese is not alone in his interpretation of these resonance processes as simulation. Jeannerod and Pacherie (2004, p. 113) 'argue in favor of a simulation hypothesis that claims that actions, whether overt or covert, are centrally simulated by the neural network, and that this simulation provides the basis for action recognition and attribution'. A growing number of neuroscientists endorse this view. Marco Iacoboni states: 'When you see me perform an action – such as picking up a baseball – you automatically simulate the action in your own brain' (cited in Blakeslee 2006). Giacomo Rizzolatti writes: 'Mirror neurons allow us to grasp the minds of others not through conceptual reasoning but through direct simulation. By feeling, not by thinking' (in Blakeslee 2006). And Ramachandran and Oberman claim that MNs 'not only send motor commands but also enable both monkeys and humans to determine the intentions of other individuals by mentally simulating their actions' (2006, p. 65; also see Oberman and Ramachandran 2007).
3   See our discussion of 'naked intentions' in the previous chapter.
4   This use of the term consequently differs from Stueber's recent discussion, where he explicitly defines empathy as a form of 'inner or mental imitation' (2006, p. 28; see also Zahavi, forthcoming-a).
5   Some empirical research suggests that the expression of a number of basic emotions, such as anger, happiness, disgust, contempt, sadness, fear, and surprise, are cross-cultural and universal, though there are, of course, culturally specific rules about how to manage expressions in public

(Ekman 2003, pp. 4, 10, 58). The suggestion that basic emotional expressions are innate is further corroborated by the fact that even congenitally blind children normally exhibit the relevant facial expressions.

6   In citing Gopnik and Meltzoff's claim about the necessity for innate mappings we are not thereby endorsing their theory-theoretic construal of what this involves. Indeed, much of the evidence developed by Meltzoff and cited by Gopnik and Meltzoff supports the idea of a strong intersubjective perceptual capacity in the infant.

7   Our understanding of the performance of mimes who work without props depends on their excellent ability to express intentions in their movements, but also on our familiarity with contexts. The mime's talent for expressive movements is clearly demonstrated in contrast to what we often experience in the game of charades or pantomime when we haven't a clue about what the player is trying to represent.

8   This is not to deny that theories have their own historical contexts, in terms of how they get developed, and in terms of their employment by theorists. Theory, however, tends to ignore just such contexts. More importantly, however, because of their general nature, theories ignore the context of the person we are trying to understand – call it the context of application. To the degree that theory remains general and dependent on predetermined rules or predictions, it downplays the importance of the particular aspects of the situation under consideration. If theorists of mind do worry about the context of application, it's not clear how they are able to understand it except by appealing to narrative aspects of the situation (see Gallagher 2011).

FURTHER READING

Anita Avramides, *Other Minds*. London: Routledge, 2001.

Aron Gurwitsch, *Human Encounters in the Social World*. Trans. F. Kersten. Pittsburgh: Duquesne University Press, 1979.

Edmund Husserl, *Cartesian Meditations: An Introduction to Phenomenology*. Trans. D. Cairns. The Hague: Martinus Nijhoff, 1999.

Daniel D. Hutto, *Folk Psychological Narratives: The Socio-cultural Basis of Understanding Reasons*. Cambridge, MA: MIT Press, 2008.

Søren Overgaard, *Wittgenstein and Other Minds: Rethinking Subjectivity and Intersubjectivity with Wittgenstein, Levinas, and Husserl*. New York and London: Routledge, 2007.

Matthew Ratcliffe, *Rethinking Commonsense Psychology*. London: Palgrave-Macmillan, 2007.

Jean-Paul Sartre, *The Emotions: Outline of a Theory*. Trans. B. Frechtman. New York: Philosophical Library, 1948.

Max Scheler, *The Nature of Sympathy*. Trans. P. Heath. London: Routledge & Kegan Paul, 1954.

Anthony Steinbock, *Home and Beyond*. Evanston: Northwestern University Press, 1995.

Michael Theunissen, *The Other*. Trans. C. Macann. Cambridge, MA: MIT Press, 1986.

Evan Thompson (ed.), *Between Ourselves: Second-Person Issues in the Study of Consciousness*. Exeter: Imprint Academic, 2001.

Dan Zahavi, *Husserl and Transcendental Intersubjectivity*. Athens: Ohio University Press, 2001.

10 Self and person

The phenomenological and ontological status and nature of the self are controversial issues that are currently debated in a variety of different fields, including philosophy of mind, social theory, cultural studies, psychiatry, developmental psychology, and cognitive neuroscience. Among the topics discussed are questions like the following. What is a self? Does it exist for real, or is it a mere social construct or perhaps a neurologically induced illusion? If something like a self exists, what role does it play in our conscious lives, and when and how does it emerge in the development of the infant?

The scientific community is rather split on the issue concerning the scientific and philosophical legitimacy of the notion of self. There is currently no consensus about whether the self has an experiential reality or whether it is nothing but a theoretical fiction. Some claim that the sense of self is an integral part of consciousness (see Damasio 1999) and that this is something which the ongoing search for the neural correlates of consciousness must necessarily take into account. Others argue that it is neither necessary nor rational to assume the existence of a self, since it is a theoretical entity that fulfils no indispensable explanatory function (see Metzinger 2003). Currently, both sides have ardent defenders. Where should one start, if one wants to make headway?

A first step is to recognize that there is no widespread philosophical consensus about what exactly it means to be a self. The concept is characterized in a variety of ways throughout the literature. The disparity of conceptions can be glimpsed by considering an incomplete inventory of terms that have come to proliferate in philosophical and psychological accounts:

- Material self, social self, spiritual self (James 1890/1950).
- Ecological self, interpersonal self, extended self, private self, conceptual self (Neisser 1988).
- Autobiographical self, cognitive self, contextualized self, core self, dialogical self,

embodied self, empirical self, fictional self, minimal self, neural self (see, for example, Damasio 1999; G. Strawson 1999).

This disparity, which is both problematic and productive, is directly related to the variety of methodological approaches taken within philosophy and in related interdisciplinary studies of the self. They include introspection, phenomenological analysis, linguistic analysis, the use of thought experiments, empirical research in cognitive and brain sciences, and studies of exceptional and pathological behaviour. One problem to be posed in this light is whether different characterizations of self signify diverse aspects of a unitary concept of selfhood, or whether they pick out different and unrelated concepts. This problem of 'inter-theoretical coherency' is addressed below. Regardless of how one answers this problem, however, the variety of approaches and definitions found in studies of the self productively reinforces the idea that human cognition involves complex and varied aspects that are not easily reducible to one set of principles.

NEUROSCEPTICISM AND THE NO-SELF DOCTRINE

The legitimacy of the notion of self has been questioned throughout the history of philosophy. In one tradition, the claim has been that the positing of a conscious self or subject is descriptively unwarranted. If we describe the content of our consciousness accurately, if we actually pay attention to what is given, we do not find any self. This is the standard interpretation of Hume's reflections on the self. It follows that, rather than having experiential reality, the self must be classified as a linguistic construct or as a product of reflection. This is also – perhaps somewhat surprisingly – a view one can find in phenomenology. In the first edition of *Logical Investigations*, Husserl defends what is known as a non-egological theory of consciousness. On this view there is no pure identical ego-pole that is shared by all experiences or that conditions their unity. Experiences are not states or properties of anybody, but mental events that occur without a subject. Whereas we can distinguish between a red sports car and the experience of a red sports car, we are unable to locate a third element, a pure ego that is directed at the sports car through the experience.

Sartre later adopted a similar view. It has occasionally been argued that mental life would dissipate into the chaos of unstructured and separate sensations if it were not supported by the unifying, synthesizing, and individuating function of a central and atemporal ego. However, as Sartre pointed out in one of his early essays, *The Transcendence of the Ego*, this reasoning misjudges the nature of the stream of consciousness; it does not need an exterior principle of individuation, since it is *per se* individuated. Nor is consciousness in need of any transcendent principle of unification, since it is, as such, a flowing unity. As we saw in Chapter 4, it is exactly as temporal that consciousness unifies itself. Thus, a correct account of time-consciousness will show that the contribution of an ego is unnecessary; the ego consequently loses its *raison d'être* (Sartre 1957, p. 40).

Furthermore, Sartre claimed that a correct phenomenological investigation of lived consciousness will simply not find an ego, whether understood as an inhabitant in or possessor of consciousness. One occasionally says of a person who is absorbed in something that he has 'forgotten' himself. This way of speaking contains a truth. When I am absorbed in reading a story, I have a consciousness of the narrative and a pre-reflective self-awareness of the reading but, according to Sartre, I do not have any awareness of an ego. As long as we are absorbed in the experience, *living* it, no ego will appear. The ego emerges only when we adopt a distancing and objectifying attitude to the experience in question, that is, when we *reflect* upon it. As Sartre put it, the ego appearing in reflection is the object and not the subject of reflection. When I engage in a reflective exploration of this object, I will be examining it as if it were the ego of another person (ibid., p. 87). It is in this sense that the ego is transcendent and it is exactly for this reason that Sartre, in an attempt to bypass the problem of solipsism, denied that my ego is something about which I enjoy a special certitude: 'My I, in effect, is *no more certain for consciousness than the I of other men*. It is only more intimate' (ibid., p. 104).

This phenomenologically motivated self-scepticism has recently been matched by a rather different kind of scepticism. According to a view that is gaining popularity among some neuroscientists and philosophers, what is crucial is not whether or not the self is a given in experience. Whether something is real is neither a question of its appearance, nor a question of its being experienced as real, rather it is a question of whether it fits into our scientific world view. According to this criterion, the concept of the self has been weighed and has been found wanting.

One prominent exponent of this neuroscepticism is Thomas Metzinger, who in *Being No One* offers us a representationalist and functionalist analysis of what a consciously experienced first-person perspective is. The conclusion he reaches is quite unequivocal: 'no such things as selves exist in the world: Nobody ever *was* or *had* a self' (2003, p. 1). For all scientific and philosophical purposes, the notion of a self can safely be eliminated. It is neither necessary nor rational to assume the existence of a self, since it is a theoretical entity that fulfils no indispensable explanatory function. In reality, the self is not an actually existing object, and it is certainly not an unchangeable substance, rather it is what Metzinger calls a representational construct. Biological organisms exist, but an organism is not a self. Some organisms possess self-models, but such self-models are not selves; they are merely complex brain states (ibid., p. 563). All that really exist are certain types of information-processing systems that are engaged in operations of self-modelling, and we should not commit the mistake of confusing a model with reality (ibid., pp. 370, 385, 390). Or to be more precise, the self-representing system is caught up in a naive-realist self-misunderstanding (ibid., pp. 332, 436–37, 564). Properly speaking, there is no one who confuses herself with anything, since there is no one who could be taken in by the illusion of a conscious self (ibid., p. 634).

It is obviously possible to speak of the self or ego the way Husserl, Sartre, and Metzinger do. One problem with their sceptical reservations, however, is that they all presuppose rather specific concepts of self, which they then proceed to criticize. Yet is it at all clear what, precisely, a self is?

VARIOUS NOTIONS OF SELF

What we intend to do in the following is to contrast a rather classical understanding of the self (the self as a pure identity pole), which, to a large extent, is targeted by the non-egological criticism, with two alternative and more contemporary ways of conceiving of the self (the self as a narrative construction, and the self as an experiential dimension).

The self as a pure identity pole

This traditional view insists on distinguishing between the identical self on the one hand and the manifold of changing experiences on the other. In a sequential order I can taste a single-malt whisky, smell a bunch of violets, admire a painting by Picasso, and recollect a visit to Venice. We are here faced with a number of different experiences, but they also have something in common; they all have the same subject, they are all lived through by one and the same self, namely myself. Whereas experiences arise and perish in the stream of consciousness, the self remains as one and the same through time. More specifically, the self is taken to be a distinct *principle of identity* that stands apart from and above the stream of changing experiences and which, for that very reason, is able to structure it and give it unity and coherence.

The notion of self at work here is obviously a very formal and abstract one. It is always the case that experience is lived through *by* a certain subject; it is always an experience for a certain subject. The self is, consequently, understood as the pure subject, or ego-pole, to which any episode of experiencing necessarily refers back. It is the subject of experience rather than the object of experience. Instead of being something which can, itself, be given as an object for experience, it is a necessary condition of possibility for (coherent) experience. We can infer that it must exist, but it is not, itself, something that can be experienced. It is an elusive principle, a presupposition, rather than a datum or something that appears in the stream of experience. If it did make a phenomenal appearance, it would be an appearance for someone, i.e. it would be an object, and therefore no longer a self (see Natorp 1912, pp. 8, 40). As Kant already pointed out in his *Critique of Pure Reason*, 'It is ... evident that I cannot know as an object that which I must presuppose to know any object' (1956/1999, p. A402).

The self as a narrative construction

A quite different way of conceiving the self takes its point of departure in the fact that self-comprehension or self-knowledge, rather than being something that is given once and for all, is something that has to be appropriated and can be attained with varying degrees of success. As long as life goes on, there is no final self-understanding. The same, however, can also be said for what it means to be a self. The self is not a thing, it is not something fixed and unchangeable but rather, something evolving. It is an achievement rather than a given. It is something that is realized through one's projects and actions and it therefore cannot be understood independently of one's own self-interpretation. In short, one is not a self in the same way one is a living organism. One does not have a self in the same way that one has a heart or a nose (Taylor 1989, p. 34).

According to this view, which has become increasingly popular lately, the self is constructed in and through narrative self-interpretations. When confronted with the question 'Who am I?' we will tell a certain story and emphasize aspects that we deem to be of special significance, to be what constitutes the *leitmotif* in our lives, what defines who we are, what we present to others for recognition and approval (Ricoeur 1988, p. 246). This narrative, however, is not merely a way of gaining insight into the nature of an already existing self, since there is no such thing as a pre-existing self, one that just awaits being portrayed in words. To believe in such a prelinguistic given is quite literally to have been misled by stories.

The narrative account is quite explicit in emphasizing the *temporal dimension* of selfhood (see also Chapter 4). Human time is the time of our life stories; a narrated time structured and articulated by the symbolic mediations of narratives (ibid., p. 244). Events and experiences that occur at different times are united by being incorporated into a single narrative. Whether or not a particular action, experience, or characteristic counts as mine is a question of whether or not it is included in my self-narrative. As MacIntyre puts it, the unity of the self 'resides in the unity of a narrative which links birth to life to death as narrative beginning to middle to end' (1985, p. 205).

The narrative account also stresses the *social dimension* of selfhood (see Chapter 9). Narration is a social process that starts in early childhood and continues for the rest of our lives. I come to know who I am and what I want to do with my life by participating in a linguistic community. Others are called upon to hear and to accept the narrative accounts we give of our actions and experiences. Furthermore, as Bruner points out, our self-making stories are not made up from scratch; they pattern themselves on conventional genres. When I talk about myself, my selfhood becomes part of the public domain, and its shape and nature are guided by cultural models of what selfhood should and shouldn't be (Bruner 2002, p. 65). To come to know oneself as a person with a particular life history and particular character traits is, consequently, both more complicated than knowing one's immediate beliefs and desires and less private than it might initially seem (Jopling 2000, p. 137). When I interpret myself in terms of a life story, I might be both the narrator and the main character, but I am not the sole author. The beginning of my own story has always already been made for me by others and the way the story unfolds is only in part determined by my own choices and decisions. In fact, the story of any individual life is not only interwoven with the stories of others (parents, siblings, friends, etc.), it is also embedded in a larger historical and communal meaning-giving structure (A. MacIntyre 1985, p. 221). Whether I come to understand myself as the inheritor and continuer of various traditions, or not, my story is caught up in such traditions.

Who we are depends upon the story we (and others) tell about ourselves. The story can be more or less coherent, and the same holds true for our self-identity. The narrative self is, consequently, an open-ended construction which is under constant revision. It is pinned on culturally relative narrative hooks and organized around a set of aims, ideals, and aspirations (Flanagan 1992, p. 206). It is a construction of identity that starts in early childhood and continues for the rest of our lives, always involving a complex social interaction. Who one is depends on the values, ideals, and goals one has, and on one's actions; it is a question of what has significance and meaning for one, and this, of course, is conditioned by the community of which one is part. Thus, as has often been claimed, one cannot be a self on one's own, but only together with others, as part of a *linguistic* community. This narrative connection to others goes two ways; not only does it shape our own selves, but, as we indicated in the previous chapter, it also provides a framework for understanding others.

It is worthwhile noticing that the narrative account can on a certain reading turn into a version of the no-self doctrine. In effect, one might consider the extended narrative self as simply a fiction, albeit a useful one because it lends a practical sense of continuity to life, but a fiction nonetheless. Dennett (1988, 1991) offers an example of this view, which he sees as consistent with recent developments in our understanding of how the brain functions. The consensus from contemporary neuroscience is that neurological processing is for the most part distributed across various brain regions. There is consequently no real unified neurological centre of experience, nor is there any real identity across time that we could label the self. Humans, however, do have language. And with language we begin to make our experiences relatively coherent and integrated over extended time periods. We use words to tell stories, and according to Dennett it is with these stories that we create what we call selves. We extend our biological boundaries to encompass a life of meaningful experience. Two things are to be noted from Dennett's account. First, we cannot prevent ourselves from 'inventing' our selves. We are hard-wired to become language users, and once we are caught up in the web of language and begin spinning our own stories, we are not totally in control of the product. As Dennett puts it, 'Our tales are spun, but for the most part we don't spin them; they spin us' (1991, p. 418). Second, an important product of this spinning is the narrative self. The narrative self, however, is nothing substantially real. Rather, according to Dennett, it is an empty abstraction. Specifically, Dennett defines a self as an abstract 'center of narrative gravity', and likens it to the theoretical fiction of the centre of gravity of any physical object. In the case of narrative gravity, however, an individual self consists of the abstract and movable point where the various stories (of fiction or biography) that the individual tells about himself, or are told about him, meet up.

The self as an experiential dimension

In *The Feeling of What Happens*, Damasio claims that a sense of self is an indispensable part of the conscious mind. As he writes: 'If "self-consciousness" is taken to mean "consciousness with a sense of self," then all human consciousness is necessarily covered by the term – there is just no other kind of consciousness' (1999, p. 19). When I think thoughts, read a text, perceive a melody, a red sports car, or a steaming cup of hot chocolate, I automatically and implicitly sense that I, rather than anyone else, am doing it. I sense that the objects I now perceive are being apprehended from my perspective and that the thoughts formed in my mind are mine and not anyone else's. Thus, as Damasio puts it, there is a constant, but quiet and subtle, presence of self in my conscious life (ibid., pp. 7, 10, 127).

Consciousness is not a monolith, however, and Damasio finds it reasonable to distinguish a simple, foundational kind of consciousness, which he calls *core consciousness*, from a more complex kind, which he calls *extended consciousness*. Core consciousness has a single level of organization and remains stable across the lifetime of the organism. It is not exclusively human (non-human animals may have a core consciousness) and does not depend upon conventional memory, reasoning, or language. In contrast, extended consciousness has several levels of organization. It evolves across the lifetime of the organism and depends upon both conventional and working memory. It can be found in a basic form in some non-humans, but only attains its highest peak in language-using humans. According to Damasio, these two kinds of consciousness correspond to two kinds of self. He calls the sense of self that emerges in core consciousness the core self and refers to the more elaborate sense of self provided by extended consciousness as the *autobiographical self* (1999, pp. 16–17, 127). From a developmental perspective, there are little more than simple states of core self in the beginning, but as experience accrues, memory grows and the autobiographical self can be deployed (ibid., p. 175).

From a purely descriptive point of view, however, there is nothing new in the analyses offered by Damasio. We are dealing with a reformulation of ideas already found in classical phenomenology. To put it differently, the most explicit defence and analysis of what might be called the *experiential dimension of selfhood* is precisely to be found in classical phenomenology. Thus, it is important to realize that both Husserl and Sartre subsequently distanced themselves from the non-egological position they had originally defended. Or to be more precise, the notion of self they came to embrace was not the concept they had earlier rejected; rather, they came to realize that there is more than one legitimate notion of self.

Sartre argues that consciousness is at bottom characterized by a fundamental self-appearance or self-referentiality which he terms *ipseity* (selfhood, from the Latin *ipse*) (1956, p. 103). When Sartre speaks of a self, he is referring to something very basic, something characterizing (phenomenal) consciousness as such. It is something that characterizes my very mode of existence, and although I can fail to articulate it, it is not something I can fail to be. As Sartre also puts it, 'pre-reflective consciousness is self-consciousness. It is this same notion of *self* which must be studied, for it defines the very being of consciousness' (ibid., 76).

Merleau-Ponty occasionally speaks of the subject as realizing its *ipseity* in its embodied being-in-the-world (1962, p. 408). However, he also refers to Husserl's investigations of inner time-consciousness and writes that the original temporal flow must count as the archetypical relationship of self to self and that it traces out an interiority or *ipseity* (ibid., p. 426). A few lines later, Merleau-Ponty adds that consciousness is always affected by itself and that the word 'consciousness' has no meaning independently of this fundamental self-givenness (1962, p. 426).

As Husserl points out, consciousness exists as a stream, and it appears to itself as a stream. But how the stream of consciousness is capable of being conscious of itself, how it is possible and comprehensible that the very being of the stream is a form of self-consciousness, is the enduring question (2001b, pp. 44, 46). Indeed, Husserl's investigation of temporality is very much motivated by his interest in the question of how conscious ness manifests itself to itself. His analysis of the structure of inner time-consciousness (protention–primal impression–retention) is precisely to be understood as an analysis of the (micro)structure of the pre-reflective self-appearance and *ipseity* of our experiences (Husserl 1966a/1991; Zahavi 1999, 2003b). What we find in Husserl is ultimately a sustained investigation of the relationship between selfhood, self-experience, and temporality.

Michel Henry repeatedly characterizes selfhood in terms of an interior self-affection (e.g. Henry 1973, p. 682). Insofar as subjectivity reveals itself to itself, it is a self (Henry 2003, p. 52). Or as he puts it in his early work *Philosophy and Phenomenology of the Body*: 'The interiority of the immediate presence to itself constitutes the essence of ipseity' (Henry 1975, p. 38). It is because consciousness is as such characterized by a primitive, tacit, self-consciousness, that it is appropriate to ascribe a fundamental type of *ipseity* to the experiential phenomena. More precisely, Henry links a basic notion of selfhood to the first-personal givenness of experiential life.

The crucial idea propounded by all of these phenomenologists is that an understanding of what it means to be a self calls for an examination of the structure of experience, and vice versa. Thus, the self is not something that stands opposed to the stream of consciousness, it is not an ineffable transcendental precondition, nor is it a mere social construct that evolves through time; it is taken to be an integral part of the structure of our conscious lives. More precisely, the claim is that the (minimal or core) self possesses experiential reality, and is in fact identified with the first-personal character of the experiential phenomena. At its most primitive, self-experience is simply a question of being pre-reflectively aware of one's own consciousness. As we have indicated in previous chapters, this is what makes experience *subjective*. Although there are different types of experiences (smelling hay, seeing a sunset, touching an ice cube, etc.), and although there are different types of experiential givenness (perceptual, imaginative, and recollective, etc.), there are common features as well. One such common feature is the quality of *mineness*. With the possible exception of certain pathological states (but see below), experiences that I live through in the first-person perspective are *my* experiences. When I think about Paris, smell crushed mint leaves, listen to Prokofiev's *Romeo and Juliet*, or move my left arm, all these various experiences seem to share a certain feature; they are all felt as *mine*; they carry a subtle presence of self. To speak of *mineness* is not meant to suggest that I own the experiences in a way that is even remotely similar to the way I possess external objects of various sorts (a car, my trousers, or a house in Sweden). The mineness or for-me-ness in question is not a quality like yellow, salty, or spongy. It doesn't refer to a specific content of experience, to a specific *what*, but to the unique mode of givenness or *how* of experience. It refers to the first-personal perspectival character of experience; it refers to the fact that experiences I am living through present themselves differently (but not necessarily better) to me than to anybody else. Although I live through various different experiences, there is consequently something experiential that in some sense remains the same, namely, their distinct first-personal character.

Whether a certain experience is experienced as mine or not does not depend on something apart from the experience itself. If the experience is given in a first-personal mode of presentation, from a first-person perspective for me, it is experienced as my experience, otherwise not. Incidentally, this view makes it clear that self-experience is not to be understood as an experience of an isolated, worldless self; nor is the self located and hidden in the head. To have a self-experience is not to interrupt the experiential interaction with the world by turning one's gaze inwards; on the contrary, self-experience is always the self-experience of a world-immersed, embodied agent. The self is present to itself when it is engaged in the world. It would consequently be a decisive mistake to interpret the phenomenological notion of a core, or minimal self as a Cartesian-style mental residuum, that is, as some kind of self-enclosed and self-sufficient interiority. The phenomenological notion of self is fully compatible with a strong emphasis on the fundamental intentionality, or being-in-the-world, of consciousness.

This third notion of self is a minimalist notion, and it is obvious that there are far more complex forms of selves to consider. With this said, however, the experiential notion remains fundamental in the sense that nothing that lacks this dimension deserves to be called a self. Some have argued that no organism can survive or act without being able to distinguish between self and non-self (see Dennett 1991, pp. 174, 414), even if on a non-conscious level. According to the phenomenological conception of the minimal self, however, selfhood requires more than merely a non-conscious differentiation between oneself and the environment. In fact, the crucial idea is that some minimal form of self-*experience* is essential for selfhood.

SOCIALITY AND PERSONALITY

What is the relation between the narrative self – a self linked to sociality, memory, and language – and the experiential self, a self linked to the basic structures of experience and action? The two different notions of self are not necessarily at odds. They can be seen as complementary notions. But in this case, it is important to clarify their exact relation. Is the experiential core self a (logical and temporal) precondition for the extended narrative self? Is the extended self a higher-order construction, perhaps even a (useful) fiction? Or is the core self, on the contrary, a subsequent abstraction; is it simply a stripped-down version of what must count as the genuine and original self?

The experiential self, although constantly accommodating changing experiences, has a structure (defined by temporality and embodiment) that remains stable across the lifetime of the organism. In contrast, the narrative self evolves across the lifetime of the organism. From a developmental perspective, there are little more than simple states of core self in the beginning, but as experience accrues, memory grows and the autobiographical/narrative self develops.

On the phenomenological view, the experiential core self is not a product of our narrative practices. It is an integral part of the structure of phenomenal consciousness and must be regarded as a prelinguistic presupposition for any narrative practices. We should recognize the existence of a primitive, pre-conceptual self(-experience) from early in ontogenesis. Furthermore, experiences and actions must already be given as mine if I am to worry about how they hang together or make up a coherent life story. Only a being with a first-person perspective could consider her own aims, ideals, and aspirations as her own and tell a story about them. When speaking of a first-person perspective, one should consequently distinguish between having such a perspective and being able to articulate it linguistically. Whereas the latter obviously presupposes mastery of the first-person pronoun, the former is simply a question of the first-personal, subjective manifestation of one's own experiential life.

One option is to distinguish between an experiential self and a narrative self (as above, and as a number of philosophers have done). Another option is to opt for a deeper termin-ological differentiation. When dealing with the experiential self, one might retain the term 'self' since we are dealing precisely with a primitive form of self-experience or self-referenti-ality. By contrast, it may be helpful to speak not of the self, but of the *person* as a narrative construction. After all, what is being addressed by a narrative account is the nature of my personal character or personality, a personality that evolves through time and is shaped by the values I endorse, my moral and intellectual convictions and decisions, and my actions. The etymology of the term 'person' speaks strongly in favour of this view. The Latin *persona* refers to masks worn by actors and is related to the expression *dramatis personae*, which designates the characters in a play or a story.[1]

The fact that narrative personhood presupposes experiential selfhood (but not vice versa) does not diminish the significance of the former, especially when it comes to questions of personal identity. Due to the first-person and embodied nature of experience, our experi-ential life might be inherently individuated. As such, a description of my experiential self will not differ significantly from a description of your experiential self, except, of course, insofar as the first is a description of me, the second a description of you. By contrast, a more tangible and differentiating kind of individuality manifests itself in my personal history, in my moral and intellectual convictions and decisions, in all of those things found in my self-narrative and in others' narratives about me. It is through my actions that I define who I am, thereby distinguishing myself from others; actions have a character-shaping effect.[2] I remain the same as long as I adhere to my convictions; when they change, *I* change (Hart 1992, pp. 52–54). Ideals and convictions are identity defining; acting against one's ideals or convictions can mean the disintegration (in the sense of a dis-integrity) of one's wholeness as a person (see Moland 2004).

Persons do not exist in a social vacuum. To exist as a person is to exist socialized into a communal horizon, where one's bearing on oneself is appropriated from other people. As Husserl writes,

> The *origin of personality* lies in empathy and in the *social acts* which are rooted in the latter. To acquire a personality it is not enough that the subject becomes aware of itself as the center of its acts: personality is rather constituted only when the subject establishes social relations with others.
>
> (1973a, p. 175)

I become a person through my life with others in our communal world. Usually, the self under consideration is already personalized or at least in the process of developing into a full-blown person. In this respect, although a narrow focus on the experiential core self might be said to involve a certain amount of abstraction, there is no reason to question its reality, it is not a mere abstraction. Normally, our self-understanding is interwoven with and understood in the light of a self-narrative, but there is self-experience in the minimal sense defined above even when one's capacity to weave a narrative of oneself has not yet developed or has been diminished or lost through a neurological disease or psychiatric disorder. This is borne out by empirical science.

A DEVELOPMENTAL STORY

All healthy infants have an innate rooting response. When the corner of the infant's mouth is touched, the infant turns her head and opens her mouth toward the stimulation. By recording the frequency of rooting in response to either external tactile stimulation or tactile self-stimulation it was discovered that newborns (24 hours old) showed rooting responses almost three times more frequently in response to external stimuli. Philippe Rochat concludes from this that even newborns can pick up the intermodal invariants that specify self- versus non-self-stimulation, and, thereby, have the ability to develop an early sense of self (2001, pp. 40–41). Infants are in possession of proprioceptive information from birth and as Rochat argues, proprioception is 'the modality of the self par excellence' (ibid., p. 35; see also, Gallagher 2005a; Gallagher and Meltzoff 1996). Thus, long before they can pass any mirror self-recognition tasks, not to speak of any false belief tasks, infants have a sense of their own bodies as organized and environmentally embedded entities and, hence, an early perceptually based sense of themselves. Following in the footsteps of Gibson and Neisser, Rochat calls this early sense of self the infant's ecological self (ibid., pp. 30–31, 41). For Rochat, the ecological self is clearly a bodily self and he argues that the infant's self-experience is initially a question of the infant's experience of its own embodied self. It is through their early explorations of their own bodies that infants specify themselves as differentiated agents in the environment, eventually developing a more explicit awareness of themselves. More precisely, infants have an inborn inclination to investigate their own bodies. This inclination forms the cradle of self-perception and constitutes the developmental origin of self-knowledge (ibid., pp. 29, 39, 74).

Proprioceptive awareness, as we indicated in Chapter 7, provides an immediate experiential access to my pre-reflective, embodied self, even when I, as an agent, am not reflectively seeking myself, but am engaged in pragmatically and socially contextualized action. Although much of the detail about bodily position and movement *vis-à-vis* the environment, detail which is absolutely essential for motor control and physical action, is not conscious, whatever is conscious does not present itself as detailed information about various parts of my body. Rather, it manifests itself as an integrated or global sense of where I am spatially in relation to the immediate environment, and what, in any particular situation, I am capable of doing. Proprioceptive awareness, in the broad sense, includes what Gibson calls visual proprioception and kinaesthesis – the sense of self-movement that I get from vision. Such ecologically situated experience provides a pre-reflective sense of the self as a spatial presence and a set of embodied capabilities. When my attention or conscious activity is directed toward the environment or toward some project, the content of proprioceptive awareness, in this Gibsonian sense, tells me, for example, whether I am moving or staying still, whether I am sitting or standing, whether I am reaching or grasping or pointing, whether I am speaking or maintaining silence.

The Gibsonian notion of an ecological self thus involves the idea that the information I receive about the world includes, implicitly, information about my own self (specifically about egocentric perspective and spatial embodiment). My perception of the world is at the same time shot through with information about my own embodied position in that world. In this sense, all perception involves a coexperience of self and environment – information about the relation between perceiver and perceived (Gibson 1986, p. 126). Gibson's theory has found confirmation in a number of empirical studies, for instance in the so-called 'moving room experiment' (Lee and Aronson 1974). The subject (Lee and Aronson conducted the experiment with toddlers) is standing on a solid floor, but is surrounded by walls hanging from the ceiling. If the walls are then moved towards or away from the subject, the subject will sway or fall. For example, the optical flow created by moving the facing wall towards the subject gives him the impression that he is himself falling forward. The muscular readjustments undertaken to compensate for this apparent sway cause him to fall back (Neisser 1988, pp. 37–38).

A further example can be found in developmental psychology. An infant as young as a few weeks can discriminate between objects that are within its reach and objects that are just outside its reach. The infant is far less inclined to reach out for an object that is just outside its reach. Of course, for the infant to be able to make this distinction is for the infant to be aware of the position of the object in relation to *itself*. This is not to say, however, that infants are already, at this stage, in possession of an explicit representation of self, rather, they are able to perceive a distinctive kind of affordance involving *self-specifying information*. Thus, even very young infants pick up the information that specifies the ecological self. They respond to optical flow, discriminate between themselves and other objects, and easily distinguish their own actions and their immediate consequences from events of other kinds. They experience themselves, they experience where they are, how they are moving, what they are doing, and whether a given action is their own or not. These achievements appear already in the first weeks and months of life, and testify to the existence of a primitive but basic form of self-experience (Neisser 1993, p. 4).

PATHOLOGIES OF THE SELF

In *Making Stories*, Jerome Bruner – an ardent defender of a narrative approach to the self – admits that certain features of selfhood are innate and that we need to recognize the existence of a primitive, pre-conceptual self. At the same time, however, he maintains that dysnarrativia (encountered in Korsakoff's syndrome or Alzheimer's disease) is deadly for selfhood and that there would be nothing like selfhood if we lacked narrative capacities (Bruner 2002, pp. 86, 119). Bruner is quite right in assuming that a reference to pathology can be illuminating, but the question is whether his own observations are really to the point. Alzheimer's disease is a progressive, degenerative brain disorder that results in profound memory loss, changes in behaviour, thinking, and reasoning as well as a significant decline in overall functioning (Snyder 2000, p. 44). The person suffering from Alzheimer's will consequently have a wide range of cognitive impairments; the comprehension and expression of speech (and narratives) will only be one of the areas affected. So even, and to put it in an odd but pointed way, *if* no self remains in the advanced stages of Alzheimer's, one cannot without further ado conclude that dysnarrativia was the cause of death. (If one were on the lookout for a disorder that specifically targeted narrative capacities, global aphasia might be a better choice – but then again, who would want to claim that those struck by global aphasia cease being selves?) Furthermore, there is a big *if*. It is by no means obvious that Alzheimer's disease brings about a destruction of the first-person perspective, a complete annihilation of the dimension of mineness or that any experience that remains is merely an anonymous and unowned experiential episode, so that the 'subject' no longer feels pain or discomfort as his or her own. In fact, it is hardly insignificant that experienced clinicians report that no one person with Alzheimer's disease is exactly like another (ibid., p. 72). But if this is true, and if Alzheimer's disease does in fact constitute a severe case of dysnarrativia, we should draw the exact opposite conclusion from Bruner. We would be forced to concede that there must be more to being a self than what is addressed by the narrative account. This is in fact the conclusion drawn by Damasio, who explicitly argues that neuropathology provides empirical evidence in support of the distinction between core self and autobiographical self. Neuropathological impairments of the autobiographical self do not impair the core self, whereas impairments that begin at the level of the core self do cause problems with the autobiographical or narrative self (Damasio 1999, pp. 115–19).

Other questions abound. Are the senses of agency and ownership for actions and experiences the result of a self-ascriptive metacognitive operation employing conceptual and linguistic resources, or are actions and experiences implicitly and prelinguistically sensed as one's own? Does explicit and conceptual self-reference rest on an implicit sense of self? If senses of agency and ownership are part of the experiential self, are disruptions of these senses, e.g. in schizophrenia, anarchic hand syndrome, alien hand syndrome, or unilateral neglect, for example, fatal for the experiential self?[3] These are questions currently debated in philosophy, psychology, and cognitive neuroscience. There is, however, a growing awareness of the fact that these issues concerning self-reference cannot be settled by empirical means alone and that there is an acute need for a philosophical clarification of the different notions and experiences of self. Not only can the cognitive neuroscience of the self benefit from a clarification of the notions of self and of the possibility of an implicit self-representation, but the philosophical investigation can certainly also profit from an engagement with neuropsychological and -pathological findings.

Still, within both the philosophical and cognitive neuroscientific discussions one finds divisions on such issues. For example, on one side, the distinction between the *sense of ownership* and the *sense of agency* (defined in Gallagher 2000a, and discussed above in Chapter 8) is a distinction made on the level of first-order experience associated with the experiential or minimal self. Engaged in some action I implicitly feel the action to be mine and I have a sense of generating it and controlling it – I don't have to reflectively attribute it or evaluate it in regard to the coherency of my intentions. In regard to the sense of agency, it certainly feels different If I walk across the room on my own volition than if I am pushed across the room. If I am pushed or if I am undergoing involuntary spasms, I will still experience the movement as mine – I, rather than somebody else, am the one moving – but I will lack a sense of agency; I will lack an experience of being the agent or initiator of the movement. On the other side, some philosophers and scientists claim that ownership or agency is a matter of explicitly deciding to whom the mental event or process should be ascribed – is this my action (or thought) or not (Jeannerod and Pacherie 2004; Stephens and Graham 2000)? Scientists who support the first, implicit view argue that the second, explicit view is too demanding and tends to reduce the sense of the self in action to a *post hoc* construction. Instead, they claim that the acting self has an implicit sense of self-agency, which is simultaneous with acting (Haggard and Clark 2003; Tsakiris and Haggard 2005). In their respective arguments, the opposing sides draw on various investigations of neuro- and psychopathological disorders (Jeannerod 1999; Rossetti and Rode 2002).

Let us look at a more dramatic case of disturbed self-experience, namely schizophrenia. Although the most recent versions of the psychiatric diagnostic systems (DSM-IV and ICD-10) do not include a reference to the self, varieties of self-disorders have always figured, at least implicitly, as an important component in the clinical picture of schizophrenia. As early as 1913, the concept of '*Ichstörungen*' (disturbances of the self) was used by Jaspers. One year later Berze proposed that a basic transformation of self-consciousness was at the root of schizophrenia. But the most detailed analyses of schizophrenic self-disorders are to be found in phenomenologically oriented psychiatry (Minkowski 1927; Conrad 1959; Laing 1960/1990; Blankenburg 1971; Tatossian 1979/1997; Sass 2000; Parnas 2003; Parnas et al. 2005). As Minkowski wrote: 'The madness ... does not originate in the disorders of judgment, perception or will, but in a disturbance of the innermost structure of the self' (1997, p. 114).

Parnas has argued that all of these complaints point to a diminished *ipseity*, where the sense of self no longer automatically saturates the experience (Parnas 2003; Parnas et al. 2002). We are faced with an experiential disturbance on a pre-reflective level that is far more basic than the kind of feelings of inferiority, insecurity, and unstable identity that we find in personality disorders outside the schizophrenic spectrum (Parnas et al. 2005).

Some patients are able to articulate these subtle disturbances better than others. One of Parnas' patients reported that the feeling that his experiences were his own always came with a split-second delay; another that it was as if his self was somehow displaced a few centimetres backwards. A third explained that he felt an indescribable inner change that prevented him from leading a normal life. He was troubled by a very distressing feeling of not being really present or even fully alive. This experience of distance or detachment was accompanied by a tendency to observe or monitor his inner life. He summarized his affliction by saying that his first-personal life was lost and replaced by a third-person perspective (Parnas 2003, p. 223).

More generally speaking, Parnas and Sass have argued that these self-disorders may even be ascribed a generating, pathogenic role. They antecede, underlie, and shape the emergence of later psychotic pathology and may thus unify what, from a purely descriptive psychiatric standpoint, may seem to be unrelated or even antithetical syndromes and symptoms (Sass and Parnas 2006).

It is not difficult to find first-person statements about schizophrenic symptoms of thought insertions or delusions of control, which (if taken in isolation and at face value) seem to offer ample evidence in support of the claim that some experiential states completely lack the quality of mineness or the sense of ownership. However, subjects who experience thought insertions or delusions of control clearly recognize that they are the subjects in whom the alien episodes occur. The patients are not confused about where the alien movements or thoughts occur – the sites of such movements or thoughts are their own bodies and minds. Some sense of ownership is still retained, and that is the basis for their complaint (see Gallagher 2000b, p. 230; Stephens and Graham 2000, pp. 8, 126). Even if the inserted thoughts or alien movements are felt as intrusive and strange, they cannot lack the quality of mineness completely, since the afflicted subject is quite aware that it is he himself rather than somebody else who is experiencing these alien thoughts and movements. When schizophrenics assert that their thoughts or movements are not their own, they do not mean that they themselves are not having the thoughts, or that it is not their own body that is being moved, but rather that someone else is inserting the thoughts or controlling the movements and that they themselves are not responsible for generating them. Thus, rather than involving a complete lack of a sense of ownership, passivity phenomena like thought insertions primarily involve a lack of a sense of self-agency and a misattribution of agency to someone or something else.

This seems to indicate that some sense of ownership survives even in schizophrenic delusions. It has been suggested, however, that schizophrenic experiences such as thought insertion and delusions of control represent a violation of the principle of 'immunity to error through misidentification' (IEM) (Campbell 1999; Jeannerod and Pacherie 2004). The IEM principle is related to what Wittgenstein (1958) called the use of the first-person pronoun 'as subject'. He suggested that if a person says that she is having a certain experience, it would be nonsensical to ask 'are you sure that it is *you* who are having the experience?' That is, if you claim to have a toothache, it makes no sense to ask, 'Are you sure that it is *you* who have the toothache?' This is nonsensical, not primarily because of the way language works, but because of the character of experience. Shoemaker (1968) makes it clear that IEM applies to forms of self-reference in which there is no identification required, and thus no chance of misidentification. In other words, we are immune to error in this regard, not because we are infallible at judging who we are, but because this kind of self-awareness doesn't involve a judgement of identification at all. According to this view, IEM would seem to apply equally to both the sense of ownership and the sense of agency. My sense of agency or ownership does not require me to verify that I meet certain criteria in order to judge, on the basis of observation, that I am the one who is acting or experiencing something bodily.

In contrast to uses of the first-person pronoun *as subject*, uses of the first-person pronoun *as object*, where I am ascribing a property to myself on the basis of a perceptual observation – as exemplified in the statement 'I have dirty feet' – is often taken to be subject to the error of misidentification. There are several issues to be sorted out here. First,

IEM is usually distinguished from 'guaranteed self-reference' of the sort argued for by P. F. Strawson (1994; see also Castañeda 1968). Guaranteed self-reference pertains to the fact that whoever says 'I' cannot help but refer to himself or herself. Even uses of first-person pronoun *as object* cannot be mistaken in this sense. When I look in the mirror and say 'I have dirty feet' I may be wrong about who has dirty feet, but the word 'I' refers to no one other than myself – and that's precisely why my judgement is mistaken. I can misidentify myself (or perhaps more precisely, I can misattribute some characteristic to myself) only because the 'I' is guaranteed to self-refer. In this sense it is impossible to be thinking an I-thought (i.e. to be making a self-conscious judgement) and not be referring to oneself. Even if I am mistaken (my feet are in fact clean), or radically deluded ('I am 4 meters tall') in my self-ascription, I am still ascribing the property to *myself*.

It is important to understand that IEM also pertains to experiences that do not involve use of the first-person pronoun. Indeed, it is precisely tied to the prepredicative first-person perspective, which in the first place allows one to generate first-person *as-subject* statements. Being in the first-person perspective involves what Albahari (2006) calls a 'perspectival ownership' of experience; it anchors my experiences unmistakably to me, underwriting my pre-reflective awareness of myself as subject. Again, when I see dirty feet in the mirror, and mistakenly say 'I have dirty feet', I'm not wrong about *who* it is to whom I attribute the dirty feet; I attribute them to myself, the one who is not only the speaker, but also the perceiver, and it is precisely for that reason I make a mistake. But that is a mistaken attribution; it is not a mistake about who is having the experience of looking in the mirror – namely, I the perceiver, even if I am not the perceived in this case. In other words, whenever there is a misattribution or misidentification of self *as object* there is always a subject who is perceiving or acting, and sometimes speaking, *as subject,* and for whom IEM and guaranteed self-reference remain intact.

John Campbell has suggested that we can find violations of IEM in schizophrenic symptoms. He writes:

> What is so striking about the phenomenon of thought insertion as described by schizophrenic patients is that it seems to involve an error of identification. ... A patient who supposes that someone else has inserted thoughts into his mind is right about which thoughts they are, but wrong about whose thoughts they are. So thought insertion seems to be a counterexample to the thesis that present-tense introspectively based reports of psychological states cannot involve errors of identification. Frith himself puts the point succinctly.
>
> (Campbell 1999, pp. 609–10)

Campbell then quotes Chris Frith (1992, p. 80):

> Thought insertion, in particular, is a phenomenon that is difficult to understand. Patients say that thoughts that are not their own are coming into their head. This experience implies that we have some way of recognising our own thoughts. It is as if each thought has a label on it saying 'mine'. If this labelling process goes wrong, then the thought would be perceived as alien.

We can clarify this by considering Shoemaker's observation that 'whereas the statement "My arm is moving" is subject to error through misidentification, the statement "I am waving my arm" is not' (1984, p. 8). Shoemaker's claim clearly requires some qualification. Even if I am somehow tricked into mistakenly thinking that my arm is moving, this is an error of misattribution rather than one of misidentification. Moreover, even if one is experimentally fooled into thinking that one's arm is moving in a way that it is not (as done, for example, in experiments that use muscle vibration techniques), or even if there is no arm (as in the case of a phantom arm) – in such cases I may be wrong about what my arm is doing, or even that it is an arm that is doing it, but I could not be wrong about the fact that it is I who experience it.[4] What the statement 'My arm is moving' means in such cases is 'I *feel* my arm is moving', and one cannot sensibly ask, 'Are you sure that it is *you* who feel your arm moving?'

When the schizophrenic reports that certain thoughts are not his thoughts, and that someone else is generating these thoughts, he is also indicating that these thoughts are being manifested, not 'over there' in someone else's head, but within his own stream of consciousness, a stream of consciousness for which he claims perspectival ownership. In other words, his complaint with regard to inserted thoughts is not that he is suddenly telepathic, but that someone else has invaded his own mind. For that reason the schizophrenic should provide a positive answer to what he might rightly regard as a nonsensical question: Are you sure that *you* are the one who is experiencing these thoughts? After all, this is precisely his complaint. He is experiencing thoughts that seem to be generated by others. He ascribes agency to someone or something else, but the experience remains his own.

In cases of involuntary movement, or in cases of involuntary pain, where I lack a sense of agency, there is still a sense that the movement or the pain is mine, so I cannot deny that I experience my arm moving, or that it is my tooth that is aching. In such cases IEM, which is linked to the sense of perspectival ownership, remains intact.[5] In some cases, however, the sense of ownership for one's body does in fact go missing or does become confused. This is, for instance, the case in somatoparaphrenia, where stroke patients claim that their left arm is not theirs, and that it belongs to someone else. Clearly the sense of ownership for the body part has failed, but even here there is no violation of IEM since the body part at stake is being viewed 'as-object' rather than as the perceiving embodied subject.[6] In other words, the patient is not misidentifying herself when she says 'This arm is not mine', since the 'mine' refers to no one other than herself.

CONCLUSION

Whether the self is real or fictional, one thing or many, it is clearly something that needs explanation, for at least two reasons. First, there is an undeniable sense of self that accompanies experience and action. If this phenomenology points to something real, then a full explanation of cognition would require some account of the self. As for those who claim that the self has a fictional status, they still need to explain why the fiction arises, and for whom. In either case, one is led back to the phenomenology, and to neuropsychological accounts involving the mechanisms responsible for the implicit (ecological and proprioceptive) structures of perception and action, for autobiographical memory, and for the generation of narratives.

As Galen Strawson has argued, if we wish to answer the metaphysical question concerning whether or not the self is real, we will first need to know what a self is supposed to be. To establish this, our best chance will be to look at self-experience, since self-experience is what gives rise to the question in the first place by giving us a vivid sense that there is something like a self. Thus, as Strawson readily concedes, the metaphysical investigation of the self is subordinate to the phenomenological. The latter places constraints on the former. Nothing can count as a self unless it possesses those properties attributed to the self by some genuine form of self-experience (2000, p. 40). Of course, this move could be countered by the neurosceptics who might argue that it would be a fallacy to conclude to the literal properties of the self from the content and structure of phenomenal self-experience. For the sceptics, our self-experience, our primitive, pre-reflective feeling of conscious selfhood, is never truthful, in that it does not correspond to any single entity inside or outside of the self-representing system (see Metzinger 2003, p. 565). But it remains rather unclear why the reality of the self should depend upon whether it faithfully mirrors either subpersonal mechanisms or external (mind independent) entities. If we were to wholeheartedly endorse such a restrictive metaphysical principle, we would declare most of the world we live in and know and care about, illusory. For someone to declare everything peculiar to human life fictitious simply because it cannot be grasped by a certain mode of scientific comprehension, not only reveals one's prior commitment to a naive scientism, according to which (natural) science is the sole arbiter of what there is, one also self-defeatingly (no pun intended) runs the risk of undermining the very scientific realism that one champions. After all, science is itself a human enterprise. So why not rather insist that the self is real if it has experiential reality and that the validity of our account of the self is to be measured by its ability to be faithful to experience, by its ability to capture and articulate (invariant) experiential structures (Zahavi 2003d, 2005a, 2005b)?

Interdisciplinary approaches that focus on a single aspect or dimension of the complex problems of self are more likely to mitigate problems of intertheoretical coherency. Neuroscientists, psychologists, psychiatrists, and roboticists, as much as philosophers, have an interest in developing a model of the self (see Gallagher and Shear 1999; Kircher and David 2003; Zahavi 2000). The neuropsychology of dissociative disorders and the neuroscience of the split brain, for example, as well as the cognitive linguistics of narrative structure and a hermeneutically inclined phenomenology, may throw light on how narrative generates a seemingly unified self in normal humans. A variety of approaches, including phenomenology, the neuroscience of motor action, animal studies, and developmental psychology, are needed to understand aspects of self-experience, self-recognition, agency, and social interaction, and how such things contribute to the generation of self-identity. In the end, if good explanations of these various aspects of experience are developed, a cognitive science that incorporates the insights of phenomenology has the potential to recast the central philosophical questions about the self.

NOTES

1   This is neither to suggest that persons are after all mere fictions nor that they are masks that somehow conceal the primitive core self. The point is simply that there is an etymological link between narratives and the original concept of persons.

2   Our actions shape our character, but the influence goes the other way as well, of course (see Gallagher 2007; Gallagher and Marcel 1999). The actions we perform and the choices we make are partially explained by our character. In fact, as Anscombe has argued, the activity of giving reasons for actions comes to a stop with 'because that's the kind of person I am (she is)' (1957).

3   Marchetti and Della Sala (1998) have made an important distinction between 'alien hand syndrome' and 'anarchic hand syndrome'. Anarchic hand involves a disruption in the sense of agency, but the subject still acknowledges that it is his own hand performing the seemingly goal-directed movement. In the case of alien hand syndrome, by contrast, the sense of ownership is disrupted as well and the subject denies that the hand is actually his (see Gallagher and Vævver 2004).

4   Proprioception (sense of limb position) and nociception (pain sensation) cannot be wrong about whose body it is (they deliver information only about the subject's own body), although proprioception can be wrong about what posture the body is in, and nociception can be wrong about where the cause of the pain is located (Gallagher 2003b; also Jeannerod and Pacherie 2004).

5   It is not clear why Jeannerod and Pacherie (2004) equate the sense of ownership with 'the self as object'. And this equation seems important in their claim about immunity to error through misidentification: 'In a nutshell then, the bad news for philosophers is that self-identification is after all a problem. In the domain of action and intention at least, there is no such thing as immunity to error through misidentification, whether for the self as object (sense of ownership) or for the self as agent (sense of agency)' (p. 141). It's also not clear why this would be bad news for philosophers rather than for ordinary people who normally depend on this kind of immunity, even if they don't know it.

6   This also applies to the sense of ownership that we may have for a rubber hand in certain experimental situations, most famously in Botvinick and Cohen (1998; also see Tsakiris and Haggard 2005). In this case, too, the attribution of ownership is 'as object' and based on vision, and not 'as subject'.

FURTHER READING

Shaun Gallagher (ed.), *The Oxford Handbook of the Self*. Oxford: Oxford University Press, 2011.

Shaun Gallagher and Jonathan Shear (eds), *Models of the Self*. Exeter: Imprint Academic, 1999.

Tilo Kircher and Anthony David (eds), *The Self in Neuroscience and Psychiatry*. Cambridge: Cambridge University Press, 2003.

Paul Ricoeur, *Oneself as Another*. Trans. K. Blamey. Chicago: Chicago University Press, 1994.

Philippe Rochat (ed.), *The Self in Infancy*. New York: Elsevier, 1995.

Jean-Paul Sartre, *The Transcendence of the Ego*. Trans. F. Williams and R. Kirkpatrick. New York: Noonday Press, 1957.

Dan Zahavi (ed.), *Exploring the Self*. Amsterdam: John Benjamins, 2000.

Dan Zahavi, *Subjectivity and Selfhood*. Cambridge, MA: MIT Press, 2005.

11 Conclusion

In a recent introduction to cognitive science, Friedenberg and Silverman devote ten lines (out of 529 pages) to phenomenology. They write that phenomenology refers to subjective experience rather than objective description, and that phenomenological description differs from introspection in that it focuses on the immediate and subjective perception of an external stimulus and does not require training or an intensive examination of one's internal state (Friedenberg and Silverman 2006, p. 77). As should be clear from the preceding chapters, this is not only a very misleading description of what phenomenology amounts to and what it has to offer the study of the mind, it also reflects a rather strange prioritization, or lack of one. In fact, in our view — but this should hardly come as a surprise at this stage – any contemporary introduction to the cognitive sciences should include a substantial discussion of phenomenology. This is so, not only because phenomenology has made quite substantial contributions to the study of the mind, but also because contemporary discussions in the cognitive sciences are becoming increasingly aware of the rich possibilities offered by phenomenological approaches to certain central issues, and any timely introduction to this area of research ought to reflect this.

The problem, of course, is that although a small number of prominent figures in philosophy of mind and the cognitive sciences have recently started to take philosophical phenomenology seriously, the vast majority of researchers are not using the term in its technical sense when they talk of phenomenology, but are still identifying phenomenology with some kind of introspectionism. As we have tried to make clear, however, phenomenology is not just another name for a kind of psychological self-observation; rather, it is the name of a philosophical approach that can offer much more to contemporary consciousness research and cognitive sciences than a simple compilation of introspective data. Phenomenology refers to the tradition of philosophy that originated in Europe and includes the work of Husserl, Heidegger, Merleau-Ponty, Sartre, and other more recent thinkers. By ignoring this tradition and the resources it offers, contemporary cognitive research risks missing out on important insights that, in the best of circumstances, will end up being rediscovered decades or centuries later (see Zahavi 2004d).

Phenomenology involves a rich set of approaches with many different practitioners, and it would have been impossible to do justice to all of the various relevant issues in an introduction of this size. We have consequently been forced to be selective. We have focused on topics that are of particular importance for contemporary discussions in philosophy of mind and cognitive science – topics such as consciousness and self-consciousness, intentionality, the temporal nature of experience, perception, embodiment, action, and our understanding of self and others – topics that can and should be investigated, prior to deciding the larger metaphysical issues that often dominate philosophical discussions. This list is not exhaustive; there are many other areas where phenomenology has made contributions with direct relevance for ongoing discussions in the cognitive sciences; we could mention the debate about mental imagery, the analysis of the cognitive value of emotions, and the criticism of AI as examples of some of the issues we haven't been able to cover. But hopefully our presentation will stimulate the reader to pursue further readings.

One of the frequent claims made by defenders and detractors alike is that the distinguishing feature of a phenomenological approach to the mind is its sustained focus on the first-person perspective. As we have also tried to show, however, this is an overly narrow definition. Phenomenological analyses of the nitty-gritty details of action, embodiment, intersubjectivity, and so on, provide more than simply a description of first-person experience. In numerous investigations of how the subjectivity of others manifests itself in gestures, expressions, and bodily behaviour, phenomenologists have also provided detailed analyses from the second-person perspective, thereby providing a more sophisticated and nuanced understanding of how to heterophenomenologize than one finds among avowed heterophenomenologists. Contrary to the claim made by Dennett, classical phenomenology already stresses the interdependency of auto- and heterophenomenology (Zahavi 2007). Accordingly, it would be a serious mistake to limit subjectivity to what might only be accessible from a first-person perspective. To quote from the preface to Merleau-Ponty's *Phenomenology of Perception*:

> Hitherto the *Cogito* depreciated the perception of others, teaching me as it did that the I is accessible only to itself, since it defines me as the thought which I have of myself, and which clearly I am alone in having, at least in this ultimate sense. For the 'other' to be more than an empty word, it is necessary that my existence should never be reduced to my bare awareness of existing, but that it should take in also the awareness that *one* may have of it; and thus include my incarnation in some nature and the possibility, at least, of a historical situation.
>
> (1962, pp. xii–xiii)

Concerning many of the issues that we have considered we think that phenomenology offers alternatives to views that are standard in philosophy of mind and the cognitive sciences. It seems appropriate to conclude with a brief and pointed review.

- **Methodology:** phenomenology is distinct from both introspection and heterophenomenology; it offers philosophically informed methodological tools that can disclose significant – but frequently overlooked – dimensions of experience; it can help to define good empirical questions and contribute to the design of behavioural and brain-imaging experiments; and it can frame interpretations of empirical data in ways that are scientifically rigorous without being reductionistic.
- **Consciousness and self-consciousness:** phenomenology offers a clear alternative to higher-order theories of consciousness, and contributes to an account of experience which has wide ramifications for empirical science (including developmental psychology, ethology, and psychiatry) and for our understanding of cases ranging from common and everyday ones, like driving a car, to the more exotic aspects of non-conscious perception and blindsight.
- **The temporality of experience:** phenomenology offers a detailed analysis of one of the most important, but also one of the most neglected aspects of consciousness, cognition, and action – the intrinsic temporal nature of experience that is the phenomenological complement to the dynamical nature that underpins our brain–body–environment system.
- **Perception:** in contrast to various representationalist models of perception, phenomenology defends a non-Cartesian view that emphasizes the embodied, enactive, and contextual nature of perception.
- **Intentionality:** phenomenology offers a developed non-reductionist account of the intentionality of experience that stresses the co-emergence of mind and world and suggests an alternative to the standard choice between internalism and externalism.
- **Embodied cognition:** perhaps more than any other approach, phenomenology has consistently championed an embodied and situated view of cognition. Although insisting on the phenomenological distinction between the lived body and the objective body, phenomenology also shows that biology, even beyond neuroscience, is important for understanding our mental life.
- **Action and agency:** phenomenologically sensitive distinctions between kinds of movement, and between the sense of agency and the sense of ownership, can provide important tools for a more adequate account of action and for the understanding of certain pathologies where the sense of agency or the sense of ownership is lacking. Such distinctions can also inform various neuroimaging experiments.
- **Intersubjectivity and social cognition:** phenomenology offers a non-mentalizing alternative to theory-of-mind explanations, complements evidence from developmental psychology, and suggests a reinterpretation of the neuroscience of resonance systems.
- **Self and person:** phenomenology offers clarifying analyses about self-experience and different concepts of the self that can inform the recent and growing interest in these questions in cognitive neuroscience. Specifically, phenomenology shows that the self is significantly involved in all aspects of experience, including intentionality, phenomenality, temporality, embodiment, action, and our interaction with others.

Thus, in the preceding chapters, we have emphasized how counterproductive it would be to ignore the insights of the phenomenological tradition, but this should obviously not be misinterpreted as simply the expression of a backward-looking nostalgia. Our suggestion is obviously not that the right way to proceed when it comes to attaining a more satisfying account of the mind is by turning our backs on recent conceptual clarifications and empirical discoveries in order to return to classical phenomenology. We do think that the cognitive sciences can profit from considering the detailed analyses and conceptual clarifications provided by phenomenology, but the relation between phenomenology and cognitive science is not a one-way enterprise. It is not merely a question of applying ready-made phenomenological distinctions and concepts, as if there were no reciprocity, no feedback, or as if such applications would not lead to modifications of the original ideas. Rather, our guiding idea has been the notion of mutual enlightenment.

In his *Consciousness Explained*, Daniel Dennett provides a rather amusing description of the difficulties of interdisciplinary cooperation:

> I have grown accustomed to the disrespect expressed by some of the participants for their colleagues in the other disciplines. 'Why, Dan,' ask the people in Artificial Intelligence, 'do you waste your time conferring with those neuroscientists? They wave their hands about "information processing" and worry about *where* it happens, and which neuro-transmitters are involved, and all those boring facts, but they haven't a clue about the computational requirements of higher cognitive functions.' 'Why,' ask the neuroscientists, 'do you waste your time on the fantasies of Artificial Intelligence? They just invent whatever machinery they want, and say unpardonably ignorant things about the brain.' The cognitive psychologists, meanwhile, are accused of concocting models with *neither* biological plausibility nor proven computational powers; the anthropologists wouldn't know a model if they saw one, and the philosophers, as we all know, just take in each other's laundry, warning about confusions they themselves have created, in an arena bereft of both data and empirically testable theories. With so many idiots working on the problem, no wonder consciousness is still a mystery.
>
> (1991, p. 255)

As Dennett then goes on to argue, however, there really is no alternative to this collaboration. And here we would agree. Empirical data can serve to challenge and validate theoretical analyses. Conversely, conceptual analysis can provide directions and tools for the empirical scientists and might also help in the design and development of experimental paradigms. If real progress is to be made in the study of the mind, it requires a collaborative effort that draws on all the available resources and that integrates a variety of theoretical and empirical disciplines and methods.

Having said this, let us add two caveats. The first is that although empirical data are important, we obviously shouldn't overlook the fact that they are open to interpretation. Their interpretation will usually depend upon the framework within which one is operating. Thus, the theoretical impact of an empirical case is not necessarily something that can be easily determined. Although it might be argued that phenomenology should pay attention to empirical findings, this doesn't entail that it should accept the (metaphysical and epistemological) interpretation that science gives of these findings.

Secondly, although we think it is important to encourage the exchange between phenomenology and empirical science, the possibility of a fruitful cooperation between the two should not make us overlook their difference. There is no incoherence in claiming that phenomenology should be as informed by the best available scientific knowledge, while insisting that the ultimate transcendental philosophical concerns of phenomenology differ from those of positive science.

Let us conclude, then, by wholeheartedly endorsing the renewed focus on subjectivity. An investigation of the first-person perspective is of paramount importance not only for philosophy of mind, but also for a number of related disciplines including social philosophy, psychiatry, developmental psychology, and cognitive neuroscience. Ultimately, what we need is an account of the first-person perspective that (among other things) addresses its significance (the role it plays) and systematic import, describes its structure, delineates the methodology that we should employ when investigating it, and finally clarifies its ontological or metaphysical status. However, as we have tried to argue, it would be highly unfortunate if the long overdue recognition of the importance of the first-person perspective took the form of a return to a Lockean-style account of consciousness. What do we mean by a Lockean-style account? In this context, we are mainly thinking of a pre-Kantian and pre-Wittgensteinian view on consciousness, that is, one that ignores transcendental considerations, thereby viewing consciousness merely as yet another object in the world, and one that defines subjectivity as something inner and private, thereby disregarding the extent to which it is visible to others in our meaningful behaviour, the extent to which our subjectivity is influenced, shaped, and formed by our interaction and engagement with others, and by our shared forms of life.

References

We have quoted from English translations where available. If no translations were available we have provided our own translations. In the case of quotations from Husserl and Heidegger, the following convention has been used. In those cases where the English translation includes the German page number in the margin, only the German page number is provided, and the years following the author's name refer to the publication date of the German original and the English translation, respectively. For example, Husserl 1966a/1991, p. 124, refers to page 124 in Husserl's *Zur Phänomenologie des inneren Zeit-bewußtseins* (published in German in 1966 and in English translation in 1991).

Albahari, M. (2006). *Analytical Buddhism: The Two-Tiered Illusion of Self*. New York: Palgrave Macmillan.

Allison, T., Puce, Q., and McCarthy, G. (2000). Social perception from visual cues: Role of the STS region. *Trends in Cognitive Sciences* 4/7, 267–78.

Anscombe, G. E. M. (1957). *Intention*. Oxford: Blackwell Publishers.

Armstrong, D. M. (1968). *A Materialist Theory of the Mind*. London: Routledge & Kegan Paul.

——(1981). *The Nature of Mind, and Other Essays*. Ithaca, NY: Cornell University Press.

Asemissen, H. U. (1958/59). Egologische reflexion. *Kant-Studien* 50, 262–72.

Augustine (1955). *Confessions*. Philadelphia, PA: Westminster Press.

Avramides, A. (2001). *Other Minds*. London: Routledge.

Bach-y-Rita, P., Collins, C. C., Saunders, F., and Scadden, L. (1969). Vision substitution by tactile image projection. *Nature* 221, 963–64.

Bach-y-Rita, P., Tyler, M. E., and Kaczmarek, K. A. (2003). Seeing with the brain. *International Journal of Human–Computer Interaction* 15/2, 285–95.

Baillargeon, R., Scott, R. M., and He, Z. (2010). False-belief understanding in infants. *Trends in Cognitive Sciences* 14/3, 110–18.

Baird, J. A. and Baldwin, D. A. (2001). Making sense of human behavior: Action parsing and intentional inference. In B. F. Malle, L. J. Moses, and D. A. Baldwin (eds), *Intentions and Intentionality: Foundations of Social Cognition* (pp. 193–206). Cambridge, MA: MIT Press.

Baker, L. R. (2000). *Persons and Bodies*. Cambridge: Cambridge University Press.

Baldwin, D. A. (1993). Infants' ability to consult the speaker for clues to word reference. *Journal of Child Language* 20, 395–418.

Baldwin, D. A. and Baird, J. A. (2001) Discerning intentions in dynamic human action. *Trends in Cognitive Sciences* 5/4, 171–78.

Baldwin, D. A., Baird, J. A., Saylor, M. M., and Clark, M. A. (2001). Infants parse dynamic action. *Child Development* 72/3, 708–17.

Bartlett, F. (1932). *Remembering: A Study in Experimental and Social Psychology*. Cambridge: Cambridge University Press.

Baron-Cohen, S. (1995). *Mindblindness: An Essay on Autism and Theory of Mind*. Cambridge, MA: MIT Press.

Baron-Cohen, S., Leslie, A., and Frith, U. (1985). Does the autistic child have a 'theory of mind'? *Cognition* 21, 37–46.

Bennett, M. R. and Hacker, P. M. S. (2003). *Philosophical Foundations of Neuroscience*. Oxford: Blackwell.

Bermúdez, J. L. (1995). Transcendental arguments and psychology: The example of O'Shaughnessy on intentional action. *Metaphilosophy* 26, 379–401.

——(1998). *The Paradox of Self-Consciousness*. Cambridge, MA: MIT Press.

Bertenthal, B. I., Proffitt, D. R., and Cutting, J. E. (1984). Infant sensitivity to figural coherence in biomechanical motions. *Journal of Experimental Child Psychology* 37, 213–30.

Bisiach, E. (1988). Language without thought. In L. Weiskrantz (ed.), *Thought Without Language* (pp. 464–84). Oxford: Oxford University Press.

Bisiach, E. and Luzzatti, C. (1978). Unilateral neglect of representational space. *Cortex* 14, 129–33.

Blakemore, S. J., Wolpert, D. M., and Frith, C. D. (2002). Abnormalities in the awareness of action. *Trends in Cognitive Sciences* 6/6, 237–42.

Blakeslee, S. (2006). Cells that read minds. *New York Times*, 10 January, at: http://www.nytimes.com/2006/01/10/science/10mirr.html

Blanke, O., Landis, T., Spinelli, L., and Seeck, M. (2004). Out-of-body experience and autoscopy of neurological origin. *Brain* 127/2, 243–58.

Blankenburg, W. (1971). *Der Verlust der natürlichen Selbstverständlichkeit: Ein Beitrag zur Psychopathologie symptomarmer Schizophrenien*. Stuttgart: Enke.

Block, N. (1997). On a confusion about a function of consciousness. In N. Block, O. Flanagan, and G. Güzeldere (eds), *The Nature of Consciousness* (pp. 375–415). Cambridge, MA: MIT Press.

Blumental, A. L. (2001). A Wundt primer: The operating characteristics of consciousness. In R. W. Rieber and D. K. Robinson (eds), *Wilhelm Wundt in History: The Making of a Scientific Psychology* (pp. 121–44). New York: Kluwer Academic/Plenum Publishers.

Botterill, G. (1996). Folk psychology and theoretical status. In P. Carruthers and P. K. Smith (eds), *Theories of Theories of Mind* (pp. 105–18). Cambridge: Cambridge University Press.

Botvinick, M. and Cohen, J. (1998). Rubber hands feel touch that eyes see. *Nature* 391, 756.

Braddon-Mitchell, D. and Jackson, F. (2006). *Philosophy of Mind and Cognition: An Introduction*, 2nd edn. Oxford: Blackwell

Brandom, R. (1994). *Making It Explicit: Reasoning, Representing, and Discursive Commitment*. Cambridge, MA: Harvard University Press.

Brentano, F. (1973). *Psychology from an Empirical Standpoint*, trans. A. C. Rancurello, D. B. Terrell, and L. L. McAlister. London: Routledge & Kegan Paul.

Brook, A. (1994). *Kant and the Mind*. Cambridge: Cambridge University Press.

Brooks, R. A. (1990). Elephants don't play chess. *Robotics and Autonomous Systems* 6, 3–15.

——(2002). *Flesh and Machines: How Robots Will Change Us*. New York: Pantheon Books.

Bruner, J. (1986). *Actual Minds, Possible Worlds*. Cambridge, MA: Harvard University Press.

——(2002). *Making Stories: Law, Literature, Life*. Cambridge, MA: Harvard University Press.

Buttelmann, D., Carpenter, M., and Tomasello, M. (2009) Eighteen-month-old infants show false belief understanding in an active helping paradigm. *Cognition* 112, 337–42.

Buytendijk, F. J. J. (1974). *Prolegomena to an Anthropological Physiology*, trans. A. I. Orr et al. Pittsburgh, PA: Duquesne University Press.

Cabanis, P. (1802). *Rapports du physique et du moral de l'homme*. Paris: Crapart, Caille et Ravier.

Cabestan, Ph. (1996). La constitution du corps selon l'ordre de ses apparitions. *Épokhè* 6, 279–98.

Campbell, J. (1999). Schizophrenia, the space of reasons and thinking as a motor process. *Monist* 82/4, 609–25.

Campos, J. J., Bertenthal, B. I., and Kermoian, R. (1992). Early experience and emotional development: The emergence of wariness of heights. *Psychological Science* 3, 61–64.

Carr, D. (1999). *The Paradox of Subjectivity: The Self in the Transcendental Tradition*. Oxford: Oxford University Press.

Carruthers, P. (1996). *Language, Thoughts and Consciousness: An Essay in Philosophical Psychology*. Cambridge: Cambridge University Press.

——(1998). Natural theories of consciousness. *European Journal of Philosophy* 6/2, 203–22.

——(2005). *Consciousness: Essays from a Higher-Order Perspective*. Oxford: Oxford University Press.

Cassam, Q. (1997). *Self and World*. Oxford: Clarendon Press.

Castañeda, H.-N. (1968). On the Phenomeno-Logic of the I. *Proceedings of the XIVth International Congress of Philosophy*, vol. 3 (pp. 260–66). Vienna: Herder.

Caston, V. (2006). Comment on A. Thomasson, 'Self-Awareness and Self-Knowledge'. *Psyche* 12/2, 1–15.

Catmur C., Walsh V., and Heyes, C. (2007). Sensorimotor learning configures the human mirror system. *Current Biology* 17/17, 1527–31.

Chalmers, D. (1995). Facing up to the problem of consciousness. *Journal of Consciousness Studies* 2/3, 200–19.

——(1996). *The Conscious Mind: In Search of a Fundamental Theory*. New York: Oxford University Press.

——(1997). Moving forward on the problem of consciousness. *Journal of Consciousness Studies* 4/1, 3–46.

——(ed.) (2002). *Philosophy of Mind: Classical and Contemporary Readings*. Oxford: Oxford University Press.

Chaminade, T. and Decety, J. (2002). Leader or follower? Involvement of the inferior parietal lobule in agency. *Neuroreport* 13/1528, 1975–78.

Chiel, H. J. and Beer, R. D. (1997). The brain has a body: Adaptive behavior emerges from interactions of nervous system, body and environment. *Trends in Neurosciences* 20, 553–57.

Chisholm, R. M. (1967). Brentano on descriptive psychology and the intentional. In E. N. Lee and M.

Mandelbaum (eds), *Phenomenology and Existentialism* (pp. 1–23). Baltimore, MD: Johns Hopkins Press.

Clark, A. (1997). *Being There: Pulling Brain, Body, and World Together Again*. Cambridge, MA: MIT Press.

Cole, J. (1995). *Pride and a Daily Marathon*. Cambridge, MA: MIT Press.

Cole, J., Sacks, O., and Waterman, I. (2000). On the immunity principle: A view from a robot. *Trends in Cognitive Sciences* 4/5, 167.

Conrad, K. (1959). *Die beginnende Schizophrenie: Versuch einer Gestaltanalyse des Wahns*. Stuttgart: Thieme.

Costall, A. (2004). From Darwin to Watson (and cognitivism) and back again: The principle of animal–environment mutuality. *Behavior and Philosophy*, at: http://www.findarticles.com/p/articles/miqa3814/is200401/ain9383857

——(2006). Introspectionism and the mythical origins of modern scientific psychology. *Consciousness and Cognition* 15, 634–54.

Crane, T. (2001). *Elements of Mind: An introduction to the Philosophy of Mind*. Oxford: Oxford University Press.

Crick, F. (1995). *The Astonishing Hypothesis*. London: Touchstone.

Csibra, G. (2005). Mirror neurons and action observation. Is simulation involved? ESF Interdisciplines, at: http://www.interdisciplines.org/mirror/papers/

Csibra, G. and Gergely, G. (2009). Natural pedagogy. *Trends in Cognitive Sciences* 13, 148–53.

Currie, G. and Ravenscroft, I. (2002). *Recreative Minds*. Oxford: Oxford University Press.

Dainton, B. (2000). *Stream of Consciousness: Unity and Continuity in Conscious Experience*. London: Routledge.

——(2003). Time in experience: Reply to Gallagher. *Psyche* 9/12, at: http://psyche.cs.monash.edu.au/symposia/dainton/gallagher-r.pdf

Damasio, A. R. (1994). *Descartes' Error: Emotion, Reason, and the Human Brain*. New York: Grosset/Putnam.

——(1999). *The Feeling of What Happens*. San Diego, CA: Harcourt.

Danziger, S., Levav, J., and Avnaim-Pesso, L. (2011). Extraneous factors in judicial decisions. PNAS 108/17, 6889–92.

Davidson, D. (2001). *Subjective, Intersubjective, Objective*. Oxford: Oxford University Press.

DeCasper, A. J. and Spence, M. J. (1986). Prenatal maternal speech influences newborns' perception of speech sounds. *Infant Behavior and Development* 9, 137–50.

de Gelder, B. 2010. Uncanny sight in the blind. *Scientific American* 302, 60–65.

de Haan, S. and de Bruin, L. (2010) Reconstructing the minimal self, or how to make sense of agency and ownership. *Phenomenology and the Cognitive Sciences* 9/3, 373–96.

Dennett, D. C. (1979). On the absence of phenomenology. In D. Gustafson and B. Tapscott (eds), *Body, Mind, and Method* (pp. 93–113). Dordrecht: Kluwer.

——(1981). Where am I? In D. R. Hofstadter and D. C. Dennett (eds), *The Mind's I: Fantasies and Reflections on Mind and Soul* (pp. 217–29). New York: Basic Books.

——(1982). How to study human consciousness empirically, or, nothing comes to mind. *Synthese* 53, 159–80.

——(1987). *The Intentional Stance*. Cambridge, MA: MIT Press.

——(1988) Why everyone is a novelist. *Times Literary Supplement*, 16–22 September, pp. 1016, 1028–29.

——(1991). *Consciousness Explained*. Boston, MA: Little, Brown & Co.

——(1993a). Caveat emptor. *Consciousness and Cognition* 2, 48–57.

——(1993b). Living on the edge. *Inquiry* 36, 135–59.

——(2000). Re-introducing *The Concept of Mind*. In G. Ryle, *The Concept of Mind* (pp. vii–xvii). London: Penguin.

——(2001). *The Fantasy of First-Person Science*. Nicod Lectures. Tufts University website, at: http://ase.tufts.edu/cogstud/papers/chalmersdeb3dft.htm

——(2003). Who's on first? Heterophenomenology explained. *Journal of Consciousness Studies* 10/9–10, 19–30.

——(2007). Heterophenomenology reconsidered. *Phenomenology and the Cognitive Sciences* 6/1–2, 247–70.

Dennett, D. C. and Kinsbourne, M. (1992) Time and the observer. *Behavioral and Brain Sciences* 15/2, 183–247.

de Vignemont, F. (2004). The co-consciousness hypothesis. *Phenomenology and the Cognitive Sciences* 3/1, 97–114.

——(2009). Knowing other people's mental states as if they were one's own. In S. Gallagher and D. Schmicking (eds), *Handbook of Phenomenology and Cognitive Science* (pp. 283–300). Dordrecht: Springer.

Dewey, J. (1896). The reflex arc concept in psychology. *Psychological Review* 3, 357–70.

Dilthey, W. (1992). Der Aufbau der geschichtlichen Welt in den Geisteswissenschaften. In *Gesammelte Schriften*, vol. 7. Göttingen: Vandenhoeck & Ruprecht.

Dinstein, I., Thomas, C., Behrmann, M., and Heeger, D. J. 2008: A mirror up to nature. *Current Biology* 18/1, R13–R18.

Dokic, J. (2003). The sense of ownership: An analogy between sensation and action. In J. Roessler and N. Eilan (eds), *Agency and Self-Awareness: Issues in Philosophy and Psychology* (pp. 321–44). Oxford: Oxford University Press.

Dretske, F. (1995). *Naturalizing the Mind*. Cambridge, MA: MIT Press.

Dreyfus, H. L. (1967). Why computers must have bodies in order to be intelligent. *Review of Metaphysics* 21/1, 13–32.

——(1972). *What Computers Can't Do*. Cambridge, MA: MIT Press.

——(1991). *Being-in-the-World*. Cambridge, MA: MIT Press.

——(1992). *What Computers Still Can't Do*. Cambridge, MA: MIT Press.

——(2005). Overcoming the Myth of the Mental: How Philosophers Can Profit from the Phenomenology of Everyday Expertise. *Proceedings and Addresses of the American Philosophical Association* 79/2, 47–65.

——(2007a). The return of the myth of the mental. *Inquiry* 50/4, 352–65.

——(2007b). Response to McDowell. *Inquiry* 50/4, 371–77.

Dreyfus, H. L. and Kelly, S. D. (2007). Heterophenomenology: Heavy-handed sleight-of-hand. *Phenomenology and the Cognitive Sciences* 6/1–2, 45–55.

Drummond, J. J. (1990). *Husserlian Intentionality and Non-foundational Realism*. Dordrecht: Kluwer.

——(1992). An abstract consideration: De-ontologizing the noema. In J. J. Drummond and L. Embree (eds), *The Phenomenology of the Noema* (pp. 89–109). Dordrecht: Kluwer Academic Publishers.

——(2003). The structure of intentionality. In D. Welton (ed.), *The New Husserl: A Critical Reader* (pp. 65–92). Bloomington and Indianapolis: Indiana University Press.

Ekman, P. (2003). *Emotions Revealed: Understanding Faces and Feelings*. London: Weidenfeld & Nicolson.

Engel, A. K., Fries. P., and Singer, W. (2001). Dynamic predictions: Oscillations and synchrony in top-down processing. *Nature Reviews Neuroscience* 10, 704–16.

Evans, G. (1982). *The Varieties of Reference*. Oxford: Clarendon Press.

Farrer, C. and Frith, C. D. (2002). Experiencing oneself vs. another person as being the cause of an action: The neural correlates of the experience of agency. *NeuroImage* 15, 596–603.

Farrer, C., Franck, N., Georgieff, N., Frith, C. D., Decety, J., and Jeannerod, M. (2003). Modulating the experience of agency: A positron emission tomography study. *NeuroImage* 18, 324–33.

Fifer, W. P. and Moon, C. 1988. Auditory experience in the fetus. In W. P. Smotherman and S. R. Robinson (eds), *Behavior of the Fetus* (pp. 175–88). Caldwell, NJ: Telford Press.

Flanagan, O. (1992). *Consciousness Reconsidered*. Cambridge, MA: MIT Press.

Fodor, J. (1987). *Psychosemantics*. Cambridge, MA: MIT Press.

Frankfurt, H. (1988). *The Importance of What We Care About: Philosophical Essays*. Cambridge: Cambridge University Press.

Friedenberg, J. and Silverman, G. (2006). *Cognitive Science: An Introduction to the Study of Mind*. London: Sage.

Friedman, W. (1990). *About Time: Inventing the Fourth Dimension*. Cambridge, MA: MIT Press.

Frith, C. D. (1992). *The Cognitive Neuropsychology of Schizophrenia*. Hillsdale, NJ: Lawrence Erlbaum Associates.

Frith, U. and F. Happé (1999). Theory of mind and self-consciousness: What is it like to be autistic? *Mind & Language* 14, 1–22.

Frith, C. D., Blakemore, S., and Wolpert, D. M. (2000). Explaining the symptoms of schizophrenia: Abnormalities in the awareness of action. *Brain Research Review* 31/2–3, 357–63.

Froese, T. and Gallagher, S. 2010. Phenomenology and artificial life: Toward a technological supplementation of phenomenological methodology. *Husserl Studies* 26/2, 83–107.

Gallagher, S. (1979). Suggestions towards a revision of Husserl's phenomenology of time-consciousness. *Man and World* 12, 445–64.

——(1986). Lived body and environment. *Research in Phenomenology* 16, 139–70. Reprinted in D. Moran and L. Embree (eds), *Phenomenology: Critical Concepts in Philosophy*, vol. 2. London: Routledge, 2004.

——(1996). The moral significance of primitive self-consciousness. *Ethics* 107/1, 129–40.

——(1997). Mutual enlightenment: Recent phenomenology in cognitive science. *Journal of Consciousness Studies* 4/3, 195–214.

——(1998). *The Inordinance of Time*. Evanston, IL: Northwestern University Press.

——(2000a). Philosophical conceptions of the self: Implications for cognitive science. *Trends in Cognitive Sciences* 4/1, 14–21.

——(2000b). Self-reference and schizophrenia: A cognitive model of immunity to error through misidentification. In D. Zahavi (ed.), *Exploring the Self: Philosophical and Psychopathological Perspectives on Self-Experience* (pp. 203–39). Amsterdam and Philadelphia: John Benjamins.

——(2001). The practice of mind: Theory, simulation, or interaction? *Journal of Consciousness Studies* 8/5–7, 83–107.

——(2003a). Phenomenology and experimental design. *Journal of Consciousness Studies* 10/9–10, 85–99.

——(2003b). Bodily self-awareness and object-perception. *Theoria et Historia Scientiarum: International Journal for Interdisciplinary Studies* 7/1, 53–68.

——(2003c). Sync-ing in the stream of experience: Time-consciousness in Broad, Husserl, and Dainton. *Psyche* 9/10, at: http://psyche.cs.monash.edu.au/v9/psyche-9-10-gallagher.html

——(2005a). *How the Body Shapes the Mind*. Oxford: Oxford University Press.

——(2005b). Metzinger's matrix: Living the virtual life with a real body. *Psyche: An interdisciplinary journal of research on consciousnesss*, at: http://psyche.cs.monash.edu.au/symposia/metzinger/Gallagher.pdf

——(2006). The intrinsic spatial frame of reference. In H. Dreyfus and M. Wrathall (eds), *The Blackwell Companion to Phenomenology and Existentialism* (pp. 346–55). Oxford: Blackwell.

——(2007). Simulation trouble. *Social Neuroscience* 2/3–4, 353–65.

——(2010a). Time in action. In C. Callender (ed.), *Oxford Handbook on Time* (pp. 419–37). Oxford: Oxford University Press.

——(2010b). Multiple aspects of agency. *New Ideas in Psychology*, at: http://dx.doi.org/10.1016/j.newideapsych.2010.03.003 (online publication April 2010).

——(2011). Narrative competency and the massive hermeneutical background. In Paul Fairfield (ed.), *Hermeneutics in Education* (pp. 21–38). New York: Continuum.

Gallagher, S. and Cole, J. (1995). Body schema and body image in a deafferented subject. *Journal of Mind and Behavior* 16, 369–90.

Gallagher, S. and Hutto, D. (2007). Understanding others through primary interaction and narrative practice. In J. Zlatev, T. Racine, C. Sinha, and E. Itkonen (eds), *The Shared Mind: Perspectives on Intersubjectivity*. Amsterdam: John Benjamins.

Gallagher, S. and Marcel, A. J. (1999). The self in contextualized action. *Journal of Consciousness Studies* 6/4, 4–30.

Gallagher, S. and Meltzoff, A. (1996). The earliest sense of self and others: Merleau-Ponty and recent developmental studies. *Philosophical Psychology* 9, 213–36.

Gallagher, S. and Shear, J. (eds) (1999). *Models of the Self*. Exeter: Imprint Academic.

Gallagher, S. and Væver, M. (2004). Disorders of embodiment. In J. Radden (ed.), *The Philosophy of Psychiatry: A Companion* (pp. 118–32). Oxford: Oxford University Press.

Gallagher, S. and Varela, F. (2003). Redrawing the map and resetting the time: Phenomenology and the cognitive sciences. *Canadian Journal of Philosophy* 29 (suppl.), 93–132.

Gallese, V. L. (2001). The 'shared manifold' hypothesis: From mirror neurons to empathy. *Journal of Consciousness Studies* 8, 33–50.

——(2005). 'Being like me': Self–other identity, mirror neurons and empathy. In S. Hurley and N. Chater (eds), *Perspectives on Imitation I* (pp. 101–18). Cambridge, MA: MIT Press.

Gallese, V. L. and Goldman, A. (1998). Mirror neurons and the simulation theory of mind-reading. *Trends in Cognitive Sciences* 2, 493–501.

Gellhorn, E. (1943). *Autonomic Regulations: Their Significance for Physiology, Psychology, and Neuropsychiatry*. New York: InterScience Publications.

Georgieff, N. and Jeannerod, M. (1998). Beyond consciousness of external events: A 'who' system for consciousness of action and self-consciousness. *Consciousness and Cognition* 7, 465–77.

Gibbs, R. W. (2006). *Embodiment and Cognitive Science*. Cambridge: Cambridge University Press.

Gibson, J. J. (1986). *The Ecological Approach to Visual Perception*. Hillsdale, NJ: Lawrence Erlbaum Associates.

Goldman, A. I. (1970). *A Theory of Human Action*. New York: Prentice Hall.

——(2000). Folk psychology and mental concepts. *Protosociology* 14, 4–25.

——(2005). Imitation, mind reading, and simulation. In S. Hurley and N. Chater (eds), *Perspectives on Imitation*, vol. 2 (pp. 79–94). Cambridge, MA: MIT Press.

Goldman, A. and Sripada, C. S. (2005). Simulationist models of face-based emotion recognition. *Cognition* 94, 193–213.

González, J. C., Bach-y-Rita, P., and Haase, S. J. (2005) Perceptual recalibration in sensory substitution and perceptual modification. *Pragmatics & Cognition* 13/3, 481–500.

Gopnik, A. (1993). How we know our minds: The illusion of first-person knowledge of intentionality. *Behavioral and Brain Sciences* 16, 1–14.

Gopnik, A. and Meltzoff, A. (1997). *Words, Thoughts, and Theories*. Cambridge, MA: MIT Press.

Gordon, R. and Cruz, J. (2006). Simulation theory. In L. Nadel (ed.), *Encyclopedia of Cognitive Science*. Published Online 15 January 2006, Doi: 10.1002/0470018860.s00123

Graham, G. and Stephens, G. L. (1994). Mind and mine. In G. Graham and G. L. Stephens (eds), *Philosophical Psychopathology* (pp. 91–109). Cambridge, MA: MIT Press.

Gregory, R. L. (1997). *Mirrors in Mind*. Oxford and New York: W. H. Freeman.

Grèzes, J. and Decety, J. (2001). Functional anatomy of execution, mental simulation, and verb generation of actions: A meta-analysis. *Human Brain Mapping* 12, 1–19.

Grush, R. (2006). How to, and how *not* to, bridge computational cognitive neuroscience and Husserlian phenomenology of time consciousness. *Synthese* 153/3, 417–50.

Gurwitsch, A. (1966). *Studies in Phenomenology and Psychology*. Evanston, IL: Northwestern University Press.

——(1979). *Human Encounters in the Social World*, trans. F. Kersten. Pittsburgh, PA: Duquesne University Press.

Haggard, P. and Clark, S. (2003). Intentional action: conscious experience and neural prediction. *Conscious Cognition* 12/4, 695–707.

Hamm, A. O., Weike, A. I., Schupp, H. T., Treig, T., Dressel, A., and Kessler, C. (2003). Affective blindsight: Intact fear conditioning to a visual cue in a cortically blind patient. *Brain* 126/2, 267–75.

Hart, J. G. (1992). *The Person and the Common Life*. Dordrecht: Kluwer Academic Publishers.

Haugeland, J. (1998). *Having Thought: Essays in the Metaphysics of Mind*, Cambridge, MA: Harvard University Press.

Head, H. (1920). *Studies in Neurology*, vol. 2. London: Oxford University Press.

Heidegger, M. (1964). The origin of the work of art. In A. Hofstadter and R. Kuhns (eds), *Philosophies of Art and Beauty* (pp. 649–701). Chicago: Chicago University Press.

——(1975). *Die Grundprobleme der Phänomenologie*, ed. F.-W. von Herrmann. Vol. 24 of *Heidegger Gesamtausgabe*. Frankfurt am Main: Vittorio Klostermann. Trans. by A. Hofstadter as *The Basic Problems of Phenomenology*. Bloomington: Indiana University Press, 1982.

——(1976). *Logik: Der Frage nach der Wahrheit*, ed. Walter Biemel. Vol. 21 of *Heidegger Gesamtausgabe*. Frankfurt am Main: Vittorio Klostermann.

——(1978). *Metaphysische Anfangsgründe der Logik im Ausgang von Leibniz*, ed. K. Held. Vol. 26 of *Heidegger Gesamtausgabe*. Frankfurt am Main: Vittorio Klostermann.

——(1979). *Prolegomena zur Geschichte des Zeitbegriffs*, ed. P. Jaeger. Vol. 20 of *Heidegger Gesamtausgabe*. Frankfurt am Main: Vittorio Klostermann.

——(1986). *Sein und Zeit*. Tübingen: Max Niemeyer. Trans. by J. Stambaugh as *Being and Time*. Albany, NY: SUNY, 1996.

——(1993). *Grundprobleme der Phänomenologie (1919/1920)*, ed. H.-H. Gander. Vol. 58 of *Heidegger Gesamtausgabe*. Frankfurt am Main: Vittorio Klostermann.

——(1994). *Phänomenologische Interpretationen zu Aristoteles: Einführung in die phänomenologische Forschung*, ed. W. Bröcker and K. Bröcker-Oltmanns. Vol. 61 of *Heidegger Gesamtausgabe*. Frankfurt am Main: Vittorio Klostermann.

——(2001). *Einleitung in die Philosophie*, ed. O. Saame and I. Saame-Speidel. Vol. 27 of *Heidegger Gesamtausgabe*. Frankfurt am Main. Vittorio Klostermann.

Heil, J. (2004). *Philosophy of Mind: A Contemporary Introduction*. London: Routledge.

Henry, M. (1973). *The Essence of Manifestation*, trans. G. Etzkorn. The Hague: Martinus Nijhoff.

——(1975). *Philosophy and Phenomenology of the Body*, trans. G. Etzkorn. The Hague: Martinus Nijhoff.

——(2003). *De la subjectivité*. Paris: Presses Universitaires de France.

Hickok, G. (2008). Eight problems for the mirror neuron theory of action understanding in monkeys and humans. *Journal of Cognitive Neuroscience* 21, 1229–43.

Hobson, R. P. (1993). *Autism and the Development of Mind*. Hove: Psychology Press.

——(2002). *The Cradle of Thought*. London: Macmillan.

Hodgson, S. (1870). *The Theory of Practice*. London: Longmans, Green, Reader & Dyer.

Hodgson, D. (1996). The easy problems ain't so easy. *Journal of Consciousness Studies* 3/1, 69–75.

Horton, H. K. and Silverstein, S. M. (2011). Visual context processing deficits in schizophrenia: Effects of deafness and disorganization. *Schizophrenia Bulletin* 37/4, 716–26.

Hotton, S. and Yoshimi, J. (2010). The dynamics of embodied cognition. *International Journal of Bifurcation and Chaos* 20/4, 1–30.

——(2011). Extending dynamical systems theory to model embodied cognition. *Cognitive Science* 35, 444–79

Hurley, S. (1998). *Consciousness in Action*. Cambridge, MA: Harvard University Press.

——(2005). The shared circuits hypothesis: A unified functional architecture for control, imitation, and simulation. In S. Hurley and N. Chater (eds), *Perspectives on Imitation: From Neuroscience to Social Science*, vol. 1 (pp. 177–94). Cambridge, MA: MIT Press.

Husserl, E. (1950). *Cartesianische Meditationen und Pariser Vorträge*, ed. Stephan Strasser. Husserliana I. The Hague: Martinus Nijhoff. Trans. in part by P. Koestenbaum as *The Paris Lectures*. The Hague: Martinus Nijhoff, 1964; and in part by D. Cairns as *Cartesian Meditations: An Introduction to Phenomenology*. The Hague: Martinus Nijhoff, 1999.

——(1952). *Ideen zu einer reinen Phänomenologie und phänomenologischen Philosophie, Zweites Buch: Phänomenologische Untersuchungen zur Konstitution*, ed. Marly Biemel. Husserliana IV. The Hague: Martinus Nijhoff. Trans. by R. Rojcewicz and A. Schuwer as *Ideas Pertaining to a Pure Phenomenology and to a Phenomenological Philosophy, Second Book: Studies in the Phenomenology of Constitution*. Dordrecht: Kluwer Academic Publishers, 1989.

——(1959). *Erste Philosophie II (1923–24), Zweiter Teil: Theorie der phänomenologischen Reduktion*, ed. Rudolf Boehm. Husserliana VIII. The Hague: Martinus Nijhoff.

——(1962). *Phänomenologische Psychologie*, ed. Walter Biemel. Husserliana IX. The Hague: Martinus Nijhoff. Trans. by J. Scanlon as *Phenomenological Psychology: Lectures, Summer Semester, 1925*.

The Hague: Martinus Nijhoff, 1977; and by T. Sheehan and R. E. Palmer in *Psychological and Transcendental Phenomenology and the Confrontation with Heidegger* (1927–31). Dordrecht: Kluwer Academic Publishers, 1997 (pp. 237–340, 517–26).

——(1966a). *Zur Phänomenologie des inneren Zeitbewußtseins (1893–1917)*, ed. Rudolf Boehm. Husserliana X. The Hague: Martinus Nijhoff. Trans. by J. Brough as *On the Phenomenology of the Consciousness of Internal Time (1893–1917)*. Dordrecht: Kluwer Academic Publishers, 1991.

——(1966b). *Analysen zur passiven Synthesis*, ed. Margot Fleischer. Husserliana XI. The Hague: Martinus Nijhoff.

——(1970). *The Crisis of European Sciences and Transcendental Phenomenology: An Introduction to Phenomenology*, trans. D. Carr. Evanston, IL: Northwestern University Press.

——(1971). *Ideen zu einer reinen Phänomenologie und phänomenologischen Philosophie, Drittes Buch: Die Phänomenologie und die Fundamente der Wissenschaften*, ed. Marly Biemel. Husserliana V. The Hague: Martinus Nijhoff. Trans. by T. E. Klein and W. E. Pohl as *Ideas Pertaining to a Pure Phenomenology and to a Phenomenological Philosophy, Third Book: Phenomenology and the Foundations of the Sciences*. The Hague: Martinus Nijhoff, 1980.

——(1973a). *Zur Phänomenologie der Intersubjektivität. Texte aus dem Nachlass, Zweiter Teil: 1921–1928.*, ed. Iso Kern. Husserliana XIV. The Hague: Martinus Nijhoff.

——(1973b). *Zur Phänomenologie der Intersubjektivität. Texte aus dem Nachlass, Dritter Teil: 1929–1935*, ed. Iso Kern. Husserliana XV. The Hague: Martinus Nijhoff.

——(1973c). *Ding und Raum: Vorlesungen 1907*, ed. Ulrich Claesges. Husserliana XVI. The Hague: Martinus Nijhoff. Trans. by R. Rojcewicz as *Thing and Space: Lectures of 1907*. Dordrecht: Kluwer Academic Publishers, 1997.

——(1976). *Ideen zu einer reinen Phänomenologie und phänomenologischen Philosophie, Erstes Buch: Allgemeine Einführung in die reine Phänomenologie*, ed. Karl Schuhmann. Husserliana III. The Hague: Martinus Nijhoff. Trans. by F. Kersten as *Ideas Pertaining to a Pure Phenomenology and to a Phenomenological Philosophy, First Book: General Introduction to a Pure Phenomenology*. The Hague: Martinus Nijhoff, 1982.

——(1979). *Aufsätze und Rezensionen (1890–1910)*, ed. Bernhard Rang. Husserliana XXII. The Hague: Martinus Nijhoff.

——(1984). *Einleitung in die Logik und Erkenntnistheorie* ed. Ullrich Melle. Husserliana XXIV. The Hague: Martinus Nijhoff.

——(1987). *Aufsätze und Vorträge (1911–21)*, ed. Thomas Nenon und Hans Rainer Sepp. Husserliana XXV. Dordrecht: Martinus Nijhoff.

——(2001a). *Logical Investigations*. 2 vols, trans. J. N. Findlay. London: Routledge.

——(2001b). *Die Bernauer Manuskripte über das Zeitbewußtsein (1917–18)*, ed. Rudolf Bernet und Dieter Lohmar. Husserliana XXXIII. Dordrecht: Kluwer Academic Publishers.

——(2002). *Zur phänomenologischen Reduktion. Texte aus dem Nachlass (1926–35)*, ed. Sebastian Luft. Husserliana XXXIV. Dordrecht: Kluwer Academic Publishers.

——(2003). *Transzendentaler Idealismus. Texte aus dem Nachlass (1908–21)*, ed. Robin D. Rollinger with Rochus Sowa. Husserliana XXXVI. Dordrecht: Kluwer Academic Publishers.

Hutto, D. D. (2004). The limits of spectatorial folk psychology. *Mind & Language* 19/5, 548–73.

——(2007). The narrative practice hypothesis: Origins and applications of folk psychology. In D. Hutto (ed.), *Narrative and Understanding Persons* (pp. 43–68). Cambridge: Cambridge University Press.

——(2008). *Folk Psychological Narratives: The Socio-cultural Basis of Understanding Reasons*. Cambridge, MA: MIT Press.

Huxley, T. H. (1874). On the hypothesis that animals are automata, and its history. *Fortnightly Review*, 16, 555–80.

Jack, A. I. and Roepstorff, A. (2002). Introspection and cognitive brain mapping: From stimulus–response to script–report. *Trends in Cognitive Sciences* 6/8, 333–39.

James, W. (1890/1950). *The Principles of Psychology*. 2 vols. New York: Dover.

Jeannerod, M. (1997). *The Cognitive Neuroscience of Action*. Oxford: Blackwell Publishers.

——(1999). To act or not to act: perspectives on the representation of actions. *Quarterly Journal of Experimental Psychology* 52A/1, 1–29.

Jeannerod, M. and Pacherie, E. (2004). Agency, simulation, and self-identification. *Mind & Language* 19/2, 113–46.

Jensen, R. (2008). *Perception and Action: An Analogical Approach*. Dissertation. University of Copenhagen.

Johnson, M. (1987). *The Body in the Mind: The Bodily Basis of Meaning, Imagination, and Reason*. Chicago: University of Chicago Press.

Johnson, S. C. (2000). The recognition of mentalistic agents in infancy. *Trends in Cognitive Sciences* 4, 22–28.

Johnson, S. C., et al. (1998). Whose gaze will infants follow? The elicitation of gaze-following in 12-month-old infants. *Developmental Science* 1, 233–38.

Jopling, D. A. (2000). *Self-Knowledge and the Self*. London: Routledge.

Editors (1997). Editorial: The future of consciousness studies. *Models of the Self*. Special Issue of *Journal of Consciousness Studies* 4/5–6, 385–88.

Kant, I. (1755–70/1992). Concerning the ultimate ground of the differentiation of directions in space. In *Theoretical Philosophy, 1755–1770*, ed. D. Walford and R. Meerbote (pp. 365–72). The Cambridge Edition of the Works of Immanuel Kant. Cambridge: Cambridge University Press.

——(1956/1999). *Kritik der reinen Vernunft*. Hamburg: Felix Meiner. Trans. by P. Guyer and A. W. Wood as *Critique of Pure Reason*. Cambridge: Cambridge University Press, 1999.

Keller, P. (1999). *Husserl and Heidegger on Human Experience*. Cambridge: Cambridge University Press.

Kelso, J. A. S. and Engstrøm, D. A. (2006). *The Complementary Nature*. Cambridge, MA: MIT Press.

Kim, J. (2005). *Philosophy of Mind*. Boulder, CO: Westview Press.

Kircher, T. and David, A. (eds) (2003). *The Self in Neuroscience and Psychiatry*. Cambridge: Cambridge University Press.

Kriegel, U. (2003). Consciousness as intransitive self-consciousness: Two views and an argument. *Canadian Journal of Philosophy* 33/1, 103–32.

——(2004). Consciousness and self-consciousness. *Monist* 87/2, 185–209.

Laing, R. D. (1960/1990). *The Divided Self*. Harmondsworth: Penguin Books.

Lakoff, G. and Johnson, M. (1980). *Metaphors We Live By*. Chicago: University of Chicago Press.

Lakoff, G. and Núñez, R. E. (2001). *Where Mathematics Comes From: How the Embodied Mind Brings Mathematics into Being*. New York: Basic Books.

La Mettrie, J. O., de. (1745). *Histoire naturelle de l'âme*. The Hague: Jean Neaulme.

Leder, D. (1990). *The Absent Body*. Chicago: University of Chicago Press.

Lee, D. N. and Aronson, E. (1974). Visual proprioceptive control of standing in human infants. *Perception & Psychophysics* 15, 529–32.

Legerstee, M. (1991). The role of person and object in eliciting early imitation. *Journal of Experimental Child Psychology* 51, 423–33.

Legrand, D. (2006). The bodily self: The sensorimotor roots of pre-reflexive self-consciousness. *Phenomenology and the Cognitive Sciences* 5, 89–118.

Leslie, A. M. (1987). Children's understanding of the mental world. In R. L. Gregory (ed.), *The Oxford Companion to the Mind* (pp. 139–42). Oxford: Oxford University Press.

Le Van Quyen, M. and Petitmengin, C. (2002). Neuronal dynamics and conscious experience: An example of reciprocal causation before epileptic seizures. *Phenomenology and the Cognitive Sciences* 1, 169–80.

Le Van Quyen, M., Martinerie, J., Navarro, V., Baulac, M., and Varela, F. (2001). Characterizing the neurodynamical changes prior to seizures. *Journal of Clinical Neurophysiology* 18, 191–208.

Lévinas, E. (1979). *Le temps et l'autre*. Paris: Fata Morgana.

Lewis, M. (2003). The development of self-consciousness. In J. Roessler and N. Eilan (eds), *Agency and Self-Awareness* (pp. 275–95). Oxford: Oxford University Press.

Lipps, T. (1900) Ästhetische Einfühlung. *Zeitschrift für Psychologie und Physiologie der Sinnesorgane* 22, pp. 415–50.

Locke, J. (1975). *An Essay Concerning Human Understanding*, ed. Peter H. Nidditch. Oxford: Oxford University Press.

Lotze, R. H. (1887). *Metaphysic in Three Books: Ontology, Cosmology, and Psychology*, trans. B. Bosanquet, 2nd edn. Oxford: Clarendon Press.

Lutz, A. (2002). Toward a neurophenomenology as an account of generative passages: A first empirical case study. *Phenomenology and the Cognitive Sciences* 1, 133–67.

Lutz, A. and Thompson, E. (2003). Neurophenomenology: Integrating subjective experience and brain dynamics in the neuroscience of consciousness. *Journal of Consciousness Studies* 10, 31–52.

Lutz, A., Lachaux, J.-P., Martinerie, J., and Varela, F. J. (2002). Guiding the study of brain dynamics using first-person data: Synchrony patterns correlate with ongoing conscious states during a simple visual task. Proceedings of the National Academy of Science, USA 99, 1586–91.

Lycan, W. G. (1987). *Consciousness*. Cambridge, MA: MIT Press.

——(1997). Consciousness as internal monitoring. In N. Block, O. Flanagan, and G. Güzeldere (eds), *The Nature of Consciousness* (pp. 754–71). Cambridge, MA: MIT Press.

Lyons, W. (1986). *The Disappearance of Introspection*. Cambridge, MA: MIT Press.

McClamrock, R. (1995). *Existential Cognition: Computational Minds in the World*. Chicago: University of Chicago Press.

McCulloch, G. (2003). *The Life of the Mind: An Essay on Phenomenological Externalism*. London: Routledge.

McDowell, J. (1992). Putnam on mind and meaning. *Philosophical Topics* 20/1, 35–48.

——(1996). *Mind and World*. Cambridge, MA: Harvard University Press.

——(1998). *Meaning, Knowledge, and Reality*. Cambridge, MA: Harvard University Press.

——(2006). Conceptual capacities in perception. In G. Abel (ed.), *Kreativität. Sektionsbeiträgee: XX. Deutscher Kongreß für Philosophie*. Hamburg: Felix Meiner, at: http://cas.uchicago.edu/

workshops/wittgenstein/files/2007/10/McDowell-Conceptual-Capacities-in-Perception-1.pdf (accessed 17 October 2011).

——(2007). What myth? *Inquiry* 50/4, 338–51.

——(2008). Avoiding the myth of the given. In J. Lindgaard (ed.), *John McDowell: Experience, Norm and Nature* (pp. 1–14). New York: John Wiley & Sons.

McGinn, C. (1991). *The Problem of Consciousness*. Oxford: Blackwell.

MacIntyre, A. (1985). *After Virtue: A Study in Moral Theory*. London: Duckworth.

McIntyre, R. (1999). Naturalizing phenomenology? Dretske on Qualia. In J. Petitot, F. J. Varela, B. Pachoud, and J.-M. Roy (eds), *Naturalizing Phenomenology* (pp. 429–39). Stanford, CA: Stanford University Press.

McTaggart, J. M. E. (1908). The unreality of time. *Mind*, n.s., 17/68, 457–74.

Majid, A., Bowerman, M., Kita, S., Haun, D. B. M., and Levinson, S. C. (2004). Can language restructure cognition? The case for space. *Trends in Cognitive Sciences* 8/3, 108–14.

Marbach, E. (1993). *Mental Representation and Consciousness: Towards a Phenomenological Theory of Representation and Reference*. Dordrecht: Kluwer Academic Publishing.

Marcel, A. J. (1983). Conscious and unconscious perception: An approach to the relations between phenomenal experience and perceptual processes. *Cognitive Psychology* 15, 238–300.

——(1993). Slippage in the unity of consciousness. In G. R. Bock and J. Marsh (eds), *Experimental and Theoretical Studies of Consciousness* (pp. 168–80). Ciba Foundation Symposium 174. New York: Wiley.

——(1998). Blindsight and shape perception: Deficits of visual consciousness or of visual function? *Brain* 121, 1565–88.

——(2003). The sense of agency: awareness and ownership of action. In J. Roessler and N. Eilan (eds), *Agency and Awarness* (pp. 48–93). Oxford: Oxford University Press.

Marcel, A. J. and Bisiach, E. (eds) (1988). *Consciousness in Contemporary Science*. Oxford: Oxford Science.

Marchetti, C. and Della Sala, S. (1998). Disentangling the alien and anarchic hand. *Cognitive Neuropsychiatry* 3/3, 191–207.

Marion, J.-L. (1998). *Etant donné: Essai d'une phénoménologie de la donation*, 2nd edn. Paris: Presses Universitaires de France.

Maund, B. (1995). *Colours: Their Nature and Representation*. New York: Cambridge University Press.

Maurer, D. and Barrera, M. E. 1981: Infants' perception of natural and distorted arrangements of a schematic face. *Child Development* 52/1, 196–202.

Mead, G. H. (1962). *Mind, Self and Society. From the standpoint of a Social Behaviorist*. Chicago: University of Chicago Press.

Meltzoff, A. N. (1995). Understanding the intentions of others: re-enactment of intended acts by 18-month-old children. *Developmental Psychology* 31, 838–50.

Meltzoff, A. N. and Brooks, R. (2001). 'Like me' as a building block for understanding other minds: Bodily acts, attention, and intention. In B. F. Malle, L. J. Moses, and D. A. Baldwin (eds), *Intentions and Intentionality: Foundations of Social Cognition* (pp. 171–91). Cambridge, MA: MIT Press.

Meltzoff, A. N. and Moore, M. K. (1977). Imitation of facial and manual gestures by human neonates. *Science* 198, 75–78.

——(1994). Imitation, memory, and the representation of persons. *Infant Behavior and Development* 17, 83–99.

Merleau-Ponty, M. (1962). *Phenomenology of Perception*, trans. C. Smith. London: Routledge & Kegan Paul.

——(1963). *The Structure of Behavior*, trans. A. L. Fisher. Pittsburgh, PA: Duquesne University Press.

——(1964). *Signs*, trans. R. C. McCleary. Evanston, IL: Northwestern University Press.

——(1968). *The Visible and the Invisible*. Evanston, IL: Northwestern University Press.

——(2003). *Nature: Course Notes from the Collège de France*. Evanston, IL: Northwestern University Press.

Metzinger, T. (2003). *Being No One*. Cambridge, MA: MIT Press.

Millikan, R. (2004). *Varieties of Meaning: The 2002 Jean Nicod Lectures*. Cambridge, MA: MIT Press.

Minkowski, E. (1927). *La schizophrénie: Psychopathologie des schizoïdes et des schizophrènes*. Paris: Payot.

——(1997). *Au-delà du rationalisme morbide*. Paris: Éditions l'Harmattan.

Mohanty, J. N. (1972). *The Concept of Intentionality*. St Louis, MO: Warren H. Green.

Moland, L. L. (2004). Ideals, ethics, and personhood. In H. Ikäheimo, J. Kotkavirta, A. Laitinen, and P. Lyyra (eds), *Personhood* (pp. 178–84). Jyväskylä: University of Jyväskylä Press.

Moore, D. G., Hobson, R. P., and Lee, A. (1997). Components of person perception: An investigation with autistic, non-autistic retarded and typically developing children and adolescents. *British Journal of Developmental Psychology* 15, 401–23.

Moore, G. E. (1903). The refutation of idealism. *Mind* 12, 433–53.

Moran, D. (2001). Analytic philosophy and phenomenology. In S. Crowell, L. Embree, and S. J. Julian (eds), *The Reach of Reflection: Issues for Phenomenology's Second Century* (pp. 409–33). West Hartford, CT: Electron Press.

Moran, R. (2001). *Authority and Estrangement: An Essay on Self-Knowledge*. Princeton, NJ: Princeton University Press.

Muir, D. W. (2002). Adult Communications with Infants through Touch: The Forgotten Sense. *Human Development* 45/2, 95–99.

Murray, L. and Trevarthen, C. (1985). Emotional regulations of interactions between two-month-olds and their mothers. In T. M. Field and N. A. Fox (eds), *Social Perception in Infants* (pp. 177–97). Norwood, NJ: Ablex Publishing.

Myin, E. and O'Regan, J. K. (2002). Perceptual consciousness, access to modality and skill theories. *Journal of Consciousness Studies* 9/1, 27–45.

Nagel, T. (1974). What is it like to be a bat? *Philosophical Review* 83, 435–50.

Nahab, F. B., Kundu, P. Gallea, C., Kakareka, J., Pursley, R., Pohida, T., Miletta, N., Friedman, J., and Hallett, J. (2011). The neural processes underlying self-agency. *Cerebral Cortex* 21, 48–55.

Natorp, P. (1912). *Allgemeine Psychologie*. Tübingen: J. C. B. Mohr.

Neisser, U. (1988). Five kinds of self-knowledge. *Philosophical Psychology* 1/1, 35–59.

——(1993). The self perceived. In U. Neisser (ed.), *The Perceived Self: Ecological and Interpersonal Sources of Self-Knowledge* (pp. 3–21). New York: Cambridge University Press.

Nelson K. (2003). Narrative and the emergence of a consciousness of self. In G. D. Fireman, T. E. J. McVay, and O. Flanagan (eds), *Narrative and Consciousness* (pp. 17–36). Oxford: Oxford University Press.

Newman-Norlund, R. D., Noordzij, M. L., Meulenbroek, R. G. J., and Bekkering, H. 2007: Exploring the brain basis of joint attention: Co-ordination of actions, goals and intentions. *Social Neuroscience* 2/1, 48–65.

Noë, A. (2004). *Action in Perception*. Cambridge, MA: MIT Press.

——(2007a). The critique of pure phenomenology. *Phenomenology and the Cognitive Sciences* 6/1–2, 231–45.

——(ed.) (2007b) *Dennett and Heterophenomenology*. Special double issue of *Phenomenology and the Cognitive Sciences* 6/1–2.

Oberman, L. M. and Ramachandran, V. S. (2007). The simulating social mind: The role of the mirror neuron system and simulation in the social and communicative deficits of autism spectrum disorders. *Psychological Bulletin* 133/2, 310–27.

Onishi, K. H. and Baillargeon, R. (2005). Do 15-month-old infants understand false beliefs? *Science* 308/5719, 255–58.

O'Shaughnessy, B. (1980). *The Will: A Dual Aspect Theory*. Cambridge: Cambridge University Press.

——(1985). Seeing the light. *Proceedings of the Aristotelian Society* 85, 193–218.

——(1995). Proprioception and the body image. In J. Bermúdez, A. J. Marcel, and N. Eilan (eds), *The Body and the Self* (pp. 175–203). Cambridge, MA: MIT Press.

Overgaard, S. (2005). Rethinking other minds: Wittgenstein and Lévinas on expression. *Inquiry* 48/3, 249–74.

Paillard, J. (2000). The neurobiological roots of rational thinking. In H. Cruse, J. Dean, and H. Ritter (eds), *Prerational Intelligence: Adaptive Behavior and Intelligent Systems without Symbols and Logic*, vol. 1 (pp.343–55). Dordrecht: Kluwer Academic Publishers.

Parnas, J. (2003). Self and schizophrenia: A phenomenological perspective. In T. Kircher and A. David (eds), *The Self in Neuroscience and Psychiatry* (pp. 217–41). Cambridge: Cambridge University Press.

Parnas, J. and Zahavi, D. (2002). The role of phenomenology in psychiatric diagnosis and classification. In M. Maj, W. Gaebel, J. J. López-Ibor, and N. Sartorius (eds), *Psychiatric Diagnosis and Classification* (pp. 137–62). New York: Wiley.

Parnas, J., Bovet, P., and Zahavi, D. (2002). Schizophrenic autism, clinical phenomenology and pathogenetic implications. *World Psychiatry* 1/3, 131–36.

Parnas, J., Møller, P., Kircher, T., Thalbitzer, J., Jansson, L., Handest, P., and Zahavi, D. (2005). EASE: Examination of anomalous self-experience. *Psychopathology* 38, 236–58.

Petitot, J., Varela, F., Pachoud, B., and Roy, J.-M. (eds) (1999). *Naturalizing Phenomenology: Issues in Contemporary Phenomenology and Cognitive Science*. Stanford, CA: Stanford University Press.

Phillips, W., Baron-Cohen, S., and Rutter, M. (1992). The role of eye-contact in the detection of goals: Evidence from normal toddlers, and children with autism or mental handicap. *Development and Psychopathology* 4, 375–83.

Plato (1985). *Phaedo*. In *Plato: The Collected Dialogues*, ed. E. Hamilton and H. Cairns. Princeton, NJ: Princeton University Press.

Pöppel, E. (1988). *Mindworks: Time and Conscious Experience*. Boston, MA: Harcourt Brace Jovanovich.

Premack, D. and Woodruff, G. (1978). Does the chimpanzee have a theory of mind? *Behavioral and Brain Sciences* 4, 515–26.

Price, D. D. and Aydede, M. (2005). The experimental use of introspection in the scientific study of pain and its integration with third-person methodologies: The experiential-phenomenological approach.

In M. Aydede (ed.), *Pain: New Essays on Its Nature and the Methodology of Its Study* (pp. 243–73). Cambridge, MA: MIT Press.

Putnam, H. (1977). Meaning and reference. In S. P. Schwartz (ed.), *Naming, Necessity and Natural Kinds* (pp. 119–32). Ithaca, NY: Cornell University Press.

Ramachandran, V. S. and Blakeslee, S. (1998). *Phantoms in the Brain: Probing the Mysteries of the Human Mind*. New York: William Morrow.

Ramachandran, V. S. and Oberman, L. M. (2006). Broken mirrors. *Scientific American* 295/55, 63–69.

Ramsey, W. M. (2007). Representation *Reconsidered*. Cambridge: Cambridge University Press.

Richardson, L. (2011). Bodily sensation and tactile perception. *Philosophy and Phenomenological Research*. Doi: 10.1111/j.1933–1592.2011.00504.x (first published online 21 July 2011).

Ricoeur, P. (1966). *Freedom and Nature: The Voluntary and the Involuntary*. Evanston, IL: Northwestern University Press.

——(1988). *Time and Narrative*. 3 vols, trans. K. Blamey and D. Pellauer. Chicago: Chicago University Press.

Rizzolatti, G., Fadiga, L., Matelli, M., Bettinardi, V., Paulesu, E., Perani, D., and Fazio, G. (1996). Localization of grasp representations in humans by PET. 1. Observation compared with imagination. *Experimental Brain Research* 111, 246–52.

Robinson, H. (1994). *Perception*. London: Routledge.

Rochat, P. (2001). *The Infant's World*. Cambridge, MA: Harvard University Press.

Rodemeyer, L. (2006). *Intersubjective Temporality: It's About Time*. Dordrecht: Springer.

Rosenthal, D. M. (1986). Two concepts of consciousness. *Philosophical Studies* 94/3, 329–59.

——(1993a). Thinking that one thinks. In M. Davies and G. W. Humphreys (eds), *Consciousness: Psychological and Philosophical Essays* (pp. 197–223). Oxford: Blackwell.

——(1993b). Higher-order thoughts and the appendage theory of consciousness. *Philosophical Psychology* 6, 155–66.

——(1993c). State consciousness and transitive consciousness. *Consciousness and Cognition* 2/4, 355–63.

——(1997). A theory of consciousness. In N. Block, O. Flanagan, and G. Güzeldere (eds), *The Nature of Consciousness* (pp. 729–53). Cambridge, MA: MIT Press.

Rossetti, Y. and Rode, G. (2002). Reducing spatial neglect by visual and other sensory manipulations: non-cognitive (physiological) routes to the rehabilitation of a cognitive disorder. In H. O. Karnath, A. D. Milner, and G. Vallar (eds), *The Cognitive and Neural Bases of Spatial Neglect* (pp. 375–96). Oxford: Oxford University Press.

Rowlands, M. (2003). *Externalism: Putting Mind and World Back Together Again*. Montreal and Kingston: McGill-Queen's University Press.

——(2006). *Body Language*. Cambridge, MA: MIT Press.

Roy, J.-M., Petitot, J., Pachoud, B., and Varela, F.J. (1999). Beyond the gap: an introduction to naturalizing phenomenology. In J. Petitot, F. J. Varela, B. Pachoud, and J.-M. Roy (eds), *Naturalizing Phenomenology* (pp. 1–83). Stanford, CA: Stanford University Press.

Rudd, A. (1998). What it's like and what's really wrong with physicalism: A Wittgensteinian perspective. *Journal of Consciousness Studies* 5/4, 454–63.

——(2003). *Expressing the World: Skepticism, Wittgenstein, and Heidegger*. Chicago: Open Court.

Ruffman, T. and Perner, J. (2005) Do infants really understand false belief? Response to Leslie. *Trends in Cognitive Sciences* 9/10, 462–63.

Ryckman, T. (2005). *The Reign of Relativity: Philosophy in Physics 1915–1925*. New York: Oxford University Press.

Ryle, G. (1949). *The Concept of Mind*. New York: Barnes & Noble.

Sartre, J.-P. (1956). *Being and Nothingness*, trans. H. E. Barnes. New York: Philosophical Library.

——(1957). *The Transcendence of the Ego*, trans. F. Williams and R. Kirkpatrick. New York: Noonday Press.

——(1967). Consciousness of self and knowledge of self. In N. Lawrence and D. O'Connor (eds), *Readings in Existential Phenomenology* (pp. 113–42). Englewood Cliffs, NJ: Prentice Hall.

Sass, L. (2000). Schizophrenia, self-experience, and the so-called 'negative symptoms'. In D. Zahavi (ed.), *Exploring the Self* (pp. 149–82). Amsterdam: John Benjamins.

Sass, L. and Parnas, J. (2006). Explaining schizophrenia: the relevance of phenomenology. In M. Chung, W. Fulford, and G. Graham (eds), *Reconceiving Schizophrenia* (pp. 63–96). Oxford: Oxford University Press.

Schacter, D. L. (1996). *Searching for Memory: The Brain, the Mind, and the Past*. New York: Basic Books.

Schacter, D. L., Reiman, E., Curran, T., Sheng Yun, L., Bandy, D., McDermott, K. B. and Roediger, H. L. (1996). Neuroanatomical correlates of veridical and illusory recognition memory: evidence from positron emission tomography. *Neuron* 17, 1–20.

Scheler, M. (1954). *The Nature of Sympathy*, trans. P. Heath. London: Routledge and Kegan Paul.

Schenk, T. and Zihl, J. (1997). Visual motion perception after brain damage. I. Deficits in global motion perception. *Neuropsychologia* 35, 1289–97.

Scholl, B. J. and Tremoulet, P.D. (2000). Perceptual causality and animacy. *Trends in Cognitive Sciences* 4/8, 299–309.

Schooler, J. W. and Schreiber, C. A. (2004). Experience, meta-consciousness, and the paradox of introspection. *Journal of Consciousness Studies* 11/7–8, 17–39.

Schutz, A. (1967). *Phenomenology of the Social World*, trans. G. Walsh and F. Lehnert. Evanston, IL: Northwestern University Press

Searle, J. R. (1983). *Intentionality: An Essay in the Philosophy of Mind*. Cambridge: Cambridge University Press.

——(1992). *The Rediscovery of the Mind*. Cambridge, MA: MIT Press.

——(1998). *Mind, Language and Society*. New York: Basic Books.

——(1999a). Neither phenomenological description nor rational reconstruction: Reply to Dreyfus, 30 January, at: http://istsocrates.berkeley.edu/~jsearle/replytodreyfus13099.rtf

——(1999b). The future of philosophy. *Philosophical Transactions of the Royal Society of London B: Biological Sciences* 354, 2069–80.

Seigel, J. (2005). *The Idea of the Self: Thought and Experience in Western Europe Since the Seventeenth Century*. Cambridge: Cambridge University Press.

Sellars, W. (1963). *Science, Perception and Reality*. London: Routledge & Kegan Paul.

Senju, A., Johnson, M. H., and Csibra, G. (2006). The development and neural basis of referential gaze perception. *Social Neuroscience* 1/3–4, 220–34.

Sheets-Johnstone, M. (1990). *The Roots of Thinking*. Philadelphia, PA: Temple University Press.

Sheets-Johnstone, M. (1999). *The Primacy of Movement*. Amsterdam: John Benjamins.

Shoemaker, S. (1968). Self-reference and self-awareness. *Journal of Philosophy* 65, 556–79.

——(1984). Personal identity: a materialist's account. In S. Shoemaker and R. Swinburne (eds), *Personal Identity*. Oxford: Blackwell.

Siewert, C. P. (1998). *The Significance of Consciousness*. Princeton, NJ: Princeton University Press.

——(2005). Attention and sensorimotor intentionality. In T. Carman and M. B. N. Hansen (eds), *The Cambridge Companion to Merleau-Ponty*. Cambridge: Cambridge University Press.

——(2006). Consciousness and intentionality. In E. N. Zalta (ed.), *Stanford Encyclopedia of Philosophy* (Spring 2007 edition), at: http://plato.stanford.edu/archives/spr2007/entries/consciousness-intentionality

Simons, D. J. and Chabris, C. F. (1999). Gorillas in our midst. *Perception* 28, 1059–74.

Smith, D. W. (1989). *The Circle of Acquaintance*. Dordrecht: Kluwer Academic Publishers.

——(2003). Phenomenology. In E. N. Zalta (ed.), *Stanford Encyclopedia of Philosophy* (Winter 2003 edition), at: http://plato.stanford.edu/entries/phenomenology

Smith, D. W. and McIntyre, R. (1982). *Husserl and Intentionality*. Dordrecht: D. Reidel.

Snyder, L. (2000). *Speaking our Minds: Personal Reflections from Individuals with Alzheimer's*. New York: W. H. Freeman.

Song, H.-J., Onishi, K. H., Baillargeon, R., and Fisher, C. (2008) Can an agent's false belief be corrected by an appropriate communication? Psychological reasoning in 18-month-old infants. *Cognition* 109/3, 295–315.

Southgate, V., Chevallier, C., and Csibra, G. 2010: Seventeen-month-olds appeal to false beliefs to interpret others' referential communication. *Developmental Science* 13/6, 907–12.

Stein, E. (1989). *On the Problem of Empathy*, 3rd rev. edn, trans. by W. Stein. Washington, DC: ICS Publishers.

Stephens, G. L. and Graham, G. (2000). *When Self-Consciousness Breaks: Alien Voices and Inserted Thoughts*. Cambridge, MA: MIT Press.

Straus, E. (1966). *Phenomenological Psychology*. New York: Basic Books.

Strawson, G. (1994). *Mental Reality*. Cambridge, MA: MIT Press.

——(1999). The self and the SESMET. In S. Gallagher and J. Shear (eds), *Models of the Self* (pp. 483–518). Thorverton: Imprint Academic.

——(2000). The phenomenology and ontology of the self. In D. Zahavi (ed.), *Exploring the Self* (pp. 39–54). Amsterdam: John Benjamins.

Strawson, P. F. (1959). *Individuals*. London: Methuen.

——(1994). The first person – And others. In Q. Cassam (ed.). *Self-Knowledge* (pp. 210–15). Oxford: Oxford University Press.

Stroud, B. (2000). *The Quest for Reality*. Oxford: Oxford University Press.

Stueber, K. R. (2006). *Rediscovering Empathy*. Cambridge, MA: MIT Press.

Tatossian, A. (1979/1997). *La phénoménologie des psychoses*. Paris: L'Art du comprendre.

Taylor, C. (1989). *Sources of the Self*. Cambridge, MA: Harvard University Press.

Thomas, A. (1997). Kant, McDowell and the theory of consciousness. *European Journal of Philosophy* 5/3, 283–305.

Tomasello, M. (1999). *The Cultural Origins of Human Cognition*. Cambridge, MA: Harvard University Press.

Thomasson, A. (2006). Self-awareness and Self-knowledge. *Psyche* 12/2, 1–15.

Thompson, E. (2001). Empathy and consciousness. *Journal of Consciousness Studies* 8/5–7, 1–32.

——(2005). Empathy and human experience. In J. D. Proctor (ed.), *Science, Religion, and the Human Experience* (pp. 261–85). New York: Oxford University Press.

——(2007). *Mind in Life: Biology, Phenomenology, and the Sciences of Mind*. Cambridge, MA: Harvard University Press.

Thompson, E. and Varela, F. (2001). Radical embodiment: Neural dynamics and consciousness. *Trends in Cognitive Sciences* 5/10, 418–25.

Thompson, E., Lutz, A., and Cosmelli, D. (2005). Neurophenomenology: An introduction for neuro-philosophers. In A. Brook and K. Akins (eds), *Cognition and the Brain: The Philosophy and Neuroscience Movement* (pp. 40–97). New York and Cambridge: Cambridge University Press.

Tooby, J. and Cosmides, L. (1995). Foreword to S. Baron-Cohen, *Mindblindness: An Essay on Autism and Theory of Mind* (pp. xi–xviii). Cambridge, MA: MIT Press.

Toussaint, B. (1976). Comments on C. H. Seibert's paper: On the body phenomenon in *Being and Time*. *Proceedings of the Heidegger Circle* (175–78). DePaul University conference, private circulation.

Trevarthen, C. (1979). Communication and cooperation in early infancy: A description of primary inter-subjectivity. In M. Bullowa (ed.), *Before Speech: The Beginning of Interpersonal Communication* (pp. 321–47). Cambridge: Cambridge University Press.

Trevarthen, C. and Hubley, P. (1978). Secondary intersubjectivity: Confidence, confiding and acts of meaning in the first year. In A. Lock (ed.), *Action, Gesture and Symbol: The Emergence of Language* (pp. 183–229). London: Academic Press.

Tronick, E., Als, H., Adamson, L., Wise, S., and Brazelton, T. B. (1978). The infant's response to entrapment between contradictory messages in face-to-face interaction. *Journal of the American Academy of Child Psychiatry* 17, 1–13.

Tsakiris, M. (2005). On agency and body-ownership. Paper presented at the Expérience subjective pré-réflexive et action (ESPRA) conference, CREA, Paris, 12–14 December.

Tsakiris, M. and Haggard, P. (2005). The rubber hand illusion revisited: Visuotactile integration and self-attribution. *Journal of Experimental Psychology: Human Perception and Performance* 31/1, 80–91.

Tye, M. (1995). *Ten Problems of Consciousness*. Cambridge, MA: MIT Press.

Van Gelder, T. J. (1999). Wooden iron? Husserlian phenomenology meets cognitive science. In J. Petitot, F. J. Varela, J.-M. Roy, and B. Pachoud (eds), *Naturalizing Phenomenology: Issues in Contemporary Phenomenology and Cognitive Science* (pp. 245–65). Stanford, CA: Stanford University Press.

Van Gulick, R. (1997). Understanding the phenomenal mind: Are we all just armadillos? In N. Block, O. Flanagan, and G. Güzeldere (eds), *The Nature of Consciousness* (pp. 559–66). Cambridge, MA: MIT Press.

——(2000). Inward and upward: Reflection, introspection, and self-awareness. *Philosophical Topics* 28/2, 275–305.

——(2006). Mirror mirror – Is that all? In U. Kriegel and K. Williford (eds), *Self-Representational Approaches to Consciousness* (pp. 11–39). Cambridge, MA: MIT Press.

Varela, F. J. (1995). Resonant cell assemblies: A new approach to cognitive functioning and neuronal synchrony. *Biological Research* 28, 81–95.

——(1996). Neurophenomenology: A methodological remedy to the hard problem. *Journal of Consciousness Studies* 3, 330–50.

——(1999). The specious present: A neurophenomenology of time consciousness. In J. Petitot,

F. J. Varela, J.-M. Roy, and B. Pachoud (eds), *Naturalizing Phenomenology: Issues in Contemporary Phenomenology and Cognitive Science* (pp. 266–329). Stanford, CA: Stanford University Press.

Varela, F. J. and Depraz, N. (2000). At the source of time: Valance and the constitutional dynamics of affect. Arobase: *Journal des Lettres et Sciences Humaines* 4/1–2, 143–66.

Varela, F. J., Toro, A., John, E. R., and Schwartz, E. (1981). Perceptual framing and cortical alpha rhythms. *Neuropsychologia* 19, 675–86.

Varela, F. J., Thompson, E., and Rosch, E. (1991). *The Embodied Mind: Cognitive Science and Human Experience*. Cambridge, MA: MIT Press.

Varela, F. J., Lachaux, J. P., Rodriguez, E. and Martinerie, J. (2001). The brainweb: Phase-synchronization and long-range integration. *Nature Reviews Neuroscience* 2, 229–39.

Velmans, M. (2000). *Understanding Consciousness*. London: Routledge.

Waldenfels, B. (2000). *Das leibliche Selbst: Vorlesungen zur Phänomenologie des Leibes*. Frankfurt am Main: Suhrkamp.

Walker, A. S. (1982). Intermodal perception of expressive behaviors by human infants. *Journal of Experimental Child Psychology* 33, 514–35.

Watson, J. (1913). Psychology as the behaviorist views it. *Psychological Review* 20, 158–77.

Weiskrantz, L. (1986). *Blindsight*. Oxford: Oxford University Press.

——(1997). *Consciousness Lost and Found: A Neuropsychological Exploration*. Oxford: Oxford University Press.

Weiskrantz, L., Warrington, E. K., Sanders, M. D., and Marshall, J. (1974). Visual capacity in the hemianopic field following a restricted occipital ablation. *Brain* 97, 709–28.

Wellman, H.M., Cross, D., and Watson, J. (2001). Meta-analysis of theory-of-mind development: The truth about false belief. *Child Development* 72, 655–84.

Welton, D. (2000). *The Other Husserl: The Horizons of Transcendental Phenomenology*. Bloomington: Indiana University Press.

Wheeler, M. (2005). *Reconstructing the Cognitive World*. Cambridge, MA: MIT Press.

Wider, K. (1997). *The Bodily Nature of Consciousness*. Ithaca, NY: Cornell University Press.

Williams, B. (2005). *Descartes: The Project of Pure Enquiry*. London: Routledge.

Wittgenstein, L. (1958). *Ludwig Wittgenstein: The Blue and Brown Books*. Basil Blackwell.

——(1980). *Remarks on the Philosophy of Psychology*, vol. 1. Oxford: Blackwell.

——(1992). *Last Writings on the Philosophy of Psychology*, vol. 2. Oxford: Blackwell.

Wolpert, D. M. and Flanagan, J. R. (2001). Motor prediction. *Current Biology* 11/18, 729–32.

Woodward, A. L. and Sommerville, J. A. 2000: Twelve-month-old infants interpret action in context. *Psychological Science* 11, 73–77.

Wundt, W. (1900). *Völkerpsychologie: Eine Untersuchung der Entwicklungsgesetze von Sprache, Mythus und Sitte*. Leipzig: Kröner.

Yarbus, A. (1967). *Eye Movements and Vision*. New York: Plenum Press.

Yoshimi, J. (2007). Mathematizing phenomenology. *Phenomenology and the Cognitive Sciences* 6/3, 271–91.

——(2011). Phenomenology and connectionism. *Frontiers in Theoretical and Philosophical Psychology* 2, 288. doi: 10.3389/fpsyg.2011.00288

Zahavi, D. (1992). *Intentionalität und Konstitution: Eine Einführung in Husserls Logische Untersuchungen*. Copenhagen: Museum Tusculanum Press.

——(1994). Husserl's phenomenology of the body. *Études Phénoménologiques* 19, 63–84.

——(1997). Horizontal intentionality and transcendental intersubjectivity. *Tijdschrift voor Filosofie* 59/2, 304–21.

——(1999). *Self-Awareness and Alterity: A Phenomenological Investigation*. Evanston, IL: Northwestern University Press.

——(ed.) (2000). *Exploring the Self: Philosophical and Psychopathological Perspectives on Self-Experience*. Amsterdam: John Benjamins.

——(2001a). Beyond empathy: Phenomenological approaches to intersubjectivity. *Journal of Consciousness Studies* 8/5–7, 151–67.

——(2001b). *Husserl and Transcendental Intersubjectivity*. Athens: Ohio University Press.

——(2002). First-person thoughts and embodied self-awareness: Some reflections on the relation between recent analytical philosophy and phenomenology. *Phenomenology and the Cognitive Sciences* 1, 7–26.

——(2003a). *Husserl's Phenomenology*. Stanford, CA: Stanford University Press.

——(2003b). Inner time-consciousness and pre-reflective self-awareness. In D. Welton (ed.), *The New Husserl: A Critical Reader* (pp. 157–80). Bloomington: Indiana University Press.

——(2003c). Husserl's intersubjective transformation of transcendental philosophy. In D. Welton (ed.), *The New Husserl: A Critical Reader* (pp. 233–54). Bloomington: Indiana University Press.

——(2003d). How to investigate subjectivity: Heidegger and Natorp on reflection. *Continental Philosophy Review* 36/2, 155–76.

——(2003e). Phenomenology and metaphysics. In D. Zahavi, S. Heinämaa, and H. Ruin (eds), *Metaphysics, Facticity, Interpretation* (pp. 3–22). Dordrecht: Kluwer Academic Publishers.

——(2004a). Husserl's noema and the internalism–externalism debate. *Inquiry* 47/1, 42–66.

——(2004b). The embodied self-awareness of the infant: A challenge to the theory-theory of mind? In D. Zahavi, T. Grünbaum and J. Parnas (eds), *The Structure and Development of Self-Consciousness: Interdisciplinary Perspectives* (pp. 35–63). Amsterdam: John Benjamins.

——(2004c). Back to Brentano? *Journal of Consciousness Studies* 11, 66–87.

——(ed.) (2004d). *Hidden Resources: Classical Perspectives on Subjectivity*. Special double issue of *Journal of Consciousness Studies* 11/10–11.

——(2004e). Phenomenology and the project of naturalization. *Phenomenology and the Cognitive Sciences* 3/4, 331–47.

——(2005a). *Subjectivity and Selfhood: Investigating the First-Person Perspective*. Cambridge, MA: MIT Press.

——(2005b). Being someone. *Psyche* 11/5, 1–20.

——(2006). Merleau-Ponty on Husserl: A reappraisal. In T. Toadvine (ed.), *Merleau-Ponty – Critical Assessments of Leading Philosophers*, vol. 1 (pp. 421–45). London: Routledge.

——(2007). Killing the strawman: Dennett and phenomenology. *Phenomenology and the Cognitive Sciences* 6/1–2, 21–43.

——(ed.) (2008a). *Internalism and Externalism in Phenomenological Perspective*. Special issue of *Synthese* 160/3,

——(2008b). Phenomenology. In D. Moran (ed.), *Routledge Companion to Twentieth-Century Philosophy* (pp. 661–92). London: Routledge.

——(2008c). Simulation, projection and empathy. *Consciousness and Cognition*, 17, 514–22.

Zahavi, D. (2010). Empathy, embodiment and interpersonal understanding: From Lipps to Schutz. Inquiry, 53/3, 285–306.

——(Forthcoming-a). Empathy and mirroring: Husserl and Gallese. In R. Breeur and U. Melle (eds), *Life, Subjectivity and Art: Essays in Honor of Rudolf Bernet*. Dordrecht: Springer.

——(Forthcoming-b). Mindedness, Mindlessness and First-Person Authority. In J. Schear (ed.): *Mind, Reason and Being-in-the-World: The Dreyfus-McDowell Debate*. London: Routledge.

Zahavi, D. and Parnas, J. (2003). Conceptual problems in infantile autism research: Why cognitive science needs phenomenology. *Journal of Consciousness Studies* 10/9, 53–71.

Zahavi, D. and Stjernfelt, F. (eds) (2002). *One Hundred Years of Phenomenology: Husserl's Logical Investigations Revisited*. Dordrecht: Kluwer Academic Publishers.

Zajac, F. E. (1993). Muscle coordination of movement: a perspective. *Journal of Biomechanics* 26 (suppl. 1), 109–24.

Zeki, S. (2002). Neural concept formation and art: Dante, Michelangelo, Wagner. *Journal of Consciousness Studies* 9/3, 53–76

Zihl, J., von Cramon, D., and Mai, N. (1983). Selective disturbance of movement vision after bilateral brain damage. *Brain* 106, 313–40.

Index